WARLORDS
Ancient ~ Celtic ~ Medieval

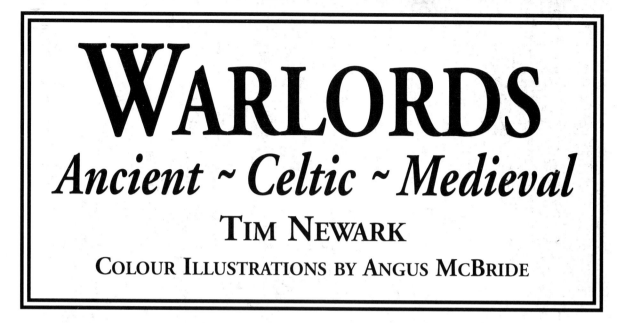

WARLORDS
Ancient ~ Celtic ~ Medieval
TIM NEWARK
COLOUR ILLUSTRATIONS BY ANGUS MCBRIDE

BROCKHAMPTON PRESS
LONDON

Arms & Armour Press
An Imprint of the Cassell Group
Wellington House, 125 Strand
London WC2R OBB

Text copyright © 1996 Tim Newark

ISBN 1 86019 8902

This edition published 1998 by Brockhampton Press,
a member of Hodder Headline PLC Group

This is an omnibus edition of
The Barbarians (1985), *Celtic Warriors* (1986) and
Medieval Warlords (1987) published by Blandford

British Library Cataloguing-in-Publication Data:
a catalogue record of this book is available from the
British Library

Typeset by Graphicraft Typesetter Ltd., H.K.

Printed at Oriental Press, Dubai, U.A.E.

Frontispiece: European man
has always feared raiding
horse-archers from the
eastern plains. This late
19th century illustration
emphasises the power of
the oriental composite bow.

ACKNOWLEDGEMENTS

Illustrations are reproduced by courtesy of following:
All colour illustrations by Angus McBride.
All black and white illustrations from Peter Newark's
Historical Pictures, except the following:
Archaeological Institute of the Czechoslovak Academy
of Sciences, Brno 124
British Museum, London 15, 22, 54, 56, 57, 58, 59,
60, 61, 74, 81, 85, 87, 89, 94, 103, 122–3, 127, 130,
131, 143, 169, 170, 172 top, 177, 186, 195, 201,
202, 210, 279, 284, 303, 308, 329, 332, 333, 334,
338, 341, 342, 344, 345, 346, 349, 350, 362

Chesca Potter 148, 149, 150
Hermitage Museum, Leningrad 16, 17
National Museum of Antiquities, Helsinki 112
Schleswig-Holstein Landesmuseum 115
State Prehistorical Collection, Munich 33, 34, 36, 37,
69, 71.
The National Museum of Wales, Cardiff (pages 187,
189, 213, 234);
The National Museum of Antiquities of Scotland,
Edinburgh (page 181).
Via Stephen Turnbull 287, 292, 293

Contents

Introduction

This omnibus edition of three Tim Newark volumes is presented for the reader who wants to gain, from one volume, a broad background to warfare and warriors of the two thousand years prior to 1600 AD.

The vivid accounts which follow will entertain as well as educate, they will serve both the adult and novice historian, and will surely enthuse those who like their heroes to be larger-than-life. Though we have suffered two World Wars in this century, the distant days recorded here were seldom as peaceful as we find life to be today. Not only were the smallest plots regularly fought over but only the fittest, strongest and most belligerent - and those who attached themselves to such leaders - survived. The slightest waning in your master's fortunes prejudiced your very existence.

The battles these warlords fought were vicious, remorseless and crude, and yet they were also more colourful. Weapon technology advanced slowly, leaving battlefield ingenuity and daring to hold sway; strategy was limited by the pace of cavalry or the march of the soldier and the man of lower rank was a disposable item of war material in comparison with his king, lord or leader.

As warfare is inevitably part of our world history, so the warlord is a fascinating subject of study.

Ancient Warlords

Barbarian was a derogatory name. An insult. The Greeks used the word for all those people living beyond their frontiers. It was in imitation of the foreigners' incomprehensible, ba-ba-babbling way of talking. Later, the Romans and their heirs applied the word to European and Asian races living outside their empires who did not inhabit sophisticated urban settlements. These Barbarians were viewed as wild, savage people. From their archetypal appearance, the Latins derived their word for a beard, *barba*.

The general image we now have of the Barbarians is still very much one derived from Latin historians. Barbarians are seen as the antithesis of civilisation. Destroyers. For this reason, it has been said, our advanced societies must always be on their guard against Barbarian elements or lapses into Barbarism. This nightmare vision of the anarchic, savage warrior is represented by several dramatic 19th century illustrations reproduced throughout this book. It is an image that has persisted for over 2,000 years.

This century, however, has seen historical research begin to reveal a version of the Barbarian invasions in which the *status quo* of our civilisation was disturbed far less than has been supposed. The times were violent and much was destroyed, but essential power structures remained intact. The Barbarians simply adapted and adopted the systems they overran. Against that background, this book traces the means by which the Barbarians challenged the military might of a strong Mediterranean culture. It tells the story of a thousand years of armed competition.

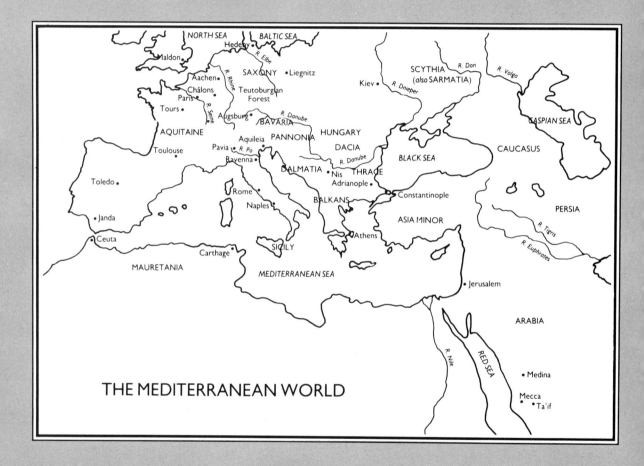

THE MEDITERRANEAN WORLD

The most terrible of all

THE HUNS
AND
EASTERN
GERMANS:
THE
4th TO 5th
CENTURIES

In AD 448, a group of ambassadors rode out from Constantinople on a mission to the land of the Huns. After 13 days, they reached Sofia. Over a dinner of lamb and beef, the members of the party discussed the merits of their leaders. The Romans praised their Emperor. The Huns exalted their King. Bigilas, a high-ranking interpreter, brought the argument to a head. 'Anyway, it is not fitting to compare a God with a man.' His Emperor being the God. The Huns were insulted. Tempers flared. Hands gripped hilts. Slowly, after gifts of Chinese silk and Indian jewels, the Huns were pacified. The mission would continue.

Reaching Nis, the devastation brought by the Barbarian raiders became clear. The city was deserted. Piles of human bones lay scattered by dogs and wolves. Passing that night amongst the ghosts, the ambassadors then rode on to the river Danube, the northern frontier of the eastern Roman Empire. They journeyed through rough, rocky terrain and lost their bearings. A servant cried out, the sun was not in the right place. Strange events were anticipated. On the banks of the Danube, the anxious became excited. Ferried across in primitive, hollowed-out logs, the Romans were now passing into alien territory. A few hours into the Barbaricum, the most important Huns rode ahead of the party to prepare their leader for the envoys. The next day, Barbarian guides brought the Romans to their King's encampment. The land in which this confrontation took place is now called Transylvania. The Barbarian King, for centuries afterwards, was represented in western portraits with dog's ears and goat's horns.

At first, the King of the Huns would not talk to the Romans. Only after sensitive negotiations were they led into his royal tent. The King sat on a simple wooden seat: no gilded throne. From his boots hung no precious beads: from his sleeves no little gold plates: on his head no sparkling diadem: no sword hung from his side. In contrast to the splendid Hun nobles that flanked him, the Barbarian King wore the plainest of clothes. This man was Attila. In later centuries, he was believed to be a monster. Today he is the most notorious of Barbarians. Such a reputation derives from failure.

9

Although highly successful in his initial command of the Huns, Attila never took his people into the Roman Empire to settle among the rich villa estates: the aim of all Barbarians. Attila never became absorbed in the Latin way of life. And yet, because of this life of raiding, he maintained an image as a barbaric outsider long after triumphant Germanic warlords had been accommodated within the Empire. Whether he would have become Romanised eventually is an open question, but dying as he did, in the wastes of the Barbaricum, he has remained the archetypal Barbarian. But what of his people? The Huns possess a notoriety to equal that of their master. And like Attila, their story is laced with tales of the supernatural.

Wild rumours reached the Romans in AD 376 of a new race of Barbarians. Witches expelled from amongst the Goths had coupled with the weird spirits that inhabit the wilderness beyond the Maeotic marshes to produce a savage people. Such tales were at first ignored by Romans familiar with fantastic reports from the Barbaricum. But then came news that the Germanic kingdom of the Ostrogoths had been shattered by a race of men never seen before. Sub-human, like centaurs, these warriors seemed indistinguishable from the beasts they rode. Their faces were hideous to behold; skulls deformed by binding when young and slits for eyes. Swollen cheeks disfigured by scars and covered in wispy hair. Soon the Visigoths were begging to be allowed within the Empire to escape the new horror from the steppes. Clearly the Romans had been wrong to doubt the existence of such a people. Churchmen, forever predicting the coming of the Antichrist, at last seemed vindicated. The Huns had arrived in Europe.

Swift in movement and ferocious in attack, the Huns must indeed have appeared to be the Horsemen of the Apocalypse. Of course, Europeans have always feared mounted raiders from the eastern plains. The Greeks wrote of horsemen from Scythia who devoured strangers and used their skulls as drinking cups. Germanic kings had to defend their Christian realms against pagan Avars and Magyars. While the Mongols very nearly made Europe a mere appendage of an Oriental empire. In the 20th century, this traditional sense of menace has been transferred from the horses and bows of Asian nomads to the 'eastern' tanks and missiles of Communist Russia. It is still the Huns, however, who remain the most terrible of all Barbarians.

Such dread was elaborated in the minds of victims and chroniclers. From the 4th century onwards, the Huns were demonised. To the Romans, the Huns were the most distant, and therefore the first and most ferocious people in a chain-reaction that hurtled Barbarian against Barbarian in the story of Imperial decline. The disintegration of the Empire meant the end of the world and so, for Christians, the Huns were the calamity that would precede the Second Coming. They were the forces of Gog and Magog: the Scourge of God. Reports of the alien Oriental features of the Huns contributed greatly to their fiercesome image. They were the stuff of nightmares and live on in folk tales as ogres covering vast distances in seven-league boots. Even the Avars, thought to be descendants of the hordes of Attila, were believed to use magic to create illusionary effects in battle. Some opposing armies probably wavered under the pyschological impact of the Huns alone. Although much of this terror was in retrospect — the imagination of writers — and most professional warriors must have confronted the Huns with little regard for their reputation or alien appearance.

A great part of the success of the Huns lay in their prowess as horse-warriors. For as nomads, travelling across hundreds of miles of Eurasian steppe, horses had always been essential to them. And in order to control their herds of sheep and cattle, they had naturally developed horsemanship to a high standard. From these skills evolved the martial techniques of the Huns. Even the lasso became a deadly weapon. 'While the enemy are guarding against wounds from sword-thrusts,' recorded a Roman officer, Ammianus, 'the Huns throw strips of cloth plaited into nooses over their opponents so that they are entangled and unable to ride or walk.' The Huns spent so much of their life on horseback that they had difficulty walking. Like American cowboys, they developed a bowlegged gait. In battle, if ever dismounted, they considered themselves dead. Virtually every activity was conducted from horseback. Sometimes they sat side-saddle to carry out specific tasks. Negotiations with Roman diplomats were nearly always debated in the saddle. The horses the Huns rode were tough, shaggy ponies with short legs, common to the steppes. They were muscular and had great stamina. Their smallness gave the Huns considerable control over them and thus provided a stable base for archery as well as hand to hand fighting. Many of the stallions were gelded to make them easier to handle.

The excellent horsemanship of the Huns has often been ascribed to their use of stirrups. No such devices have been found that are attributable to the Huns. Instead, archaeological evidence indicates that stirrups originated in the Far East and only by the 7th century were in use in the Near East and eastern Europe. Besides, the Huns did not need stirrups. Their innate skill and small mounts gave them an advantage over most Western horsemen. The riding equipment of the Huns was primitive. They did not use spurs but urged their horses on with whips. Very few wooden saddles have been found and it must be assumed that the majority of Huns rode on simple stuffed leather pillows. To protect their legs from the sharp blades of long steppe grass, they wore goat-skin chaps.

When the Huns first burst into European history on the plains north of the Black Sea, they clashed with a group of steppe people called the Alans. Defeated, the Alans then allied themselves with the Huns and moved against the eastern Goths — the Ostrogoths — who in turn gave way before the invaders. History says that four hundred years earlier, the Goths had migrated from Sweden across eastern Europe eventually to settle in the grassland of Eurasia. The truth behind this epic journey has been questioned. The story is told by Jordanes in his 6th century Goth chronicle, but how could collective memory and oral history stretch back so far?

Hideous to behold, the Huns were 'demonised' from the 4th century onwards. This war trophy of a head hanging from the saddle was a practice originally ascribed to the Alans. From Guizot's *L'Histoire de France*, 1870.

12

Through its occurrence in other late Germanic chronicles, it seems that Scandinavia was a favoured home land in German folk-lore, whether true or not. For the northern lands were seen as strange and wild, and the home of so many mythical beings. It is possible, however, that the Goths did travel from the Baltic to southern Russia in much the same way as did the Swedes several hundred years later, sailing along the extensive waterways of Eurasia. Like the Swedish Vikings, the Goths were efficient sailors and their ships were already terrorising Black Sea ports by the 3rd century.

Living along the waterways of what the ancient Greeks had called Scythia, the eastern Germans became firmly established. They were no less fierce than the Sarmatian people they lived amongst. The Alans were reputed to wear the heads and flayed skins of their dead enemies on their horses as trophies. The Germans did not, however, fight in the same way as the oriental tribesmen who lived around them, and this may account for the shock defeats inflicted upon them by the Huns. Though adapting themselves partly to the bow and horse warfare of Eurasia, they strongly retained the instinct of their Germanic forefathers for fighting with spear and sword. They readily adopted the long lances of the Sarmatians but not their bows. The Ostrogoths probably also wore the heavy armour that was a characteristic of the Sarmatians. Made of overlapping scales of bone, horn and iron, it was sewn together with the sinews of horses or oxen. Some

Scenes from Scythian life. The upper drawing shows horsemanship typical of all Eurasian nomads. The lower drawing demonstrates the stringing of a bow as well as rudimentary medical measures. Both drawings are of friezes on electrum vases from the 3rd and 4th centuries BC, found in the steppeland just north of the Black Sea and now in the Hermitage, Leningrad.

armour was made from the hoofs of mares, split to resemble the scales of a dragon. 'Anyone who has not seen a dragon,' suggested the geographer Pausanias, 'is best advised to compare the appearance of a warrior clad in such armour to a green fir cone'.

The Sarmatians, an Iranian-speaking people, had dominated south-west Russia for several centuries but now, with the coming of the Huns, were in decline. It was among these tribes that the myth of the Amazons originated. Wearing men's clothes, long trousers and soft leather boots, Sarmatian wives were believed to join their husbands in hunting and battle. Virgins were not allowed to marry until they had killed an enemy in combat. Young girls had their right breasts scorched with a hot iron so that these might not prevent the girls using their right arms in fighting. Such stories are not without foundation. Ancient graves discovered in Russia have shown women lying next to spearheads, arrows and suits of scale armour.

The Huns were a wholly nomadic people. Driving their grazing herds before them, they trundled onwards with their families and felt-tents packed in huge wagons. Their origin is a mystery. Most often they have been identified with the Hsiung-nu Mongolians who terrorised the Chinese but were eventualy thrown back into central Asia. That these Mongolians then trekked across the whole of Asia seems a needlessly epic undertaking. They could have continued their activities much closer to home. Indeed, it was probably the Hsiung-nus switching of raids to peoples to the west of them, that then encouraged these people to move out of the Mongolian

Scythian archer on horseback, firing backwards. Greek bronze, c 500 BC, from the British Museum, London.

sphere of influence. Alternatively, it may have been a series of particularly devastating droughts – a regular hazard on the steppes – that broke the usual grazing cycles of tribesmen around the Aral and Caspian seas and spurred them on to new pastures, and thus clash with the Alans and Goths. On this basis, it seems likely that the Huns were an essentially Turkish confederation of tribes. A relatively open association, that no doubt also included tribes from further afield, like Mongolia. Such a force would have been totally horse-borne. It would also have been full of expert plunderers, for such a large unsettled group of people depended on raids and rustling to supplement its own drought-ravaged resources.

The Goth horsemen who first observed the relentless caravans of hostile, hungry people invading their territory must have been awestruck. To defend their homeland, they gathered together all able-bodied men in a roughly hewn army. The majority of these warriors were farmers and others engaged in settled pursuits. Unlike the professional raiders and marauders who comprised the armed retinues of their leading warriors and chieftains, these men did not own horses or swords, but fought on foot with anything to hand. When battle was joined, such men were hopelessly equipped to deal with the large numbers of Hun horse-archers. Refusing to engage in

A Eurasian horse-warrior clad in characteristic Sarmatian fashion. He wears scale armour and carries his lance in both hands, as did most horsemen of this period. This warrior appears on a marble stele found at Tanais, at the mouth of the River Don on the coast of the Sea of Azov. Now in the Hermitage, Leningrad.

close combat, the Huns preferred to pour a hail of arrows into the crowd of Goths. Howling and screaming, the Huns dashed about in wild bands, evading the charges of the lance-carrying Goth horse-warriors and then suddenly turning to pelt them with more arrows. Only when weakened and scattered by such attacks did the Huns then plunge amongst the enemy and swing sword against spear. These were the classic tactics of all true steppe warriors.

The bow the Huns used so effectively was the composite bow. The most deadly missile weapon in the Ancient and Medieval World, it was the primary weapon of all Oriental horsemen. It outdistanced the longbow and could penetrate armour at 100 yards/metres. So valued was it, that Hun nobles gave each other gilded bows as a sign of authority. The power of the composite bow derived from the combined strength of several materials. A wooden core was backed with layers of sinew and bellied on the inside with strips of horn. All these materials were then sandwiched together with an animal glue in a process which took much practice and was not easily mastered. The gluing of horn to wood was usually carried out in winter when cooler, humid conditions slowed – and thus toughened – the setting. Glue-soaked sinew was better applied on a warm spring day. The bow

17

would be left to set for two months at least. After its use, throughout the summer and autumn, it was unstrung and reconditioned. The combination of wood, sinew and horn produced a highly flexible bow which allowed a far longer draw than was usual from a short bow. It was thus ideal for use on horseback. Longer bows were more accurate, even if they became more susceptible to stress, but demanded a firm foothold and so were rarely used by horse-archers. The most powerful bows were stressed near to breaking point and needed to be warmed for an hour before being strung. Such easily-snapped bows were used for sport, while more sturdy and reliable bows were used in battle. Average range for use of a composite bow fired from horseback at the gallop was ten yards/metres. When standing still, a maximum effective range of 250 yards has been claimed. A major improvement in the design of the composite bow was devised in the Far East and Central Asia. The adding of strips of bone to the tips of the bow, holding the string, increased greatly its strength. This bone-reinforced bow was the weapon used by the Huns. Roman and German warriors highly prized any such bows picked up on the battlefield intact although they frequently lacked the expertise to use them effectively.

By AD 376 the Huns dominated Eurasia as far as the Danube. The Alans had been absorbed into the horde, while the Goths that had escaped asked permission of the Eastern Emperor to be allowed within the relative safety of the Empire. Such an entreaty was welcomed by the Emperor Valens as the Goths promised to fight with the Roman army. This influx of new recruits meant that money instead of conscripts could now be accepted from provincial landowners who preferred to part with gold rather than labourers. So enthusiastic were the Romans that they made boats available to ferry the refugees across the Danube. Roman officers escorted the Barbarians to ensure that they had disarmed as ordered. Such a condition of entry to the Empire was a severe blow to the Goth armoury, for their collection of weapons had been built up over years of manufacture, trade and plunder and could not easily be replaced. Valens even restricted Goth merchants to specific market towns where arms could not be bought. Fortunately for the Goths, most of the Romans escorting them were more interested in chasing good-looking women and picking up cheap slaves rather than enforcing the arms ban. Many Barbarian warriors slipped into Roman territory with their weapons hidden.

The shifting of a whole people is a massive operation. At one stage, rumours of the Huns being close at hand, sent the refugees into panic. Some desperately cut down trees, hollowed them out and tried to row across the rain swollen river. Many drowned. Once in the Balkans, the situation deteriorated. Corrupt Roman officials diverted supplies of food intended for the Goths and sold what little did reach them at highly inflated prices. Some Goths were reduced to offering their fellow tribesmen as slaves in exchange for dogs to eat. Famine and disease spread amongst the refugee camps. In their frustration, warriors began to ransack the surrounding countryside

Gilt bronze belt plaque showing two wild horses fighting. Characteristic of Eurasian steppe culture, it comes from the Ordos region of China.

and soon the Goths were in revolt. Marauding bands of Barbarian horsemen looted villas and ravaged the farmlands of Thrace. The consequences of the Hun migration were becoming dangerously clear.

On hearing this news, the Emperor Valens returned from the Near East in 378 with a veteran army and began to hunt down the freebooting Goths. Saracen horsemen with lances were sent out to harass the Barbarians. They were successful and brought back many heads. Next, the guerilla war was stepped up with a force of 2,000 picked troops installed in several walled cities. These Romans, carrying only swords and small, light shields, crept up on Goth gangs while they were foraging, resting, or drunk on their spoils, and efficiently butchered them. Such tactics slowly but surely curtailed the Barbarian raiding. Despite this, political rivals envious of the success of the task force commander, urged Valens to commit all his forces in one great battle to end the menace once and for all. Valens agreed and on the outskirts of Adrianople, receiving information that underestimated the strength of a nearby horde, he prepared for battle. He was advised to wait for the extra troops that his nephew Gratian, Emperor of the West, would soon bring. But impatient for military glory to equal that of this nephew, he ignored good counsel and left the security of his fortified camp.

It was a hot August day and approaching noon when Valens' legions spied the Goth encampment. In typical Barbarian fashion, the Goths had arranged their great four-wheeled wagons in a defensive laager. Within the wagon circle, the Goths yelled insults and war-cries as the Imperial army drew up into battle formation. Roman horsemen gathered on the right wing but those meant to secure the left flank of foot-soldiers were still scattered along the roads leading to the battlefield. Some Roman archers began to pelt the Barbarian wagons while legionaries clashed their shields. Anxiety began to spread amongst the Goths despite their initial ferocity, for a significant

19

number of their horse-warriors were away foraging. Intermingled as they were with their women and children, their aggression must have been tempered with concern. Fritigern, the Goth chieftain, tried to buy time with proposals of peace. As envoys travelled backwards and forwards, his warriors started fires on the parched plain to increase the discomfort of legionaries already sweltering under the afternoon sun. For a group of Armenian auxiliaries the strain proved too much and they broke ranks, rushing against the Barbarian laager. The clash was short and hasty, and they were forced to withdraw ignominiously. The Romans considered it an ill omen.

The wait before battle must have been demoralising. Nerves, exhaustion and thirst would have stifled any remaining impetus amongst the lower Roman ranks to crush the raiders. Much of that day seems to have been spent waiting. Fritigern's delays were no doubt proving strenuous to both sides. Then, suddenly, all hell broke loose. The Goth horse-warriors had returned from plundering and now bore down on the weary Roman troops. Surprised and tired out, the Roman cavalry broke before the charging Barbarians and were soon joined by fellow foot-soldiers they had thus left exposed. With no massed ranks of shields and spears to discourage their horses, the Goths could dash among the disintegrating legions and use superior mobility and height to savage those on foot. Goths with lances rushed after fleeing legionaries as if pig-sticking. Those foot-soldiers who struck back suffered from the downward, crushing slashes of the Barbarians' long double-edged sword, the *spatha*. But this alone did not guarantee the Goth horse-warriors victory, for concerted spearmen can ensnare cavalry and determined swordsmen, with no fear of flailing hoofs, can cut and stab at both rider and mount. Chaos, however, had gripped the Romans and thrown their formations into a stampeding crowd. In the crush to escape the slaughter, soldiers were packed so closely that those who retained their weapons could hardly raise them. Many suffocated. Clouds of dust enshrouded the struggling, shrieking masses. Arrows struck from nowhere. Gangs of horse-warriors appeared suddenly to swoop murderously on isolated groups of legionaries. Those Goths waiting within the wagon defences now joined in the fury that threatened to engulf the Romans. Foot-soldiers with spears and clubs, anything to hand, slogged away at the Roman front and pushed it back. As escape proved increasingly remote, many legionaries returned to the offensive. In their desperation, in the crowd, Roman wounded Roman. The battle dragged on until exhaustion reduced all remaining resolve. Stimulated by victory, the Barbarians pressed forward across the heaps of dead and dying and pursued the routed Imperial forces. The Roman reserve of German cavalry had already disappeared. Emperor Valens was lost amongst his soldiers and killed in the chase that continued into the night.

Barely a third of the Imperial army escaped the disaster outside Adrianople. The Goths must have suffered heavy losses too but they had won a remarkable victory. On this battlefield, military historians have claimed that medieval warfare began. The supremacy of the horse-warrior had eclipsed the infantry-based tactics of the Mediterranean Ancient World. Such a neat formula is far from the truth. Before and after the 4th century, disciplined infantry could soundly defeat horse-borne armies. In 507 at Vouillé, Frank warriors on foot, wielding axes, broke a force of Goth cavalry armed with lance and sword, just like that above. Adrianople itself was not simply a clear-cut victory of Barbarian horsemen over legionary infantry. The Goth foot-soldiers that emerged from behind their wagons carried the weight of sheer hard fighting that capitalised on the surprise of their horsemen. Besides, the majority of Goths always fought on foot. The decisive factors against the Romans in this battle were the exhaustion of their troops, the shock of the returning Goths and then the ensuing chaos in which they could not offer an effective defence against the enemy, whether on foot or horseback. In addition, the Emperor Valens, by not waiting for extra military support, had proved himself an incompetent commander. The Roman army was not exclusively composed of foot-soldiers, and by the 4th century it included many fine horse-warriors, usually recruited from the Barbarians and frequently armed similarly to their adversaries. If the Roman cavalry at Adrianople had not panicked, they might well have proved equal, perhaps superior, to the Goths, as they did on many other occasions.

Free from Imperial restraint, the Goths rampaged through the Balkans. They attacked the city of Adrianople as the dead Emperor's treasure was believed to be hidden there. Apparently the Goths lacked the expertise in siege warfare to overcome the walls and met stiff resistance. To prevent the Barbarians from re-using the arrows fired at them, the citizens partly cut the cords securing the barbs to the shafts so that they remained in one piece in flight but on impact broke up. The Romans also used artillery mounted on the walls to great effect. One machine, called a 'scorpion' from the way its lethal catapult leapt into the air, flung a huge rock amongst the crowd of warriors recklessly charging forward. Though it crashed to the ground missing the enemy, it spread terror amongst the Barbarians. Beneath this storm of stone, javelins, and slabs of columns ripped from within the city, the Goths became discouraged and eventually withdrew. They continued to plunder the open country. Attacking only towns without walls or those given up to them by deserters. The Goths, however, could not resist the possibility of capturing Constantinople – capital of the Eastern Empire, with riches to exceed even those of Rome – and they rode optimistically towards this jewel. In this endeavour, the historian Ammianus claims they were joined by Huns and Alans.

Awe-inspiring in its wealth, Constantinople also presented a terrific bastion of walls and fortifications. Nevertheless, the Barbarians rushed forward with their scaling ladders and began the assault. They were assisted most probably by Roman prisoners and deserters who helped them to build siege machines. Amongst the Roman garrison, however, was a group of Saracen horsemen. Bursting out from the city gates, they engaged the Goths in fierce hand to hand fighting. The mad action of one Saracen so appalled the Barbarians that it passed into legend. Riding into the midst of the enemy, this Saracen with long hair and naked except for a loin-cloth, thrust his dagger wildly into a Goth. Howling terribly, he then leapt from his horse and bit the neck of the dying warrior, sucking the blood that flowed out. Shaken by this vampiric act, the determination of the Barbarians was further undermined by the sheer technical superiority of the defending Romans. The Goths left as swiftly as they had arrived.

To deal with the Goths, Theodosius, a renowned general, was called back from retirement in Spain. In the winter of 378, he arrived in the Balkans with an army probably similar to that slaughtered at Adrianople and inflicted defeat upon the Barbarians. Eventually, Theodosius was made Emperor of the East and concluded a peace treaty with the Visigoths which gave them substantial tracts of land within the Empire. Many were recruited into the army. Similarly, those Goths who had split from the forces of Fritigern after Adrianople, known as the Ostrogoths, advanced westwards into Pannonia and were accepted in peace by the Western Emperor Gratian. The Romans now hoped that the Goths would act as a buffer between them and the bulk of the Huns who dominated the Barbaricum north of the Danube.

After their initial inroad into eastern Europe, the Huns appear to have lost their impetus. Throughout the rest of Theodosius' long reign and into the first decades of the 5th century, the western Huns settled into a semi-nomadic existence. Raising their tents in Hungary, they were content to limit their movements to sporadic raids across the Danube. Factions grew amongst the Huns and they no longer acted as a unified force. Many were employed in Roman armies to defeat the invasions of German barbarians to the west of them. Others joined the gangs of bandits, deserters and refugees that continued to terrorise the Balkans. During this period, the Alans seceded from the horde and joined the Vandals in their surge towards Spain. A more cohesive and enterprising campaign was carried out by those Huns who remained north of the Black Sea. In the summer of 395, the eastern Huns tore through the passes of the Caucasus and broke into Persia and the Roman provinces of Asia Minor and Syria. They were rigorously defeated. Persian and Roman armies of horse-archers confronted them on equal terms and forced them back through the mountains. In that summer the Huns demonstrated the speed and range of their raids, descending as far as the Euphrates and Antioch.

By the middle of the 5th century, the robber bands of the Huns were welded once more into a single force strong enough to attempt an ambitious campaign. The western Huns were now led by two supreme chieftains – two kings – Bleda and his younger brother, Attila. Both these warriors began their reign by securing dominance over the northern tribes of

Bronze plaque in form of man. Thought to be Hunnic, though bearing Caucasian features, possibly Germanic. From the Ordos region, 1st century BC, now in the British Museum, London.

22

Sarmatia. From there, they glanced across the border towards an Empire that offered them more material riches than they could ever obtain in the Barbaricum. While a man could spend his whole life scraping a living in the forests and plains of Eurasia, any freebooter daring within the Empire could dress himself in gold cloth, eat bread and meat, have a hot bath, and get drunk whenever he wished. These were the prizes of civilisation!

In 441 the Huns violated a trade agreement by capturing a border market town. In justification of their act they claimed that the bishop of Margus had crossed the Danube and stolen treasure from Hun tombs. This was a frequent occurence, even amongst clergy. The Huns demanded the handing over of the bishop as well as any escaped prisoners harboured by the Romans. After several more frontier towns were devastated, the bishop agreed to his fate. But in the end he saved his own skin by promising Attila to betray the city of Margus. The bishop slipped back into his city, opened the gates, and allowed it to be annihilated. The season's raiding ended with a great gap rent in the Danube defences. The next year the Romans gained a respite through patching up a treaty. But in 443 they felt strong enough to defy the Huns' call for tribute money. Again Attila and Bleda invaded the borderland and this time they plunged into the interior. Town and country were wrecked as far as Constantinople where, outside the walls, the Huns were confronted by an army led by Romanised German generals. The Romans were beaten. The Emperor was forced to sue for peace and treble the annual tribute to 2,100 pounds of gold.

Within the horde, such success brought with it rivalry and in 445 Attila murdered Bleda and assumed absolute command of the Huns. To reinforce

Goth refugees crossing the Danube into the Roman Empire to escape from the Huns. From Guizot's *L'Histoire de France*, 1870.

his position he proclaimed that an ancient rusty sword, dug up and brought to him by a peasant, was the sword of Mars. He now had the approval of the God of War. Such a supernatural power seemed demonstrated when Attila launched a second, greater attack on the Eastern Empire in 447. Before the invasion, earthquakes shattered the land. Towns were swallowed up. The walls of Constantinople collapsed. Storms and plague followed. And then came Attila. The Romans decided to gather their forces together and meet the Huns in one final decisive conflict. They lost. Attila had broken the Balkans. But, that said, resistance must still have been strong enough to deter him and his people from settling there permanently, for they retreated back to Hungary laden with booty.

The victories of the Huns at this stage cannot be ascribed to the military superiority or inferiority of either side. Both forces fought with a similar armoury. Horse-archers supported by heavier armoured lancers formed the basis of most eastern European armies during this period. Advantage lay in numbers, morale and leadership, and this was frequently determined simply by the fortunes of war. In addition to these factors, the Romans suffered particularly from continuing economic crises and the draining demands of the Persian frontier. The Huns had little to lose and were driven on by the promise of plunder.

The composition of the Hun horde in this period was highly cosmopolitan. Warriors from all conquered races fought under Attila: Turks, Persians, Sarmatians, Germans and Romans. During his stay at the camp of Attila, envoy and chronicler Priscus was approached by a man dressed as a Hun nobleman. The man spoke Greek and revealed that he had been captured by the Huns in 441. He had fought well for his new masters against the Romans and been allowed to marry a Hun woman. He now dined with the leading warriors and led a life more prosperous than he had ever had as a Roman merchant constantly threatened by tax extortion and Imperial corruption. The number of horsemen fighting under Attila has often been fantastically exaggerated. Hordes of half a million have been claimed by chroniclers determined to make them seem overwhelming in order to excuse Roman defeats or glorify victories. Instead, it has been suggested what the average raiding force probably numbered about a thousand horse-warriors at the most. Attila's army would have been considerably large than this, but there again at any one time many contingents would have been engaged in separate plundering expeditions, like the Ostrogoths at Adrianople.

For three years Attila enjoyed the booty and tributes of the Eastern Empire, then, in 450, he turned his attention to the West. He proposed to march as an ally of the Western Emperor Valentinian and rid Roman landowners of the Visigoths that had settled in the south of France. By such a move, he intended to displace the Romano-Barbarian warlord Aetius as protector of the West and thus control Gaul and the Western Empire with the permission of the Emperor. A craving for plunder had been replaced by

Attila observes the savage battle of the Catalaunian Plains in northern France, AD 451. His demonic likeness is based on Renaissance woodcut portraits. From Ward Lock's *Illustrated History of the World*, 1885.

more sophisticated power politics. Attila seemed ready at last to leave his raiding and accommodate himself within the Empire. Relations with the Emperor soured, however, after Valentinian refused to give up his sister in marriage to Attila and with her half of his Empire.

In Gaul, dynastic struggles among the Franks saw one faction side with Aetius and the other with the Huns. When Attila crossed the Rhine, he faced a western coalition of Franks and Gallic tribes, Visigoths under Theoderic, and a Romano-German force led by Aetius. It was an uneasy alliance. Theoderic and Aetius had been bitter enemies for years. At first Theoderic was prepared only to defend his lands around Toulouse, but envoys from the Emperor managed to convince him of the need to present a combined front and save the whole of Gaul. As for Aetius, he had been a life-long friend of the Huns and fought with them on many occasions against Germans. Indeed, his use of the Huns to annihilate the Burgundians sparked off a tradition of epic poetry which culminated in the tale of the *Nibelungenlied*, preserving a Germanic dread of the Huns long after the event. In his youth, Aetius had spent much time with the Huns as an Imperial hostage and become a skilled archer and horseman. He knew their ways very well.

The two forces clashed in a titanic battle somewhere in Champagne called the Catalaunian Plains or *locus Mauriacus*. This is generally believed to have been near the town of Chalons-sur-Marne. Numerous peoples and tribes gathered here in June 451. Jordanes, Goth chronicler, wrote of the events of that day as if describing Armageddon. 'What just cause can be found for the encounter of so many nations,' he wondered, 'what hatred fired them all to take arms against each other? It is evident that the human race lives for its kings. At the mad impulse of one mind, a slaughter of nations takes place. At the whim of a haughty ruler, that which nature has taken so long to create is destroyed in a moment.'

The battle began towards the end of the day. Horse-warriors rode from both sides to seize a ridge above the plain. Roman horse-archers clad in mail and scale armour dashed forward. Joined by Visigoth nobles and their retainers, wielding lance and sword, they captured one side. Along the other slope charged the Huns with allied German tribes. A great struggle now ensued for the crest of the hill. Archers let fly from afar while Germanic warriors thrust and hacked at each other. A contingent of Alans confronted the Huns, their former masters. Their loyalty was in doubt and so Aetius placed them between the Romans on the left wing and the Visigoths on the right. Now they could not so easily run away. Attila positioned his bravest and finest warriors in the centre, with Ostrogoths and other subject Germans on their flanks. As the fight for the hill intensified, foot-soldiers joined in. Those Franks allied with the Romans, hurled their famed tomahawk axes at the enemy before running into close combat. Other Germans, Romans, and Huns just battered away with spear and shield.

Eventually the Romans and Visigoths gained the upper hand and threw the Huns back down the hill. Attila rode amongst the action and rallied his men with words of strength. 'Let the wounded exact in vengeance the death of his foe,' he bellowed. 'Let those without wounds revel in the slaughter of the enemy! No spear shall harm those who are sure to live. And those who are sure to die-Fate overtakes anyway in peace!' Warriors hammered each other until exhaustion or pain overcame them. Theoderic, an old and venerable chieftain, encouraged his Visigoths against their kinsmen, the Ostrogoths. They fought furiously and in the crowd Theoderic was struck down dead. Angered by such a loss, the Visigoths pushed back their adversaries and fell upon the majority of the Huns. Many Huns and their allies now took flight while Attila and the body of his army retreated behind the bulky wagons of their encampment. As dusk drew on, fighting became confused in the half light, gradually ceasing as weary warriors made their way back to their camps. During the night, it was claimed, the ghosts of the fallen continued the battle.

The next day, each side awoke to the awful spectacle of a battlefield heaped with the slain and wounded. Slashed and cut warriors stumbled back to their tribal groups. If bound cleanly, their lacerations would heal. Those pierced by lance and arrow, bursting vital organs, stood little chance. Arrows with barbed heads ripped great holes in the skin. Those fired by the Huns were believed to be tipped with poison. Though this is probably not true, they most certainly did carry ordinary infection deep into the body. Inflammation and putrefaction set in and warriors groaned as sickness or disease claimed many still left alive after the shock of combat. Undeterred by the carnage, the Visigoths demanded to finish off the Huns. They burned to avenge their chieftain. Attila prepared for a last stand. Determined not to be taken alive, he piled saddles within his wagons to form a fire, upon which he would fling himself. But as the Visigoths grieved for their dead king and readied themselves for battle, Aetius consulted their leaders. He believed that with the Huns totally vanquished, the Visigoths, drunk with victory, would overrun the whole of Gaul. Therefore, he advised the son of Theoderic that others might sieze power in his homeland if he suffered badly in the forthcoming fight. Apparently accepting this counsel, the Visigoths left immediately for Toulouse. Aetius used a similar argument to recommend the withdrawal of the Franks. Attila and his mauled forces were thus allowed to retreat eastwards. It seems likely that Aetius wished to maintain the Huns as a force he could play against the Germans, as against the Burgundians. But he had made an error of judgment, for the Huns were not going to fade away until he needed them. Furious at his defeat, Attila and his horde rode into Italy.

From Aquileia to Milan, northern Italy was devastated. Such depredations only added to the famine and plague that already dominated the countryside. So that when news reached Attila of an attack on his territory by the Eastern Empire, he speedily returned to Hungary, sparing the rest of Italy. On the steppes of Eurasia, Attila planned a campaign against Constantinople that would ensure the tribute of the Romans forever. The opportunity never came. Celebrating the addition of another woman to his harem, Attila lay flat out drunk in his tent. He was not conscious of the nose-bleed that ran down into his throat and choked him. In the power struggle that followed, the sons of Attila and the leaders of subject tribes tore the great Barbarian's kingdom apart. In a series of ferocious battles, the majority of the Huns were crushed by the Germans and fled back to the steppeland north of the Black Sea − the scene of their first victories eighty years before.

The Huns had ceased to be a threat to Europe and the Roman Empire, but the spirit of the Huns was not dead. Over the next few centuries, their infamy was absorbed by each new terror from the East. Although these were different confederations of tribes, led by other strong men, the West still called the steppe warriors Huns. Europe would not forget Attila. Despite their ferocity, however, and their damaging campaigns, the Huns did not destroy the Roman Empire. They had not even established themselves on Imperial territory. They were raiders not invaders. Like all other oriental nomads, before and after, they only scratched the surface of the European world. It was left to the German tribes to transform the Empire into great estates held by their warlords. The raids and invasions of the Germans grew in momentum over hundreds of years. From the 1st century to the 5th century. An assault not as dramatic as that of the Huns, but far more profound.

Fear in the forest

Six years after their slaughter by German tribesmen, the remains of governor Varus and three Roman legions – 15,000 men – lay scattered among the brushwood and bracken of the Teutoburgian Forest. Pausing in the middle of a retaliatory campaign across the Rhine, Germanicus and his legionaries solemnly surveyed the location of this disaster. It must have been a chilling series of discoveries: heaps of bleached bones and splintered weapons. On surrounding tree trunks the skulls of Roman prisoners had been nailed as a ferocious warning that Arminius, German chieftain, still dominated the forest. Survivors of the butchery pointed out the forest altars upon which captured tribunes and centurions had had their throats slit, in sacrifice to the northern gods of War.

Tacitus, the historian of this scene, felt that such a paying of respects served only to terrify even further Roman troops far away from their Gallic camps in the dank dark Teutoburger Wald. It is a tribute to the steady command of Germanicus that he managed to conduct the rest of his punitive expedition with some success. Fear can break an army. German warriors chanted on the battlefield before fighting. The tone of their shouts indicated whether they were terrifying their enemy or becoming scared themselves and thus foretold the outcome of combat. Some warriors held their shields in front of their mouths to amplify this noise. The Roman legions managed to reduce the natural fear of battle through uniform discipline and practised tactics. But in AD 9 in the western German forestland, such composure had given way.

Varus and his troops had crossed the Rhine and entered what they believed to be friendly territory on their way to putting down an uprising. This guarantee was given by Arminius, a young chieftain of the Cherusci, who had served with the Romans on several expeditions and been granted citizenship. Arminius, however, was a deceiver and wished to crush the governor Varus for hastily trying to impose Roman laws and taxes upon his people. Apparently reassured by Arminius, Varus dispersed many of this soldiers to assist in local village affairs while the main body of troops,

THE
WESTERN
GERMANS:
THE
1st TO 4th
CENTURIES

Germanicus buries the
remains of the three Roman
legions slaughtered by
Arminius in AD 9. From Ward
Lock's *Illustrated History of
the World*, 1885.

wagons and camp followers trundled forward. Where secret forest paths
proved insufficient, trees were felled and undergrowth cleared. Heavy rain
fall made the ground slippery and treacherous. Ravines and marshland had
to be bridged. As Varus advanced deeper into the dismal wood, Arminius
excused himself from the main force and joined his gathering warriors.
With the Roman soldiers scattered amongst wagons and pack animals, and
bogged down in a sludge of roots and mud, the Cherusci attacked.

Howling and screaming, the Germans pounced upon the isolated groups
of legionaries. At first, spears were hurled from the thickets. But then, as
the Romans fell back in disarray, the tribesmen closed in and used the same
spears as stabbing weapons. The dense forest and the shock of ambush
prevented the Romans from assuming their battle formations and allowed
the Germans to catch legionaries by themselves. In close combat, the
physical presence of the Barbarians undoubtedly proved intimidating to
those recruits from Mediterranean countries. Of a larger build, with an alien
pale skin and red hair, the Germans frequently fought semi-naked, with
chests adorned only with scars or tattoos, or wrapped in animal skins. Other
wild sights confronted the Romans. Some young tribesmen, having let their

29

hair and beards grow long so as to cover their face in accordance with a vow of manhood, now stood over a slain enemy and slashed at their hair. At last, through this blood of their foe, they had become worthy of their parents and homeland and could show their face. Exposed to such terrific attacks in a chaotic four-day running battle of relentless ambush, it is little wonder that few survivors of those original three legions emerged from the Teutoburgian Forest. Varus killed himself before capture by falling on his sword. His head was cut off and sent to Roman leaders south of the Rhine.

The Varian Disaster was a tremendous Barbarian victory over the Roman Empire and halted its expansion significantly. When news of the defeat reached Rome, soldiers had to be posted throughout the city to prevent a riot. Emperor Augustus and his subjects had been speaking of the recently explored land between the Rhine and the River Elbe as their latest province of Germania. Now all this was shattered, and Germany north of the Rhine never became part of the Roman Empire. Of course, the Romans could not leave this humiliation as it stood and over the next years conducted many retaliatory campaigns across the Rhine, not least of them the expedition of Germanicus. But essentially the German tribes remained unconquered.

The calamity of AD 9 was not the first the Germans had inflicted upon the Romans. 'Neither by the Samnites, the Carthaginians, Spain or Gaul, or even the Parthians,' remarks Tacitus, 'have we had more lessons taught us.' Earlier in the reign of Augustus, a legionary standard had been lost embarrassingly to raiders from across the middle Rhine. A hundred years before that, two roving German tribes, the Cimbri and Teutones, had threatened an invasion of Italy itself and defeated several Republican armies. But were the Germans superior as warriors to the neighbouring, defeated Celts of Gaul? With regard to military technology they were considerably inferior. For centuries, the Germans had imported finer iron weapons from the Celtic tribes of central Europe. The beautifully worked helmets and shields of the Celts were virtually unknown among the Germans; as was the Celtic use of chariots, which so impressed the Romans. Fortified earthworks like those of the Britons and Gauls were rare north of the Rhine. So why should the Celtic peoples of Spain, France, Britain and central Europe have fallen so completely to the Romans while conquest of the Germanic lands remained elusive?

Caesar's conquest of Gaul had succeeded partly because of dissension among the Celtic tribes. Many Gauls fought as auxiliaries with the Romans. Similarly, the invasion of Britain in AD 43 was undertaken because the Celtic Britons had become increasingly Romanised through their contact with Gaul. Invitations to intervene in their politics from factions amongst the Britons led Emperor Claudius to assume that here was a relatively easily-obtained feather in his cap. When the Celtic Britons did present a concerted opposition, as in the rebellion of Queen Boudicca, the Romans had a much tougher time.

In contrast to their southern neighbours, the Germans were not as familiar with the benefits of Imperial life. They lacked the sophisticated contacts that the Celts had with Mediterranean culture. They were less inclined to invite the intervention of the Romans. After all, it was their general hostility to the Romans over hundreds of years that maintained their cultural independence long after the Celts had become submerged in the Empire and lost their national identity. And yet, the Germans were tempted by the material wealth of the Empire and tapped it constantly through trading and raiding. In the end, it was the appeal of life within the Empire that spurred on the great invasions of later centuries. As for the fatal discord of the Celts, intertribal conflict was endemic among the Germans and many leading German chieftains sided with the Romans against their fellow countrymen. Opportunites were there to divide and conquer.

At this point, then, it must be remembered that the Romans had already conquered part of Germany. By 9 BC, Drusus, stepson of Augustus had conducted a series of successful campaigns beyond the Rhine and subdued the region as far as the River Elbe. Other Roman generals followed and all the main tribes had apparently submitted to Imperial rule. But this was

A late 19th century vision of the Teutoburger Wald as it would have looked when Governor Varus met his death there. In the foreground is an auroch, a species of wild cattle whose bulls, according to Caesar, grew to the size of elephants.

virgin territory. The slow process of Romanisation had only just begun when Arminius and his tribesmen threw out the remnants of Imperial occupation in the wake of the Varian Disaster. It was possible to defeat the Germans, but the problem was the maintenance of Roman rule. Strabo, a contemporary geographer, said that the Germans were like the Celts in every way, except that they were fiercer. This may have been true, although such a belief probably derived from the fact that the Germans were remoter and more primitive than the Celts. The decisive factor does seem to have been the guerilla warfare of Arminius. After such a calamitous defeat in AD 9, the Romans looked again at the strategic and logistical cost of re-invading Germany and decided it was simply not worth it. Gaul was near to Italy, a neighbouring land, whereas Germany vastly over-extended the supply routes of the Empire, and required a great investment of resources and troops. Besides, what was to be gained materially from colonisation of these inhospitable tracts of northern Europe? The Roman Empire was essentially a Mediterranean-centred economic community, and trade could always be conducted across the Rhine and Danube. And so, in the absence of any major weakness in the opposition of the Germans – such as existed among the Celtic Britons – the great rivers would provide a convenient natural frontier.

The victory of Arminius in the Teutoburgian Forest was won against all odds. The Roman army was superior in almost every way to its Barbarian

German warriors ambush Roman legionaries in the forests of western Germany. Guerilla warfare was the most successful opposition to Roman expansion in Northern Europe. From Ward Lock's *Illustrated History of the World*, 1885.

adversaries. The Romans frequently amazed their enemies with their advanced military technology. Caesar records the astonishment of the Gauls at Roman bridge-building, siege engines and warships. The Gallic chieftain Vercingetorix comforted his defeated warriors by concluding, 'The Romans have not conquered us through their courage in pitched battle, but with ingenuity. As in their knowledge of siege operations in which the Gauls have no experience.' Roman campaign management was overwhelming. There was a constant back up of food and weapons. The Germans, however, did not organise supply systems and relied on reaching enemy territory so that they could plunder for food. Every man took care of himself. Romans forewarned of a raid would stockpile all food in their area, so that Barbarians would be defeated by famine before battle was joined.

Even in close combat – the favoured test of arms and courage of the German warrior – the Romans possessed a superiority in weapons and armour. Germanicus encouraged his soldiers with a description of the military poverty of the enemy. 'The Germans wear neither breastplate nor helmet,' he claimed. 'Their shields are not even strengthened with metal or hide but are made of wickerwork, or thin, painted wood. They carry only spears and many of these are simply fire-hardened pointed sticks. Their bodies, while grim enough to behold, are powerful only for a short-lived onset and lack the stamina to bear a wound.' Certainly, in hand to hand fighting, the iron mail or plate armour of the Roman legionaries gave them a distinct advantage over near-naked Germans. The main weapon of the Germans was the spear, called *framea* by the Romans, and though this could be a primitive affair, many had short, narrow iron blades. These spears

Celtic bronze helmets from southern Germany, now in the State Prehistorical Collection, Munich. The Celts were far more sophisticated than their Germanic neighbours and possessed a superior military technology.

were either thrown or used in close combat as stabbing weapons. To this extent, spears had a longer reach than the Roman short sword and could have proved more useful for penetrating armour than a slashing sword. The Roman javelin, the *pilum*, could not be used as a thrusting weapon and this disadvantaged the Romans. Some historians refer to the Germans using 'long lances', by which they must mean pikes. Such long spears are most useful when the warriors carrying them maintain a strict close formation and present a phalanx of spear-heads. But there is no evidence that the Germans possessed the cohesion to carry out such tactics successfully and long spears would have proved unwieldy in guerilla warfare.

The German shield, so denigrated by Germanicus, was essentially a rounded wooden construction sometimes reinforced with an iron boss as much as 5 in. (12cm) long which could always be used as a punching weapon in the last resort. On most occasions, after having flung at the enemy the spears they had brought with them, German warriors depended upon picking up discarded weapons on the battlefield. When these proved scarce, they would fight with any rock or branch to hand. The battle-site

Celtic bronze swords from southern Germany, now in the State Prehistorical Collection, Munich. Many such weapons were imported or stolen by the Germans who then modelled their own arms after them.

Gallic horseman. Such warriors frequently fought as auxiliaries with the Romans. A proud engraving from Guizot's *L'Histoire de France*, 1870, showing how a 19th century nationalistic interest in the ancient glories of both France and Germany encouraged a Romantic image of the noble Barbarian.

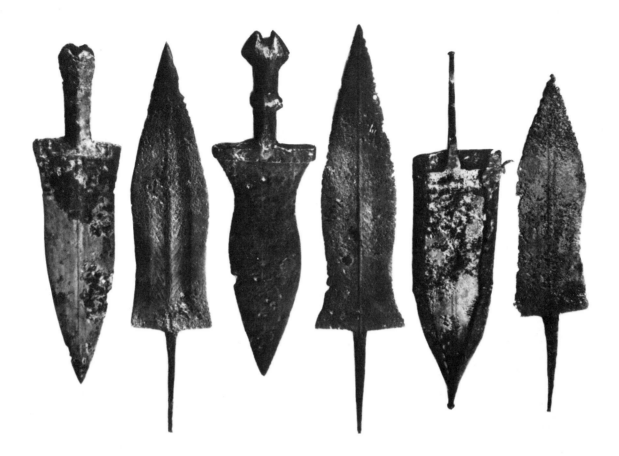

after a victory was a treasure trove of weapons and many warriors must have combined Roman and Celtic arms with their native garb. Swords were rare amongst the Germans and, as they were expensive items, often imported, they would have been used by leading warriors only. Such swords as have been discovered fall into two distinct types. A short, single-edged sword or knife of native origin, and a double-edged thrusting sword like the Roman *gladius*. As the years passed and Roman contacts increased, Roman-style swords became widespread.

The majority of German warriors fought on foot as few tribes could bring large numbers of cavalry into the battlefield. The Batavi and the Tencteri were the only people noted for their horsemanship, the former serving as auxiliaries with the Romans. The growth of horsemanship amongst a people is partly determined by the landscape they inhabit. The plains of north Germany and the heathland, in areas where forest had been cleared for cultivation, no doubt encouraged mastery of the horse. Spurs and harnesses discovered in these locations reinforce this supposition. Cavalry in forests and marshland, however, is less effective and it seems that the subsistence living of most Germans did not encourage them to keep horses. Among these tribes, the few horses available became the preserve of chieftains and

Roman daggers of the 3rd century AD, now in the State Prehistorical Collection, Munich. Despite arms embargoes, these weapons found their way into Barbarian hands.

36

Silver decorated dagger belonging to a Roman officer of the 1st century AD, now in the State Prehistorical Collection, Munich. Roman daggers and short swords influenced Germanic weapon design.

thus denoted high status. The general standard of German horsemanship was thus not nearly as high as amongst the nomads of the steppes. German horsemen fought with spears, swords and shields, not bows, the supreme weapon of the horse-warrior. Indeed, archery appears to have fallen into neglect amongst Germans of the early Imperial period and was revived only in part in later centuries.

It seems likely that once German horsemen had ridden into battle, they preferred to fight on foot. Such a belief is fuelled by Caesar's account of a cavalry skirmish against Germans in which the enemy leapt from their mounts and began to stab at the Roman horses, thus bringing the riders down. Frequently, fleet-footed warriors accompanied groups of horsemen into battle, so it is unlikely that the horsemen acted as highly manoeuvrable cavalry contingents independent of foot-soldiers. In addition, the Romans observed that indigenous German horses were of a low quality, and they often had to mount their auxiliaries on horses imported from Italy.

With such primitive military resources, it seems baffling that the Germans managed to provide any resistance to the Romans at all. In such circumstances, a leader can only hope to make the most of the fighting spirit of his warriors through guerilla tactics. Having served with the Romans, Arminius must have observed how easily legionaries in strict order could absorb the headlong rush of the Barbarians and then employ troops on their flanks, or cavalry, to cut down the impetuous warriors. The Germans depended very much on the initial shock of their running attack. If this first charge failed to break the Roman line, the Barbarians usually came off second best to superior weaponry and tactics. On some occasions, as Caesar noted about the Gauls, the Barbarians ran over such distances, sometimes even up hill, that when they reached the Romans, they were utterly exhausted. Arminius preserved the wild energy of his warriors and exploited their familiarity with the treacherous German terrain through relentless short, sharp ambushes which eventually wore down the opposition. In their struggle against Germanicus, the Germans constantly tried to force the Romans onto swampy ground where, according to Tacitus, the water affected the Romans' ability to balance their javelins for a throw. The Barbarians even went to the extent of diverting streams so as to flood the ground the Romans stood upon. When beaten back by Germanicus, some Germans sought protection up trees, though these were later shot down by mocking Roman archers.

An important aspect of guerilla warfare is the spreading of terror. Atrocities like that described by Tacitus in the Teutoburgian Forest, though terrible, instilled dread amongst those advancing through 'Indian territory'. Indeed, Tacitus reflected Roman outrage at these brutal acts by calling them *barbarae*: savage. At this stage, however, one must question how shocking such incidents would really have seemed to Romans regularly attuned to the cruelty of the arena. While on campaign, the Romans were not adverse to wholesale slaughter. Caesar's massacres of complete German tribes are

37

notorious. Still, Roman soldiers did not look upon the prospect of serving on the northern frontier with pleasure, as the individual ferocity of the German warrior was renowned.

Like most primitive people, German men expressed aggressive masculinity through their appearance. Skin-tight trousers, animal skins and rough cloaks created a wild image. Some warriors shaved parts of their head to increase the bizarreness of their looks. Others, like the Suebi, gathered their hair into a distinctive knot standing erect on the crown of the head. If not naturally red, hair would by dyed. Caesar once surprised a band of Germans as they were bathing in a river and dyeing their hair. Above all, however, Germans judged a man by his courage in battle. German warriors fought as much for the respect of their kinsmen as to defeat the enemy. This can, of course, be said of the Romans who equally valued individual bravery. But whereas the Romans rewarded valour with military decorations, for the Germans their daring determined their very social standing. The hardest and most feared warriors held positions of power amongst their people. Commanders achieved the respect of their men through example rather than the authority of their rank. It was a disgrace for a chief to be surpassed in courage by his followers. Generally, it was regarded weak and dismal to obtain slowly through labour what could be achieved immediately through the spilling of blood. Cowards were despised. Barred from religious ceremonies and tribal assemblies, many ended their shame by hanging themselves. To this extent, aside from a few ruling families, the German tribe was a hierarchy of hardmen. This explains the wedge-shaped battle groups mentioned by Tacitus and called *cunei* by the Romans. Later historians have described these almost as if they were a sophisticated tactical formation, but it seems more likely that they were simply groups or clans of warriors tied together by kinship, with the few bravest at the front, and the rest sloping away to the back according to their bloodlust. In an environment where leading warriors could idle away a day feasting while others worked the land, individual violence was regarded as the only way to betterment. Such was the motivation of the warrior on the battlefield.

Though the Germans together presented a threat to the Roman Empire, they were not a united people. On one occasion, Romans were even invited to watch one tribe annihilate a neighbouring people. 'More than 60,000 were killed and not by Roman swords,' Tacitus enthused. 'Long, I pray, may Barbarians persist, if not in loving us, at least in hating each other.' But this was the inter-tribal warfare that had always gone on and always would. During the Imperial period, some Germans received Roman assistance. It was Imperial policy to create buffer zones of friendly tribes, and envoys were sent with gifts to those chiefs the Romans thought susceptible to such advances. Many German chiefs accepted an alliance with Rome more as an opportunity to defeat rival tribes than out of any love for the Roman way of life. Even within a single tribe, loyalties could be split by the possibility of employing the Empire against an enemy.

Among the Cherusci, Arminius began a feud by abducting the daughter of another chieftain, Segestes. As Governor Varus advanced to his death in the Teutoburgian Forest, it was Segestes who continually warned him not to trust Arminius. Later, Segestes was forced to flee to the Romans as the majority of tribesmen stood by Arminius. In his escape, he kidnapped the wife of Arminius, who was with child. As Segestes urged Germanicus in his campaign against the Cherusci, Arminius railed furiously at the Romans, 'Before my sword, three legions, three generals have fallen. I wage war not with the help of treason nor against pregnant women, but in open day and against men who carry arms!' After having maintained the German tribes in coalition against Germanicus and compelled the Romans back across the Rhine, Arminius marched against Maroboduus, one of the few German chiefs to rival Arminius in influence and skills of military command. If Arminius and Maroboduus had united their peoples they could have taken the Germans deep into the Empire. Instead, Arminius inflicted a heavy defeat on Maroboduus who was forced to take refuge with the Romans. For Arminius, success proved his downfall. He was killed in AD 19 by his own warriors who feared a leader too powerful to control.

With the fall of Arminius and Maroboduus, the Romans enjoyed a respite from the northern Barbarians. But the Romans never stopped regarding the Germans as a primary military threat; and throughout the 1st century the greatest concentration of legions in the Empire were stationed along the Rhine frontier and the Danube. During the reign of Augustus, a mere 1,200 men at Lyons were deemed sufficient to control Gaul, whereas eight legions, approximately 40,000 men, guarded the Rhine. These armies were composed of regular troops (largely Roman citizens) and auxiliaries, recruited from German tribes allied to the Empire. The auxiliaries often fought with their own native weapons and under the command of German chieftains with Roman names. It was through these warriors that the Barbarisation of the Roman army over the next few centuries was to take place. In the short term, however, they could prove as much of a threat to the Romans as a useful ally.

In AD 69, Julius Civilis united the Batavi with independent German tribes in a mutiny against Roman authority under the pretext of supporting a particular Imperial faction. He was joined by a Gallic chieftain who proclaimed an Empire of the Gauls. Eventually the unlikely alliance of Gauls and Germans broke down. No doubt because the freedom the Germans most wanted was the liberty to plunder Gaul. Both forces were defeated. In response to this rebellion, auxiliary troops were removed from their areas of origin to far flung frontiers and their command transferred to Roman officers. This could only be a temporary measure. By the 2nd century, the scarcity of legionary recruits from Italy meant that the regular army as well as the auxiliaries were made up largely of provincial warriors.

Fortunately for the Empire, the 2nd century proved a relatively quiet period along the Rhine. Under the Emperor Domitian, the frontier linking

Fanciful illustration of an ancient Pict with body tattoos. Engraved by Theodor de Bry after a drawing by John White, from the 1590 edition of Thomas Harriot's *The New Found Land of Virginia*. The intention was to show that the British had once been as barbaric as the native Americans were believed to be in the 16th century.

T·B·J·

the Rhine to the Danube was advanced to incorporate the Black Forest and
the Taunus mountains into its defences. The main threat to the Empire in
the 2nd century came across the Danube in the form of eastern Germans,
steppe warriors, and the Dacian tribes. Of the eastern Germans, the
Marcomanni, the Quadi, and the Vandals were the most vociferous. Causing
considerable havoc in the provinces of central Europe, these Germans
crossed the Italian frontier and raided as far as Aquileia before being chased
back across the Danube by Marcus Aurelius.

By the middle of the 3rd century, the northern Barbarians had coalesced
into the various peoples that would eventually fragment the Empire and
were carrying out audacious raids. The Franks overran the lower Rhine,
obtaining firm footholds in Gaul. Saxons and other tribes from the
Netherlands and Denmark, harried the coasts of England. Crossing the

German tribesmen of the first
few centuries AD. From
Costumes of All Nations, 1907,
originally published between
1861 and 1890 by Braun und
Schneider, Germany.

Rhine and the Danube, the Alamanni plunged into Italy. In the east, the Goths ravaged the Balkans and Asia Minor. All these incursions were either defeated or controlled by Roman forces, but the routes of a future, permanent invasion had very clearly been laid. To some extent, the Germans had changed since described by Tacitus two hundred years earlier. Many of the old tribes named by Tacitus had broken down and fused into larger groups. The Cherusci suffered from prolonged internal discord after the death of Arminius and eventually disintegrated. Similarly, the Chatti and other north-western tribes on the frontier dissolved, to be reborn along with the Cherusci in the confederation of the Franks. Several pressures brought about this transition: not least being Roman diplomacy. The Empire constantly tempted German chieftains with the luxuries and higher standards of living south of the Rhine. Some Germans acquiesced and settled down in Gallic Roman cities: others did not. The resulting strain between those factions urging collaboration and those maintaining re-sistance frequently led to fighting, and split many prominent tribes. Another development altering the structure of several German tribes, was a greater centralisation around a warrior elite.

The close proximity of the Empire inevitably touched the day to day life of the Germans. Tribesmen had always raided the Celts, a wealthier people, but with the Celts' Romanisation and the presence of the Romans them-selves, this activity accelerated. Trade also increased. In return for the sophisticated, manufactured products of the Romans and Gauls, the Germans could offer animal skins and amber. But these were luxury items, gathered only in particular parts of Germany. More readily available commodities were cattle and, above all, slaves. Both items were easily gained through raiding and war, with slaves becoming the primary export of the Germans. Such trade led to an increase in intertribal conflict as tribes launched slaving wars on each other. The Roman appetite for slaves was insatiable. At first, the Germans had little use for slaves: after battle, warriors returned to work the land themselves. But as the income from raiding and trading increased, the chieftains and their best warriors devoted all their time to this activity, leaving the less effective warriors and women to continue the farm labour. These were later joined by slaves, not sold, but given a little patch of land and expected to hand over a portion of their crop to their masters. A two-tier system now evolved in which chieftains and their followers became professional warriors while weaker men, women and slaves were confined to farming.

A successful chieftain rewarded his followers – his retinue – with the spoils of war: horses, cattle, slaves, weapons and food. Land was not yet part of the pay-off. In this way, wealth became concentrated among a warrior elite and was not shared with the whole tribe. The more successful a chieftain, the greater the number of retainers he attracted. Soon, these groups of warriors loyal to one charismatic leader, began to displace the old war bands based around the clan and kinship. Now, only in a time of great crisis – if a whole people were in danger – would the entire tribe take to arms. But as full-scale invasions by the Romans ceased to be a threat, any fighting in the tribe was carried out by these gangs of professional warriors. Because of their increased wealth, a chieftain and his retainers could afford to ride a horse, wear armour and wield a sword, thus furthering their status as a martial elite. The special sword favoured by these horse-warriors was a long, two-edged slashing weapon – the *spatha* – ideally suited to fighting from horseback. This became increasingly widespread amongst both Barbarian and Roman soldiers in the the late Imperial period. If, as in some of the later migratory invasions of the Germans, the whole fighting force of a tribe was needed, the lesser, common warriors continued to fight on foot with spears or whatever came to hand. Because of the authority and professionalism of the elite warriors, more sophisticated tactics, manoeuvres, and discipline could be expected from the Germans. The northern Barbarians were no longer near-naked savages.

With the accumulation of wealth and military power in the hands of the most successful war leaders, their political influence increased. Sometimes, such power was in opposition to the desires of the rest of the tribe and wayward retinues were exiled. In other circumstances, a particularly strong warlord could subject the rest of this people to his control. Such a dictatorial centralisation of power occurred in the 1st century under Maroboduus who ruled the Marcomanni almost as effectively as a medieval king. It happened also under Arminius, though he was killed before he could become an absolute tyrant. These were prototypes for later developments. The growth of a powerful military class separate from the rest of the tribe, is clearly a forerunner of medieval feudalism and knighthood. Such a process, however, occurred only among the most advanced German societies, those nearest to the Roman frontier. These tribes had the greater opportunity to obtain the superiority of arms and wealth needed to maintain a martial elite and subjected lesser German tribes to their control. From this action, larger associations of tribes evolved around the most successful warlords to form the great tribal confederations of the 3rd and 4th centuries. It was these warlords and their retainers who spearheaded the Barbarian campaigns of the 5th century.

Business as usual

'Most sacred Emperors,' appealed a man who felt sure he could save the Roman Empire. 'It must be admitted that wild Barbarian tribes, screaming everywhere, surround and threaten every stretch of our frontiers. These savages are sheltered by forests and snow-bound mountains. Some are nomads and protected by deserts and the blazing sun. Others, hidden amongst marshes and rivers, can not even be located and yet they shatter our peace and quiet with surprise attacks. Tribes of this kind must be assaulted with a variety of ingenious armed devices.' Addressing the Emperor Valens sometime between 367 and 369, the anonymous Latin writer went on to describe a series of weird and marvellous military machines. On one page he described a chariot pulled by *cataphractarii* – rider and horse clad in steel scale armour. Driven into battle at high speed, the chassis and axle were fitted with knives and very sharp scythes to slash the ham-strings of a fleeing enemy. Elsewhere in the tréatise, powerful *ballistae* were outlined. One, the 'thunderbolt', was strong enough to throw an iron arrow across the width of the Danube. Another, was mounted on four wheels for ease of movement on the battlefield. A javelin designed with spikes around its neck had a dual purpose. For if it failed to impale an enemy, it would fall to the ground and act as a caltrop, sticking in his feet instead. Further on, the anonymous author suggested a pontoon bridge in which calf-skin bladders could be stitched together to form a platform for soldiers to cross, with hair mats laid on top to prevent a slippery surface. Finally, a huge warship was proposed, powered by oxen inside the hull, turning gears which turned paddles. Such a ship would crush all before it.

Some of the weapons in this treatise were not as fantastic as they might first seem. The *ballistae* were versions of equipment already in service. Both the pontoon bridge and the animal-powered paddle boat have been utilised and adapted in later centuries. That said, aside from the *ballistae*, none of the other devices were constructed, let alone used in warfare on the frontier. They remained the imaginative solutions of one Roman citizen sufficiently disturbed by the Barbarian incursions of the late 4th century to try and do something about them. If only the Emperors of the East and West would listen to him, he must have thought, then the Empire could be saved. But the Romans were not lacking in their military technology. The wars against the Barbarians in the 4th and 5th centuries were well fought by Roman forces, often better equipped and supplied than their adversaries. It was other factors – political, social and economic – in the maintenance of a vast association of countries and peoples that saw the Empire slip piece by piece from the control of the Romans. Some of these problems were mentioned in the anonymous treatise. The author criticised extortionate taxes ruining farmers in the provinces. He wished to root out corruption amongst tax-collectors, cut extravagant expenditure, and prevent the fraudulent debasement of the currency. Certainly the Empire was being weakened through mismanagement. But it was also, more to the point, changing its character.

Frequent Barbarian raids forced many towns to erect sturdy walls. In their haste and with little money to spare, pillars, monuments and tombstones were ripped up and incorporated into ring-walls linking massive buildings, such as a basilica or an amphitheatre, into their defences. Only the essential administrative and financial institutions could be thus protected and towns visibly shrank. Harassed by Barbarian bandits and

Scythed chariots, equipped with automatic whips to goad on the horse. From the 1552 edition of an anonymous 4th century treatise *De Rebus Bellicis*, in which the author proposed several fantastic machines with which to combat Barbarian marauders.

Scythed chariot driven by a horse clad in scale armour. Also from the 1552 edition of *De Rebus Bellicis*.

Four-wheeled ballista strong enough to hurl a bolt across the Danube. A screw device allows the aim of the machine to be raised or lowered. From the 1552 edition of *De Rebus Bellicis*.

tyrannical officials, those craftsmen, traders and small landholders who could not find security within town-walls, fled to the country estates of the great landlords. Here, fantastically wealthy landowners absorbed even more land from their frightened, powerless neighbours. Tenant farmers now surrendered their freedom, becoming serfs tied to the land, in return for the protection and prosperity of their landlords. Self-sufficient estates evolved around fortified villas. Private armies were raised by landlords to protect their stretch of the frontier. In the towns, citizens took to arms to defend themselves. The armies of the government had become independent forces, either living off the land or taking over towns. These forces traded, farmed and set up industries, creating their own state within a state. They defended their property against both Barbarian maurauders and Imperial tax-collectors. Power rested in the hands of landlords and warlords and these were the men, in the 4th and 5th centuries, who stood against the Barbarians in order to save their own individual privilege and prosperity. The saving of the Empire as a whole was a mere ideal harboured by a few historically minded writers.

With decentralisation came Barbarisation. Barbarian troops had long been incorporated into Roman armies. At first, they were auxiliaries armed and disciplined as legionaries. Then they fought under the Imperial eagle as allied, federated forces, brandishing their own weapons and led by their own chieftains. Finally, provincial armies were composed almost totally of native troops defending their borderland against neighbouring Barbarians envious of their greater material wealth. The armies of the late Empire looked and fought like their enemies. In the 4th century, an Egyptian woman wrote apologising for non-payment of her taxes with the excuse that her son had 'gone away to the Barbarians'. By this she meant that her son had joined the regular Imperial army. Even in the most Barbarian-dependent days of the Empire, however, Roman infrastructure still meant that Imperial armies were better supplied with arms and provisions than those of their adversaries.

Successful Barbarian chieftains, fighting on behalf of the Romans, rose to great power within the Imperial hierarchy. They had Latin names, lived the life of Latin aristocracy and were frequently sponsored by Emperors as official 'Defenders of the Empire'. But they were still essentially Barbarian. The famous Aetius and Stilicho were both Germanic landowners supported by bands of Barbarian warriors. Even the most notorious Barbarian kings, such as Alaric and Theoderic, were open to accommodation with the Empire and propped up their part of the frontier against further incursions. It was more to their advantage, more profitable, to settle Imperial land in return for services rendered, and live as a Roman grandee, than destroy everything Imperial just because it was Roman. Trade, agriculture and industry could all be enjoyed by the Barbarian who grabbed his land and towns, settled it and then defended it against others. Indeed, Barbarians were not keen simply to *steal* the land. They had not risked their lives against other

Barbarians and government troops merely to set themselves up in a bandit refuge. They wished to be legitimate. They wanted security and the legal acknowledgement that they were entitled to land within the Empire. Only by working within the law could Germanic chieftains hope to exploit and pass on their estates without being harassed by government troops. Tracts of land taken by the government from private Roman landowners and granted to the Barbarians were the most prized form of payment for military services rendered. In addition, these allotments were tax free. A great

Late 19th century drawing of a tombstone from Mainz, featuring a Roman horse-warrior (probably a German auxiliary). He carries a long cavalry sword, *spatha*, and tramples down a barbarian. Many details have now been obscured on the original tombstone.

49

incentive for Barbarians to toe the Imperial line and settle down. Which is what many did. Tax evasion could not be absolute, and it was Theoderic who stressed to his Goth followers that though they need not pay anything on land given by the Empire, if they then invested in extra land they would be subject to the same taxes as the Romans. After all, Theoderic had as much to gain from efficient tax collection as any Imperial magnate. Wrangles over deeds of settlement and taxation fuelled much of the conflict between Empire and Barbarian throughout the invasions of the 5th century and later.

'Invasion' is itself an overestimation of several Barbarian movements within the Empire. Frequently, Barbarian confederations were allowed or invited on to Imperial territory. That said, in many regions of the Empire groups of Barbarian raiders did find themselves to be the dominant force and took control of activities in these areas through violence and intimidation. These invasions increased in their magnitude as Imperial authority retreated, until warlords had absolute command of huge stretches of land. In such circumstances, Roman legality and attention to correct tax assessment could go to hell! When the last Roman Emperor of the West was deposed in 476, it was not a sudden cataclysm but acknowledgement of the established fact that the Empire had been broken up into independent estates ruled by Germanic warlords. It was dangerous to pretend otherwise.

Claims to the Imperial title could lead to civil war, as in the past, which would prevent Barbarian chieftains from enjoying their newly-acquired wealth. The Germans wanted peace and security as much as anyone, but on their terms. This then is the 'Fall of the Roman Empire'. As Abbé Galliani wrote in 1744, 'Empires being neither up nor down, do not fall. They change their appearance.' The Germans were not just vandalic raiders. They wished to transform the Roman into a German Empire, or more properly, into an assembly of Germanic kingdoms. In this they succeeded. Power was handed from Roman landlords to German landlords.

With these concerns in mind, Barbarian migrations throughout the Empire were not so much raging floods of anarchy as ambitious quests for position and possession within the Roman system. Of course, military power had to be demonstrated and towns, especially on the frontier, were devastated. But German chieftains realised that to destroy the very fabric of the Empire was to reduce it to the impoverished conditions of the Barbaricum, which they had thankfully left far behind. Such a view did not always agree with the desires of their warriors. On the banks of the Danube in 376, Goths swore to smash the Empire in revenge for the sufferings they had endured from the Romans before being allowed within the frontier. In the years following they savaged substantial areas of the Balkans. The Romans, however, frequently achieved in peace and subterfuge what they failed in war. After Adrianople, the Emperor Theodosius made increasingly attractive overtures to the Barbarian leaders. They were invited to sumptuous feasts within the walls of Constantinople. Goth chieftains saw for themselves all the wondrous goods that flowed into this city. Spices and silk from the Far East: grain and oil from Africa: gold and silver from all round the Mediterranean. The full panoply of the Imperial army paraded before them. Clad in mail and scale armour from head to foot, Roman horse-warriors carried banners in the shape of dragons which twisted and hissed in the wind. 'The Emperor is God on earth,' exclaimed one excited Goth, 'anyone who raises a hand against him commits suicide.'

Laden with Imperial gifts, many Goth chieftains returned to their warriors and urged them to forget their Barbaric oaths of destruction. Instead, they should work with the Empire and relish a higher standard of living. Not surprisingly, the rank and file warriors were less than happy with this compromise, as it was their chieftains who benefited most while the rest came off second best to the Roman citizens with whom they were supposed to share their land. Tensions grew. With their chieftains ensconced in the luxury of Constantinople, many Goth warriors and their families were put to work on the farms of Roman landowners. They had become slaves while their rulers advanced up the Imperial ladder. Rebellions broke out. Goths joined with Roman peasants in an attempt to overthrow the state. But Goth chieftains, now risen to high office in the Roman army, rode out and crushed the rebels – once fellow tribesmen, now merely wretched slaves spoiling the status quo.

Barbarians on the move. The classic vision of whole tribes migrating into the Roman Empire. From Guizot's *L'Histoire de France*, 1870.

51

Dwelling within the palatial apartments of the Imperial capital, it was hard for Barbarian nobles to resist the internal politics of the Empire. Byzantine factions depended on the muscle the Germans could bring to their machinations. Stilicho, a Vandal by birth, enjoyed the patronage of Theodosius and became his leading general. Unfortunately, on the death of Theodosius, Stilicho was in Italy installing one of the dead man's sons as Emperor of the West. The other son shakily assumed the Imperial diadem in the East. Stilicho's rivals took advantage of his absence and one of them, Alaric, broke away from the Roman army and rampaged through Greece. Surrounded at first by a retinue of Romanised Goth warriors, he was joined by those Barbarians and peasants who saw their only salvation in the looting of villas and sacking of towns. In AD 395, this robber army elected Alaric, King of the Visigoths. Whether they were all true Visigoths is unlikely but it gave them a legitimate facade for their activities. The warriors that presented Alaric with this title were in no mood for compromise with the Empire. Regardless of any notions he may have had of strengthening his position within the Imperial hierarchy through a display of violence, his men roamed westward in search of plunder. They clashed several times unsuccessfully with Italian forces led by Stilicho and for a decade their advance faltered and lingered in present-day Yugoslavia.

The Visigoths that followed Alaric were largely a gange of marauders, which constantly changed as it overran new estates and absorbed the peasants and armed retinues of Roman landlords. It was forces such as these that carried out the more adventurous of the Barbarian migrations of the 5th century. A picture of hundreds of thousands of Barbarian families – wives, children and parents – moving as a whole to new lands does not ring true. Only in Gaul, where the Franks, Vandals and Burgundians had control of the borderlands, is it acceptable that their people should then cross the frontier and follow their warriors into land vacated by the Romans. After all, the population of Gaul was not enormous and its farmland had for a long time proved attractive. In this way, the Franks increasingly won – and settled permanently – large districts of northern Gaul. But those Barbarians, like the Vandals and Goths, who journeyed far through Italy, Spain and Africa, must have long left their native people behind. Only a few unrelated camp followers can have rumbled along with them in their wagons. Most of these wagons being full of arms, booty and valuable prisoners, with perhaps only the families of the ruling chieftains in tow. The majority of wariors took their women and wealth from the land they were given by their lords or granted by the Romans. Besides, a number of the warriors fighting with the Barbarians at any one time were likely to be disaffected local men; tenants bonded to their land and now taking revenge against their masters; runaway slaves and bandits seeking better opportunities for outlawry.

All such wild elements within the Barbarian horde had to be kept well under control. For though their fury was useful in battle, they could prove

Eight hundred years before the sack by Alaric, the Celtic Gauls sacked Rome in 390 BC. The Capitol held out for seven months. According to legend the citizens of the Capitol were alerted to a Celtic night attack by the honking of the sacred geese of Juno. A late 19th century engraving, from a painting by Henry Motte.

a handicap to negotiations with Imperial authorities when a chieftain
eventually wanted to set himself up in a provincial landholding. This
conflict of interests, one which had fractured the Goths in the Balkans,
proved a constant problem to Alaric and an annoyance to his men. In
addition, a string of defeats by Stilicho had badly shaken his leadership. So
that the treaty finally agreed with Stilicho, in which Alaric received an
Imperial subsidy to defend his province against other Barbarians, seemed
like the last straw to many adherents. These now rode off to join a horde of
Germans streaming through the Alps. Stilicho had got the better of Alaric,
neutralising him just when Italy was at its most threatened. He could now
deal with the latest Barbarian raiders without having to worry about the
Visigoths. But just when Alaric was beginning to settle down with his
Imperial pension in Dalmatia, news reached him of Stilicho's assassination
in 408. The opportunity for an almost unopposed advance into Italy proved
too great. Alaric snatched it and rode into central Italy towards Rome. What
little Imperial defence remained was centred around Ravenna, the newly
established capital of the Western Empire, safe behind the marshes of the Po
delta. Rome, the very symbol and heart of the Empire, had been left exposed.

As Alaric and his followers approached the great city, the magnitude of
their endeavour suddenly struck them. Rome had not seen an enemy within
its walls since Celts from Gaul had assailed it in 390 BC. For eight centuries
the Imperial capital had been the storehouse of a vast treasure collected
from its Mediterranean provinces. It was the most glittering city: the centre
of the Empire: the centre of the world. Powerful politicians, multi-
millionaire merchants, all lived within its walls, decorating their own
palaces as well as creating some of the most remarkable and famous
buildings in the Ancient World. In the 4th century, the city's walls had

been renewed and raised. This does not seem to have filled the Emperor Honorious with much confidence. For it was he who moved the political, if not the spiritual capital of the Western Empire, to Ravenna. With him travelled many of Rome's richest citizens, thus denuding the city of part of its moveable wealth. Still, enough of the splendour and legend of Rome remained to inspire awe in those Goths riding towards it. A thunderstorm gathered over the surrounding countryside. Many Goths felt that the old Classical Gods had not deserted their home. One warrior proclaimed that he saw, 'Thunderbolts hurled against us. Divine fire flickered in front of the walls. Heaven, or was it Rome herself, raged in the storm.' But there was no need to worry. The Barbarians would not have to do battle with the Gods. Mortal treachery opened the gates of Rome without a struggle.

When Alaric entered Rome in AD 410, centuries of preserved treasures greeted the gaze of his warriors. According to chroniclers, Alaric allowed his troops to loot the city but not destroy it. He risked his leadership and life if he denied his men the rewards of pillage, their only payment, but he does seem to have wished to save the structure of the city. Perhaps he envisaged it as his own capital. Or perhaps he wished to make peace with the Emperor and this was a sign of his good intentions. Perhaps the city was just too vast and its buildings too well built for him to bother with their destruction. Jordanes, Christian Goth apologist, suggests that Alaric restrained the excesses of his wild men so as to protect churches and holy places. But, though a Christian, Alaric was an Arian. A member of a heretic faith that believed in the divinity of God the Father but not of Christ. Like other Arian Germans, he did not have much respect for Catholic shrines. Indeed, in later years, there were bitter religious wars between Arians and Catholics, with the latter only emerging triumphant by a narrow margin. For Roman Christians, the arrival of the Visigoths was as bad as that of any pagans. Fortunately for them, Alaric and his followers did not relish their occupation of Rome for long. They moved southwards after only a few months: their chief concern being food. Italian towns, especially Rome, depended heavily on grain and oil shipments from Africa and these had been stopped once news of the Barbarian invasion had reached Romans there. Food supply had always been a weak point in the campaigns of the Barbarians, and now there was no food even to plunder. The Visigoths were forced to ride southwards, and planned to sail to Sicily and then Africa. But as they prepared for their voyage, Alaric died. The great chieftain was buried with all his weapons and personal treasure. And so that no one might know where he lay, the diggers were slaughtered and the waters of a river diverted over his grave to obscure the place forever.

The Visigoths never sailed to Africa. Athaulf, their new king, turned back through Italy. Desperate for food supplies and land his men could farm, Athaulf began to negotiate with the Emperor for estates they could peacefully settle. The Barbarian king took advice from Romans within his entourage, married a Roman princess, wore Roman dress and renounced his

Replica of the warlord's helmet found at Sutton Hoo, made by the Tower of London Armourers. Panels decorating the side of the helmet show mounted warriors, lances in their hands, trampling down enemies. Elsewhere, dismounted warriors wear helmets with fantastic horns.

Helmet of iron, with gilt bronze face mask. Probably made in Sweden in the 6th century. Found at the ship burial of Sutton Hoo.

determination to smash *Romania* and set up *Gothia* in its place. In return for his support against other Barbarians, the Emperor granted the Visigoths a great chunk of southern France. Such a transition from foe to friend was not a smooth one. Athaulf could not control all his warriors. Those who still desired the life of a freebooter menaced southern France and had to be forcibly restrained. Assisted by their private armies, Romano-Germanic landowners spent much energy crushing the more anarchic members of their former Barbarian hordes. Throughout this period, the more remote corners of the land remained under the dominance of masterless bandits acting outside the interests of both the Emperor and German kings.

Alongside the mass accommodation of Barbarian tribes within the Empire, individual warriors offered their services to the Romans. Some acted as bounty-hunters, utilising their local knowledge to root out Barbarian marauders. Working outside the state, they were hired by groups of citizens or landowners to clear a certain district. Others were employed by the government, and information survives about one such man-hunter, Charietto. A German of fearsome reputation and appearance, he operated as a raider along the frontier near Trier with other Franks. Having exhausted the easy pickings, he rode into the provincial capital in the hope of hustling some money off citizens or troops in exchange for any form of service. Scouting, interpreting or perhaps, if he was lucky, even recruitment as an auxiliary with regular pay, food and a place to sleep. No official work offered itself, however, so he acted freelance. Realising very well that the surrounding countryside was plagued by Barbarian brigands – he had been among the most notorious of them – he set about making his experience pay. One night, he disappeared into the German forests and made for familiar bandit haunts. Around the dying embers of one camp-fire, he fell upon raiders drunkenly asleep after a successful day's work. He cut off their heads and, no doubt, snatched a few valuables for himself. Back in Trier he displayed the Barbarian heads and stirred the interest of the citizens. With a payment for each head delivered, Charietto embarked on a systematic annihilation of local outlaws. Soon his reputation persuaded others to stay away. At the same time, former bandits joined his gang of manhunters. Julian, commander of Roman forces along the Rhine, heard of Charietto's success and invited him to discuss tactics. The Franks, easily enough defeated in open confrontation, were resorting most sensibly to guerilla raids and proving elusive. Julian decided to harass the tribesmen during the day and then allow Charietto to stalk them at night. This combined pressure proved triumphant and Charietto rose to dizzy heights within the Imperial army. After a good ten years, however, his luck ran out in a bitter encounter with the Alamanni. Trying to encourage his fleeing men by confronting the enemy alone, he perished under several spears. Charietto was not an isolated example. Official bounty-hunting existed under the Emperor Valens who, during his war against the Goths, also offered a reward to anyone who brought in the heads of Barbarians.

Southern France was a vital part of the Western Empire. In the interior lay rich farmlands managed by some of the most powerful and wealthy Roman landlords. On the coast, the ports were an invaluable link in the chain of Mediterranean trade, the life-blood of the Empire. Weakened by civil wars that tore its armies apart and by Barbarian incursions that sprung up everywhere, the Imperial governors of Gaul abandoned a frontier policy. They could now no longer afford, or even admit it possible, to draw a line between the Barbaricum and the Empire. Instead, they rationalised the situation and saw that an Empire could still thrive – or rather, that its ruling class could endure – by adopting a new approach, an alternative definition of survival. The Empire invited Barbarians onto its territory. In this way, German chieftains then shared a common interest with Roman magnates in defending their way of life against the wreckers – savages with no respect for property or civilisation: although these 'savages' were merely those Barbarians who missed out on Roman patronage and were determined to

Pattern-welded sword in scabbard. Late 6th or early 7th century, from Sutton Hoo, Suffolk. Now in the British Museum, London.

Iron hammer also found at Sutton Hoo.

gain a little treasure for themselves, with or without Imperial permission.

In the first half of the 5th century, the Visigoths were settled in Aquitaine around Toulouse. The Burgundians were invited into Savoy, south-eastern France, while groups of Alans were established in central France around Orleans. The Barbarians had not conquered these areas. They had been set up on Roman land in order to maintain a semblance of order and security, so that southern Gaul would remain an economically useful part of the Empire. For much of the time the Romanised Barbarians were not required to defend estates against invaders, but were used to crush the frequent revolts of heavily oppressed peasants and native Celts. To the outsider, it may have seemed as if France had fallen to the Barbarians but for Roman magnates and their German associates, it was, on the whole, business as usual. Only die-hard Imperialist historians, with their minds on an Augustan ideal of the 1st century, could really call this their blackest period. After all, the time spans discussed here were decades and warring was not constant. There were long stretches between major conflicts during which both Barbarian and Roman could concentrate on farming and trade. Then, the only fighting would have been riots and feuds sparked off by drunken disagreements between neighbouring landlords and their retinues. Even major confrontations, in truth, only involved warbands of a few hundred strong. The tribe in arms, a whole people taking the offensive, was a phenomonen of the past: and even then had been rare.

For German landholders and their supporters, war had become a professional occupation. They no longer fought to defend their families against Roman invaders. They no longer put down their plough to take up any weapon close to hand. From simple raiders they had emerged as a separate class, a ruling order of nobles and retainers. They no longer fought for cattle or slaves to sell to the Romans – their Gallic underlings dirtied their hands with soil and manure – they fought for the security of their property and landed income. Their weaponry reflected this privilege and pride. Leading German warriors wore shirts of mail. Long worn in the Roman army, mail was still a valuable item, and Frankish laws were later to proclaim a coat of mail worth two horses or six oxen. The making of mail took time and required special skills and tools. Roman mail workshops were well established, but it is not known to what extent this specialisation occurred amongst the Barbarians.

The construction of mail during this period probably differed little from later medieval examples. Essentially a defence of interlinked metal rings, one method of assembling mail used rows of solid rings linked with rings made from wire and closed with rivets. These latter rings were made by drawing metal wire through the progressively smaller holes of either a swage or a draw-plate. The wire was drawn through by hand or with a windlass. It was then coiled round an iron rod and cut up to form rings. Before being flattened for riveting, the ends of the rings were overlapped by being punched through a tapering hole in a steel block. The rings were

59

worked cold in all the processes so far described. As soon as the metal became hard through working, it had to be heated red hot and left to cool. The next stage, the flattening of the rivet joint, was achieved by placing the ring between two steel dies and striking the top die with a hammer, thus forcing the joint of the ring to take shape. Holes to take the rivets were punched through the joints of the ring. Finally, the rings were opened and linked together into the required formation. The rivets were then inserted and closed. Each ring was linked with four others and was dense enough to prevent the penetration of arrows or the slash of a sword. Surviving examples of Roman mail are riveted and it is likely that much Barbarian mail was as well. Oriental mail, however, had rings which are not overlapped and riveted, but simply butted and some eastern Barbarian tribes may have used this kind.

Early mail-makers used a soft iron ore. In order to toughen it, as was done with swords and spear-heads, it was case-hardened. This was done by rolling up the finished mail shirt in crushed charcoal and then placing it in a forge until red-hot. The carbon in the charcoal turned the outside of the iron into steel, the layer getting deeper the longer it was left. Weapons and armour were rarely made of steel throughout, as this was likely to crack. In the High Middle Ages, mail was decorated with rows of brass rings and this was probably so in earlier centuries. Some of these brass rings were stamped with talismanic words, these being hung near the most vulnerable spots. Other rings were stamped with Christian monograms or the maker's mark. The construction of a mail-shirt was undertaken by several people. Apprentices did the repetitive, boring processes, while the master craftsmen actually 'knitted' it together. It is little wonder that a product of such labour and technological expertise was highly valued and passed on from father to son. Helmets were also precious. They were generally *Spangenhelme*, built around an iron headband from which sprung strips of metal to

Vandal noble with hound depicted on a 6th century mosaic from Carthage. His horse is branded with an elaborate cross. Mosaic now in the British Museum, London.

60

Vandal horseman lassos a deer. Hunting scene from North African mosaic of the 6th century.

form a rounded cone. To this were riveted four to six bronze or iron plates. Hinged cheek-pieces, a strip of metal to protect the nose and a neck-guard of mail, were frequently added. Such a helmet was very strong and it is not surprising that this is the most characteristic helmet to survive from the period. As it was worn by kings and chieftains, it was often decorated with crests in the shape of boars, ravens and wolves. Images of power and magic.

Equally prestigious were the pattern-welded swords that belonged only to leading warriors. These blades had peculiar serpentine marks running down them that fired the imagination of their owners, leading to the swords being called names such as *Fishback* and *Dragonsword*. These blades were the result of the process of pattern-welding. When good quality steel was in short supply, smiths made blades out of a combination of light case-hardened iron and darker soft iron. These alternating layers of metal were sandwiched together, twisted and welded into one piece. Cutting edges of steel were separately welded onto this core. Half the total weight was then removed through grinding and the cutting edge filed. Finally, the blades were treated with an acid, anything from sour beer to urine, and the characteristic wavy pattern on the blade highlighted by etching and polishing. Some blades were made with a groove. Traditionally, this was supposed to allow the victim's blood to be channelled down the blade. Actually, its main function was to give extra strength to the edges without gaining weight or losing flexibility. A recent reconstruction of a pattern-welded sword took one craftsman 75 hours to complete, – from blade to belt-fittings. In Roman sword factories, such processes were handled by a team of artisans. Many such famous sword and armour workshops were taken over by the Barbarians in Italy and elsewhere.

Unlike other Barbarians, the Vandals found it difficult to settle down within the Empire. At the beginning of the 5th century, they along with Alans and the Suebi tore through Gaul and burst into Spain. Here they were

61

harassed by Goths allied with Romans and pushed further into the peninsula. Compared to the Goths little is known about the Vandals. It seems likely that they, with an amalgam of other eastern Germans, operated as hordes of horse-warriors. Their action in Spain was far from a complete conquest. Areas held by strong Hispanic-Roman landlords channelled them towards weaker targets. Some cities held out against them. Their citizens riding out to hunt down isolated packs of the invaders. Occasionally the Empire sponsored other Barbarians, namely the Visigoths, to regain control of vital districts of the Mediterranean coast. Fighting was sporadic. Here and there a gang of raiders would be confronted by Spanish farmers or Imperial Germans. The Vandals do not appear to have gained the confidence of the Empire sufficiently to be employed themselves, or to be given land to defend. They were probably quite content to range over the wide lands of the peninsula as plunderers. Only twenty years after their first appearance south of the Pyrenees, a restless young generation pushed on across the sea to Africa. Apparently, they had been invited by a rebellious Roman warlord who then changed his mind – too late.

What the north-European Vandals made of the strange, hot lands of Africa is unknown. Though at this stage they were probably joined by rootless, marauding Spaniards and Moors who were more familiar with the new territory. Certainly, the Vandals were treated to yet another Roman province untouched by previous Barbarians and full of food and booty. But Africa was also over-flowing with fervent Catholicism and the conflict there soon developed into a desperate religious war between the bishops of each city along the Mediterranean coast and the fiercely Arian Vandals. The renowned Saint Augustine, bishop of Hippo, died during that city's siege. With the fall of each port, food supplies were cut to the rest of the Empire. Finally, with the seizure of Carthage, the Vandals were provided with a vast fleet, ready built and manned. Years before, the Romans had issued an edict promising death to anyone who revealed the secrets of shipbuilding to the Barbarians. Now the Vandals were fully equipped for a life of piracy. They raided Sicily and the coasts of Italy. Realising that his ports would be next, the Eastern Emperor dispatched two great armies to Africa: and this at a time when Constantinople was threatened by the Huns. The crisis escalated with the failure of these two expeditions. The Vandals in Africa were proving far more dangerous than they had ever been in Spain.

The main reason for the success of the Vandals lay in their king. Lame since a riding accident, Gaiseric was a highly able and respected statesman as well as warlord. He ruled for fifty years and led his people to their greatest victory. In 455, the Vandals sacked Rome. The whole of the Mediterranean was at their mercy. Western and eastern Roman fleets were crippled and destroyed. All the skills of naval warfare were revealed to them by captured Roman and Moorish sailors: including the secret of Greek Fire. Consisting of crude oils, pitch, fats, resins, sulphur and other inflammable, noxious ingredients, the mixture was poured into earthen-

The Vandals sack Rome in AD 455. From Ward Lock's *Illustrated History of the World*, 1885. Although nearly always depicted as northmen, the majority of the Vandal force would probably have been composed of native Spaniards and north Africans.

ware pots and ignited. Flung from ship-board catapults, the pots exploded on contact spraying a sticky, clinging, fiery substance over wood, canvas and skin. It even burnt on water, only sand could extinguish the flames. With their loss of Africa, and thus command of the Mediterranean, Roman Emperors began to comprehend that the Barbarians they felt sure they could control were now in a position to dictate the fate of the Empire to them. Such a suspicion became stone-cold fact in 476.

While Attila's kingdom was at its zenith, two men worked for him whose sons would play out the final drama of the Western Empire. One was a Roman, Orestes, who served as Attila's secretary, dealing with written requests sent to his illiterate master. The other was a Hun, Edeco, a respected warrior and leader of the horde. With Attila's death in 453, the two men were displaced in the anarchic power struggle that followed. Edeco joined the vagabond gangs of Huns who battled savagely with the Germans over food and territory. His son, Odoacer, fought at his side. Orestes made straight for the Western Empire where he served successfully in a military capacity. So useful was he that the Emperor gave him supreme command of the army in 475. But such power is too tempting and Orestes rebelled, setting up his son, Romulus, as Emperor. The boy was nicknamed Augustulus, 'little Augustus', because he was so young for the office. In the meantime, Odoacer had entered the army of Orestes as a promising captain. Ten months after the boy Emperor had been placed upon the throne, German soldiers under Odoacer protested that they should be allowed to have land to farm in Italy like the Visigoths had received in France. Orestes refused. Orestes was murdered. Mercifully, his young son was allowed to retire to a castle in the bay of Naples. He had no supporters. Romulus Augustulus was the last Roman Emperor of the West.

At the time, this deposition was considered nothing special. Contemporary chroniclers were not struck by it, for there had been gaps in the Imperial succession before. It was only with the passing of decades that the importance of the date was realised. By the next century, it was recognised as the end of the Western Empire. With no Imperial candidate and no Italian force strong enough to challenge him, Odoacer was proclaimed leader by his warriors. The Germans then settled their desired estates and Roman landlords soon accepted them in return for the stability and protection they provided. The Emperor of the East was politely informed that there was no need to look for a successor to his western counterpart. Odoacer would prefer to maintain his loyalty to one Emperor only. Although still legally part of the Empire, in reality, Italy had become a German kingdom. Admittedly a highly Latinised Barbarian domain, with Pope and senators still exercising influence, but nevertheless the peninsula could no longer be regarded as the heart of the Roman Empire. This was now wholly preserved in Constantinople. From there, the Empire prepared to strike back.

Alan and Sarmatian attacked by Hun. Eurasian steppeland, late 4th century. The Huns destroyed the realms of both the Alans and the Sarmatians.

Goth horse-warrior and foot-soldier ensnare a Roman legionary. Battle of Adrianople, AD 378.

Hun nobleman and raider ambushed by Balkan farmers, middle of the 5th century. The Huns carried bone-tipped composite bows.

Germans of the Cherusci tribe attack a Roman baggage train. Teutoburgian Forest, AD 9.

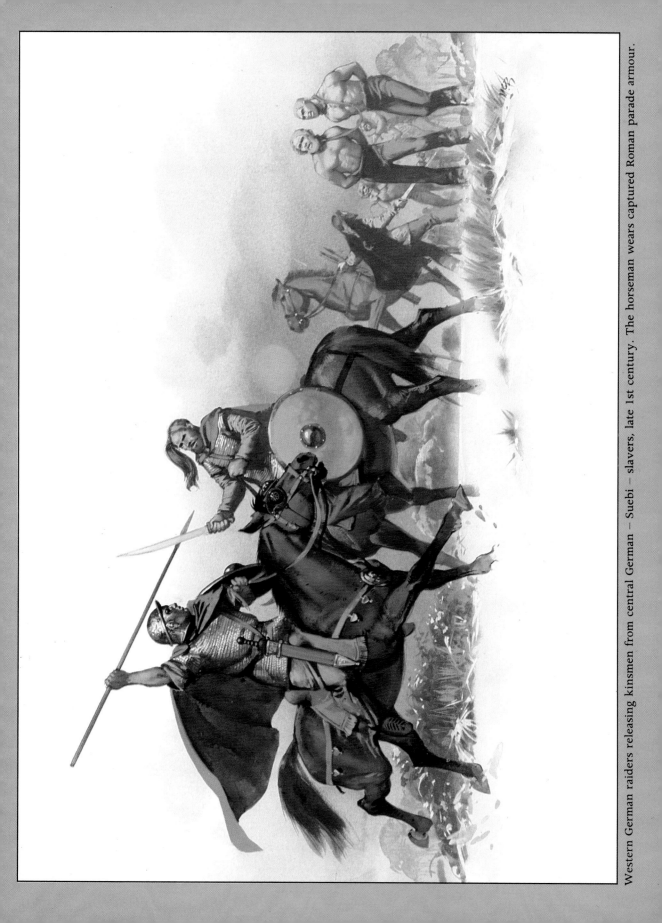

Western German raiders releasing kinsmen from central German – Suebi – slavers, late 1st century. The horseman wears captured Roman parade armour.

Visigoth bandits and runaway slaves ransack an Italian villa, early 5th century. The leading bandit has exaggerated his Barbarian image.

Gallo-Roman landlord hands over property rights to a Burgundian warlord, late 5th century.

Ostrogoths assault the Temple of Hadrian (now Castel S. Angelo), against a defence by citizens and Byzantine warriors. Siege of Rome, AD 537.

Franks attacking Byzantine warriors at the Battle of Casilinum, AD 554. Axe-wielding Frank foot-soldiers suffered heavily from enemy arrows.

Vandal raider shies away from Moorish warrior, Libyan desert, early 6th century. The Moors used camels within their tactical groups.

Muslim Arab warrior and his Ethiopian slave tackle a Sasanid Persian *clibanarium*. Mesopotamian desert, early 7th century.

Berber lancer and Arab archer clash with a Frank nobleman between Tours and Poitiers, AD 732. By this time some horsemen used stirrups.

Danish Viking chieftain and raider confronted by local Franks, Northern France, late 9th century. Viking raiders rode their stolen horses deep inland.

Swedish Vikings – Rus – board a Byzantine ship which is spraying Greek Fire through a dragon-shaped tube. The Black Sea, early 10th century.

Avar horse-warriors clash with the Carolingian Frank horsemen of Charlemagne, early 9th century, Bavaria.

German knights of the Teutonic Order confront heavily-armoured Mongol horse-warriors at the Battle of Liegnitz, 1241.

The Empire fights back

THE OSTROGOTHS AND FRANKS: THE 6th CENTURY

Behind the mosquito-infested marshes that surrounded and shielded Ravenna, Odoacer sat tight. Zeno, Emperor of the East, had broken the uneasy peace that lay between him and the West, and sent a Barbarian, Theoderic, to restore direct Imperial rule in Italy. Odoacer renounced all pretence of allegiance to Zeno and planned to make his own son Emperor of the West. By 489, Theoderic had Odoacer shut up in Ravenna. The siege dragged on for four years around the waters of the Po estuary until, in 493, a surrender was agreed. The two Barbarians were to rule as equals, but Theoderic could not forget the animosity and deaths that had separated them for so long. He invited Odoacer, now 60, to a feast. There, two men knelt before the veteran warlord and clasped his hands as they petitioned him for assistance. Thus shackled, warriors emerged from recesses in the walls of the Palace and prepared to strike the old man dead. They could not do it. Theoderic himself was forced to leap up and draw his sword. 'Where is God?' cried Odoacer. Tensing his muscles, Theoderic announced, 'I avenge my murdered friends so!' He brought his sword smashing down on Odoacer's collar-bone and cut deeply into his torso. Surprised at the depth of his blow, Theoderic bellowed, 'Indeed, this miserable man has no bones!'

For over thirty years, Theoderic ruled Italy as King of the Ostrogoths, the name given to the ragbag band of warriors that supported him. The Emperor of the East was no nearer to extending his control over the West than he had been under Odoacer. Theoderic reigned in all but name as Emperor of the West. As custodian of Italy for the Empire, he was careful to preserve Roman laws and estates, for while he was in command such administration was as beneficial to him as an efficient bureaucracy was to a medieval king. On the face of it, the Italians had little reason to overthrow their German master, particularly if it was only to exchange an approachable tyrant for one not even based on their own soil. Theoderic's pleas for tolerance, however, could not still the racial hatred that bubbled and often boiled over between Italian and German. Frequently, he had to compensate Roman land-owners for the unruly behaviour of his lower ranks. Gangs of

65

German warriors still roamed the peninsula in search of action and easy pickings, and were a constant irritation to the ruling order of Goths.

Unfurling a map of Europe, the new Emperor of the East, Justinian, and his Byzantine courtiers could see that more than half of the old Empire had been lost to the Barbarians. Britain was an assemblage of Saxon kingdoms: France was dominated by the Franks and Spain by the Visigoths: Africa was a firm base for the Vandals: while Italy was now under the sway of the Ostrogoths. Well, the Germans could keep Britain, it had always been a prestigious luxury, more trouble than it was worth. Similarly, the remoter tracts of France and central Europe were of little importance to the maintenance of Mediterranean trade. It was the coastal regions that had to be secured if the Empire was to enjoy continued economic supremacy. After having pacified the Persian frontier, Justinian sent his leading general to north Africa. In a lightning campaign, Belisarius, fast winning a reputation for exceptional military command, routed the Vandal kingdom and repossessed Africa. From there, all eyes focused on Italy. Could Justinian really rebuild the Roman Empire?

Like Germans before them, the Ostrogoths had a problem with Romanisation. Even before coming to Italy, Theoderic had enjoyed himself as a Roman patrician within the beguiling walls of Constantinople. So much so was he removed from the hardships of his people settled in the Balkans that he almost let slip his lordship of the Ostrogoths and had to drag himself away from the princely life of the Byzantines to lead his warriors westwards. Amongst his successors in Italy, that fatal attraction proved even more divisive. Theoderic's wife, Amalasuntha, roused the enmity of chief Goths by educating their son and hier as a civilised Roman. 'If fear of the schoolmaster's strap should overcome our young leader,' they argued, 'how could he possess the strength to defy the swords and spears of his enemies?' Amalasuntha, ruling as regent, despaired of the Barbaric interests of her inferiors and entered into secret negotiations with Justinian to return Italy to him. Likewise, other Goth magnates tried to sell Italy to the Byzantines for a guaranteed income and palace in Constantinople. All the fight had gone out of them. All they wanted was to retire in the lap of luxury and leave the suppression of peasants and marauders to the Emperor. Eventually, the murder of Amalasuntha before she could return Italy to him and the obvious dissension among the Goths, encouraged Justinian to embark on the reconquest of Italy.

Fresh from his success in Africa, Belisarius was appointed overall commander of the invasion force. In addition to his own private bodyguard – his retainers – his army of just over 7,000 men included regular Byzantine troops, Barbarian mercenaries, Isaurian mountain-men from Asia Minor armed with javelins, and small detachments of Moors and Avars. It was given out that his fleet was sailing to Carthage via Sicily. When Belisarius landed in Sicily, the reconquest had begun. In the meantime, to soften up the target, Justinian wrote to the Franks and offered them money if they would join in a general purging of the peninsula. The Franks hated the Goths and agreed. In Dalmatia, Imperial forces marched against Barbarians stationed there. In Sicily, all major cities yielded to Belisarius except one. A Goth garrison within Palermo refused to give up so easily. It was a strongly defended port and Belisarius decided to assault it from the sea. His ships sailed into the harbour and anchored right next to the city walls. The ships' sails overlooked the fortifications and the Byzantines exploited this ready advantage by hauling archers in little rowing boats way up to the top of the masts. From there the archers poured a hail of arrows into the Goths, and soon after the city opened its gates. By 536, Belisarius was lord of all Sicily.

Unfortunately for the Goths, at this time of crisis, their self-appointed leader was Theodatus. A wholly Romanised Barbarian, he was more interested in the philosophy of Plato than the defence of his people. Panicking, he wrote to Justinian with the plea, 'Let me hand over to you the whole of Italy, for I would rather live the life of a farmer free from all cares than persist in the dangers of remaining a king.' Justinian promised Theodatus a hefty annual pension and all the honours the Romans could bestow on him. For a moment, it seemed as if the reconquest of Italy would be an easier task than anticipated. However, as ambassadors took over from

The classic image of axe-wielding, fur-clad Barbarians, probably Franks. From Guizot's *L'Histoire de France*, 1870.

soldiers, news of a Goth counter-attack in Dalmatia emboldened Theodatus. It was now left to Belisarius to bring the Goths to heel.

On the mainland, the Byzantines were greeted by Italians from town and country. This may have been because few of the cities were fortified or garrisoned, and could not withstand Belisarius anyway. What Goths there were in the vicinity were surrendered immediately by their leader, in return for a boat to Constantinople. The Byzantines advanced along the west coast, accompanied by their fleet just offshore, until they reached Naples. The city was both fortified and garrisoned so Belisarius decided to enter into negotiations with the leading citizens to see if both sides could come to a mutually acceptable arrangement. One of the Neapolitans explained their situation frankly 'We are guarded by Barbarians and so cannot oppose them even if we wanted. These Goths, in turn, have left their families behind under the protection of Theodatus and so are not at liberty to betray him. It would be wiser for you to conquer Rome first, for then we would be encouraged to join you without a struggle. Otherwise, if you do not take Rome, you cannot expect to hold Naples'. Belisarius replied that he was determined on the capture of Naples and would rather treat the Neapolitans as friends than enemies – guaranteeing them safety from pillage. To the Goths, he offered either service with the Emperor or the freedom to go home to their farms. In addition, Belisarius promised the Neapolitan envoy great reward if he inspired good-will within the city.

The Neapolitans were divided. One side maintained that by remaining loyal to the Goths, they would not only be well treated if the Goth defenders were victorious but also in the event of defeat at least they would not be renowned as traitors, and so could be depended upon by the Emperor to accept the new regime without oppression. The Goth garrison promised these citizens a strong defence, while the Jewish community in the city made all their merchandise available. Belisarius was told to leave while the going was good. Enraged, the Byzantines flung themselves at the walls of Naples in an attempt to overcome it quickly. After this failed, they cut the aqueduct. The citizens survived from wells within the city.

As time rolled by, Belisarius despaired whether he would ever be rid of the Neapolitans, for he wished to engage Theodatus before the winter season. He prepared to leave the city. But then one of his warriors discovered a hole leading from the aqueduct into the city. This was made bigger and at night a contingent of Byzantines struggled through the tunnel. It was a covered aqueduct, supported by brick arches which carried it right into the middle of the city. Unable to emerge from it until they reached the end, the Byzantines then found themselves only able to get out of the tunnel by climbing on to an overhanging olive tree. This they did and advanced quietly through the streets to a tower in the wall. The defenders were slain and the Byzantines outside called to the wall. It was then discovered that their scaling ladders were too short. Carpenters had misjudged the height from afar, so they had to rope several together before the troops could ascend. The Byzantines on the wall patiently kept their cool and preserved their foothold. Fighting continued throughout the morning. The Neapolitan Jews, fearing an intolerant Christian regime, put up the stiffest resistance. Eventually, the city gates were thrown open and the whole Byzantine army burst in. The massacre, that Belisarius had hoped to avert, swept through the city as Imperial soldiers expended their frustration on the citizens. The Avars were said to be the most savage.

In Rome the Goths became openly dissatisfied with their leader when they heard that Naples had fallen. Theodatus seemed concerned only to remain as safe as possible, with as much money as possible. Sensing the increased animosity Theodatus fled – only to be tipped out of his carriage on the road to Ravenna where the fat man was murdered like an upturned turtle. A warrior, Vittigis, was then elected King of the Ostrogoths. Not a fool, he decided to finish off the conflict against the Franks before engaging in strength with Belisarius. He therefore gave up Rome to the advancing Byzantines and retreated to Ravenna. Vittigis had hoped that the Romans would remain loyal to him as he had treated them well, but on fearing that the fate of the Neapolitans would be inflicted on them if they held out, the citizens of Rome welcomed Belisarius through their gates. After sixty years, Rome was back under the direct control of the Empire.

Immediately, Belisarius set about restoring Rome's walls and fortifications. A deep moat was dug. Surrounding farmers were ordered to bring all their food to the great storehouses of the city. To this was added the grain the Byzantine fleet had brought from Sicily. Though impressed by the efficiency of these measures, the citizens were somewhat anxious at the prospect of a siege. Their walls were too long to be defended at all points and provisions could not reach them from the sea. Compared with Naples, Rome was a sitting target. That said, the majority of Italians accepted the rule of Belisarius and were joined in this also by some Goths. Having strengthened their position up to and around the Tiber, the Byzantines now raided Tuscany and won several towns. Vittigis was being hemmed in. No longer content to sit it out in Ravenna, he sent a force to Dalmatia to recruit warriors from the Suevi, and to reclaim land lost by the Goths to the Empire. He bought a peace treaty with the Franks. Vittigis then gathered a massive army, claimed to be 150,000 strong, though this is obviously a wild exaggeration by Procopius, secretary and chronicler to Belisarius.

As Vittigis inspected his leading warriors, clad in mail which also covered their horses, he was furious that he had left it to this late stage to crush the invaders. He had heard that the Byzantine army was small and wished to march on Rome before Belisarius could retreat before his mighty horde. (Again, this may be Procopius underestimating his own forces so as to emphasise the generalship of his master.) It is likely that Belisarius' army was fairly large, as he would have been able to bolster his ranks with local men. Nevertheless, the Byzantine commander was apparently anxious at the speed of the Goth advance for he was expecting Imperial reinforcements. To slow down the Barbarians, he placed a garrison in a tower defending a bridge across the River Anio. The Goths camped before it, planning to storm it the next day. They were saved the trouble. That night, some of the terrified garrison, Barbarian by birth, deserted to the Goths, while others fled into the countryside. In the morning, unaware of his troop's desertion, Belisarius rode out with some horsemen to reinforce the bridge tower. Suddenly he was attacked by the Goths. Feeling his men waver, Belisarius charged into the midst of the action and engaged the enemy in combat. Deserters fighting with the Goths pointed out the general and soon all Barbarians were aiming their spears at the distinctive dark grey horse with white-flashed face. Belisarius' bodyguard desperately raised their shields around their master, for both sides knew that if he fell, the battle was over. Splattered in gore, Belisarius and his warriors turned this way and that as they hacked and thrust at the Goths. Eventually, the Byzantines fought their way back to the city. Many of Belisarius' closest and noblest warriors had fallen and though he had saved his troops from total annihilation, his actions were considered foolish by the Romans.

After this initial clash, the Goths settled in for a siege. They could not surround the entire length of the city walls and so throughout the spring of AD 537 they constructed six camps on the opposite side of the Tiber, where the Vatican now stands. The camps were fortified with trenches and mounds of earth in which were placed great numbers of wooden stakes. The Barbarians demolished some 14 ancient aqueducts that supplied the city with water and powered its mills. To obviate this, Belisarius set up the mill wheels on boats in the Tiber. The Goths simply broke these by throwing tree trunks and dead bodies into the river. This was countered by hanging great chains from a bridge that lay within the walls and thus collecting the rubbish.

Psychological warfare is particularly potent during a siege. The Goths realised this and exploited it fully. One night, a Goth chieftain rode up to the walls and denounced the Romans for their disloyalty to the Goths. 'Instead you have entrusted your father-land,' he shouted, 'to the Greeks. And the only Greeks you have seen before the arrival of Belisarius were thieving sailors and travelling actors!' Later, on hearing that the Romans were beginning to lose confidence in the Byzantines and resent Byzantine involvement of them in a siege, the Goths sent envoys into the city. 'Repent from your rashness,' urged the messengers, as if preaching to sinners. 'We have no argument with you. For have not the Goths in the past allowed you to live a life of freedom and luxury.' The citizenry were uncertain what to do. It was true that the oppression they now suffered under the military regime of the Byzantines was no better than the tyranny of the Goths which at least had allowed them to carry on their lives relatively free from rationing and assault. But they said nothing, no doubt afraid of the Byzantines, and the envoys returned to Vittigis saying that Belisarius was firm in his command of Rome.

The Goths prepared to storm the city. They revealed a competent knowledge of siegecraft and built great wooden, moveable towers, scaling ladders and battering rams. They filled in the moat with wood and reeds and on the eighteenth day of the siege began a general assault. On seeing the massive towers rumbling towards them, the Romans were dismayed. But Belisarius merely laughed. He ordered his archers to shoot at the oxen that pulled them forward. The great animals fell under the hail of arrows and prevented the towers from moving any nearer the walls. Those warriors who tried to remove the carcasses were also plied full of shafts. The towers stood there uselessly. Undeterred, at other points the Goths assembled in dense masses and rolled their battering rams against the walls. The Romans, in turn, activated their engines of war. One, called 'the wolf', consisted of iron-pointed beams which were suddenly allowed to fall on Barbarians nearest the wall. The beams plunged down and impaled many men on their metal beaks. On other occasions, they were used to smash the heads off battering rams.

Along some stretches of the wall, Vittigis commanded that his warriors restrain themselves from assault but just fire arrows at the battlements to prevent the Byzantines from moving along them and reinforcing other sections under attack. By so doing, the Barbarians made themselves vulnerable to the Romans' *ballistae* and catapults. Firing iron-tipped shafts with double the power of a normal bow, the *ballistae* proved lethal. One Goth, a noble warrior wearing a breastplate, separated himself from his comrades and stood against a tree trunk. From there he placed many arrows accurately amongst the defenders. Aggravated, some Byzantines directed

Silver-inlaid sword hilt of the 7th century. From southern Germany, now in the State Prehistorical Collection, Munich.

71

their *ballista* at this sharpshooter. A few moments later, a bolt flashed out and plunged through the Goth's armour with such force that it pinned him against the tree, leaving the dead man suspended. His fellow warriors moved out of range.

The Romans and the Byzantines considered themselves supreme at siege-warfare and accounts of Barbarian incompetence while assaulting towns frequently have the air of black comedy about them. Dexippus described a siege of Philippopolis in which the Goths spent much time painstakingly constructing wooden shelters covered with hides to protect them against the fiery missiles of the defenders. Their warriors got inside the boxes and were wheeled to the city gates. Here, the citizens simply heaved great stones up onto the battlements and dropped them on their attackers. Both boxes and Barbarians were crushed. But were the Barbarians always that stupid? On many occasions they do seem to have been overawed by superior Roman military technology and tended to restrict their initial campaigns to raiding easier targets: countryside villas and towns without walls. By the 5th century, however, the Barbarians did attack major cities and with success. Even the Huns, supposedly the most primitive and least equipped Barbarians made city gates shake.

When Attila invaded France, Orleans nearly fell to his battering rams. Later, major urban centres of northern Italy were devastated. Priscus, a highly reliable chronicler of events in his own day, records a successful Hun assault on the city of Naissus in 441. The Huns brought great engines of war against the circuit walls. Wooden planks mounted on wheels allowed Hun archers to be pushed forward under cover of screens made of interwoven willow twigs and rawhide. Other engines included massive metal-tipped battering rams swinging on chains. Men at the back of a ram, protected again by screens, pulled back ropes attached to the beam and then let it crash against the wall. Eventually parts of the city walls were broken down and Huns with scaling ladders brought the siege to a bloody conclusion. At this stage, one might suspect that the Barbarians were helped in technological matters by Roman prisoners and deserters. This may be true but it is also likely that the majority of Barbarians did have a good grasp of siegecraft and that the continued Roman denigration of Barbarian achievements was merely prejudiced elitism. Besides, there were many other ways a city could fall into the hands of the enemy. Surprise, panic, mismanagement, blockade and treachery all brought cities to their knees. In the 6th-century siege of Rome, however, the Ostrogoths were confident enough of their skills to hope for victory by direct assault.

While Roman war machines kept many Barbarians away from the walls, the Goths had more success elsewhere, around the Tomb of Hadrian. A massive marble monument surmounted by statues, the mausoleum had been incorporated as a tower into the city's defences. While their archers tried to clear the battlements, the Goths rushed forward. Some, partly hidden by a colonnade leading from the church of St Peter, held very long, man-size shields. These proved highly effective against the defenders' arrows and allowed them to raise their ladders against the walls. The Byzantines manning the Tomb were almost surrounded and out of desperation they began to break up the statues they had been pushed back amongst. Hurling lumps of marble down on the Goths, the attackers were battered, crushed and forced back. Where Goths tried to under-mine the walls, Byzantines fought hand to hand through the holes and threw them out. By the end of the day, the Goths were licking their wounds while the Romans were singing loudly the praises of Belisarius.

Though pleased with the action so far, Belisarius realised he needed more men and wrote urgently to Justinian. To bolster his forces, before the arrival of reinforcements, Belisarius enrolled all able-bodied Romans into his army. At the same time, to save their scanty food supplies, Belisarius ordered the evacuation of all women and children to Naples. This could be done because the Goth forces were not large enough to surround the whole city. Indeed, to protect themselves from Byzantine counter attacks they had restricted themselves to a few fortified camps on just one side of the city. In order to capitalise on this fear, the Byzantines sent out gangs of Moors with hunting dogs to pounce upon isolated groups of Barbarians. The Moors, renowned for their savagery, stripped their victims and then ran speedily back to the walls. Such a situation allowed Rome to receive regular provisions.

To prevent the city being given up by treachery, Belisarius banished all suspect Romans and changed the locks of the gates frequently. To Vittigis, it seemed as if the siege could go on forever. In his frustration, he slaughtered many hostages he had captured before the war. News of this only strengthened the citizens resolve. So Vittigis decided to cut some of the Byzantine supply routes and successfully captured the port of Rome some miles from the city. Belisarius had been unable to spare any troops to garrison it. At this dire moment, Byzantine reinforcements suddenly arrived. Not a major force – sixteen hundred Slav and Avar horsemen – but it was enough for Belisarius to consider carrying the battle outside the walls and against the Goths. In the following skirmishes, the essential differences between Western and Eastern warfare were clearly demonstrated.

A few hundred Byzantine horsemen dashed out of the city and rode towards the Goth camps. They were given strict instructions not to engage the Barbarians in close combat but to use their bows only. Provoked, the Goths grabbed any weapon to hand and rushed out to meet them. The Byzantines evaded their charges and rode onto a hill from where they shot arrows at the advancing crowd of Goths. As soon as their quivers were exhausted, they galloped back to the city walls, chased hotly by wounded and furious Barbarians. From their battlements, the Romans covered their horsemen with *ballistae* bolts. Yet more Goths fell under the vicious storm. Twice more Belisarius executed this tactic with great loss to Vittigis. If Procopius is to be believed, and he is most certainly an eye-witness to the

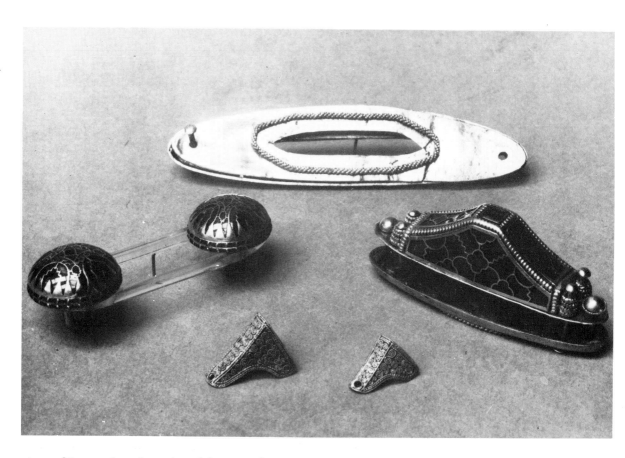

Gold sword fittings inlaid with garnets from the Sutton Hoo ship burial. Late 6th or early 7th century, possibly Swedish.

siege of Rome, then the point of these confrontations was that the Goths did not possess horse-archers with which to counter the Byzantines. Like all western German tribes – the Franks and Saxons included – Goth horse-warriors wielded sword and spear only, while the majority of their armed forces fought on foot with spears. Though they had lived for many years in eastern Europe, in close contact with the horse-archers of the Huns and Sarmatians, the Goths do not seem to have adopted the bow as a weapon worthy of the mounted warrior. Bows were used by Goth foot-soldiers and appear throughout the siege of Rome, though these were most probably simple wooden bows, like those found in northern Europe, and not composite bows. The fact remains, however, that Goth horse-warriors resolutely refused to combine the power and range of the bow with the mobility of their mount.

The reason for this prejudice among German horse-warriors against using bow and arrow appears to be a purely cultural affectation. It seems to have been deeply inbred among the aristocratic ranks of Germanic Barbarians that it was not manly to fire at the enemy from afar. Martial glory could only be obtained through the slogging exchange of sword against spear. This western aversion to the mounted archer defied all military logic and experience. Again and again, when keeping at a distance, horse-archers from the East – whether Hun, Byzantine or Avar – soundly thrashed their Germanic counterparts.

Such a social prejudice against the bow determined the whole nature of western warfare for the next thousand years. Throughout the Middle Ages, it was considered unseemly for a knight to use a bow and arrow, and in later centuries this applied to firearms. Even when the Crusader knights fought in the Holy Land against highly effective Turkish horse-archers, they clung faithfully to their swords and lances. It was left to their foot-soldier underlings to return fire with bow and crossbow. It is a peculiarity of medieval western European warfare that the high social standing of the horse-warrior – the knight – meant that he could not contemplate using the weapons of his inferiors. Elsewhere in the world, where the riding of a horse was somewhat less of a mark of social rank, the bow was an essential arm of even the most noble warrior: the most excellent and decorated bows being highly prized. In the west, there were no decorated or gilded bows. The only occasion when a western aristocrat might bring himself to touch a bow was in hunting or sport. But never in battle. As a result, exceptions to this rule stand out. In his 6th century Frank chronicle, Gregory of Tours mentions that Count Leudast wore a quiver hanging round his mail shirt. In all other respects, the Count was patently a member of the elite warrior class – his breastplate, his helmet, his mail – and yet he also carried a bow. Perhaps this detail was intended to show that he was a parvenu: he had risen quickly from cook to stablemaster to count and so did not possess the decorum of truly noble men. Perhaps the social and military situation during this period was sufficiently fluid to allow for such a transgression: military snobbery became more rigid throughout the Middle Ages. Whatever the explanation, this was most unusual and the noble horse-warrior, with sword and lance only, dominated western, Germanic warfare for centuries to come. With such a fundamental handicap, it is remarkable that the Goths ever won any conflict with eastern warriors. But they did, maintaining the war against the Byzantines for many years. The answer to this lies in the fact that few military combats are planned, text-book battles. Surprise and a rapid rush into hand-to-hand fighting quashed any advantage horse-archers might have possessed over Germanic horsemen.

Elated by the success of their skirmishes against the Goths, the Romans wished to finish the siege of their city with a pitched battle outside the walls. Belisarius was reluctant to risk his whole army in such an engagement, but eventually acceded to the enthusiasm of the citizens. For several days, the battle was delayed because Byzantine deserters kept informing the Barbarians of the offensive. When the confrontation at last began, a lack of professionalism and control proved crucial to the outcome. Belisarius wished to fight a cavalry battle and many of his foot-soldiers rode on captured horses. Their archery proved effective and slew great numbers of the massed Barbarians. Elsewhere on the battlefield, crowds of Roman citizens, demanding to carry arms and fight alongside the regular Byzantine troops, became excited at the apparent defeat of the Goths and rushed upon them. Surprised, the Goths fell back. The charging mob of Roman citizens, servants, sailors and artisans pursued them as far as their camps, but allowed the Goths to retreat into the hills while they looted their wagons and tents. Seeing the collapse of the Roman advance into a chaos of pillage, the Barbarians, full of fury and shouting terribly, dashed down the hill-sides and savaged the plunderers. At the same time, the initial onslaught of the Byzantines had come to a halt and now Goth horse-warriors galloped to assault them with spears and lances. The lighter spears were thrown, while the heavier lances were held in two hands and carried into close combat. A general retreat soon escalated into a rout as horrified Romans threw the Byzantines into disorder in their sprint to the safety of the city walls. After this disaster, Belisarius resumed his smaller, sudden sallies of horse-archers.

The siege of Rome dragged on for a year until the spring of 538. Long periods of famine and disease were broken occasionally by reports of the bold exploits of members of Belisarius' bodyguard. This elite corps frequently amazed the Romans and Byzantines with their daring acts of solitary courage. On one occasion, Chorsamantis, an Avar, wounded and drunk, rode out by himself to the Goth camp. At first, the Barbarians thought he was a deserter, but then he raised his bow. Arrows flashed towards them. Twenty Goths immediately galloped out. Chorsamantis swung his spear at these men with such ferocity that while some fell dead, others shied away. Cursing the weakness of the Germans, he turned round and trotted back to the city. Insulted, other Goths charged after him. Watching from their battlements, Byzantines shouted words of encouragement as the Avar wildly deflected the blows of the Barbarians. Swords and spears clattered against mail. The Avar seemed raving mad in his superhuman energy. Eventually he was surrounded and crumpled beneath the cuts of his team-handed adversaries. At another time, it was a Thracian who deeply impressed his fellow warriors. In order to keep the Barbarians occupied during an Imperial delivery of money for the troops, a group of Byzantine horsemen rode out to the Goth camp. In the skirmish that followed, Cutilas, another of Belisarius' bodyguard, was struck in the forehead by an arrow. Undeterred, he forced back his assailants and chased after them. Returning to the city, the whole arrow remained in the Thracian's head, waving about to the astonishment of the Romans. Clearly, the Germans were not the only people to appreciate or originate tales of heroic single-combat.

Barricaded in their fortified camps against the relentless raids of the Byzantines, the Goths felt as besieged as the Romans. Having already plundered all local farmland, the Barbarians were also suffering from famine and plague. The arrival of Byzantine reinforcements further demoralised the Goths and an armistice was called between the two forces in order to work out a compromise. The Byzantines took advantage of this pause and improved their position throughout central Italy, taking over towns

76

evacuated by the Goths. Vittigis, the Goth leader, tried a few more feeble attempts to breach the walls of Rome but eventually the Goths gave up and retreated to Ravenna. The siege of Rome ended with no titanic battle, but merely fizzled out through exhaustion. Over the next years, scattered, chaotic fighting embroiled the whole of northern Italy. Milan, the second largest city in Italy, was lost to an allied force of Goths and Burgundians. All male citizens were massacred and the women given as slaves to the Burgundians: just one of many atrocities in a savage war. Amidst this brutality, Belisarius maintained his upper hand, and finally captured Ravenna. Vittigis was sent to Constantinople.

Fearful that Belisarius had grown too powerful through his victories, and might assume control as Emperor of the West, the Emperor Justinian recalled him. Soon after Belisarius left Italy, however, the few remaining Goth strongholds broke out and defeated piecemeal the Imperial garrisons scattered throughout the land. And then in 545, the new leader of the Goths, Totila, captured Rome. All the effort and sacrifice that had gone into the reconquest of Italy had been lost in only a few years. All because of the Emperor's jealousy and suspicion.

Belisarius was sent back to Italy, but because Justinian still did not trust him, he was provided with a wholly inadequate army. Rome was re-captured, but the war degenerated into a savage game of hide and seek with the population of Italy suffering terribly at the hands of rampaging Byzantines and Goths. Again Belisarius was recalled to Constantinople and once again the Goths emerged to seize territory lost to the Imperialists. Though a statesman of great vision and enterprise, Justinian let his personal jealousies lose him any gains. Finally, however, he realised that Italy could only be secured by a major and decisive campaign. The eunuch warlord Narses was put in command of a substantial army of around 25,000. On his way to Rome in 552, he confronted a smaller force of Barbarians near the village of Taginae. Situated high in the Apennines, the Byzantines posit-ioned themselves amongst the mountain crevasses and awaited the Goths. A tactically-vital prominence was guarded by fifty Byzantine foot-soldiers. The next day, the Barbarians also realised the importance of this hill and before the main combat broke out, Totila sent forward a group of horsemen to capture it. They dashed up the mountain slope, brandishing their spears and yelping fiercely. The Byzantines, however, were drawn up in a tight phalanx. The Goth horses stopped abruptly and swerved away from the formidable wall of shields and spears. Several times the Goth horse-warriors tried to break the resolve of the foot-soldiers, but each time they were repulsed. Among the Byzantines, one soldier particularly distinguished himself. With his quiver empty and his sword bent, he grabbed the Goth spears with his bare hands and wrenched them from the Barbarians. In recognition of this bravery, Narses appointed the warrior to his personal bodyguard. Thus a warlord insured his own protection by being sur-rounded by only the most courageous warriors.

Both sides prepared for battle. Narses and his personal retainers, as well as his finest regular soldiers, positioned themselves around the hill. On each flank, Narses placed contingents of dismounted Byzantine archers. Bracing themselves on foot, these men could use stronger bows than horsemen and so had a greater range. A group of cavalry were maintained in reserve to reinforce the main body and execute encircling manoeuvres when the enemy were engaged. In the centre, between him and his right wing, Narses assembled his German mercenaries, among them both Lombards and Heruli. He dismounted this essentially horse-borne force because he felt they were untrustworthy and less likely to flee if on foot. The Lombards were such a wild tribe, ravaging and assaulting the native Italians wherever they went, that after the battle Narses was forced to send them back to their own land. Totila similarly organised his army with a phalanx of foot-soldiers flanked by bands of horse-warriors. As each side readied itself for combat, praying and chanting, a Goth rode out from his ranks and challenged the Byzantines to a duel. The Goth happened to be a Byzantine deserter and immediately one of Narses' bodyguard rode forward. The Goth charged, trying to ram his spear into the Byzantine's stomach. The Byzantine turned his horse aside and the Goth lurched past harmlessly. The Byzantine then thrust his own spear at the Barbarian's side and the Goth fell to the ground. A tremendous shout arose from the Byzantine army. They were ready to fight.

With such a dire omen, Totila wished to delay the battle and buy time as he knew reinforcements were close at hand. Desperately, Totila dashed out into the space between the two forces. Clad in gold-plated armour and with regal purple ornaments hanging from the cheek-pieces on his helmet, the Goth warlord hurled his spear into the air and caught it skilfully. At the same time, he wheeled his horse around in a kind of dance. Continuing to juggle his spear, he then leaned back on his horse and stretched out his legs, just as if a trick rider in a circus act. Amazed and somewhat bemused by this performance, the Byzantines held back. With the addition of two thousand Goths who arrived during his performance, Totila armed himself for battle. He pulled on a simple mail shirt and dressed himself as an ordinary warrior so he would not be a conspicuous target for the enemy. The armies then moved towards each other.

According to their orders, Narses' flanking archers advanced further than the rest of the Byzantines. Into this crescent galloped the Goth nobles and their horse-warriors, the foot-soldiers following behind. Rashly, and no doubt because of his Germanic pride, Totila commanded that his warriors should not use bows or any other weapon except their spears. It is difficult to believe that warriors fighting for their life would obey such a silly conceit. Perhaps this was an attempt by Procopius, the chronicler of the battle, to explain the absence of the bow amongst Goth horse-warriors. Whatever happened, the Goths were suddenly raked by a murderous rain of arrows from Byzantines on each side. Losing many warriors, the Goths clashed ineffectively with Narses' dismounted German spearmen, while

Belisarius leads his warriors against the Ostrogoths. From Ward Lock's *Illustrated History of the World*, 1885.

the Byzantine cavalry endeavoured to encircle them. As the afternoon drew to an end, those Goth horsemen that remained rushed back onto their foot-soldiers, who broke before the general advance of the Byzantines. Throughout the night, gangs of Byzantines and Germans chased fugitive Goths, amongst them Totila. Caught up with, the Goth king and his retainers were slain.

After such a victory, Narses marched on Rome. For the fifth time in Justinian's reign, the city was recaptured. From there, Narses fought a last battle with the Goths around their treasure store in the stronghold of Cumae. In the shadow of Mt Vesuvius, the two forces dismounted because of the rough terrain. The battle centred around the figure of the newly elected Goth king, Teias. After losing many men in the process, the Byzantines finally obtained the head of Teias and displayed it on a pole to

the Goths, hoping that they would then surrender. The Barbarians, however, were intent on a desperate last-stand and the fighting continued until the next day. Eventually their position was recognised as hopeless and a number of Goth chieftains swore on their swords to stop fighting in exchange for safe conduct out of the peninsula. The majority of Goths were escorted out of Italy and the reign of the Ostrogoths was broken. Italy was now ruled directly from Constantinople and was again part of the Roman Empire. This had taken twenty years to achieve and the farmers and citizens of Italy had been wracked by military savagery, famine and disease. There was nothing to celebrate. And still the war for Italy was far from over. No sooner had Narses crushed the remaining Goth outposts, than the Franks decided to embark on a major invasion of the peninsula.

The Franks were a confederation of Barbarians composed of ferocious western German tribes that Tacitus had referred to in the 1st century. 'These Franks were called *Germani* in ancient times,' Procopius announced. Like all western Germans, a majority of Franks fought on foot, while their leading horse-warriors carried spears and swords but no bows. In addition to this basic armament, the Franks were renowned for their battle-axes. The *francisca* was an iron-headed, short-handled, throwing axe. According to Procopius and Agathias, it was double-edged, although archaeological finds show that some possessed a single blade. In battle, the Franks hurled these axes at the enemy as they charged forward. The Franks were noted also for their use of a javelin, called an *ango*. This had a barbed iron head that ran someway down its shaft so that its head could not be chopped off. It was modelled on the Roman *pilum* and Agathias, writing in the 6th century, suggested that it could be used in a similar way. When the javelin struck an enemy shield, it was not easily removed and weighed down the shield, thus allowing Frankish warriors to strike the unprotected foe.

Throughout the 5th century, the Franks had made great inroads into Gaul and established it as their country. They defeated the Gallo-Roman landowners, and in 507, at the battle of Vouillé, they shattered the Visigoths settled in the south of France. The Goths retreated into Spain, where they remained during the 6th and 7th centuries. Around the beginning of the 6th century, in their wars against the Alamanni, the Burgundians and the Visigoths, the Franks were led by the energetic and ruthless Clovis. He was the grandson of Meroveus, a chieftain who had fought alongside Aetius against Attila in 451 and given his name to the Merovingian dynasty. It was Clovis who welded the Franks into a unified force and established the Merovingians as its ruling family. He killed those Franks who opposed him and absorbed their land and wealth. He commanded through terror. On one occasion he addressed his warriors on the fact that he, as chieftain, should receive more booty than the rest. One warrior disagreed and stated that they should all receive an equal share. Clovis hid his anger and passed on to other matters. Some months later, when he was inspecting his warriors' arms, he came across the warrior who had denied him his extra share.

The single-edged blade of the *francisca* throwing axe, characteristic of the Franks. Found at Howletts, Kent, now in the British Museum, London.

Criticising the condition of the warrior's spear, sword and axe, Clovis threw the latter weapon on the ground. The warrior bent to pick it up and as he did so, Clovis raised his own battle axe and split open the warrior's skull. The rest of his men took heed of this warning. With his conversion to Catholicism, and his acceptance of a consulship from the Eastern Emperor, Clovis and his clan became the official rulers of France. Clovis' attitude to religion encouraged cynicism. Of the Visigoths he said, 'I cannot bear to see those Arians occupying any part of Gaul. With God's help, we will invade them and when we have beaten them, we will take over their territory.'

The official recognition of Clovis by the Eastern Emperor was most likely a Byzantine ploy to counter the power of the Goths in the west. Throughout the reconquest, the Franks loomed over north-west Italy, changing their allegiance as it suited their ambitions. Occasionally, they carried out raids against the Byzantines as well as the Goths. With the death of Clovis in 511, his kingdom was divided equally, according to Frank law, among his four sons. Such an inheritance weakened the unity of the Franks and there was much feuding. Nevertheless, their energy was also directed against outsiders and the kingdoms of the Franks remained a strong European power. In 553, Frank warlords invaded Italy and were joined by remnants of the vanquished Ostrogoths. They rode through Italy and ravaged many

Byzantine garrisons. Narses bided his time and built up his strength. The next year, Narses confronted the Franks at the Battle of Casilinum. Horse-archers annihilated the invading troops. Remaining Frank bands were decimated by epidemic and Italy was again left to the Byzantines. For just over ten years, Italy remained free of Barbarians. Justinian, and his courtiers in Constantinople, probably marvelled at the fact that he had done more than any other late Roman Emperor to rebuild the glory of Rome. And yet Italy was too vulnerable to be long out of German hands. Shortly after Justinian's death in 565, his Empire began to crumble. Retreating before the Avars, the Lombards crossed the Alps in 568 and set in motion a series of wars with the Byzantines that lasted for two centuries and forced the Imperialists into southern Italy. Ravenna remained an isolated outpost of the Empire in the north, while the Popes in Rome stiffly resisted the Arian Lombards.

As with other German invasions, the Lombard incursion was largely a contest for the most attractive landholdings. Lombard nobles competed with Byzantine landowners, and in their wake left the ruined lives of more humble Italians. On every occasion, it was the peasants who suffered most from marauding gangs of Barbarians and Imperialists. By this time, despairing of ever aligning themselves with the right side, they maintained an open hostility to both oppressors. Italy was a land fought over, not governed. Wars of conquest merely gave way to ferocious vendettas between landlords. In between fighting, Lombard aristocrats continued the business of their predecessors: exporting and importing goods from Italian ports and maintaining trade from farm to town. In many respects, aside from the ever-present power struggle over who claimed what piece of land, the Germans, the Byzantines and the descendants of the old Imperial ruling caste settled down to a way of life that was very similar to – and a continuation of – the Roman economy. In the 7th century, however, their monopoly of the Mediterranean was severly disturbed by a new power from the East. A froce motivated by the word of God.

The force of God

THE
MOORS
AND ARABS:
THE
7th AND 8th
CENTURIES

In a cave in the mountains of western Arabia, a man received messages from God. Within twenty years of announcing these visions, Arabia had been converted to a new religion and united under this one man. Within fifty years, his successors conquered Palestine, Syria, Mesopotamia, Egypt, Persia and Afghanistan. The Persian Sasanid Empire was annihilated and the Byzantine Empire left with only one oriental province in Asia Minor. Within a hundred years of that lonely mystical experience, the followers of the Messenger of God ruled a domain that stretched from India to Spain and from the Sahara to southern France and Central Asia. In a remarkably brief period, Arabs held sway over lands on three continents: an area vaster than that controlled by the Romans at the height of their Empire. The Messenger of God was Muhammad and his religion – Islam.

For centuries before their surrender to Islam, the nomadic tribes of Arabia were considered of little importance. To the Roman and Persian empires the wild Arabs of the interior were vagabonds whose raids were ineffectual pin-pricks: nothing to worry about. Occasionally the tribes fought for Imperial forces but always they disappeared back into the desert. In the 6th century, it was the Moors, the native inhabitants of Mauretania – the western regions of north Africa – who proved the most dangerous of the southern Barbarians, but even they were dismissed by the Byzantines as the most poorly armed Barbarians the Empire had to fight. Solomon, commander of Byzantine forces in north Africa after Belisarius, described the Moors thus, 'Most of them have no armour at all. Those that have shields, have only small, poorly made ones which are not able to turn aside thrusts against them. They carry only two short spears and once they throw these, if they achieve nothing, they turn around and run.'

Solomon underrated the Moors at his own cost. Later they ambushed him and he was killed. Indeed, in the competition for power following the death of Gaiseric, the great Vandal leader, the Moors inflicted several serious defeats on the Germanic Barbarians. One of the most devastating was won by Cabaon in Libya.

For days, Cabaon had been aware that the Vandals were advancing into his territory. He had sent spies into Carthage and was well informed of the Vandal raids. In order to obtain supernatural support and also, no doubt, to gain the friendship of local inhabitants, he instructed his spies to help those Roman Christians assaulted by the Arian Germans. After each violent attack on a church or Catholic community, Cabaon's agents moved in, cleared up the damage and recompensed the holy men for their losses. In the meantime, the Moor leader ordered his warriors to abstain from all injustice, all luxurious foods and, most of all, association with women. To reinforce this order a palisade was set up between the men and women in his camp. Women and children remained with their men on campaign so they could tend horses and camels, construct stockades and sharpen weapons. When Cabaon's spies finally told him that the Vandals were fast approaching, he prepared his warriors in the usual Moorish fashion. Their camels were rounded up in a circle, twelve animals deep. Warriors, wielding swords and javelins, stood amongst them. Confronted with the sight and smell of these camels, the horses of the Vandal raiders shied away and refused to be driven towards them. Some horses panicked and threw their perplexed riders to the ground. Without bows or effective missile weapons, the Germans suffered badly from the showers of javelins hurled at their ranks. Unable to return the fire, the resolve of the Vandals disintegrated and they broke before the advancing Moors.

With the conquest of the Vandals by Belisarius, the Moors tried out the same tactics against the Byzantines. Against a more sophisticated force, they came unstuck. Quickly appreciating the effect of camels on their horses, the Byzantine cavalry dismounted and marched towards the Moors with their shields interlocked in a powerful wall of wood and iron. The light Moorish spears bounced off the heavily armoured warriors and when they reached the lines of camels, the warriors slaughtered both the animals and the men hiding behind them. The Moors fled and the Byzantine horsemen, now regaining their mounts, cut down many in the pursuit. From then on the Moors avoided pitched battles in open spaces and concentrated on damaging raids. Though unable to throw the Byzantines out of north Africa, the Moors nevertheless remained a constant problem to the Empire. When the Empire withdrew before the Arabs, the Moors joined the great surge of Islam and went on the offensive against Europe.

The Roman and Persian empires had never bothered to conquer the whole of the Arabian peninsula. In the interior, deserts and arid mountains encouraged a nomadic pastoral existence. Arabia's only source of wealth and appeal to outsiders was its many trade routes which crossed the land from the south and the Indian Ocean. Caravans laden with aromatic and exotic goods advanced from oasis to oasis along the Red Sea coast. Around these fertile pools thrived market towns that grew fat on the trade that passed through them. Frequently, neighbouring towns competed violently with each other to ensure that caravans paused with them rather than their rivals. In a battle to secure their monopoly over the middle stretch of the Incense Route, the merchants of Mecca defeated the people of Ta'if, a few miles to their east. By the beginning of the 7th century Mecca was a major commercial centre, deriving its great wealth almost exclusively from the caravan trade. To ensure its continued prosperity, Bedouin nomads from the interior were employed as guards and guides for the myriad trains of camels that passed to and fro. Occasionally, and more as a sport and demonstration of masculine prowess, Arab townsmen would engage in raids – called *razzias* – on neighbouring communities. The intention was to avoid bloody confrontation and simply rustle a few animals from their rivals.

It was into this world of high materialism that Muhammad, a man of middling status and wealth, was born. By 610, in his late middle-age, he began to preach to the citizens of Mecca about his mystical experiences. These revelations became the essential tenets of the Koran and Islam, an offshoot of the Jewish and Christian religions. Muhammad preached that God – Allah – is almighty and that he alone should be worshipped. After a

Parthian horse-archer. The Parthians had been the great eastern enemies of Rome until displaced by the Persian Sasanid dynasty. Terracotta image, 1st to 3rd century AD, now in the British Museum, London.

period of toleration, the Jews were accused of corrupting the scriptures, while the Christians were criticised for worshipping Jesus as the Son of God. Muhammad was only a prophet – a messenger – he was not of supernatural origin. In addition to this basic faith in one God, Muhammad taught that God expected his people to be generous with their wealth; to help those less fortunate than themselves. In return those people that led a virtuous life would, on the Day of Judgement, pass in to heaven, while those who had not, would be consigned to hell. Such a blatantly anti-materialist philosophy naturally excited the poor of Mecca and annoyed the ruling merchants. Irritation turned to outright hostility and in 622, Muhammad and his Muslim followers fled to Medina, the next important trade centre, 200 miles to the north of Mecca. It is from this date that Islamic history begins – year one.

Instead of settling down to a life of meditation and preaching in Medina, Muhammad at once began organising raids against Meccan caravans. Ostensibly to gain his impoverished followers a living in a new town, it seems likely that Muhammad also used these raids as a method of building up his power and respect in Medina, and amongst the western Arabs. For without an income and strength of arms, Muhammad's religion might have disappeared in the wake of other self-proclaimed prophets and their sects. After a slow start, Muhammad's raiders gained some successes and other Arabs converted to Islam and joined his horde. Despite misgivings and hostility from many of Medina's inhabitants, the activities of the Muslims inevitably embroiled that town in a war against Mecca. The first battle evolved from an unsuccessful razzia. In 624, 300 Muslims beat off 900 Meccans. The conflict had started with with a few single combats and ended with less than a hundred dead on both sides. The battle of Badr was the first notable victory of the Muslim forces, and was interpreted as a victory of faith over the unbelievers.

Within Medina, Muhammad consolidated his political position. Leading opponents were assassinated. Jews were expelled and massacred. Two Meccan attacks on Medina were repulsed and in 630, after Muhammad had assembled an unusually large force which overawed the city, the Muslims entered Mecca peacefully. Over the next years, Muhammad defeated rival tribes and towns, emerging as the most powerful man in Arabia. Undefeated tribes rallied to his side as allies. As Muhammad's strength grew, these tribes converted to Islam. Only those Arabs to the north, nearest to the Byzantine and Persian empires, remained aloof from the new enthusiasm that had seized their neighbours. A couple of years before his death in 632, Muhammad led an expeditionary force, said to be 30,000 strong, along the trade route to Iraq. It foreshadowed conquests beyond Arabia.

The Muslim forces that achieved the first victories of Islam were samll and unprofessional. Essentially they were raiders, used to attacking caravans and not prepared armies. Muhammad's supporters were towns-men from Mecca and Medina with Bedouin recruited from the interior.

Silver dish of the 5th century, showing King Bahram V on a lion hunt. Sasanid Persian weaponry and armour influenced steppe warriors such as the Huns and Turks, and later influenced the Arabs. Dish now in the British Museum, London.

Many were motivated by the prospect of booty, some by the desire of their leader to spread the new religion. The raiders and Bedouin rode horses. In large-scale confrontations, however, the majority of Muslim townsmen went into battle on foot. Camels were used mainly as pack-animals, although warriors sometimes rode them into battle but then dismounted. They do not appear to have been used in tactical formations like those of the Moors and rarely did warriors fight from their camel back. When battle was engaged, camels were usually left behind in camp where they were hobbled to prevent them from being easily rustled away by enemy raiders. The number of horses available to the Muslims was very small at first, but this grew with every victory.

Alongside the more prosperous Muslims fought their slaves. Inspired by the egalitarianism of Islam, these slaves fought particularly well. According to tradition, the first Muslim killed in battle was a black slave called Mihja. Another slave, a Persian, was credited with suggesting the digging of a ditch around Medina that saved the town from the Meccans. But aside from the promise of their new faith, slaves fought effectively in battle for other reasons. On the positive side, success in combat could bring a slave renown, promotion, favours, perhaps even liberty if he saved his master's life. On one occasion, later in the 7th century, a commander urged his massed levies of slaves onwards with the words, 'The slave who fights is free.' So encouraged, observers were astonished at the vigour of the slaves as they gained victory. Fighting also gave a slave the opportunity to prove himself a man of worth in his own right. On the negative side, fear of defeat and death, as well as fear of punishment if they did not fight well, instilled many slaves with greater martial energy. Such considerations seem to have overcome any doubts that their masters may have had in arming a potentially hostile group of men. Besides, at the beginning of their struggle for survival, Muhammad and his followers were desperate for any able-bodied recruits. Their slaves, particularly the physically strong agricultural workers, could often endure the harsh conditions of campaign better than their town-bred masters.

Some slaves rose to prominence through their efforts in battle. Wahshī was a black Ethiopian highly skilled at spear throwing. At first he was employed by his master, an opponent of Muhammad, to kill the Prophet's uncle. This he achieved in battle and thus obtained his liberty. When Mecca was taken by the Muslims, Wahshī fled to Tā'if. There, he fell in with a group of citizens who converted to Islam. He attempted to obtain forgiveness from Muhammad but was dismissed. He turned to drink and was conspicuous for wearing bright red clothes. At the battle of Yamāma, the Ethiopian seized a chance to redeem himself. Fighting with the Muslims, he charged fearlessly towards the enemy commander and struck him dead, thus saving Islam from its chief 'false prophet'. 'I killed the best of men after Muhammad,' Wahshī claimed in later life, 'and then the worst of them.' Eventually, his drinking killed him. Such slave warriors were not professional soldiers in the sense of the military slaves acquired and trained by Muslim dynasties, like the Egyptian Mamlûks, in later centuries. The systematic raising of elite corps of professional slave warriors did not become institutionalised until the 9th century. Until that time slaves only fought as occasional retainers, defending their masters in battle, much like medieval European serfs. The best that could be said of them was encapsulated by an Arabic poet thus

> 'One obedient slave is better
> than three hundred sons.
> For the latter desire their father's death,
> the former his master's glory.'

The death of the Prophet could well have been the end of Islam had not a string of remarkably strong and determined men taken over leadership of the religion and the Arabs. These leading disciples of Muhammad were known as caliphs. Not suprisingly, the main task the first caliph, Abū Bakr, had to face on his succession was to maintain the unity of the Arabs. Encouraged by the success of Muhammad, 'false prophets' sprung up throughout the country. By calling themselves 'prophets', these men hoped

Sasanid iron sword with silver scabbard from the 6th or 7th centuries. These blades were adopted by the conquering Muslim armies of Arabia. In the British Museum, London.

to detach themselves from the relentless inter-tribal suspicions and rivalries that had dogged previous attempts at greater centralisation of power. A spiritual man was seen to be above politics, unaligned to any faction, therefore only he could be a truly unbiased ruler of several tribes. Whether this had lain intentionally behind Muhammad's rise to power is uncertain, but it was a fundamental factor in his triumph. The elimination of competition by Caliph Abū Bakr in the war of the Ridda established more potently than ever before the Arabs as a single force. Under the reign of the Caliph 'Umar, this energy was directed against foreign non-Muslims. With the invasion of Mesopotamia, Palestine and Syria, the *Jihad* – or Holy War – was carried onto alien territory. Internal peace and external conquest profoundly transformed the Arabs. From an array of feuding tribes they had become a nation, a major Mediterranean power.

Much has been made of the belief that it was the strength of their faith that brought the Muslims so many spectacular victories. Certainly, today in the Middle East, the militancy of fundamentalist Muslim groups causes their more liberal neighbours to shudder as they witness the willingness of the hardliners to die for their beliefs. It can be argued, however, that such religious zeal has the authority of over a thousand years of established worship: and is frequently associated with fervent nationalism. The religion of the first caliphs was only a few decades old and must still have been widely misinterpreted and confused with other monotheistic faiths in the region. Such a newcomer to the philosophies of the Middle East would not have had the weight of tradition needed to impress many Arabs. That said, the doctrines of Jihad did promise a place in heaven to any warrior who died for Islam. This paradise was conceived as a wonderful garden running with cool streams. For a desert nomad, vulnerable to the superstitions and visions of afterlife that enveloped most people at this time, such a heaven was highly attractive. Warriors thus fearless of death would indeed have made an invincible force. And yet the West had its own spiritual promise for faithful warriors. Christianity offered its defenders an equally comforting afterlife. Even those Germans still motivated by pagan beliefs knew that to die fighting meant ascension to the glorious halls of their War Gods. But it was only the most religion-obsessed minds on all sides that truly believed such images: only a core of warrior mystics. The majority of men knew it was better to survive than be killed. Such commonsense cannot have been any less prevalent among rank and file Muslims.

Both Islam and Christianity preached the basic tenet that it was wrong to kill a man, but made an exception when that man was an infidel and opposed to one's own religion. The Jihad had its parallel in Christianity with the just wars condoned by Saint Augustine, and the crusades of later centuries. Yet Islam is still regarded as a stronger motivating force than the faith of the Byzantines or the Franks. This cannot be true, and is largely the result of Western cynicism regarding a belief close to hand, while maintaining a certain respect for a mysterious system of faith. The primary motivating force among the majority of Arab warriors was the same as that which stimulated medieval crusaders and has always excited soldiers. The prospect of booty and the licensing of outrageous behaviour. The success of the early Muslims simply encouraged many more Arabs to clamber on the wagon of ruthless enterprise. It was a campaign of conquest that made nomads rich beyond their own meagre pastoralism and transformed merchants into dynastic imperial governors. That solid material ambition underpinned much of the Muslim conquest is revealed even by Muhammad. When the Prophet placed Amr ibn al-As, the future conqueror of Egypt, in command of some warriors, he announced, 'May God keep you safe and bring you much booty.' Amr rejoined, 'I did not become a Muslim for the sake of wealth, but for the sake of submission to God.' To which the Prophet concluded, 'Honest wealth is good for an honest man.'

The most realistic and effective aspect of Islam in its conquest of half the Mediterranean world was its tolerance of Christians and Jews. Whenever subjugated by the Muslims, they were treated with respect and allowed to continue as before. For they were all People of the Book, sharing the same religious old Testament background. Such a policy meant that Christian and Jewish populations were far less hostile to the invaders than they might have been. To them it did not really matter whether their overlords were Byzantine, Persian or Arab. The Muslims only offered their adversaries 'conversion or the sword' when they were worshippers of idols or many gods. As there were few such cults around the Mediterranean, the Muslims found themselves in charge of increasing numbers of 'protected groups' or dhimmī. These People of the Book were allowed to practise their own faith in return for a regular protection payment to their conquerors. The Muslims frequently left economies to continue as before and simply lived off the taxes, thus leaving them independent, not tied to new estates. In this way, the Muslim forces were constantly funded and free to move on.

In Christian Europe, the doctrine of chivalry evolved to curb the excesses of war. Similarly, the Jihad incorporated a code of military conduct. But unlike chivalry, which was an unwritten code emerging from a general Christian aristocratic regard for honourable decency, the rules of Jihad were actually inscribed in works on Islamic law. The killing of women, children and old men was forbidden, unless they fought against Muslims. The wanton destruction of crops was discouraged. Prisoners converted to Islam were not to be killed. Other prisoners should not be tortured to death or mutilated, although they could be executed. Grants of safe-conduct and quarter must be upheld. Similarly, peace treaties and armistice agreements could be entered into with non-Muslims. Before war was embarked upon, a summons to Islam must have been issued to the enemy state. Like the vague humanity of chivalry, such a code was frequently broken in the heat of battle. In addition, there were so many differing interpretations of Islamic law that outright contradictions of many of the above measures were justified by a variety of sects.

Charles Martel, called 'the Hammer' by later historians, smashes an Arab force near Tours in AD 732. From Ward Lock's *Illustrated History of the World*, 1885.

For centuries, the Sasanid Persian Empire had been the Roman Empire's principal Eastern enemy. In the early 7th century, both forces were exhausted and recovering from their costly conflicts. On top of this, the Sasanid dynasty was politically unsteady and vulnerable to a sudden, unexpectedly powerful thrust from the south. But the Persians were no easy target: indeed, in their initial contact with the Muslims they severely defeated the invaders. The reluctance of the Arabs to give up the struggle triumphed, however, and in the end they captured a series of ancient capitals. The Barbaric behaviour of the victorious nomads shocked the more refined Persians. The Arabs tore up priceless carpets studded with jewels and shared them among each other. Dogs were fed off gold platters and luxurious aromatic substances were mistaken for food spices and tipped into soups. As the Persian Empire quickly crumbled, Arab forces launched attacks on Byzantine Palestine and Syria. With a sandstorm blowing in their enemy's faces, the Muslims tore apart a Byzantine army at the second battle of Yarmuk. Aided by the passivity of the native population the Arabs soon dominated both provinces. In 638, Muslims occupied Jerusalem. A year later, they invaded Egypt and threw out the Byzantines. This was particularly galling for the Empire as it had just expended a great deal of effort in recapturing the land from the Persians.

From their campaigns against the Persians and the Byzantines, the Arabs gained much. Their primitive warfare of enthusiasm aided by fortune was transformed into a more sophisticated system of war through acquisition and adaption. Horses had been rare amongst the Muslims before they left Arabia, but as they conquered the lands of the Persian and Byzantine empires, they acquired the finest horses of the East. The Syrian-Arab crossbreed combined weight with strength and became a vital weapon in further Islamic expansion. So much so did the Arabs take to horses that the small force of 4,000 that invaded Egypt in 639 was almost exclusively made up of horse-warriors. Among these riders the stirrup was known but was largely disdained as a sign of weakness. Only later did it become a generally accepted device. Camels and mules were still ridden while on the march to save the horses for battle.

In Arabia, the Muslims had also been poor in arms and armour. From the Byzantines and Persians, the Arabs looted mail and scale armour and witnessed the effective use of heavy cavalry so protected. Arab nobles were greatly impressed by their Sasanid counterparts clad entirely in iron. Veils of mail covering their faces gave them a dramatic appearance; while strips of iron were fastened on to their mail shirts around their torso; and yet more mail or scale armour protected their horses. Ammianus referred to earlier warriors so encased as looking 'not like men, but statues polished by the hand of Praxiteles'. Perhaps, however, leading Muslims rejected such a display as decadent. Chroniclers commented on the victorious entry of the Muslims into their cities as impressively unshowy compared to the Byzantines or Persians. This may have been because the majority of Arabs wore their mail shirts between layers of clothing: similarly, helmets were swathed in turbans. In the case of mail, covering it with linen may have been intended to deflect the direct rays of the sun, to prevent it from heating the bare metal to an unbearable condition.

Of course, not all Muslim warriors wore armour. Frequent injections of poor nomadic tribesmen meant that there were alway a great many lightly clad horsemen in all Muslim armies. This contributed to the preference of many Muslim commanders for campaigns that were a series of raids rather than pitched battles. That said, there does appear to have been a strong strain of Germanic-like chivalry in Arab warfare: a need for direct confrontation. For though the Arabs employed the composite bow as a matter of necessity, particularly when fighting against Central Asian Turks, the horse-archer did not play an overwhelming role in early Muslim warfare. Foot archers were employed to great effect but much mounted fighting was still carried out with sword and spear. Single combat was favoured and many battles were decided by hand-to-hand fighting. In the civil wars of 657, a duel between two Arab champions was recorded. Both Abbās ibn Rabiah and Irar ibn Adham dismounted to confront each other. The warriors wore coats of mail. Abbās' mail covered his head and was so long – being intended for horseback – that he had to tuck part of it into his belt. In fact, so completely protected were they by their mail that their sword blows proved fruitless. Becoming tired and desperate, Abbās suddenly noticed a gap in Irar's armour. He tore this aside with one hand and then plunged his sword into his opponent's naked chest. Irar fell dying. In later centuries heavily armoured horse-archers became the regular core of most Arab armies. The early 10th century chronicler al-Tabarī lists the following essential arms and armour for a warrior: mail, breastplate, helmet, leg-guards, arm-guards, horse armour, lance, small shield, sword, mace, battle-axe, quiver of thirty arrows, bowcase with two bows and two spare bow strings. Such a 'tank' was clearly descended from the Byzantine and Sasanid *clibanarii*, so named after the Greek word for 'oven' – obviously how many a soldier felt!

Inevitably, the continued success of the Muslims brought great strains to their unity. Civil war broke out and for a few decades their conquests faltered. By the beginning of the 8th century, however, the whole of north Africa had fallen to the Muslims. Like other warriors before them, the temptation to cross a strip of sea just eighteen miles wide and pass from continent to continent proved overwhelming. In the town of Ceuta, opposite Gibraltar, they found themselves an ally. Count Julian, perhaps a Byzantine exiled from Spain or a disaffected Visigoth, demonstrated how easy it was to tap the wealth of Romano-Goth Iberia. Accompanied by Muslims, his men raided the southern-most tip of the peninsula. Thus encouraged, a year later in 711, a force of 7,000 warriors commanded by a Berber called Tāriq, set sail in ships provided by Count Julian. For ever after, their landing place has been called Gibraltar, *Jabel Tāriq*, 'the mountain of Tāriq'. The army consisted mostly of Berbers, nomads of the Sahara who had converted to Islam and provided some of the fiercest warriors of the Arab invasions.

Racked by conflicts over succession, the Visigoth kingdom of Spain was unable to field a united front. After the Muslims had established themselves and received reinforcements, they were finally confronted by the Visigoth King Roderick somewhere north of the salt-lake of Janda. The Berbers had rustled many horses from local farms and so met the Iberian Germans on horseback. Both sides fought with swords and spears. Gangs of noble horse-warriors were supported by bands of foot-soldiers. The Berbers were veteran warriors of the Muslim African campaigns and fared well against the reluctant farmers and serfs desperately assembled as an army by Goth landlords. Roderick had already suffered from crippling desertions on his way south from Toledo. And now, as the Berbers charged forward, swathed

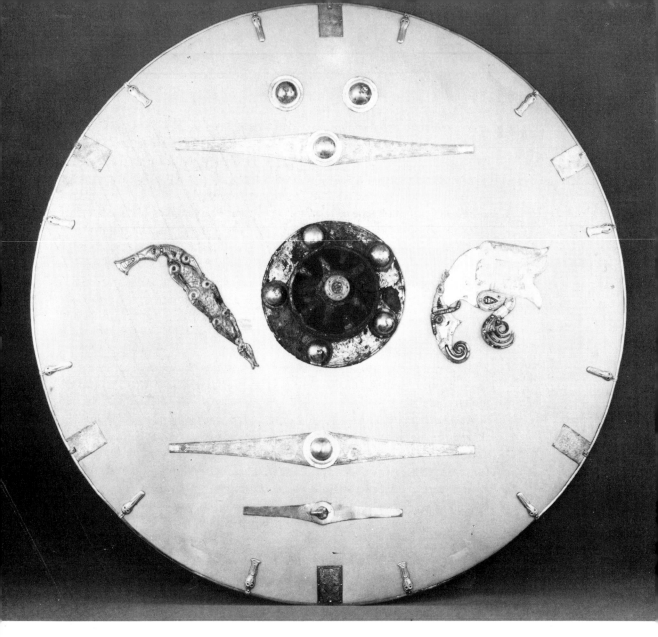

in mail and dark blue face-covering turbans, the Visigoth ranks shuddered and broke. Roderick and his retainers were killed.

The Muslim advance towards the Visigoth capital of Toledo in central Spain was rapid. The Jewish and Byzantine inhabitants of the region made no pretence of resistance. They had suffered much under the oppressive regime of the Goths and were happy to exchange it for the less intolerant rule of Islam. Indeed, the Jews, with north African allies, had organised an abortive revolt against the Visigoths in the last years of the previous century and savage massacres of the Jews had followed. Local Visigoth warlords did, of course, oppose the invaders but there was no central co-ordination and their unity had long been shattered by dynastic rivalry.

Some Goths even helped the Arabs in the hope of future political preferment. The Visigoth kingdom was spent, and in the face of a determined invader, it fell apart. Over the next few years, many more Arab warriors arrived and key cities were subdued. As with previous Barbarian invasions, not every community in a country as vast as Spain could be said to be under direct Arab control, but by 716 the conquest was complete and al-Andalus, or Andalusia, emerged as the first European province of the Muslim Empire.

Throughout their conquests, the Muslims were aided by the internal exhaustion and collapse of their chief adversaries. The Sasanids, Byzantines and Visigoths were all caught at their least dynamic. With the Muslim invasion of southern France, however, they came against a far more vigorous opponent, though this was not immediately apparent. For on the surface, if the inhabitants of France had depended on their royal family to protect them there would be Islamic palaces in Aquitaine today to equal the Alhambra. The Merovingian dynasty of Franks had kept a firm grip on the lands of Gaul for two centuries but was now in decline. Real power was held by men behind the throne, the Mayors of the Palace. This role, of defender and maintainer of the state, was assumed by the Arnulfing dynasty and was handed from father to son. From this family emerged the Carolingian monarchs.

At the time of the first Arab raids into southern France it was the illegitimate son of one of these mayors who took command in the crisis – Charles Martel. The principal landholder in north France and western Germany, Martel had one major rival – Eudo – warlord of Aquitaine. When news reached Charles of substantial Muslim conquests in and around Narbonne he could see that Eudo had his hands full and monitored the outcome with great interest. As the Arabs consolidated their position, Eudo struck back and defeated them soundly, killing their commander. But relentless as ever, the Muslims sent further expeditionary forces via the Rhone valley. For over a decade the Arab raiders plundered the rich lands of Provence until finally, in 732, the Arabs embarked on their second large scale invasion and crossed the Pyrenees. This time, Eudo was beaten and pursued into central France. Fearing an attack on his own lands, though more interested in the outcome of a victory achieved on his rival's territory, Charles Martel seized the opportunity of Eudo's rout and marched south. Joining remnants of Eudo's army just south of Tours, Charles drew up his warriors in defence of this rich religious centre. An alternative tradition, recorded by Fredegar, relates that Eudo and Charles had already clashed in several border incidents. Worsted by Charles' raiders, Eudo then invited the Arabs to join him in an attack on Martel. Therefore, in the battle that followed, Christians fought alongside Muslims against the Franks of northern France.

For a week, both forces sent raiders against each other: testing their strength. This delay allowed the Arab commander, 'Abd al-Rahmān al-

Ghāfiqī, to secure the passage of his wagons laden with booty back to safer zones. Why Charles did not employ the advantage of surprise to attack his foes immediately is unknown. According to Fredegar he did, but other records give time in which the Arabs were allowed to save their goods and prepare for battle. This week of waiting would also have allowed the Franks to ride through the district and gather local men to fight alongside the professional warriors loyal to Charles. When battle was finally begun, tradition has it that the majority of Franks fought on foot, shoulder to shoulder, in an impenetrable iron phalanx of shields and spears. This was certainly true of the hastily assembled farmhands and citizens, who could do little else but fight on foot. Many of the aristocratic retainers of the leading Frank nobles, however, would have remained on their horses in the hope of rapidly exploiting weaknesses amongst the enemy.

As a force of raiders the Muslims must have been largely mounted, and it makes sense that it was they who opened the battle. (Though hereagain, Fredegar says that it was Charles who came upon them 'like a mighty man of war'.) Such a large invasion force must have included many foot-soldiers as well, for these were still an important element of Arab warfare. Therefore, it is likely that crowds of Berbers, Arabs, recently recruited Christians and Jews, all fought side by side in a phalanx of sword and spear carriers to equal that of the Franks. There were more archers among the Arabs than the Franks, but hails of arrows were probably not a determining feature. Also, the traditional picture of lightly clad Arab horsemen hurling themselves against heavily armoured Frank foot-soldiers must be discounted. Instead it is more likely that the Muslims, veteran raiders and well supplied with looted arms from recently defeated Frank adversaries, fielded more men clad in mail and brandishing swords than the poorly equipped levies of Charles Martel.

The fighting was fierce, lasting until nightfall. Arab and Frank horsemen probably came to blows first, as the most noble horse-warriors hoped to obtain victory quickly with an initial display of daring and skill. Once exhausted, they then fell back amidst their rows of foot-soldiers. As the battle progressed, groups of warriors advanced and entrapped isolated horsemen. Prodding them with their spears, pushing them off their horses, forcing blades through gaps in their mail and ripping off anything of value. It was a battle of muscle and endurance; swords bashed against shields and spears pierced bodies. Beneath their mail many of the chief warriors suffered only battering and bruises. Blows to their spirit rather than their bodies. It was the unprotected and unprepared peasant levies who were slashed and gored, trampled and crushed, and it was these men who quit the battlefield first if suffering visibly-great losses. Indeed, considering the more professional quality of the Muslim warriors it is remarkable that the Arabs did not gain another victory. But, on returning to their camps, the Muslims learned that their commander was dead and the next day they retreated before the weary but triumphant Franks.

An early portrait of Charlemagne and his wife. Beneath is his signature from a document of AD 775. A late 19th century engraving from a Carolingian manuscript of between AD 817 and 823, now preserved at the monastery of St Paul in Carinthia, Austria.

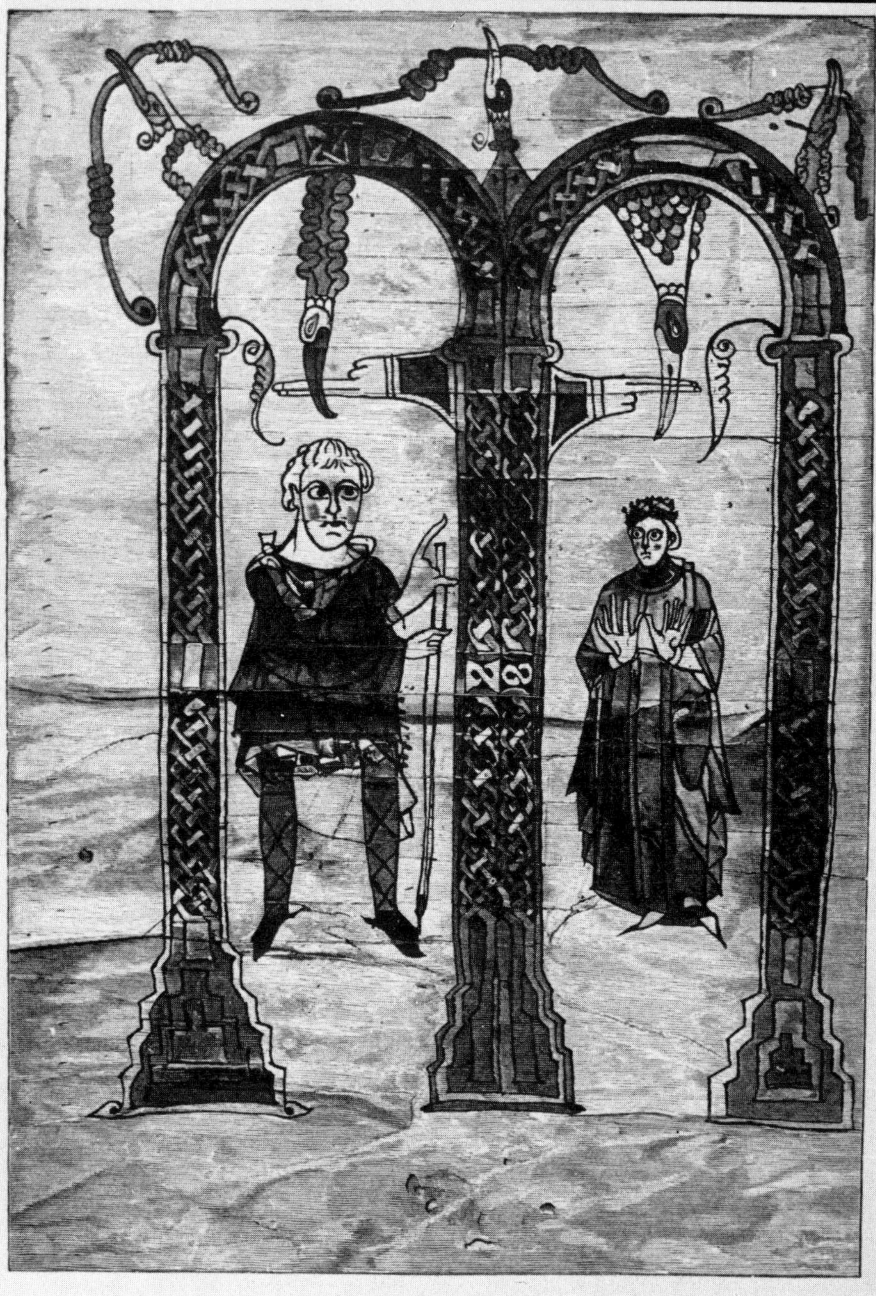

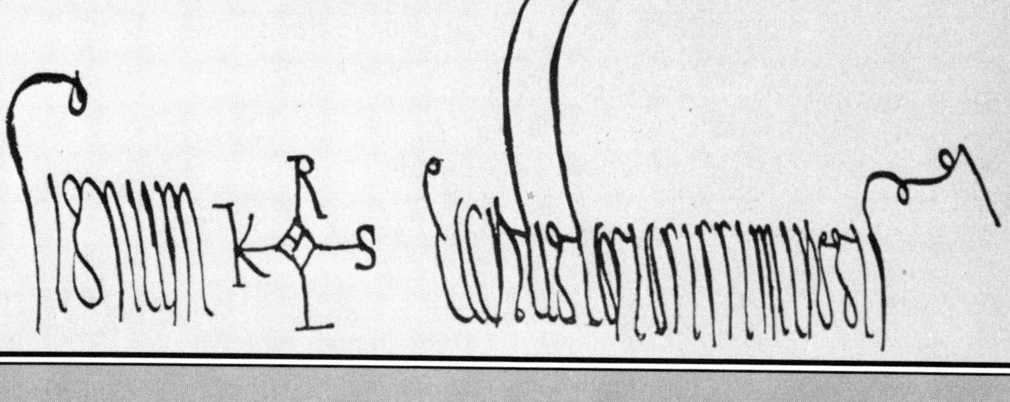

At first, the Muslims would have seen their defeat near Tours as just a temporary setback in the overall tide of Islam. But as time passed, it became clear that this was to be the furthest north into Europe the Arabs would ever penetrate. From then on, Charles Martel kept up a constant pressure on the Muslim raiders and slowly the Franks expelled them from their recent conquests north of the Pyrenees, eventually recapturing Narbonne. The tide had turned. The determination of the Franks outweighed that of the Arabs. Mass raiding north of the Pyrenees had become unprofitable, but the western reaction went further. In the mountains of north-west Spain, Visigoth warlords held out against the Muslims. From this kingdom of the Asturias sprung the warriors of the *Reconquista*. A crusader project that obsessed Christian Spain for the whole of the Middle Ages, and piece by piece recaptured the land. In the meantime, through his victory against the Muslims, Charles Martel had spread his dominion over most of southern France. The Arnulfings had risen in power and reputation to such a degree that Martel's son, Pepin III, felt confident enough to end the pretence of the Merovingians and place himself upon the throne. The Carolingians were possessed with all the energy of a new dynasty and pursued several expansionist campaigns while, in contrast, the dynamism of the Muslims was being drained by internal dispute. A revolt by the Berbers weakened the hold of the Arabs over Spain and allowed further Christian resurgence. Nevertheless, later Arab consolidation maintained the country as a principal Muslim power, and for the next few centuries the Franks and Arabs remained uneasy neighbours.

With half the old Roman Empire absorbed by followers of a new religion and culture, and the other half occupied largely by Germanic kingdoms, it seems that the Ancient World had definitely come to an end – this period is generally referred to as the Early Middle Ages – and yet this transition from era to era was far from sharply defined. Certainly the ancient unity of the Roman Empire, centred around the Mediterranean, seems to have been ripped in half. Yet this was a cultural and political division, not an economic one. Trade between all ports around the Mediterranean was vital to each ruling hierarchy and continued as before. Christian, Jewish and Muslim merchants had no qualms about dealing with each other, even though their lords were at war. Frequent punitive raids and the activities of unchecked pirates lessened the quantity of this trade, but where there was a good chance of some return on a trip to a far flung country, sailors and merchants could always be found to undertake it. Culturally and politically, Islam may have appeared alien to Christian, Graeco-Roman Europe but even here one is discussing its essence rather than the day-to-day reality. Frequently, Muslim governors were happy to see the old Roman-Byzantine bureaucracy, economy and religions they inherited carry on as before. The major impetus for the increased conversion to Islam among the majority of inhabitants in the conquered territories of the Near East, Africa and Spain was simply that they could advance further socially if they adopted the state religion.

In 8th century Europe, the links between the Ancient and Medieval worlds were maintained as often as they were broken. The Byzantine state was still officially and legally recognised as the legitimate Roman Empire. A calculated insult, often employed by the Franks, was to address the Byzantine ruler as Emperor of the Greeks and not Emperor of the Romans. Not just an heir to Imperial glory, Byzantium remained an energetic force in Eastern Europe for centuries to come. In 718, the Emperor Leo so decisively defeated the Arabs outside Constantinople that they never again tried to invade Europe via the Balkans. As regards the Germanic kingdoms of Italy and France, the determination of the northern invaders to maintain a degree of Latin civilisation — merely exchanging the authority of Roman land-owners for that of German landlords — has already been stated. The wars that followed the Barbarian invasions of the 5th century were no more disruptive than the Roman civil wars of earlier centuries. Warlords had always governed semi-autonomously throughout southern Europe and would continue to do so, whether it be under the guise of the Roman Empire or more nakedly in the Latinised kingdoms of the Germans. Therefore, to an observer unbiased by false historical divisions, early medieval Europe sustained a character similar to that of the late Roman Empire. Crucial to this continuity was the institution of Christianity which, having survived and prospered throughout virtually the entire history of the Roman Empire, was a powerful link with the Ancient World: but the most celebrated evocation of the continuing presence of the old Western. Empire was yet to come.

Outside the Christian bastion of Constantinople, the Catholic faith was championed by the Roman Papacy, which was developing its political strength and status in central Italy. It was a minor crisis in this growth that led to the spectacle of a Germanic king assuming the discarded mantle of Western Roman Emperor. All previous Germanic warlords had felt it unnecessary to fill the throne vacated years before by Romulus Augustulus, preferring the sham of allegiance to the Eastern Emperor. In the year 800, however, Pope Leo III was in dire trouble with the citizens of Rome. Narrowly escaping assassination, he had been slashed across the face by a gang of rivals and forced to flee to Germany. Receiving no help from the Eastern Empire, he wrote to the Carolingian King of the Franks and urged him to come to his rescue. Charlemagne arrived in Rome, put down the revolt, and secured the position of the Pope. In return, Leo insisted that a king of the Franks and the Lombards, with a domain covering Gaul, Germany and northern Italy, should have his imperial status recognised. Reluctant to spoil his friendly relations with the Emperor of the East, Charlemagne nevertheless agreed to be crowned Emperor and Augustus. The title of Holy Roman Emperor was not actually adopted until many centuries later, by the Germans in 1254, but in the minds of many, the Western Roman Empire had been dramatically resurrected. As one contemporary chronicler exclaimed 'He who ordains the fate of kingdoms and the march of centuries – the all-powerful Disposer of events – having destroyed one extraordinary image, that of the Romans, then raises up among the Franks the golden head of a second image, equally remarkable, in the person of Charlemagne.'

The Carolingian domain was not a Mediterranean-bound Empire, its heart had shifted to the Rhineland, but it did occupy many of the provinces once held by the Caesars. With such vast lands under its control, it was the strongest power-base in Western Europe. In the whole continent, it was second only in authority to the Byzantine Empire. As officially acknowledged 'Defender of the Church' by the Papacy, the Carolingian dynasty was perceived as a preserver of the Roman Christian tradition. As a result its wars of expansion into central Europe and its wars of defence against raiders, were considered battles against Barbarians. These new Barbarians were Avars, Slavs, Magyars and Northmen – the Vikings. They were no more Barbaric than the Carolingian warriors that slaughtered them: but they were pagan outsiders, while the Franks managed – in the eyes of western history – to be regarded as the holy agents of civilisation.

The wolves of Wodan

THE DANES
AND
SWEDES:
THE
9th AND 10th
CENTURIES

'I am a man alone,' wrote a warrior of the Dark Ages. 'As I recall the slaughter of my comrades, there is no one I can open my heart to. The man mindful of his reputation does not reveal his sadness. Ever since I buried my lord, ever since I lost my companions, I must mourn alone. Now I have left my home land, I sail the icy seas in search of a new lord. A generous giver of gold. A lord who will welcome me into his drinking-hall and divert me from my grief.

'With no friends to assist me, I remind myself of the hall full of retainers. The receiving of treasures from my lord after the feast. My youth. I remember resting my head and hands upon the knee of my lord and pledging my loyalty. Then I awake from my thoughts and see the dark waves lashing around me. The hail and snow beating down. I wish all the more to see my warrior friends, to be welcomed with song. But again these images are soon gone. It is little wonder that my spirit is darkened by the fate of man. How brave warriors, one by one, must leave the mead-hall.

'A man cannot be wise until he has endured the winters of his life. A wise man must be patient. Not easy to anger, nor loose of speech. Neither rash nor unreliable in battle. He should not lack courage, nor be greedy for plunder. He should never boast actions before he can achieve them. He must hold back his promises until he has thought them through and has no doubt. A wise man must contemplate destruction. For now, ancient walls are decaying, ravaged by wind and frost. Grand buildings, the work of giants, stand deserted. The wine-halls crumble. All the proud lords and their warriors lie dead. Falling in battle, one was carried over the sea by a raven: another was devoured by a wolf: and one was buried by his heart-broken retainer.

'So he who thinks deep about destruction and the battles of the past cannot fail to ask 'Where now is the war-horse? Where is the warrior clad in mail? Where the giver of gold and feasts? Where is the glory of my lord?' These days are long gone. All that remains is a monument carved with serpents. Where once warriors were laid down by a hail of ash-spears, now a storm of sleet batters their stone. Winter howls and the hardship of life fills men. Wealth is fleeting, comrades are fleeting. Man is transient. I wander through a wilderness.'

This passage, a prose rendering of an Anglo-Saxon poem commonly called *The Wanderer*, is a moving insight to the mind of the professional warrior. Without a lord, a warrior could not function. From a lord came all the wealth – material and emotional – that sustained a man in his martial status. With a loyalty proclaimed to one lord, on his death the faithful warrior became an exile. A masterless wanderer. It was far better that he should die in battle alongside his lord, rather than endure survival. Such a close, mutually dependent relationship was recorded by Tacitus in his 1st century description of the German tribes, and was still present a thousand years later in Germanic literature. It was the core around which all the honour and nobility of the medieval hero was constructed.

Throughout *The Wanderer*, loyalty is implicit in the warrior's sense of loss and aimlessness. In the third paragraph the author then lists other qualities desirable in retainers. But what did the warrior expect from his master? How could a warlord preserve his status as a man of supreme power? The first requirement for the maintenance of power throughout the first millennium was – as it always has been – wealth. With food, shelter, weapons, armour, horses and money, a man could gather around him a formidable bodyguard. For many landlords, the possession of wealth was enough to sustain power. However, for warriors to fight to the death for a lord, many demanded attributes in their leader that were of a physical and moral character. Retainers thrived on personal respect for their master. Such renown was recorded by chroniclers and if sufficiently outstanding would ensure the everlasting fame of the lord as well as his closest supporters. Being a man of respect was almost as potent as being a man of wealth. Courage, physical strength, skill in handling weapons, all earned the respect of other men. Important too was wisdom: the intelligence to command men effectively in battle, the wit to handle negotiations and peacetime government.

After such essential features, less weighty talents impressed many a warband. Nordic sagas are particularly full of such skills. The Norwegian warlord Olaf Tryggvason was renowned for juggling three daggers at once, catching them always by the hilts. He was able to walk from oar to oar alongside the outside of his longboat while the men were rowing. Such talents recall the circus antics of the Goth king Totila before the battle of Taginae in 552. Neither chieftains' followers were dismayed or embarrassed by such displays: they would have admired their leaders all the more. And yet, could one imagine a Roman general encouraging the respect of his men by juggling swords in the air? There seems to have been a very definite division between the bounds of decorum expected from leaders of Mediterranean soldiers and those of Germanic warriors. Indeed, the further north one goes, the less were the limits of dignity. Running, rowing, skiing and swimming were all noble demonstrations of prowess among the Scandinavians. They even considered it worthy to make their own weapons. They were proud of their technical skills and hence the inclusion of many details of weapon manufacture in nordic literature. Similarly, the skilled use of the bow, a weapon left to the lowest classes of foot-soldiers amongst the majority of Germans, was a matter of vital concern between two Norwegian kings debating their relative merits in the *Heimskringla saga*. However, such a use of the bow was confined to sport and hunting, so that when it came to battle, the spear and sword remained the primary weapons of the aristocrat. As far as Scandinavian nobles were concerned, the only pursuits that were considered unseemly for men of their rank were those skills arising from commerce and farming. Such a prejudice against the mastery of earning a living outside the bounds of pillaged or inherited wealth continued amongst aristocracy throughout the Middle Ages and after.

Aside from protecting their lords, faithful warriors were expected to be their avengers. Regardless of their Christianity, revenge was a strong motivating force among Germanic warriors, and vendettas frequently sparked off full scale campaigns. Paul the Deacon, in his 8th century *History of the Lombards*, records the private vengeance one servant undertook for the killing of his master. On an Easter Sunday, this man, a dwarf, hid himself in the font of a baptistry. When the betrayer of his lord passed through the church, the dwarf suddenly emerged and cut off the warrior's head. He himself was quickly killed but through such an action he had

Fierce carved head from the stem-post of a 4th or 5th century Danish ship found in the River Scheldt in Belgium; evidence of the presence of nordic pirates in the North Sea long before what we now know as the Viking Age. Now in the British Museum, London.

revived the honour of his lord as well as ending the humiliation of outliving him. Honour in battle is best exemplified by another Anglo-Saxon poem. In *The Battle of Maldon*, written shortly after the event, many of the fine qualities of the warrior-retainer (as mentioned above) are featured. Faults are also made plain. The Battle of Maldon took place in the south-east of England in 991. It was one of countless bloody encounters with Viking raiders in Anglo-Saxon Britain and Carolingian France throughout the 9th and 10th centuries. On this occasion, the Northmen had sailed through the Blackwater estuary in East Anglia and camped on the little island of Northey.

The poetic account of the Battle of Maldon begins with Byrhtnoth, a great English lord, commanding his warriors to dismount and advance into battle on foot. We can assume that this order only applied to his personal retinue of leading warriors. Such a decision may well have been due to the marshy terrain around the Blackwater, making effective riding impossible. Also, it seems that Byrhtnoth wished to fight a defensive battle and a dismounted band of warriors were far steadier when receiving attacks. Certainly, on this occasion, the Vikings were without horses themselves and so Byrhtnoth simply confronted them on equal terms. It has been suggested that Anglo-Saxon warfare may have been less ready to use horses and that the English were primarily foot-soldiers, like the early Franks. But with a Celtic and Roman legacy, as well as the Germanic noble status attached to horsemanship, it seems more than likely that – like any continental army – Anglo-Saxons did use horses in battle when taking the offensive and pursuing a broken enemy.

As the Anglo-Saxon warriors assembled under Byrhtnoth's orders, one young noble let his prized hunting hawk fly from his wrist. A symbolic act appreciated by the poet. Once arrayed in their position of battle, Byrhtnoth dismounted and joined his finest warriors in the shield-wall. A landlord of considerable standing, it has been estimated that Byrhtnoth was a white-haired man of about sixty. The confrontation with the Danish raiders opened with an exchange of insults. The Viking spokesmen announced that they would be happy to leave the area in return for a tribute of gold. Greatly offended, Byrhtnoth, or more likely an official messenger – a herald – shouted back, 'Listen pirates, the only tribute we shall send you is one of spear-points and veteran sword-edge. We are the guardians of our people, our land and our King. It is the heathen who shall fall.' Byrhtnoth and his warriors then strode towards the edge of the river bank. Both sides glared at each other across the water. A few arrows were let fly. Some Danes endeavoured to use a ford but the East Saxons, men of Essex, stoutly prevented them.

Wearying of the stalemate, the Vikings asked if they could have permission to cross the ford and thus begin the battle. Somewhat over-confidently, according to the poet, Byrhtnoth allowed the enemy to cross over onto the mainland. At first, such a decision appears to have a ring

of Germanic chivalry about it, but if refused a battle the Danes would simply have sailed off, and ravaged some other part of the coast which was unprotected. At least the Anglo-Saxons had the chance to finish off the Viking menace there and then. The Danes, called by the poet the wolves of Wodan, God of War, waded across the ford with their lime-wood shields and weapons held high. The Anglo-Saxons drew themselves up in a closely packed crowd, fronted by shield-carrying warriors, ready for the Viking onslaught.

When the warriors clashed, shouts and screams ripped across the countryside. Case-hardened spears were thrown. Bows were busy. In close combat, sword and spear slashed and stabbed. The majority of Anglo-Saxon soldiers were local levies and poorly equipped. Their thick leather jackets, if they possessed them, would have afforded little protection against the professional weaponry of the Vikings, collected over many raids. The Anglo-Saxon nobles and their retainers were clad in mail and parried sword blows with their metal-strengthened shields. From these ranks came the stiffest resistance. One Dane, gripping his shield and spear, closed in on Byrhtnoth. The Viking threw his weapon and wounded the Saxon lord. According to the text, the Viking's weapon was a 'southern spear', that is made in a country to the south of Scandinavia and England, which must mean France. Elsewhere, in the struggle over the ford, there is mention of a Frankish spear, *francan*. It is unlikely that this was the early Frankish *angon*, but it may well have possessed the wing-like projections from its socket, supposedly characteristic of Frankish spears. After being pierced by the spear, Byrhtnoth is said to have broken the shaft with the edge of his shield. The Anglo-Saxon lord then threw one spear which passed through the Viking's neck and another that slit open his mail. Byrhtnoth laughed and thanked God for his good fortune. But no sooner had he dealt with one enemy than another wounded him, again with a thrown spear. A retainer next to him immediately withdrew the weapon from his lord's body and hurled it back, striking the Dane. Yet another Viking advanced on the Saxon leader, this time intending to steal the mail, rings and ornamented sword of the wounded man. Desperately, Byrhtnoth swung his broad, bright-edged sword at the robber. The Dane countered and slashed at the Saxon's arm, so that his gold-hilted sword fell to the ground. Beneath the frenzied blows of the enemy, the chieftain and his two closest retainers slumped to the ground.

With the death of their leader, some leading Saxons lost heart and took flight. One, in his panic, actually mounted the horse of his lord. Cowardice was bad enough, but this act was shocking: the poet notes that Byrhtnoth had frequently given gifts of horses to this same man. Other warriors joined the flight, forgetting their loyalty to their lord and the many gifts he had bestowed upon them. The words of a noble are recalled, warning Byrhtnoth that many warriors speak keenly of their courage but in battle they prove unequal to the stress. Those warriors that remained in battle intensified their struggle, determined to avenge their lord or die. Amongst the loyal retainers was a good-will hostage, obtained from a Northumbrian family, who fought with equal courage and used bow and arrow to inflict wounds upon the common enemy. Another bold warrior crashed through the shield-carrying Danes and plunged deep amongst the marauders.

The fighting was fierce. Shields were shattered, leaving warriors to punch their opponents with the remaining metal boss. Mail shirts rang as they were splintered in the fury. Soon many of the bravest retainers had fulfilled their vows of loyalty by dying alongside their lord. The majority of Anglo-Saxons had already fled, thinking the sight of their lord's horse galloping away meant that their leader was signalling a retreat. The battle was lost. Amidst the Saxon last stand, the author of the poem chose a veteran warrior to express words of heroic loyalty that would have impressed the poet's aristocratic audience. Said the old man, 'Heart must be braver, courage the bolder, mind the firmer, as our strength becomes lesser.

The siege of Paris in AD 885 was a bitterly fought campaign. The Vikings sailed their boats right up to the walls of the island city. From Guizot's *L'Histoire de France*, 1870.

106

Here lies our lord. A noble man, in blood and mud. Those who turn their back now will regret it forever. I am old. I will not leave here. I will lie beside my lord – the man I love most dearly.'

Within a couple of decades of this combat at Maldon, the Danes had conquered the whole of England and set their king upon the Anglo-Saxon throne. Elsewhere, on the continent, Danish Vikings had set up an independent state in northern France: while the Swedes had long established themselves in Russia: and the Norwegians ruled a north Atlantic dominion including Iceland and Greenland. The Scandinavian Vikings were the last pagan Northern people to descend on Europe and ravage established regimes. To Christian chroniclers, preservers of Roman Catholic civilisation, the first Vikings were devilish destroyers. They were Barbarians. Later like all Germanic invaders the Northmen (or Normans), with the responsibility of conquest became the hardiest defenders of the culture they had once violated. It was in their 'barbarous' state, however, that the Vikings accomplished some of their most characteristic military operations.

According to conventional histories, the impact of the Scandinavians was first noted around the year 800. Around this date, ferocious raids by Northmen on British monasteries and island communities were recorded. At the same time, the completion of a savage campaign against the Saxons in north-west Germany brought the Carolingians face to face with the warriors of Denmark. Viking raids soon followed. And yet, the belief that a new race of marauders had suddenly sprung out of Scandinavia is a false one. Scandinavian tribes had long been involved in the movements of Germanic Barbarians. Most of those German tribes that had invaded England in the 5th century came from Denmark. Many notable Barbarian confederations, such as the Goths, claimed to have originated in the lands of the Baltic. Nordic pirates had always been rife in the North Sea, using shallow-draught sea-going ships. The raids of the Vikings in the 9th and 10th centuries, were only the latest in a long tradition of sea-borne Scandinavian assaults. Gregory of Tours recorded a Danish raid, on the Frankish territory of King Theuderic in the early 6th century, which has all the characteristics of later Viking attacks. A Danish fleet ran ashore, captured some local inhabitants, loaded their ships with their booty and prepared to sail home. Theuderic reacted promptly, however, and beat the invaders in a naval battle, retrieving all the lost property.

Nevertheless, by the late 8th century, certain developments occurred which, in hindsight, gave the appearance of a sudden explosion of activity among the Scandinavians. They had perfected the design of their sea-going ships – sails were added to the power of their oars – and this led to an increase in the amount of piracy in the North Sea. Short trips across strips of sea or along familiar coastlines had always been possible, but now more extensive voyages could be undertaken. At the same time, in the period from 600 to 800, the Scandinavian language underwent a profound change that transformed it from a language similar to that of the Germans, to the south of them, to one that was specifically nordic. This, combined with the fact that the Scandinavians were still a pagan people, meant that they were now viewed by their neighbouring German kingdoms as an alien race. No longer did they share a language, culture, religion or common aims. While the Scandinavians still pursued a roving, scavaging way of life, their raids increasingly threatened the settled Germanic dynasties and Christian communities. The Scandinavians and Germans were no longer allies intent on sacking a Romanised Europe, for the Germans were now part of that Latin establishment, while the Scandinavians were still outsiders. Such an explanation of the Viking phenomonen in the west is far more convincing than the suggestion that there was a sudden population explosion in Scandinavia which forced its people outwards. Certainly, populations in Scandinavia were increasing, but this was common throughout Europe. In addition to the altered perspective in which the Scandinavians were regarded in the 9th and 10th centuries, it must be remembered that the Germanic chronicles which supposedly first record Viking raids against England and France were both compiled around the dates they mention. They are not accurate historical surveys over hundreds of years, and do not record regular occurrences before the time of their compilation. That there were no frequent raids by Scandinavian warbands on England and France before 800 is difficult to believe and contrary to archaeological evidence.

On one day in 782, Charlemagne had 4,500 Saxon prisioners massacred. It is little wonder then that Godfred, King of the Danes, watched with alarm as the Franks wiped out all opposition in north-west Germany and approached his territory. With Saxony subdued, the northern-most frontier of the Carolingians ran across the base of Jutland. At the heart of this Empire was a man who increasingly saw his wars of imperialist conquest as worthy crusades against the heathen Northerners. At first, relations between the two states was cordial. Danish chieftains were received at the court of Charlemagne despite the piratical activities of their fellow countrymen along the northern coast. To curb the Danish raids, Charlemagne strengthened his coasts' guard and improved his fleet. Strongpoints were erected at all ports and at the mouths of rivers so that if any Vikings sailed into them, they could be bottled up by a special military task force. Similar defences were used in southern France and Italy against the Arabs. Indeed, it has been said that the strong coastal defences of the Franks were responsible for encouraging the Danes to venture a little further and turn to England in their search for softer targets.

By the first decade of the 9th century, the Carolingians had so far encroached on the Danes' sphere of influence that confrontation was inevitable. To prevent invasion, Godfred built an immense timber and earth rampart, called the Danework, which linked natural obstacles across Jutland from the North Sea to the Baltic. Then, in 810, he sent 200 ships into Frisian territory, recently acquired by the Carolingian Empire. The Danish seamen were unopposed and Godfred felt so confident of his powers that he

boasted that he would next invade Aachen, Charlemagne's capital. But, as Charlemagne prepared for the last campaign of his career, King Godfred was assassinated and the Danish threat melted away. A conflict had been established, however, and the two powers wrangled over the borderlands.

By the middle of the 9th century, Frisia was paying such regular protection money to the Danes that it could be considered Viking property. The Northmen therefore took their raids further afield, along the French coast and inland. There was very little the Carolingians could do. Following the death of Charlemagne, the old imperial realm had been torn by civil wars and was eventually divided into separate kingdoms, each more concerned about each other than with the raiders. Previously, the Danes had been content to run their shallow-draught boats up onto a beach, jump out, pillage a nearby community and leap back into their ships for a quick getaway. With an increase in the size of their fleets, experience of where they were going and a decrease in organised coastal defence, the Vikings grew more daring. The weakness of the Carolingian dominion encouraged an explosion of northern raiding. Once they landed, the Danes conducted small campaigns against the surrounding districts. They stole horses to ride inland and soon Viking armies were threatening major urban centres. The Franks were forced to pay massive tributes to the invaders. Even so, large stretches of land fell under direct Viking control. French peasants formed groups to ensure their own defence but were frequently crushed by Frank nobles in league with the Vikings. Many Franks hoped to ally themselves with the ascending power: the Carolingians were proving incapable of any concerted action. Often they had to resort to hiring Viking mercenaries to combat those Danes taking over their lands. At this time the efforts of Alfred the Great in England were reversing the flow of freebooters back to the continent for easy pickings.

Across both France and Germany, great cities went up in flames. Paris, situated on an island in the middle of the Seine, proved particularly attractive. It had been ravaged before but, in 885, a huge Danish army sailed upon it, probably intent on long-term conquest. With so many warriors crammed in to their dragon ships, the Danes decided to assault the city straightaway but, under the command of Count Eudes, the island fortress proved a tough nut to crack. As the Vikings clambered up their scaling ladders, clutching swords and axes, the Parisians poured boiling oil, wax and pitch upon them. The scalding liquid clung to the warriors and many, in their agony, tried to tear the burning hair from their heads. Unable to storm Paris immediately, the Danes settled in for a siege. As they endeavoured to cut the city off from the outside world, they constructed awesome engines. Massive battering rams of oak were raised onto roofed carriages having sixteen wheels. Large screens, capable of shielding four men, were covered with the skin of young bulls: holes were made in them through which burning arrows were fired. Several catapults hurled lumps of molten lead into the city.

111

The ingenuity of the Danes was matched by that of the Parisians. When the siege machines were brought forward for a major attack, heavy beams tipped with iron were lowered from the walls and crushed the engines. From the battlements, *ballistae* and stone-throwing catapults battered the Danes. The rocks smashed their shields and bashed out their brains, according to a chronicler of the conflict. The siege continued for almost a year. In that time, wagons loaded with burning turf were pushed against the city towers and blazing fire-ships tied against bridges. Several times the Danes fought off relieving armies, but all to no avail. Paris did not fall and eventually the Vikings accepted a tribute from the Frank king in return for their withdrawal.

The sophistication of Danish siege-machines may seem surprising but there is other evidence of such technology throughout this period. The continuity of Roman-style weaponry is revealed in an Anglo-Saxon riddle:

'I am the defender of my people.
Strengthened with wires and filled with gifts,
During the day I spit them forth.
The fuller I am the better I am.
I swallow dark weapons of war.
Bitter arrows and poisonous spears.
I have a good stomach.
Men seldom forget what passes through my mouth.'

Ballista is the answer. In another riddle —recorded in the 10th century, but probably far older – a battering-ram is described, 'A tree-trunk, once swathed in rich foliage, is now bound in chains and its head adorned with more sombre trappings.'

Several old English riddles are a highly imaginative interpretation of everyday objects and deal with many used in war. The harsh voice of the horn blown in battle : the shield weary of combat which can find no cure for its wounds from roots or herbs: a tree of four timbers, covered with silver and inlaid with jewels, with a goldhilted sword hanging from one of its branches. The last is a sword-rack. Many of the weapons used by both the Germans and the Scandinavians, though straight-forward in design, were skilfully adorned. Pattern-welded swords, still popular among the Vikings, were given dramatic names, according to their appearance and performance: such as 'Snake of wounds', 'Lightning flash of blood', and 'Mail-biter'. Viking swords usually had double-edged blades about 90 cm (3 ft) long. From the regularity of their mention in Scandinavian literature, it appears that Frankish swords from the Rhineland, as well as spear-blades, were strongly favoured. These imported, or stolen, blades were then given splendid hilts by native craftsmen. Straight cross-guards were made of bone, antler or ivory, which was then further encrusted with precious metals and stones according to the wealth of the warrior. Grips were

Finnish pattern-welded spearhead. The interlain iron and steel can be seen where the blade has been cleaned at the bottom. Now in the National Museum of Antiquities, Helsinki.

covered in leather while pommels were of metal, sometimes inscribed with the name of owner and maker. These swords were of such value that they could be passed on for generations.

An alternative, or addition to the sword, was the *scramasax*, a long single-edged knife. However, spears remained the commonest weapon, with lighter ones used for throwing and heavier ones for hand-to-hand. Spear-carrying and throwing horse-warriors continued to be an important element in battle and many Viking stirrups and spurs have been found. Aside from the spear, the battle-axe has emerged as the most characteristic weapon of the Northmen. Unlike the Frank throwing-axe, it was principally a broad-bladed close combat weapon that could be wielded with one hand or, with a longer shaft, become a terrifying two-handed weapon. Axe blades were also enriched and engraved. Shields, helmets and mail shirts followed much the same form as throughout the early medieval world. What certainly gave the Vikings in battle a material advantage over their adversaries was that as professional raiders they had greater access to a wide variety of ransacked weapons and armour and so, on the whole, were better equipped.

With secure bases in France and England, Vikings sailed further southwards, attacking Muslim Spain and bursting into the Mediterranean. They ransacked the city of Luna along the Italian coast, thinking it was Rome. There was little limit to the ambition of the Northmen. And yet, these achievements were largely accomplished by the Danes. The Norwegians were content to concentrate their attention on the north Atlantic and pursue daring exploration. The Swedes, on the other hand, made inroads into continental regimes like the Danes, but their chosen path was eastwards, along the rivers of Russia and eastern Europe, following perhaps the routes of earlier Germanic tribes, such as the Goths. For these warriors, the greatest pirate prizes were to be found along the coasts of the Black Sea. The Byzantines had little patience for these wild men from the North and called them plainly 'Barbarians'. Inevitably, Constantinople – still most splendid of all cities – came under siege several times from the Vikings. The city did not fall. On most occasions the Vikings were content with forcing the citizens to grant them lucrative trade concessions. Still, the Byzantines had a tough time of it and were so impressed with the Northmen as fighters that the emperors recruited them. They became the famed Varangian Guard, acting as personal bodyguards and an especially feared branch of the Byzantine army.

The daughter of one of the Eastern emperors, Anna Comnena, described the Northmen as 'Men who hung their swords and axes from their shoulders and regard their loyalty to the Emperor and his protection as a sacred duty, an inheritance to be handed from father to son.' The Greeks were impressed not only by their loyalty, but their physical size as well. They were nordic giants among Mediterranean men. The wealth to be obtained from serving the Byzantines was tremendous and whenever

Swedes returned to their homeland, the Scandinavians were deeply impressed by the travellers' rich clothes. One description of returning Varangian warriors pictures them in scarlet baggy trousers and riding on gilded saddles. Their leader wore a tunic and trousers of silk, over which hung a cloak of scarlet. His sword hilt was ornamented with gold thread wound round the grip. On his head he wore a gilded helmet and carried a scarlet shield. Wherever they stopped, native nordic women could not keep their eyes off the brilliant warriors. Another description of the eastern Vikings again mentions their baggy trousers, fastened around the knee, but adds kaftans and tall hats. The Varangian Guard was established around the end of the 10th century: for a century before this, the Northmen had been untamed marauders.

With the subjugation of various Slavonic, Finnish and Eurasian tribes, the Swedish Vikings of the 9th century became the rulers of western Russia, where they were known as the Rus. From their southern capital at Kiev, and from surrounding strongholds, several ambitious campaigns were carried out, ranging from the Caspian to the Black Sea. Not least of these were their attacks on Constantinople. Around the year 907, King Oleg of Kiev led a fleet of upwards of 200 ships against the Byzantines. Each ship carried forty men. Large as this may seem, far greater Viking forces were also recorded.

Compared to his own ships, Emperor Leo VI noted that the boats the Rus used were 'smaller, lighter, faster crafts, because sailing into the Black Sea through the rivers, they cannot use bigger ships.' Sometimes the Rus attacked overland. *The Russian Primary Chronicle,* compiled by Nestor in the 12th century, states that Oleg's assault on Constantinople was by ship and by horse. The employment of mounted warriors does suggest that this was a major campaign, although the chronicle may well be at fault. In the main, most Viking raids were from the sea. To counter these, the Byzantines drew a massive chain across the inlet of the Golden Horn to the north of their capital, but faced with such an obstacle, the Rus merely beached their boats and ravaged the surrounding communities on foot. Frequently these conflicts were settled with tributes and a trade treaty. To Oleg, the Byzantines gave brocade sails for his Viking ships and silk sails for the Slavs that fought with him. These fancy sails were soon torn by the wind and they reverted to ones of canvas.

When the Byzantines did fight back against the Rus raiders, one of their most effective weapons was Greek Fire. The pirate fleet of King Igor suffered badly from this in 941. Surrounding a smaller Byzantine force and expecting easy plunder, the Vikings were suddenly enveloped in a blazing mixture of crude oil and other combustibles pumped through metal tubes mounted on their victims' ships. With their clothes and hair aflame, Rus sailors flung themselves into the sea rather than endure the sulphurous, burning hell on board. The Viking fleet was annihilated. The terror provoked by these early flame-throwers encouraged the Rus to return home with tales maintaining that the Byzantines possessed the very lightning from heaven. Byzantine craftsmen capitalised on this awe and designed metal tubes in the shape of weird animals, so that the fire spewed from their mouths. It is little wonder that stories of fire-breathing dragons were frequent among the Northmen. It may also be that mythological accounts from Scandinavia of special tunics which made the wearer invulnerable, actually derived from the flame-proof clothes, woven from asbestos and silk, that the Byzantines are said to have devised. Interestingly, one northern saga has an alternative description of just such a protective garment. To defend himself against a fire-breathing dragon, the warrior hero dipped a coarse woollen coat in tar until it was matted and then rolled it in sand to give it an impregnable surface.

The chief fear-inducing weapon the Vikings possessed was themselves. The impression that their nordic stature and ferocity made on the Byzantines has already been mentioned but there were, however, a special group of warriors amongst the Vikings, in both the east and the west, who made even their own comrades feel uneasy. They were the hard-men in whom courage was mingled with madness. They were the *berserkr*. Wearing no armour, but clad in bear-fur and other animal skins, these terrifying

Danish decorated sword hilt from Hedeby, one of the largest Viking settlements. Now in the Schleswig-Holstein Landesmuseum.

warriors rushed into battle mowing down everyone before them. They had no fear, for their rage of bloodlust overcame the pain of their wounds. Howling like wolves, they bit their shields, and when their weapons were shattered through frenzied blows, they tore their enemies apart with bare hands in a fury of animal strength. This crazed state has been ascribed to the taking of hallucinogenics, but it seems more likely that it was simply the alcohol-enhanced action of wild men. Hardened psychopaths have accompanied every army and robber band throughout history, and it was probably the perverse thrill they obtained from violence that fuelled these warriors onto superhuman feats. Such human beasts have always been men to avoid and it is not surprising that the Vikings themselves considered these warriors to be possessed – turning into werewolves under cover of night. For most of the time, they managed to hide their dark nature, but once they got whiff of a fight, their calm character was unbalanced and these warriors became ravening animals again.

Though renowned for their ferocity, the majority of Vikings were, in reality, no more ferocious than other Barbarian warriors. The Vikings did, however, possess one unique attribute which gave them a very definite edge over many of their contemporaries. The Scandinavian mastery of water-borne warfare can be compared with the excellent horsemanship of the steppe warriors. It has been said that the seamanship of the Vikings has been overestimated: after all, the majority of their raids either closely followed the continental coasts or simply penetrated European waterways. This might have been true of the Danes and the Swedes, but the navigational feats of the Norwegians were quite remarkable. This aside, the quality of the Vikings as ocean-going warriors is hardly the point. Very few battles were actually fought at sea. One account of just such an armed encounter, around AD 1000, shows that the ensuing battle was more like an action fought on land than a battle requiring naval skills.

When Olaf Tryggvason of Norway sailed out against an alliance of Scandinavian rulers, he roped his ships together so that they were not so much a fleet as a floating platform. Fortunately for Olaf, when the two sides clashed, he had the advantage of craft with higher decks. Anchors and boathooks were hurled at the opposing ships to secure them so that warriors could charge onto each others' decks. The main missile weapons in action were the usual bows and light throwing spears employed on land. At times, stones were also used, either thrown or powered by slings. There was no attempt by either side to ram or outmanoeuvre each other. As fortunes changed, the Scandinavian alliance forced the Norwegian crews on the outermost boats to retreat inwards. Winning ship after ship, the Scandinavians slashed the ropes keeping together the ships and so increasingly isolated their opponents on the splendid carved and gilded Long Serpent ship of Olaf. A fierce last stand took place, during which many of Olaf's warriors threw themselves into the sea rather than be captured. At the end, after throwing spears with both hands and wielding his sword until it was

Vikings attack an Arab encampment. Both the Danes and the Swedes clashed with the Muslims, but they never seriously challenged their dominion of the Mediterranean. From Guizot's *L'Histoire de France*, 1870.

blunt, Olaf joined his faithful warriors and plunged to his death amongst the waves. Even such a major marine combat as this was probably not fought on the open-sea but in a bay or river mouth. It is little wonder that after their initial foray into the Mediterranean, the Danes did not try to challenge the naval might of the Arabs: or that when the Swedes decided to attack Constantinople, they waited until the Byzantine fleet was away on other business.

The strength of the Vikings lay in the amphibious nature of their raids. No other group of warriors could equal this versatility. In the West, once the Danes had sailed their ships up onto a beach, they could then take themselves deep inland on horse-back. Alternatively, once the great rivers of France proved too shallow ever for their slender craft, they took to smaller canoes and penetrated even further, finally advancing on foot to subdue a city. In the East, the Swedes were masters of the waterways of Eurasia. From their island or riverbank fortresses, they launched raiding campaigns numbering hundreds of boats against powerful bastions. If needs be, as in their assault on Costantinople in 907, they mounted their ships on rollers and let the wind fill their sails to help them overland. All this gave the Vikings the primary military advantages of speed, mobility and surprise.

Travelling deep into unknown territory, the Vikings fought a battle against the harsh environment as violent and taxing as any test of arms. The hardship and fears of this roving life are best conveyed in an Anglo-Saxon poem commonly called *The Seafarer*. Probably based on the accounts of the same warrior exile described in *The Wanderer*, it opens with the wild weather conditions endured on the North Sea. The Seafarer takes his turn at night-watch. The ship dips and rises perilously near a rocky coast-line. His feet are frozen to the deck. Icicles hang all around him. Hail stones beat down. His only comfort is the cry of the sea-birds. But these serve only to remind him of the laughter of the drinking-hall.

'How can the land dweller, living in a city and flushed with wine, know the suffering of sailing?' asks the seafarer, 'And yet, despite snow from the north, frost and hail, deep down there is a yearning to undertake a journey. To see a new land, a foreign people. But there is no man, so brave or so bold, that he does not feel fear when venturing on the sea. All thought of the joy of music, the receiving of rings, ecstasy in a woman, all worldly pleasures, are replaced by the relentless rolling of the waves. But even then, the mind travels over the sea, across the whale's domain, to strange new regions and the spirit is urged onwards. This life is fleeting and the best a warrior can hope for is to win the respect of those living after him. The finest monument is to achieve noble and daring deeds in this world so his name may be honoured by his children.'

In these lines, the wanderlust of the warrior overcoming the dread and danger of roaming in an alien, hostile world, is potently expressed. It is an impressive evocation of the essential character of the Germanic Barbarian.

The relentless plainsmen

THE AVARS,
MAGYARS
AND
MONGOLS:
THE
6th TO 13th
CENTURIES

The Huns forever lurked in the minds of medieval men. They were the most notorious of the warriors from the eastern plains: all others followed in their wake. Four centuries after their destruction, Notker, chronicler of Charlemagne, recalled a tale told to him when a boy by a veteran soldier. 'The land of the Huns used to be encircled by nine rings,' said the old man. 'These rings were fortifications. Very wide. Many miles separated them. The defences of each ring were built of logs of oak, beech and fir. These constructions were then filled with stones and heavy clay. They were eight paces deep and eight paces high. On top of the ramparts, sods of earth were piled. Small trees were then planted along each ring so that when cut back and trained to bend forward, they presented an impenetrable screen of sharp branches and dense foliage. On the land between each ring, farms and houses were laid out, but so placed that any news of invasion could be transmitted by the blowing of a horn.'

Such a system of earthworks was not beyond the capabilities of early medieval rulers, as the Danework of King Godfred demonstrated, but no evidence of these particular ramparts has been found, and this story is essentially an indication of the fantastic achievements attributed to the Huns. It is significant of the impact of the Huns that for hundreds of years afterwards, eastern mounted raiders from the steppes were still called by that name. For the warriors that Notker and his story teller called Huns were, in actual fact, another Eurasian confederation – the Avars.

The Avars were no new menace. They had ravaged the Empire of the Franks over two centuries before and fabulous reports of their origin had been heard in Constantinople. A pack of griffins, half eagle, half lion, had erupted in the wastes of Asia and before them they drove a ferocious group of warriors. No sooner had the Eastern emperors seen the last of the Huns than this next onslaught of horse-archers was upon them, perhaps driven on by droughts or the expanding campaigns of an even fiercer people. The Avars were essentially of Turkish origin, from around the Caucasus and southern Russia. Among their ranks were the descendants of the hordes of Attila who had retreated to the lands north of the Black Sea. As they pushed westwards, the Bulgars and Slavs were disturbed into action. 'These Barbarians have reduced the whole of the Balkans to a second Scythian desert,' concluded Procopius in his *Secret History* of the reign of Justinian. The region was scarred by war, disease and famine. Any major armed resistance to the raiders was quashed by the Emperor who wished to employ the various Barbarian factions against each other.

With their marauding unopposed, the Avars, Slavs and Bulgars became even more daring and outrageous. So that in the end, shocked by the sight of their ransacked farms, and with their wives and children enslaved, Balkan civilians and farmers formed themselves into groups of local resistance. Often they were successful, ambushing bandits laden with booty, but once word of this reached the Imperial authorities, government troops were sent to harass the farmers, forcing them to return the horses and plunder they had taken from the raiders. To the inhabitants of the Balkans, the Byzantines were as great a menace as the Barbarians. Within the massive walls of Constantinople, the close presence of the Eurasian nomads served only to inspire a new fashion among the wild young men of the city. To set themselves apart, one street gang – the Blues – wore bizarre clothing after the style of the 'Huns', that is, the Avars. They cut the hair on the front of their heads right back, but allowed the hair behind to hang down in a tangled mass. They wore tunics belted very tight at the waist that then spread out to their shoulders, giving them the appearance of muscle men. In addition, they wore the capes, trousers and shoes typical of steppe warriors. This gang caused much trouble in the city: robbing people at night, rioting during the day. Little was done to stop them, for the Emperor was said to favour them over the Greens, another gang deriving from opposing sports supporters.

In their wars against the Byzantines, the Avars employed guile as much as brute force. During the reign of Tiberius II, towards the end of the 6th century, the Kagan of the Avars asked the Emperor if he would be gracious enough to let him share some of the luxuries of civilisation by having Byzantine technicians build a bath house for him. No doubt seeing this as a sign of future good relations, the Emperor despatched expert craftsmen immediately. But when they arrived, it was not a complex of saunas and hot and cold pools that the Kagan was expecting them to build. He wanted a bridge across the Danube. At sword-point the Byzantines acquiesced, and the Avars surged over the river into the Balkans. On another occasion, Avar attempts to outwit the Byzantines backfired. In 562, merchant envoys were instructed to travel to Constantinople on behalf of the Avars and there acquire arms and armour skilfully manufactured by the Byzantines, thus equipping the Avars for a campaign against the self-same citizens. But Imperial intelligence was one step ahead. Once the merchants had handed over their money and bundled up the weaponry, they were seized by the Byzantine authorities and their goods confiscated. In this way, the Avars made an unwitting contribution to their enemy's balance of trade.

Pair of 9th century bronze-gilt spurs, either Avar or Slav. The prick points are decorated with helmeted heads. From Mikulcice in Czechoslovakia, courtesy of the Archaeological Institute of the Slovakian Academy of Sciences, Nitra.

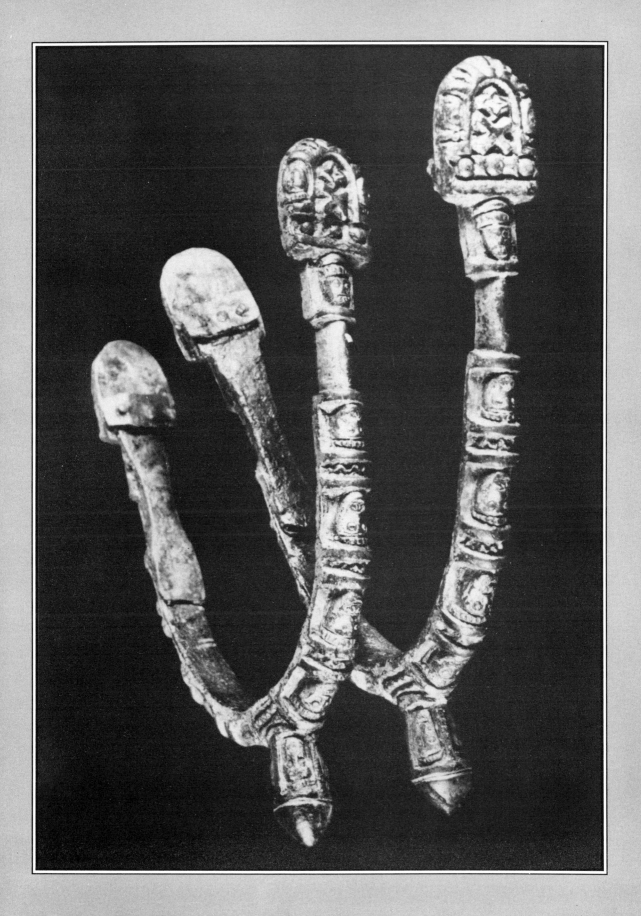

By the 8th century, the Avars had left the wealth of the Byzantines to other raiders and were in conflict with the Germanic kingdoms of the West. Settled in the old Roman province of Pannonia, the dwellings of their Khan grew splendid with all their pickings from Italy, France and Germany. The Avar raiders were naturally excellent horsemen. The use of stirrups was widespread among them, and highly ornate spurs have been found where the prick-points feature little helmeted faces. In addition to their composite bows, spears and pattern-welded swords, it appears from archaeological evidence that they may also have favoured battle-axes, perhaps adopted from the Slavic tribesmen who had followed the Germanic migrations but were now dominated by the Avars. The Franks, like all Germanic warriors, were never really happy fighting highly mobile horse-archers. With their feigned retreats and reluctance to close-in until they had emptied their quivers, the keeness of the Franks for combat with sword and spear was constantly frustrated. And yet, over the course of a decade, Charlemagne and his retainers brought the Avar menace to heel. Warfare is obviously not just a matter of the most effective fighting fashion winning through. Political and strategic factors all contribute to victory or defeat, and it seems that Charlemagne may well have caught the Avars at a time when their control of Avar terriory was weakening, while his political control was patently overwhelming. There is, however, a distinct difference in the manner of Frankish warfare under Charlemagne, which appears unique to his period.

As stated previously, the bow was not a weapon widely used by Germanic horse-warriors, for despite its obvious effectiveness, it was not considered noble enough to displace the sword and spear of the mounted man. Nevertheless, in a letter to the Abbot Fulrad, Charlemagne instructed him to supply his army with horsemen equipped specifically with shield, lance, sword, dagger, and bow and arrows. Elsewhere, in a manuscript of 803, each landlord is asked to equip their warriors with a lance, shield, a bow and two bowstrings plus 12 arrows. In this *Capitulare Aquisgranense*, there is a sentence that says that two men are required to have these weapons between them. This may suggest that a mounted warrior was expected to carry lance and sword, while a dismounted man – a squire, perhaps – used the bow. This would certainly fit the status of weapons common in Western Europe. However, the summons to Abbot Fulrad does not make this distinction and some military historians have suggested that Charlemagne armed his horse-warriors with bows especially to counter the Avars, although the skill of these Frankish archers cannot have been as refined as that of the Eurasians.

That Carolingian horse-warriors did not wholly adapt themselves to the ways of the Avars is perhaps indicated by their slow adoption of the stirrup, an oriental device. The earliest illustrations of warriors using stirrups in Western Europe come from Carolingian manuscripts illuminated in the latter half of the 9th century. Consistently in these pictures, some

Model of a horse showing an 8th century central Asian saddle. From Astana Cemetery. Now in the British Museum, London.

'FIGURE OF A HORSE
ASTĀNA CEMETERY
640 — 750 A.D.
'Innermost Asia' Ast. III. 3. 027. Plate XCVII.

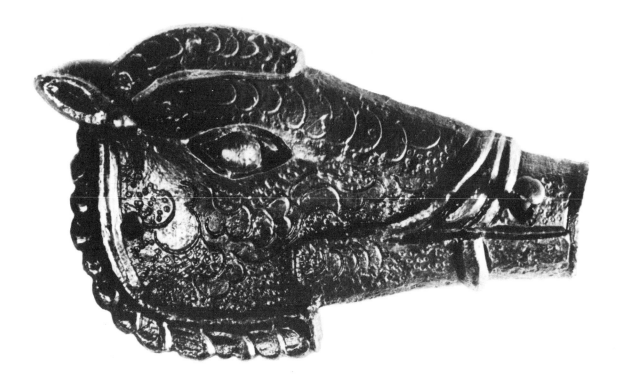

riders are shown using them and some are not. Just as amongst the Arabs over a century before, some conservative warriors probably considered the use of the stirrup a sign of weakness. Certainly, it seems that the introduction of the stirrup to Western warfare did not have as major an impact as some historians have ascribed to it. It was adopted slowly and its main influence on later mounted warriors appears to have been to encourage a stiff-legged riding posture rather than one in which legs are bent so as to clutch the horse. This meant warriors could stand in the saddle, but the introduction of the stirrup did not increase significantly the number of horse-borne warriors. Riding was largely a matter of status and wealth. Nor did it further the use of the lance among mounted men. The image of a warrior now enabled to crash into an adversary with his lance without falling off because of his stirrups is a false one. Firstly, a horse will rarely charge into a static obstacle, like a wall of shield-bearing men. Secondly, lances had in any case been used effectively before the stirrup, and were best employed in single-combat against another horseman or when pursuing a broken formation of fleeing foot-soldiers.

Despite uncertainty regarding the Frankish use of both the bow and the stirrup, the Carolingian war-machine was undoubtedly well organised. In the written instructions issued from Charlemagne's various royal residences, there are fascinating descriptions of the wagon-trains that would be used to carry the burden of his campaigns against the pagans. 'The wagons that

Avar 8th century bronze boar's-head mount. From Holiare in Czechoslovakia.

accompany our warriors as war-carts shall be well-constructed,' says one manuscript. 'Their coverings shall be made of animal skins and sewn together so that when crossing a river, the provisions inside will remain dry. It is also our wish that a goodly amount of flour and wine shall be placed in each cart.' Another manuscript lists further the equipment to be carried in each wagon, 'Food in abundance, stone handmills, adzes, axes, carpenters' tools, and slings with men who can use them properly. Stones are to brought for these slings, on 20 pack-horses if needs be ...' These latter weapons translated as slings may well be catapults or *ballistae*. With such logistical back-up, in the Roman manner, Charlemagne undoubtedly had an advantage over his less organised adversaries. This is probably what brought him victory against the Avars. That the Franks may also have possessed more sophisticated weapons and armour than their enemies is suggested by the repeated prohibition on arms trading with foreign countries. 'Concerning traders who travel in the territories of the Slavs and the Avars,' begins a *Capitulary* of 805. 'They must not take weapons and coats of mail with them to sell. If they are caught carrying them, their entire stock is to be confiscated.'

The Franks were not the only Imperialists worried about giving away their military advantages. The Greek Fire of the Byzantines was an obsessively guarded secret weapon. Emperor Constantine VII in writing to his son in the 10th century continued the tradition of secrecy. 'If you are ever asked to divulge information about the making of liquid fire discharged through tubes, you must reply, "This was revealed by God through an angel to the great and holy Constantine, the first Christian Emperor. And we are assured by the faithful witness of our fathers and grandfathers that it should only be manufactured among the Christians and in their capital city and nowhere else." For it happened once that one of our military commanders was bribed by the heathens and handed over some fire to them. God could not leave such a transgression unavenged and so when the man entered the holy church of God, a fire-ball was sent down from heaven and completely consumed him.'

From the 7th to the 9th century, the Avars dominated central Europe. Over the same period, to the east, the Bulgars controlled those parts of the Balkans they had wrestled from the Byzantines as well as the lower Danube area. To the east of them, in southern Russia, there was the mighty kingdom of the Khazars. Like the Avars, both these latter tribal confederations were essentially Turkish. Amongst them were the remnants of the Huns. In their midst, also, were Slavic tribes who, though largely subjugated, increasingly rose in revolt against their Eurasian masters. The Avars shamelessly exploited the Slaves who lived under their authority. They spent the winter with these Slavs, sleeping with their wives and daughters and living off Slav tributes. In battle, the Avars were said to herd the Slavs into their front lines, waiting for them to blunt the fighting and only then joining in the battle to insure victory and a majority of the plunder. Eventually, the half-caste sons of the Avars and their Slav women found the situation intolerable and rose successfully against the nomad bandits. Like Notker after him, the chronicler of these acts, Fredegar, also called the Avars 'Huns'.

The Bulgars and Khazars were mail-clad horse-warriors with bow, sword and spear. Frequently fighting among each other, they also clashed with the Byzantines, the Arabs, the Slavs and the Rus. The Khazars were the most powerful of the steppe confederations. Their tribes controlled land north of the Caucasian mountains, from the Black Sea to the Caspian. Because of this position, they proved a useful bulwark against any Muslim invasion of eastern Europe via the Caucasus. The Byzantines frequently entered into peace treaties with them. Because of the profit, both political and material, to be obtained from this role as neutral third power, the Khazar leaders had to think carefully about their religious status. By remaining nomadic heathens, they would gain neither the respect of the Arabs nor the Byzantines, being regarded merely as useful Barbarians. However, if they chose either Christianity or Islam, that would mean spiritual, and thus political, alignment with either Caliph or Emperor. In the event, the Khazars shrewdly chose to convert to that other faith of the People of the Book – Judaism. Subsequently, a union of nomadic Aryan Jews dominated southern Russia for several hundred years. An Arabic chronicler described some of their traits.

'When the Khazars bring back their plunder from a raid, they pool it together in the camp. The leader then takes for himself what he wishes and leaves the rest to be divided amongst his warriors. When embarking for a campaign, the Khazar leader instructs every man to carry with him a sharp stake. On halting for the night, these stakes are then placed around the camp with shields hanging from them so as to form a palisade.'

In a passage more difficult to interpret, the Arabic sources conjure up a picture of the Khazar warlord riding before his army surrounded by a vanguard carrying either lighted candles and torches or bright, reflective metal discs. Such weird illumination probably acted as a kind of signalling or as a badge of rank. It may also have had a religious signifiance.

The domination of Eurasia by the Avars, Bulgars and the Khazars came to an end at the close of the 9th century. Migrating southwards from the Ural mountains, a group of tribes closely related to the Finns entered upon the battle-ground of the steppes. These were the Magyars. At first, they were subject to the Khazars, collecting taxes for their overlords from the Slavs. During this period the Magyars mixed with the Turkish tribesmen, and would have become proficient horsemen and archers, if they had not already been. Certainly, by the last decades of the 9th century, when intertribal warfare intensified, the Magyars met their rivals on equal terms. In this ferocious activity, north of the Black Sea, a Turkish tribe – the Pechenegs – loomed large. The Byzantine Emperor Constantine VII recorded that, 'their neighbours always look on the Pechenegs with dread and are held in check by them.' Even the Rus could not carry out raids into the

Central Asian figure, 8th to 10th century, from Mingoi. Warriors such as this fought in the steppe confederations of the Khazars and their successors. In the British Museum, London.

MALE FIGURE.
MINGOI. *c.* 8TH-10TH CENT.
"Serindia". Plate CXXXIII. Mi. xi. 0064.

Black Sea unless they were at peace with these nomads. For whenever the Viking raiders reached cataracts along the southern Russian waterways, they were forced to shoulder their boats overland to quieter waters: and once caught on the riverbank by a band of hostile Pechenegs, the Rus were easily overwhelmed and cut to pieces.

The Pechenegs were described as having 'weapons in plenty, belts of silver, standards and short spears, and decorated trumpets which they sound in battle.' It was these warriors who, according to the Emperor Constantine, were responsible for shifting the Magyars into Europe. While the Magyars were away from their families, raiding the territories of the Bulgars, the Pechenegs, encouraged by the Bulgar ruler, tore into the land of the Magyars and devastated their homes, slaughtering their wives, children and the few guards left behind. With their Khazar allies in decline, and faced with the incursions of the Pechenegs and the Rus, the Magyars may well have seen their move westwards as the easiest option. Entering eastern Europe, they clashed unsuccessfully with the Bulgars. Having better luck against the Avars, already crushed and fragmented by Charlemagne, the Magyars pitched their tents in central Europe. From the plains of Hungary, the Magyars carried out relentless raids against the Germanic kingdoms of the West. A terror which lasted for over half a century.

> 'Pavia is burning.
> Winds increase the fire.
> Magyar mobs set upon citizens
> choking, fleeing from the flames.
> Pavia is burning.
> Down the streets the blaze spreads.
> Women and children are trampled down,
> a holy priest is slain.
> Pavia is burning.
> Gold melts through chests
> hidden deep in sewers.
> Streams of silver hiss
> and bubble in the gutter.
> Pavia is burning.'

In these lines from a poem by Liutprand, Bishop of Cremona, a devastation to equal that of Attila's sack of Aquileia is described. It comes from Liutprands's *Antapodosis*, a revealing account of Magyar incursions in the first quarter of the 10th century. His story begins with Arnulf, King of the eastern Carolingian territories, letting the Magyars into Western Europe. Hoping that the nomads would distract and hinder his enemies, Arnulf broke down the great earthworks that prevented the Magyars from advancing any further. Once in, the Magyars embarked on an orgy of pillage against Arnulf's enemies: but as soon as Arnulf was dead, even his own people were not safe from Magyar raids.

128

'No man ever wished more desperately for food or water than these savages desire a fight,' exclaimed Liutprand, 'their only joy is in battle.' Quoting an ancient historian, Jordanes, he then ascribed to the Magyars an old Hun custom. 'They scar their babies with knives so that they might bear the pain of wounds before receiving milk from their mothers' breasts.' Again, the latest Eurasian invaders and the Huns were seen as one and the same. Fast losing hold of his recently acquired kingdom, Louis, son of Arnulf, gathered his forces together and confronted the raiders on the plains near the city of Augsburg. It was barely daybreak when the Magyars rode on the Bavarians in their camp. Yawning and rousing themselves for the day's confrontation, German warriors were suddenly assaulted from all sides by a hail of arrows. Some never awoke – transfixed in their beds. Darting to and fro, the Magyars caused great havoc. Stumbling out of their tents, with mail only half on, warriors had their heads split by Magyar sabres. Rallying themselves amidst the panic, Louis' men dashed after a retreating band of horse-archers but, of course, in familiar fashion, this was a deception and the ambush was drawn tight. Magyars pounced on the Germans and Louis was beaten, narrowly escaping the slaughter himself. After such a defeat, Bavaria, Swabia, Saxony and eastern France lay open. Villages and monasteries were sacked and burnt, while clerics wondered what on earth their lords were doing about the Church's defence. More concerned about pursuing their dynastic feuds, however, the majority of German warlords tamely paid the Hungarians a tribute. Sitting out the storm behind the walls of their castles, the barons and dukes used this emergency as an excuse to tax their own people – part of which they kept themselves.

Italy had always proved attractive to Barbarians and was no less so to the Magyars. On their first journey south of the Alps, their scouts reported that though they were unsure of the strength of the Italians as fighters, they saw that their numbers were great and their towns well fortified. The Magyars rode back to their homeland and spent the winter in preparation for a more substantial campaign. According to Liutprand, they spent these months making armour, sharpening their weapons and training their young men with military exercises. The next spring they returned to Italy, passing through the regions of Aquileia, Verona and Pavia. Berengar, Carolingian king of northern Italy, had never even heard of the Magyars. Nevertheless, he quickly raised a force from his subjects that outnumbered the invaders three to one. Confronted by such an army, the Hungarians chose flight rather than fight, and swam across the river Adda before the might of the Italian warriors. Many Magyars were drowned in the panic and those who clambered up onto the other bank offered to return all their booty to the Christians. The Italians felt insulted and rejected this sign of weakness.

The Magyars further retreated to the plains around Verona. There, an Italian vanguard caught up with them. In the skirmish, the cocksure Italians were thrashed. But mindful of the rest of the army, the Hungarians again trekked homeward. Finally, their horses exhausted, the Magyars were forced to make camp beyond the river Brenta. The Italians jeered at them from the other side of the water. Once more, the Magyars offered to surrender their captured goods, their prisoners, arms and horses. They swore never to invade Italy and offered their sons as hostages. Sensing an easy and prestigious victory, the Italians said no, 'We do not accept pleas of surrender from dogs that have already given themselves up.' Driven to despair, and seeing no better way out, the Hungarians readied themselves for combat: they had nothing to lose for 'to fall fighting like men is not to die, but to live.' As was their manner, the Magyars took the offensive. Crossing the river surreptitiously, they surprised the Italians while the latter were resting and eating. Dismounted and scattered among their tents, they were easy prey for the Magyars. Some Italians, though equipped and ready, held back from the fray, seeing that the Magyars were conveniently annihilating their rivals. The Hungarians gave no quarter.

On the death of King Conrad (Louis' successor) the Magyars again decided on a show of strength. The election of a German king was a crucial time for the Hungarians as a new monarch frequently chose to begin his reign by refusing to continue any regular tribute. They therefore advanced into the territory of the Saxon king Henry, the new overlord of the Germans. Henry was ill at the time, but regardless of this he gathered a strong force about him: all men above the age of 13 were required to render him military service. Meanwhile, the Magyars had crossed the Saxon border enslaving women and children, and massacring all men as a warning of their ruthlesness. Magyar scouts came across the Saxon army assembled at Merseburg and at once rode back to their masters. Henry decided to deliver the message personally and his army moved swiftly upon the raiders.

Before the two forces clashed, the *Kyrie eleison* of the Christian Germans rang out, 'Lord have mercy upon us'. The heathens countered with an awesome battle-chant. By now used to the damaging tactics of the Hungarian horse-archers, King Henry ordered his horse-warriors to advance together, and not let those with faster mounts dash ahead and be swallowed up by the Magyar horde. As they thundered forward the Magyars let fly with their arrows. Expecting this, the Saxons raised their shields and caught the first volley upon them. Spurring their horses onwards, the Germans endeavoured to reach the Magyars before they could unleash another deadly cloud. Such tactics sound more impressive than they really were for surely the raising of a shield to protect oneself from arrows was common-sense. Perhaps it was the sense of order that was new. With the heavily-clad Saxons crashing towards them, the Magyars suddenly lost their courage and broke before the onslaught. The Hungarian raiders had been checked. This battle and the previous defeat of King Louis were placed by Liutprand at the beginning of both kings' reigns, giving

Central Asian warrior in scale armour or mail. The armour of the Avars, Bulgars and Khazars was influenced by their powerful eastern neighbours, and many probably looked like this. From Mingoi, now in the British Museum, London.

the Magyars a good excuse for their raids. Later historians, however, have generally placed these battles around 910 and 933 respectively.

With the German states proving too hot for comfort, the Magyars turned southwards again. In 924, a large Hungarian force invaded Italy and amidst the carnage, Pavia was burnt to the ground; Liutprand's town of birth. Times had changed, however, and western warlords were no longer willing meekly to pay tribute. Otto, another vigorous Saxon king, caught some Magyar raiders in a marsh along the Lower Elbe and savaged them. Never again would Saxony hear the hoof-beats of the Hungarians. Later, the Bavarians followed this up by smashing the raiders on their frontier and then plunging into Magyar territory. Hungarian encampments were ransacked. This time it was Magyar women and children who became part of the intensive slave trade practised by both heathen and Christian warlords. Determined to end their bad luck, the Magyars broke in upon a civil war between German princes in 954 and rode through Bavaria and into France in a major show of strength. Predictably, as the Magyars passed through, various feuding German factions could not resist trying to employ them on their side, but this time the nomads would not be diverted from their task. Unintentionally, this invasion strengthened the hand of Otto for he now marched into Bavaria at the head of a liberating army, determined to forget party politics and confront the common foe. Missing each other, the Magyars returned to their homeland determined to repeat the action.

The Hungarian horde that entered Bavaria in 955 was the biggest that central Europe had seen for many years. It seemed as if the Magyars wanted to settle once and for all their right to range unrestricted across Europe. That summer they swarmed around the city of Augsburg, the site of a previous victory. After denuding the surrounding districts, they approached the walls of the city with siege-engines; once again demonstrating that steppe warriors were no less sophisticated militarily than their town-dwelling opponents. With earthworks dug, tents pitched, the massive machines were pushed forward by Slav slaves whipped from behind. Suddenly the siege came to a halt. News had reached the Magyars that an army led by Otto was fast approaching. They readied themselves for battle. With Saxons, Bavarians, Franconians, Swabians and Bohemians riding beneath his banners, Otto made camp near the river Lech, a tributary of the Danube. Bolstered by warriors slipping out of Augsburg and numerous Slav auxiliaries, the German forces probably numbered about 5,000. Calling together their raiding parties with the aid of smoke signals, the Magyars were commonly believed to outnumber the Germans. That night, a fast was ordered among the Christians to prepare them spiritually for the coming combat: many warriors were probably too tense to eat anyway.

On the morning of battle, the German warlords swore allegiance to each other. Many a conflict in the past had been lost through rivals holding back in the expectation of their competitors being wiped out by the enemy. The Christian host then said mass and advanced with

lances and standards held high. They rode forward in eight groups, according to nationality. Otto's Saxons moved beneath the banner of Saint Michael, the heavenly vanquisher of the Devil. With the Lech to the left of them, its banks overgrown with foliage, the Germans did not notice a contingent of Magyars moving rapidly along their flank on the other side of the river. These Magyars then crossed the river and set upon the end group of Germans guarding the army's baggage train. With arrows hissing about them and the Hungarians howling like wolves, the Bohemian and Swabian rearguard faltered and fled. Disaster seemed to have struck Otto at once. With fighting already encountered in front and now a third of his army routed in the rear, encirclement appeared imminent.

Desperately, Otto despatched Duke Conrad to deal with the crisis behind him. Conrad was a bold and well respected leader and his presence rallied the remaining Franconians. They counter-attacked and freed many prisoners from the Magyars who had become diverted from battle by the task of

Magyar raiders set fire to a German homestead from a late 19th century illustration. In the 10th century the Magyars revived Western fears about horse-archers from the eastern plains.

French photograph of a Mongol warrior taken at the turn of this century. His sprouting quiver and bowcase with its composite bow – which is almost as tall as him – have always been characteristic of all Eurasian steppe warriors.

carrying away their booty. The crux of the battle now switched to the front. Here, according to a speech put into the mouth of Otto by the chronicler Widukind, the Saxon King encouraged his men with the fact that the Magyars were not as well equipped. 'They surpass us, I know, in numbers,' gasped Otto, 'but neither in weapons nor in courage. We know also that they are quite without the help of God, which is of the greatest comfort to us.' It is unlikely that anyone could have heard such a brave speech amidst the clamour and clang of fighting. But was it true? Certainly, leading German warriors would have been wrapped in a splendour of mail, with heavy shields, helmets, lances and swords. While, as steppe warriors, the Magyars may well have been more lightly armoured: depending more on the efficiency of their bows. However, most warriors at this time in both Europe and Asia wore mail, while as professional plunderers the Magyars would have been armed with the very best weapons and armour. Indeed, much of their armoury would have been the same as that of the Germans, for it was from them that the Magyars had stolen it. But whatever the relative strength in arms, the advantage in spirit and morale seems to have shifted to the Germans, who charged the Magyars successfully.

In the hard slog of hand to hand, the bravest warriors of both sides clashed fiercely while others turned and ran. It was a hot summer day and in the heat of combat, Conrad, hero of the battle, loosened the mail around his helmet. At once, an Hungarian arrow flashed through the air and struck him in the throat. He choked and fell from his horse. But now, even the strongest of the Magyar warriors were overwhelmed by the triumphant Germans, and they joined the general rout. Leaping into the river Lech, some drowned when the bank on the opposite side collapsed under their weight. Others hid in outlying villages, but were surrounded and cremated within the huts. High with victory, the Germans pursued the fleeing Magyars over the next two days. Hungarian noblemen laden with gold necklaces and silver cruciform bosses on their shields were captured and hanged like common criminals. It was this ruthless follow up to the victory on the Lechfeld that was decisive in breaking the back of the Magyars. Unfortunately for the natives of Augsburg, it was also this orgy of man-hunting that achieved a local destruction as bad as any inflicted by the Hungarians. Nevertheless, the action did bring an end to the Magyar raids.

Leaderless and with so many warriors lying dead and mutilated on the trails of Bavaria back to the eastern plains, the Magyars never again invaded German territories. The Magyars had lost their fury. Over future generations, Hungary became a settled European kingdom where Bavarian missionaries carried out a successful job of conversion. By the end of the 10th century, it was the Hungarians who were sending tributes to the Germans. The prestige of Otto and his dynasty rose considerably as a result of this victory. Acknowledging the end of a great Eurasian menace, the Byzantines sent him presents of congratulation and called him 'emperor'. From the jealous guardians. of the Eastern Roman Empire, this was high praise indeed.

With the Magyars tamed, the West remained free of steppe warriors for three hundred years. Raiding was always a problem, but this existed as much among feudal lords as more nomadic people, and on the whole no major tribal confederation from the east threatened the stability of central and western Europe. Then, in 1238 in Yarmouth, England, the price of herrings plummeted. Fifty fish could be had for just one piece of silver. That year, German merchants from across the North Sea had stayed away. They stayed away because the people of north Germany were in fear of invasion by 'a monstrous and inhuman race of men'. Matthew Paris, English chronicler, recorded the fantastic reports that reached him from the continent of this new menace.

'The men are of the nature of beasts. They thirst after and drink blood. They clothe themselves in the skins of bulls and are armed with iron lances. They are short in stature and thick-set, compact in their bodies. Their horses are very swift and able to perform a journey of three days in one.

A late 19th century Tartar horse-warrior depicted in an English newspaper from the time. The Mongols of the 13th century would have been similarly attired.

They have swords and daggers with one edge – sabres – and are excellent archers. They take their herds with them, as also their wives, who are brought up to war the same as men. Their chief is a ferocious man named Khan. The people are very numerous. The come with the force of lightning into the territories of the Christians and are believed to have been sent as a plague on mankind.' In this passage are echoes of earlier descriptions of Huns, Avars and Magyars. But this time, the oriental nomads were called Tartars, after Tartarus, a mythical place of punishment in the classical underworld. They are known today as the Mongols.

Unlike earlier tribal confederations over-running Eurasia, the Mongols were not a Turkish people but came from the far east, from the plains of Mongolia. The lands they dominated were far vaster than those of any nomadic predecessors known to the West. They reigned over the whole steppeland, from China to Eastern Europe. This may have been true of earlier confederations, and it might be only a lack of surviving records that

دیگر باز گشت وسپر از پس پشت انداخت و پیشتر و علم خویش بر گرفت واسپ را تازیانه زد و مانند برق آب بگذشت
و بدان طرف فرود زین اسپ خویش بنشاند و شمشیر را از آب پاک کیکو [...] از غایت تعجب انگشت بدندان گرفته او را
بپسران می نمود و میگفت تا پدر پسر باید که چنین آید سرا یکسی تا کنون مردوازمیان ندید [...] نه از نامداران پیشین شنیده [...] چون ایشین

جنگ کاه و فرق آب خود را ساعتی نگاهداشت و مردوازه گاه بای سپار و فتنها بی شمار بپای پشکر منوال چون اندین دیده که او بر آب زده خواستند که نعقیب
خود او فرآب بهستند گکینان گذاشت و نتایج معقد علیه آورده اند که سلطان جوی است که نقاوت ممکن نیست مشتر زن و بچه و الح حرم او از عقب
گردانید نانیل سبری نهفته و خزاین و نیز فرآب بعد ازان بر آب زده و بگذشت و لشکریان سلطان جلال الدین ثامت فضل آمد و بقول ای کو فیروز نباخ پنید

prevent us from making the connection between tribes in European annals and those of a different name in Chinese history: the Huns are believed by some to be of Mongolian origin. But what we do know is that by the beginning of the 13th century, the tribes of Mongolia had been united under the warlord Genghis Khan. Also – as opposed to earlier movements of oriental hordes, spurred onwards by drought, famine or more ferocious rivals – the expanding campaigns of the Mongols seem to have been a self-conscious effort to conquer the known world. Their dominion was imperialistic. To established Eastern and Western empires, however, they were still deadly savages. Frederick II, German Emperor, considered the Tartars *gens barbarae nationis*.

With an Asian domain left secure by Genghis Khan, his successor, Ogedei, over-looked a series of historic campaigns. In 1237, under the command of Batu (the Khan's nephew) and his leading general Subedei, a Mongol horde smashed the kingdoms of the Russians. They advanced during the winter, for in spring when the snows melted, the great rivers were swollen and the country-side a morass. In 1241, the Mongols entered Poland. Near the town of Liegnitz, Duke Henry of Silesia and the Grand Master of the Teutonic Order assembled a major force of Poles and Germans. Western knights, clad in mail, confronted the eastern marauders. At the end of the day, nine sacks of ears, cut off their European opponents, were collected by the victorious Mongols. From there the Mongol army, divided into independent forces, met up in Hungary and devastated the feudal host of King Bela at the battle of Mohi. Within a few days, the Mongols had delivered two catastrophic blows to Western defences. The Emperor Frederick now feared for the security of his own lands and wrote to his

Tartar soldiers from the mid 19th century. Although only armed with the bow and arrow, the Asian horse-warriors were still a force to be reckoned with in the last century. From Cassell's *British Battles on Land and Sea*, 1875.

fellow monarchs asking for assistance in a crisis which 'concerns not only the Roman Empire, but all kingdoms of the world that practise Christian worship'. Signs were not encouraging for concerted action against the Mongols. Only a few years earlier, Muslim leaders had sent ambassadors to the West to encourage an alliance between the two religions in order to rid the world of the infidel nomads. While the English king had pondered this request, one of his bishops interrupted, 'Let us leave these dogs – Saracen and pagan – to devour one another. So that when we proceed against those enemies of Christ that remain we will slay them and the whole world will be subject to the one Catholic Europe.' Such an attitude had brought the Mongols to the borders of the German Empire.

In his letter to all Western monarchs, Frederick outlined what little was known of the military qualities of the Mongol enemy. 'They are ready at the nod of their leader to rush into any undertaking. They wear raw hides of oxen and to these are sewn iron plates. Portable boats, also made of hide, enable them to cross over any rivers. From the spoils of conquered Christians, they are providing themselves with fine weapons so that we may be slain by our own arms. They are incomparable archers. The bow is a more familiar weapon to them than to any other people. From their regular use of it, their arms are stronger than other people and they have entirely subdued nations because of this.' The excellent archery and boiled-leather armour of the Mongols was attested by other European observers, including Marco Polo; but it was not only their clouds of arrows that devastated European warriors. Military discipline and strategy was of a very high standard among the Mongols, although it must be remembered that it was only the leading officers and commanders of the horde who were of Mongolian origin. The majority of Mongol warriors who invaded Europe in the 13th century were drawn from Turkish Eurasian tribes that had been absorbed into their confederation: no different to the previous waves of Barbarians.

Western reaction to the Mongols was feeble. Though called on to send their bravest warriors, those monarchs beyond the German Empire saw little advantage in helping their political rivals. Matthew Paris recorded that Frederick's sons did gather together an impressive force and indeed defeated the Mongols on the banks of the river Delpheos, not far from the Danube. But this has not been substantiated, and by the winter of 1241 the Mongols stood poised to invade Germany and Italy. Raiders rode into the Balkans, pursuing the Hungarian King Bela. Venice and Vienna were perilously close to being pulverised by the ingenious siege machines of the Mongols. Then, from the plains of central Asia, hard-riding messengers brought news of the death of the great Khan. Dissension between the leading Mongols made it vital for all contenders to the succession to return eastwards, and the campaign was broken off: miraculous deliverance for the West.

From what evidence we have, the military expertise of the Mongols exceeded that of any previous Eurasian eruption into Europe. The West had

With the fragmentation of Mongol unity, no Eurasian confederation was ever again to sweep into Europe from the steppelands north of the Black Sea. A late 19th century engraving.

never been as close to absolute submission to an eastern steppe confederation as it was during the 13th century. The Huns, Avars and Magyars penetrated further westward and left a greater impact on European culture than the Mongols, but they did not possess the sophisticated administration to turn their campaigns into major conquests. Fortunately for Europe, fragmentation among the Mongol royal families cut short their expansion and they lacked the dynamism to repeat their invasion of 1241. Ancient Scythia now became the western-most province of the Khanate of the Golden Horde. The steppes north of the Black Sea were never again to be a launching pad for any major nomadic incursion into Europe. That said, the terror of the Turks was not at an end. During the 14th, 15th and 16th centuries, Turks of the Ottoman confederation rampaged through Asia Minor, overran the Balkans and terrorised central Europe. With the Turkish capture of Constantinople in 1453, the Byzantines, the last direct inheritors of the Greek and Roman tradition, were swept away. Only the German Holy Roman Empire now remained to protect the West against the Turks. But because the Barbarians were essentially a creation of the Greeks and Romans, the term had lost its meaning with the ending of a Mediterranean Empire. There were no longer any outsiders – northern and eastern wildmen – battering on the frontiers of a Graeco-Latin world. The disappearance of their ancient adversaries meant that the Barbarians also ceased to exist.

139

Bibliography

THIS IS, OF NECESSITY A SELECT BIBLIOGRAPHY OF
BOTH PRIMARY AND SECONDARY REFERENCES

Primary Sources

ALL THESE TEXTS ARE AVAILABLE IN ENGLISH TRANSLATIONS IN SEVERAL
EDITIONS.

Ammianus Marcellinus, *Roman History:* 4th century account of Barbarian
invasions by a Greek 'officer and gentleman'

Anonymous, *Beowulf:* 8th century Anglo-Saxon epic poem

Anonymous, *The Wanderer* and *The Seafarer:* 10th century Anglo-Saxon
poems

Anonymous, *The Battle of Maldon:* 10th century Anglo-Saxon poetical
account of battle in 991

Caesar, *The Gallic War:* 1st century BC autobiography of campaigns against
Celts and Germans

Constantine Porphyrogenitus, *De Administrando Imperio:* 10th century
compilation of Byzantine history by Emperor Constantine VII

Einhard and Notker the Stammerer, *Lives of Charlemagne:* 9th century
accounts of the Frank Emperor. One by a courtier, the other by a monk
sometime after Charlemagne's death

Fredegar, *The Fourth Book of the Chronicle:* 6th to 8th century Frank history
by several authors

Gregory of Tours, *The History of the Franks:* 6th century chronicle of the
Franks by a Gallo-Roman bishop

Jordanes, *Getica: The Origin and Deeds of the Goths:* 6th century history of
the Goths by an Italian monk

Liutprand of Cremona, *Antapodosis:* 10th century chronicle by an Italian
bishop and ambassador to the German Emperor

Nestor, *The Russian Primary Chronicles:* 9th to 12th century history of
Russia compiled by a 12th century monk

Matthew Paris, *Historia Major:* 13th century English history including
continental affairs compiled by an English monk

Velleius Paterculus, *History of Rome:* 1st century history by a Roman army officer

Paul the Deacon, *History of the Lombards:* 8th century chronicle of the Lombards by an Italian monk

Priscus, *Fragments:* 5th century eye-witness accounts by an eastern Roman official

Procopius, *History of the Persian, Vandal, and Goth wars:* 6th century eye-witness accounts by a Greek secretary to Belisarius

Strabo, *Geographica:* 1st century description of all known peoples by a Greek traveller and writer

Tacitus, *The Annals, Histories, and Germania:* 1st century history written by a Roman politician.

Zosimus, *Historia Nova: The Decline of Rome:* 5th century eastern Roman history by a Greek official

Secondary Works

Bachrach, BS, 'Charles Martel, Mounted Shock Combat, The Stirrup, and Feudalism', *Studies in Medieval and Renaissance History*, Vol VII, p49, Lincoln, Nebraska, 1970.

Bachrach, BS, *Merovingian Military Organization 481–751*, Minneapolis, 1972.

Bachrach, BS, *A History of the Alans in the West*, University of Minnesota Press. Minneapolis, 1973.

Bivar, ADH, 'Cavalry Equipment and Tactics on the Euphrates Frontier', *Dumbarton Oaks Papers*, Vol XXVI, p273, Washington, 1972.

Blondal, S and Benedikz, BS, *The Varangians of Byzantium*, Cambridge, 1978.

Boba, I, *Nomads, Northmen and Slavs*, the Hague, 1967.

Brøgger, AW and Shetelig, H, *The Viking Ships*, Oslo, 1951.

Burgess, EM, 'The Mail-Maker's Technique', *Antiquaries Journal*, XXXIII, p48, London, 1953.

Butler, AJ, *The Arab Conquest of Egypt*, Oxford, 1902.

Czarnecki, J, *The Goths in Ancient Poland*, Miami, 1975.

Davidson, HRE, *The Sword in Anglo-Saxon England*, Oxford, 1962.

Davidson, HRE, *The Viking Road to Byzantium*, London, 1976.

Drew, KF (editor), *The Barbarian Invasions*, New York, 1970.

Dunlop, DM, *The History of the Jewish Khazars*, Princeton, 1954.

Foote, P and Wilson, DM, *The Viking Achievement*, London, 1970.

Gimbutas, M, *The Slavs*, London, 1976.

Glob, PV, *The Bog People*, London, 1969.

Goffart, W, *Barbarians and Romans*, Princeton, 1980.

Gordon, CD, *The Age of Attila*, Michigan, 1960.

Hassall, MWC, and Ireland, R (editors), 'De Rebus Bellicis', *BAR International Series*, 63, Oxford, 1979.

Havighurst, AF (editor), *The Pirenne Thesis*, Lexington, 1976.

Hoffmeyer, AB, 'Military Equipment In the Byzantine Manuscript of Scylitzes', *Gladius*, V, Granada, 1966.

Kagan, D (editor), *The End of the Roman Empire*, Lexington, 1978.

Leyser, K, 'The Battle at the Lech', 955, *History*, L, p1, London, 1965.

Maenchen-Helfen, JO, *The World of the Huns*, Los Angeles, 1973.

Macartney, CA, *The Magyars in the Ninth Century*, Cambridge, 1930.

Nicolle, D, 'Early Medieval Islamic Arms and Armour', *Gladius*, tomo especial, Madrid, 1976.

Parry, VJ and Yapp, ME (editors), *War, Technology and Society in the Middle East*, London, 1975.

Paterson, WF, 'The Archers of Islam', *Journal of the Economic and Social History of the Orient*, 9, p69, Leiden, 1966.

Pipes, D, *Slave Soldiers and Islam*, New Haven, 1981.

Rausing, G, *The Bow*, Lund, Sweden, 1967.

Russom, GR, 'A Germanic Concept of Nobility in *The Gift* and *Beowulf*', *Speculum*, LIII, p1, Cambridge, Massachusetts, 1978.

Saunders, JJ, *The History of the Mongol Conquests*, London, 1971.

Setton, KM, 'The Bulgars in the Balkans in the 7th century', *Speculum*, XXV, p502, Cambridge, Massachusetts, 1950.

Sulimirski, T, *The Sarmatians*, London, 1970.

Thompson, EA, *A History of Attila and the Huns*, Oxford, 1948.

Thompson, EA, *The Early Germans*, Oxford, 1965.

Thompson, EA, *The Visigoths in the time of Ulfila*, Oxford, 1966.

Thompson, EA, *Romans and Barbarians*, Wisconsin, 1982.

Todd, M, *The Northern Barbarians BC 100 to AD 300*, London, 1975.

Vasiliev, AA, *The Russian Attack on Constantinople in 860*, Cambridge, Massachusetts, 1946.

Vasiliev, AA, 'The Second Russian Attack on Constantinople', *Dumbarton Oaks Papers*, VI p165, Cambridge, Massachusetts, 1951.

Wallace-Hadrill, JM, *The Barbarian West 400–1000*, London, 1967.

White, L, *Medieval Technology and Social Change*, Oxford, 1962.

Bronze horse-archers form the decoration for the top of an Etrusco-Campanian cauldron, *c* 500 BC, from the British Museum, London.

144

CELTIC
WARLORDS

Celtic spearheads, arrows and bolts from Newstead, Roxborough (a); bronze Celtic sword from Cowgill, Lanarkshire (b); and mail fragment with decorated boss, from Romania (c).

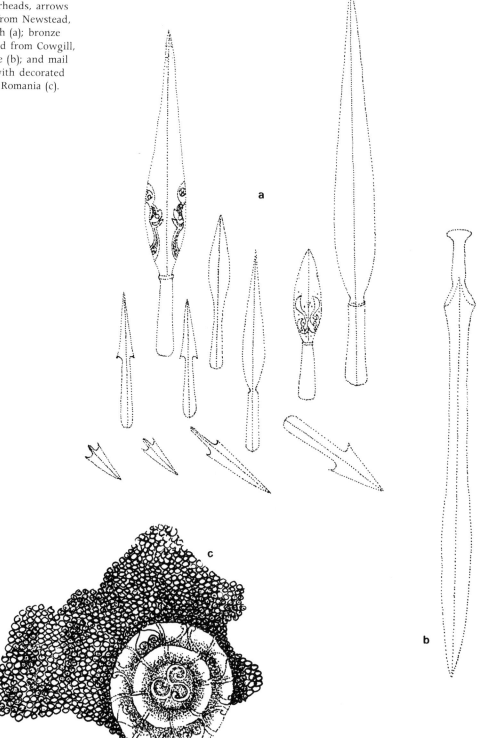

148

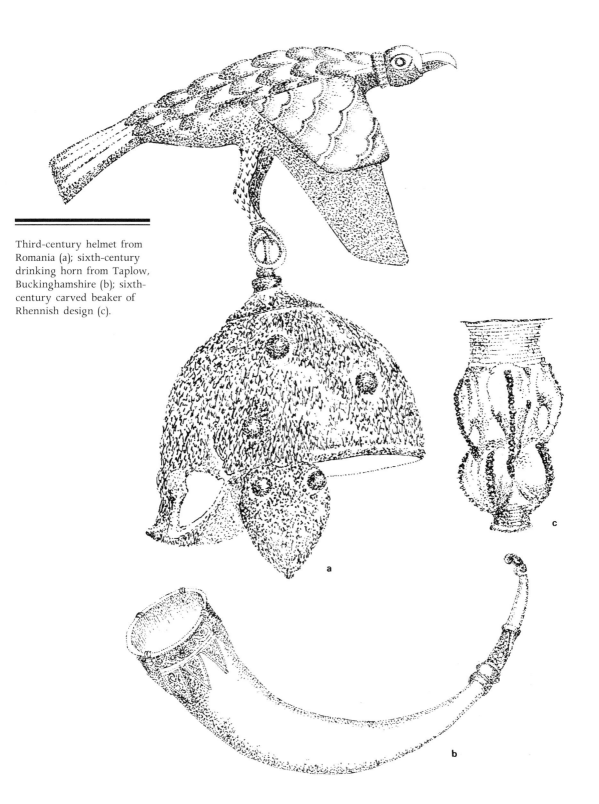

Third-century helmet from Romania (a); sixth-century drinking horn from Taplow, Buckinghamshire (b); sixth-century carved beaker of Rhennish design (c).

a

b

c

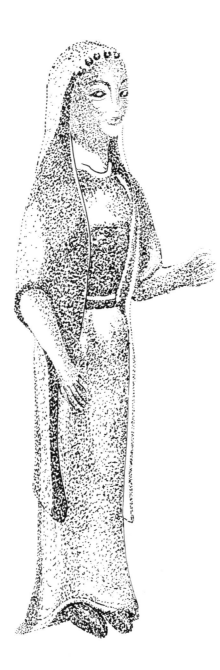

A Celtic princess, from a bronze statuette at Vix in France.

Celtic Warlords

At one time, the Celts dominated the ancient world from Spain to Turkey. They sacked Rome and invaded Greece. Their war chariots devastated all adversaries. But then it all went wrong. They were crushed by the Roman Empire. Their legendary kingdoms in Europe were no more. Only Britain remained a Celtic stronghold. And even there, the Scots, the Welsh and the Irish were forced to fight for their independence against waves of Anglo-Saxons, Vikings, and Anglo-Normans.

This book tells the heroic story of two thousand years of Celtic warfare. From four centuries before Christ to the sixteenth century, it describes the dramatic, hard-fought withdrawal before succeeding military powers and the times when the Celts struck back. It celebrates the persistent struggle of the Celtic-speaking people to retain their independence and their way of life. The occasions of unity and the defeat brought by division.

As a survey, this book serves as an introduction to Celtic military culture and it is hoped will encourage reading in depth to discover further the true character of the Celtic warrior.

The Golden Age

When Alexander the Great asked an envoy of Celtic warriors what they feared most, he expected them to say 'You, my lord.' Instead they replied: 'We fear only that the sky fall and crush us, or the earth open and swallow us, or the sea rise and overwhelm us.' A peace was made, but Alexander was furious. How dare a tribe of insignificant barbarians fear the fantastic more than his realistic military might. Fifty years later, this same confident people devastated Alexander's homeland of Macedonia.

The raiding campaign of 279 BC was an ambitious one for the Celts. Living north of the Danube, they had pillaged Thrace and Macedonia before. But this time they had killed the King of Macedonia, heir to the glory of Alexander and Philip. A fever of adventure gripped the army of raiders. This expedition would be different. Brennus, their chieftain, described the rich townships of Greece. He told his followers of the sacred sanctuaries crammed with gold and silver offerings to the Greek gods. He knew it was a good time to embark on such a campaign. The Macedonian Empire had broken up: the Greeks were a divided people. The Celts mounted their horses and rode south.

Tales of Celtic atrocities in Thessaly gradually convinced many Greeks to forget their wrangling and combine their forces. They chose to confront the Celtic warriors at Thermopylae. Almost exactly two hundred years earlier, a Greek army had fought a bitter last stand at this mountain pass against Persian invaders. The tragic outcome of that gallant defence of their homeland cannot have escaped those Greeks now guarding the narrow mountain roads. In order to prevent the Celts even reaching Thermopylae, Callippus, the Athenian commander of the Greek force, sent a detachment of horsemen to the river Spercheius. There they broke down all the bridges across the fast-running waters.

Unhindered by any major resistance, Brennus had led his warriors along the coast. Having come so far, the Celts would not be denied their booty. That same night as the Greeks camped on the bankside, a group of Celtic raiders crossed the Spercheius lower down, in slower waters. Swimming in the dark, they used their long shields as rafts. Next morning, the Greeks dashed back to Thermopylae while Brennus forced the local population to rebuild the bridges. Needing food and supplies and in no rush to confront the Greek army, the Celts were content to plunder the countryside around Heracleia. They did not even bother to attack the town. But the Greek army mustering at Thermopylae could not be avoided indefinitely. Celtic scouts and Greek deserters warned Brennus that it increased day by day.

On the day of conflict, it was the Greeks who began the battle. At sunrise they advanced quietly and in good order. Because of the rough terrain and the many streams that hurtled down the mountainside, horsemen proved useless and the majority of fighting was on foot. Despite being unarmoured except for their shields, the Celts fought with impressive ferocity. Some drew out from their wounds the spears by which they had been hit and threw them back at the Greeks. As the battle for the pass raged, the Athenian contingent rowed their triremes along the coast of Thermopylae: a coastline slowly silting up and becoming a salt-marsh. They attacked the flank of the Celts with arrows and slingshot. The Celts were hard pressed and many fell into the swamp, sinking beneath the mud. The first day of battle ended with many losses.

After a week's rest, Brennus decided to split his enemy's ranks. He sent horsemen off to the neighbouring region of Aetolia. Their plundering soon reached the ears of the Aetolian warriors camped at Thermopylae. Desperately worried by this assault on their homeland, they immediately left their Greek allies and pursued the Celtic raiders. Brennus now capitalised on the resentment of local Greeks. Fed up with the freebooters on their soil, local herdsmen were happy to see the Celts clear off along the many remote mountain paths. Acting as guides, they led Brennus and his warriors along the same tracks that had allowed the Persians to outflank the Greeks.

Obscured by a morning mist, Celtic warriors suddenly descended on the Greek guards of the mountain pass. Fighting a fierce rear-guard, the majority of the Greeks managed to clamber into Athenian ships and were evacuated from certain disaster. Thermopylae, however, belonged to the Celts and they now pressed on southwards through the mountains. The Celts had been promised the treasures of the Greek temples. But, as they approached the sacred territory of Delphi, it seemed that the very gods of the Greeks had finally rallied to protect their own people. Earthquakes shuddered beneath the raiders. Great rocks tumbled down from Mount

Bronze spearhead found in a burial mound at Snowshill, Gloucestershire, England. Early Bronze Age. The makers of this blade were a proto-Celtic people from central Europe who used their metal-working skills to spread their areas of influence and trade throughout western Europe. Their established routes of conquest were followed by later Celtic communities.

Bronze tanged and socketed spearheads found at Arreton Down, Isle of Wight, England. Early Bronze Age, 1600–1400 BC, now in the British Museum, London. Such keen-bladed weapons gave these warriors a significant advantage over the prehistoric natives of the lands they dominated.

Parnassus and bottomless crags ripped open. Thunder crashed all around. Lightning bolts engulfed individual warriors in heavenly fire. Amidst the chaos, the weird shapes of the ghosts of past Greek heroes arose.

As Delphi came within view, the supernatural forces were joined by the very real strength of a Greek army. To this were added the guerilla assaults of the local Phocians, haunting the snow-covered slopes of Mount Parnassus and pouring arrows and javelins into the Celtic ranks. In the face of all this, the Celtic warriors fought remarkably well. But that night, battered

155

and exhausted, a panic spread through their camp. In the dark, thinking they were being attacked by the Greeks, Celt killed Celt. The next day, Greek reinforcements chased the Celts back to Heracleia. During the long retreat, Brennus, already wounded, took his own life. Harried throughout Thessaly, few of the Celtic raiders returned home.

This then is the legend of the Celtic raid on Greece in 279 BC as recorded by Pausanias, a Greek historian of the second century AD. Analysing his account, one is immediately aware of several discrepancies and clichés. The Celtic raid on Delphi did not fall short of the city and end in a dismal rout. The Roman historian Livy writes several times of the pillage of Delphi while Strabo even suggests that treasure found in the sacred Celtic lake at Toulouse originated from Delphi. Moreover, after satisfying themselves in Greece, the Celts advanced back along the coast to the wealthy port of Byzantium where they crossed into Asia Minor. There they fought as mercenaries for the King of Bithynia. They then advanced further into Turkey and established themselves in territory belonging to the Phrygians, around present-day Ankara. The lands became known as Galatia and the descendants of those Celtic warriors continued to terrorise Asia Minor for over a hundred years, extracting tributes from rulers as far away as Syria.

Pausanias is guilty also of cultural cliché. His vision of the Celts is one of badly-armed, near-naked savages. Of course, he admits, they fight courageously but it is the ferocity of animals. When confronted by the cool discipline of Greek warriors, these yelping, charging wildmen have to resort to the sneaky subterfuge of the barbarian Persians: a stratagem facilitated by Greek traitors. However, even Pausanias has to admit that Brennus—for a barbarian—handled the crossing of the river Spercheius with efficiency and success. But, like all Imperialist correspondents, Pausanias greatly exaggerates the numbers of the raging savages: 200,000 Celts against 25,000 Greeks.

In reality, the Celtic force that invaded Greece was probably little stronger than those raiding parties which frequently crossed the Danube. Along the way, it may have been joined by Greek bandits but it cannot have been more than a few thousand. It would also have been divided up into numerous plundering gangs, scattered across the countryside, not at all suited to a pitched battle. Such warriors were professional raiders and augmented their own arms with a variety of stolen armour and weapons. They were better equipped and of a higher morale than the hastily assembled Greek forces that confronted them. The oldest specimen of interlinked mail yet found has been excavated from a third-century BC Celtic grave in Romania and this was probably developed from protective garments made up of rings threaded onto cords, like netting; a fragment of which has been found in an eighth-century Halstatt grave in Bohemia.

The renowned ferocity of the Celts was not all Greek myth. Livy puts a vivid description of the Galatians into the speech of Gnaeus Manlius Volso, a consul sent to crush the Asian Celts in 189 BC. 'They sing as they advance into battle,' the consul warns his troops, 'they yell and leap in the air, clashing their weapons against their shields. The Greeks and Phrygians are scared by this display, but the Romans are used to such wildness. We have learned that if you can bear up to their first onslaught—that initial charge of blind passion—then their limbs will grow weary with the effort and when their passion subsides, they are overcome by sun, dust, and thirst. And anyway, these Celts we face are of a mixed blood, part Greek. Not the Gauls our forefathers fought.' Despite references to the 'degeneracy' of the Galatians, such a description of the Galatians differs little from other

Bronze Urnfield culture swords from central Europe, Late Bronze Age, 1300–700 BC, now in the British Museum, London. The refined metalwork of the Urnfield culture allowed these Celtic people to embark on adventurous military raids throughout the Mediterranean.

accounts of Celtic and Germanic warriors in Europe. Here again, the ferocity of the Celts is respected, but it is undermined by a lack of discipline and staying power which the Romans can turn to their advantage.

Such a vision of the Celts as ferocious barbarians has endured over the centuries. In the culture war of projected images, the Celts have come off second best to Graeco-Roman propaganda. This is largely because the Celtic peoples of central Europe maintained a culture without writing. The only written accounts we have of them in the thousand years until the fifth century AD are Greek and Latin. We see the Celts through the eyes of their enemies: it is like writing a history of twentieth-century America based on Russian chronicles. Aspects of the Celts were admired, but at best they are represented as noble savages cowed by the might of classical civilization. It is a tradition mirrored in Mediterranean art. When King Attalus I of Pergamum defeated a force of Galatians in around 230 BC, he commemorated his victory with a series of sculpture. In actual fact, the victory was short-lived and the Galatians continued powerful until the next century, but the Pergamene sculptures of defeated Gauls were copied throughout the Greek and Roman world.

The most famous of these images, *The Dying Gaul*, shows a naked Celtic warrior kneeling wounded and subdued on his shield. Only the Celtic torque round his neck suggests the strength that had to be conquered to render this figure pathetic. A Roman marble copy of this sculpture now stands in the Capitoline Museum in Rome to remind us all continually of the defeated Celtic people: supposedly a naked, savage race inevitably overwhelmed by the higher civilization of the Mediterranean. Another sculpture copied from the Pergamum group, now also in Rome, shows again a Celt with characteristic wild hair and moustache (Romans and Greeks never wore moustaches without beards). This time the figure has slain his wife and is stabbing himself in the chest rather than be taken alive. A gallant and brave but eventual loser. Just as the Romans wanted them.

The true standing and culture of the pre-literate Celts can only be deduced from archaelogical discoveries. That they emerge as a recognisable collection of tribes in the first millenium BC is revealed by a series of finds in central Europe. These consist predominantly of bronze and iron metalwork and their famous hill-fort settlements. The people were called *Keltoi* by the Greeks and *Galli* by the Romans. That all these peoples of central Europe were called Celts is because from the fifth century BC onwards they were identified as speaking variations of the same Celtic tongue: an Indo-European language distinct from that of the Germans and the people of the Mediterranean, and now surviving only in the language of the Gaelic Irish and Scots, the Welsh and the Bretons.

The ancient Celts were not a unified people. They did not rule an All-Celtic Empire. Their many hill-forts attest to the fact that Celtic tribes throughout Europe fought and raided against each other as much as they did against the Romans, Greeks and Germans. Nevertheless, archaeological finds maintain that they did share a similar culture as well as a common language. That they did not develop the art of writing does not mean that this culture was any inferior to that of the Romans or Greeks. Technologically and economically, they were equal to their southern neighbours and in peace a thriving trade was continued between them. As an alternative to literature, the Celts developed highly skilled patterns of speech. Their verbal eloquence was valued and respected not only by themselves but also by the Romans and other literate races. Without doubt, however, it was the Celtic lack of written records that contributed to their apparent and real decline in influence and power from the third century BC onwards. Indeed, it is remarkable that the Celts retained any of their potent presence in European history in the face of Latin culture and warfare.

Before the Roman war-machine reached its zenith, the Celts enjoyed a golden age of martial prowess. From a heartland in central Europe, Celtic warriors carried their culture and influence into France, Spain, and Britain. Native tribesmen were unable to resist their long iron swords. By the fifth century BC, the Celts had overcome the Etruscans in northern Italy and settled the land of the river Po. In 390 BC Rome was sacked and several Roman armies humbled. Why were these Celtic warriors so successful? We are told they were fierce fighters. But, above everything else, they were horse-warriors—superb horse-warriors. So renowned were they that they were employed as mercenary cavalry by Greeks and Romans throughout antiquity. Strabo states that the Celts were better horsemen than foot-soldiers and the best mercenary cavalry the Romans ever employed: a recommendation echoed by Caesar, who almost exclusively used Celtic horsemen in his Gallic campaigns.

One of the earliest accounts of Celtic horsemanship to survive is recorded by Xenophon, a Greek historian and cavalry officer of the fourth century BC. In the war between Sparta and Thebes, he records, mercenary troops were sent by Dionysius of Syracuse to aid the Spartans. Xenophon's text makes a distinction between the Celts, Iberians, and horsemen sent, but this seems a later manuscript error and they are all one and the same: Celtic or Celtiberian horse-warriors. Xenophon describes their performance against a Theban army plundering a plain near Corinth. 'Few though they were,' he wrote, 'they were scattered here and there. They charged towards the Thebans, threw their javelins, and then dashed away as the enemy moved towards them, often turning around and throwing more javelins. While pursuing these tactics, they sometimes dismounted for a rest. But if anyone charged upon them while they were resting, they would easily leap onto their horses and retreat. If enemy warriors pursued them far from the Theban army, these horsemen would then turn around and wrack them with their javelins. Thus they manipulated the entire Theban army, compelling it to advance or fall back at their will.' Xenophon is a trustworthy chronicler of military horsemanship as he was himself a cavalry officer and wrote a treatise on the subject. Later, in his account of

Bronze ornamented mace-
heads from southern
Germany, now in the State
Prehistorical Collection,
Munich. Urnfield culture,
late Bronze Age, 1250–750 BC.

Greek wars of the 360s, he gives an example of how horsemen are best used in battle. As a force of Arcadians give way to the Spartans, a group of Celtic horsemen are sent after the fleeing Greeks, cutting down the running foot-soldiers.

Five hundred years later, Pausanias gave an equally vivid and interesting account of Celtic horsemen. 'To each horseman were attached two servants,' he wrote. 'These were themselves skilled riders and each had a horse. When the horse-warriors were engaged in combat, the servants remained behind. However, should a horse fall, then a servant brought a new horse for the warrior to mount. And if the warrior were killed, a servant mounted the horse in his master's place. If both rider and horse were hurt then one servant would ride out to replace him, while another led the wounded warrior back to camp. Thus the Celts kept up their strength throughout a battle.' This description may have been based on earlier chroniclers nearer the time of the Celtic invasion of Greece, or it may have been inspired by contemporary Celtic horsemanship in the second century AD. Whatever its source, it clearly demonstrates a sophisticated use of cavalry. It shows that Celtic horsemen possessed a high social and economic status like that of a medieval knight in relation to his squire and attendants. It suggests that Celtic horsemen fought in military units similar to the medieval 'lance' in which a heavily armed horse-warrior was supported by lighter cavalrymen who were also grooms.

The power and importance of the Celtic horse and rider is dynamically represented in Celtic art. From the great white horses carved into the chalk slopes of southern England to the tiny representations of horse-warriors on Celtic gold coins: both are symbols of dominance over the native population and the means by which it was achieved. As to the horse equipment itself, much ingenuity and craftsmanship was lavished on it. Sophisticated flexible iron horse bits from France have been dated from the fifth to the third centuries BC. In Scotland is preserved a fascinating piece of bronze armour for a horse's head. It is magnificently decorated with swirling patterns and has two curved horns attached to it. As in most societies, it appears that horsemanship was predominantly the preserve of aristocratic, wealthy warriors. An intriguing glimpse of what an ancient Celtic horse-warrior may have looked like in all his finery is provided by a relief on the Gundestrup Cauldron.

Found in a Danish peat-bog and dated to the second century BC, the cauldron depicts Celtic warriors of central Europe. The horsemen wear short, tight-fitting linen tunics. Some may also have worn the knee-length trousers of the foot-soldiers lined up beneath them. On their heads, the horsemen wear iron helmets with elaborate bird and boar crests. According to the head decorations on the Aylesford bucket, some helmets also had huge curled horns. The horsemen wear spurs but, of course, no stirrups. Bridle and harness are decorated with metal plates. Chieftains and noble soldiers probably also wore torques around their necks and shirts of mail.

Bronze antennae-hilted sword. No provenance, but probably from Urnfield groups in central Europe, now in the British Museum, London. Late Bronze Age, 1300–700 BC.

161

On the Gundestrup Cauldron, the horse-warriors are clearly in command, wearing the most expensive arms. Beneath them are foot-soldiers armed only with spears and large rectangular shields. They wear no helmets. At the end of the line of foot-soldiers is a warrior wearing a helmet with boar's head crest. He presumably belongs to the same class as the horse-warriors and is some kind of officer. Behind him are three foot-soldiers blowing on long trumpets shaped like a horse's head. This is the clearest Celtic record we have of the composition of an ancient Celtic army.

The excellence of Celtic horsemanship extended to their famous use of chariots. 'The chariots of the Britons,' wrote Julius Caesar, 'begin the fighting by charging over the battlefield. From them they hurl javelins; although the noise of the wheels and chariot teams are enough to throw any enemy into panic. The charioteers are very skilled. They can drive their teams down very steep slopes without losing control. Some warriors can run along the chariot pole, stand on the yoke and then dart back into the chariot.' Primarily, it seems, Celtic chariots were for display, intended to overawe and enemy in the prelude to battle. Once involved in combat— according to Caesar and Diodorus of Sicily—a chariot team would dismount to fight, using it more as a means of fast retreat or advance rather than as a weapon. However, those noble warriors who rode in a chariot probably did not fight on foot but mounted their horses and fought with their usual retinue of horsemen. The chariot therefore was used only for a spectacular arrival on the battlefield and was driven away when fighting commenced.

That Celtic chariots ever possessed scythes attached to their wheels seems a myth suggested by the addition of these blades to the hubs and yokes of Persian and Syrian chariots. No archaeological evidence has been discovered of scythed wheels. Although, curiously, an early medieval Irish epic tale, featuring the hero Cuchullain, does refer to a war chariot with 'iron sickles, thin blades, hooks and hard spikes. Its stinging nails fastened to the poles and thongs and bows and lines of the chariot, lacerating heads and bones and bodies.' Most Latin references to Celtic chariots mention them only as a speciality of the Britons, but the remains of chariots have been found in Celtic tombs throughout Europe.

Light, elegant two-wheeled chariots, like those that impressed Caesar, developed from heavier, four-wheeled carts found in Celtic tombs dating from before the fifth century BC. The later two-wheeled vehicles were expertly made. Their spoken wooden wheels were bound with iron tyres. The hubs were also bound with iron bands while the wheels were held on the axle by iron linch-pins. The platform was of wood, usually with curved wood or wicker sides. Two horses pulled the chariot, linked by a yoke to a wooden pole. To these basics were added splendidly crafted rein-rings, flexible bridle-bits, and harness fittings, many decorated with red, yellow and blue enamel. The best contemporary illustrations of Celtic chariots occur on Celtic coins. In the British Museum a chariot is depicted on a tiny bronze coin of the Remi tribe in northern France of the first century BC.

Such images were usually based on the chariots appearing on the reverse of Greek coins, the model for most Gallic coinage. But, in this case, the Celtic craftsman has chosen not to reproduce slavishly the realism of Greek art, but to reduce the chariot to its most vital elements. The horses are portrayed as a series of dynamic balls: muscular thighs, flaring nostrils, and plaited mane. The chariot is represented by one wheel and its semi-circular side, while the driver has been abstracted to arms holding a whip, a head, and three curved rays springing from his back, that is, his cloak flying in the wind.

The evolution of Celtic cavalry and chariotry suggests an origin for this culture in the plains of eastern Europe and Russia, the traditional home of chariot burials and excellent horsemanship. Like all Indo-European speaking people, the Celts were originally from the Eurasian steppes. That the Celts did not lose their talent for riding over their centuries of settlement in central Europe is no doubt due to their close contact with the Cimmerian and Scythian tribes that dominated eastern Europe. It is interesting to note, however, that as with the eastern German tribes of later centuries, the Celts did not adopt the deadly horse-archery characteristic of the steppe tribes. Perhaps they, like the Germans, considered it unmanly for a noble horse-warrior to kill an enemy from afar. Celtic mastery of the horse in battle is a

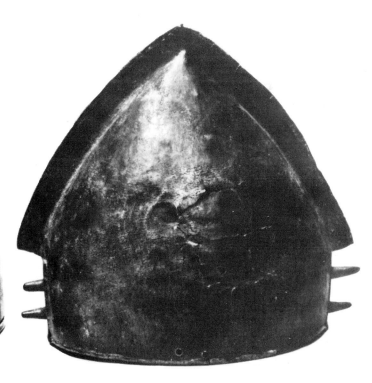

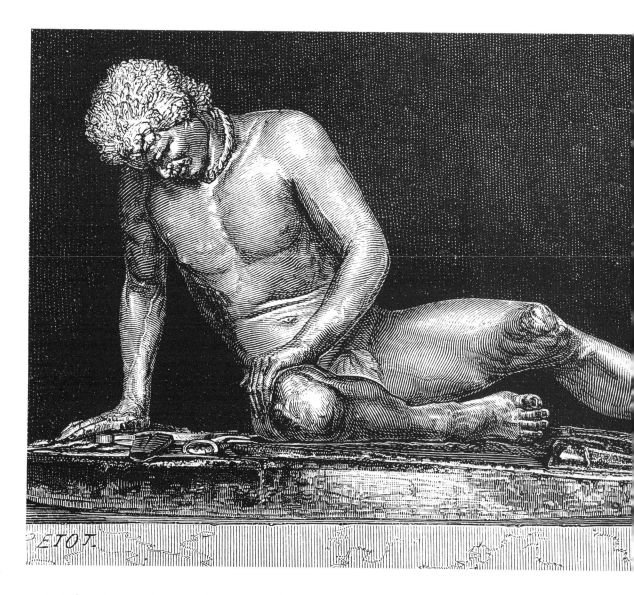

potent thread throughout the history of Celtic warfare, from antiquity to sixteenth-century Ireland. It was this horsemanship that gave the Celts the military power to establish themselves so firmly in European civilization.

For a further fifty years after that raid on Greece, Celtic warriors held absolute control over central Europe, France, Spain and Britain. It was a golden age for the Celts in which their civilization clearly rivalled that of the Greeks and Romans. But then it started to go wrong. Gradually, an ever more confident, ever more united and ambitious Roman Republic made inroads into Celtic territory. The first region to be lost was northern Italy. By 200 BC, after a fierce campaign, virtually all the Italian Celtic tribes had submitted. The Roman war-machine had not only proved superior, but the Romans had even beaten the Celts at their own game. Challenged to single

164

The Dying Gaul, a Roman copy of one of a series of sculptures commissioned by king Attalus I of Pergamum to celebrate his victory over the Celtic Galatians around 230 BC. Reproduced ever since, it has become a symbol of Celtic defeat. This version is an engraving from Duruy's *History of Rome*, 1883.

combat by the chieftain of the Insubres, M. Claudius Marcellus accepted. In the killing ground between the assembled armies, the Roman general rode forward with his shield, spear and sword. Virdomarus, the north Italian Celtic leader, bellowed that he had been born from the waters of the Rhine and would make quick work of the Roman usurper. He dashed in front of his warriors, hurling his spear. But both their spears missed and the chieftains clashed. As each side cheered his leader on, the duel came to a sudden end. A Roman sword slit the Celtic throat and his bent golden torque fell to the ground.

The next Celtic realm to lost control of its own destiny was Spain. Here, many powers converged. Celtic tribesmen had been established in Spain by the fifth century BC. They could not overwhelm the whole native population of this vast country but appear to have made themselves a ruling class over the Iberians in northern and western Spain. Over the years their cultures fused, and ancient historians generally refer to these people as Celtiberians. Along the Mediterranean coast, rivalry between Rome and Carthage over the Spanish ports exploded in war. By the start of the Second Punic War, the Carthaginians controlled most of Spain bar the north-west and Celtiberian mercenaries provided some of their fiercest warriors. However, there were other Celtiberians who resented Carthaginian exploitation of their land and welcomed the intervention of the Romans in Spain. They fought together to rid the land of the Punic invaders. It was an alliance the Celts would regret.

Although their triumphs in the Punic Wars left the Romans with unparalleled power in the Mediterranean, it also left them with many problems. The Celts of northern Italy, ignored during Hannibal's invasion, now rebelled. It took ten years to reconquer them. In Spain, the Celtiberians retained their independence and would not enter into any contract of obedience with the victorious Romans. They had not seen the back of one master merely to submit to another. If the Romans wanted the whole of Spain, they would have to conquer it by arms and not diplomacy. 'This war between the Romans and Celtiberians is called the fiery war,' wrote the contemporary historian Polybius, 'for while wars in Greece or Asia are settled with one or two pitched battles, the battles there dragged on, only brought to a temporary end by the darkness of night. Both sides refused to let their courage flag or their bodies tire.'

The war in Spain was a succession of vicious, indecisive campaigns enduring through most of the second century BC. Roman military incompetence and cruelty was particularly marked and provoked controversy among the politicians in Rome. At the siege of the Celtiberian hill-fort at Pallantia in 136, a Roman commander allowed his supplies to run out. He evacuated his position at night, but, in the hurry, wounded and sick soldiers were left behind. Retreat turned into rout when the Pallantines emerged from their fortress and chased the Romans relentlessly. This general, like many others during the wars, was recalled and deprived of his

165

command. Failure encouraged desperate savagery. Titus Didius set about his suppression of Celtiberian independence with ruthless efficiency. One tribe claimed it had been reduced to banditry because of poverty caused by the war. Didius offered them the lands of a neighbouring Celtic settlement. They agreed, having received similar booty when fighting for the Romans against the Lusitanians. They were invited to the Roman camp where Didius would apportion the land. Once disarmed and inside the stockade, Didius secured the gates and sent in his soldiers to massacre the assembled Celtic men and their families. 'For this,' remarked a disgusted and astonished Roman historian, Appian, 'Didius was actually honoured with a triumph.' Such massacres were matched by numerous military disasters and both served only to stiffen the resistance of the Celtiberians.

'They are no better than bandits,' grumbled the Roman general Scipio Africanus, frustrated yet again by their deception and treachery. 'They may be brave when devastating neighbouring fields, burning villages, and rustling cattle, but are worth nothing in a regular army. They fight with greater confidence in flight than in their weapons.' In truth, the Celtiberians were supreme guerilla warriors. Masters of their own hilly, forested landscape, they exhausted their enemies with relentless skirmishing and raids. Never hanging around long enough for a major confrontation, they humbled the reputation of many Roman generals. After half a century of indecisive conflict, few Roman officers could be found to fill the vacant command posts in Spain. It was a make or break war. But in 134, Publius Cornelius Scipio, the grandson of Scipio Africanus, rose to the challenge. When he arrived in Spain as overall commander, he found a Roman army profoundly demoralized. Discipline was non-existent. Prostitutes and traders, along with fortune-tellers, had to be expelled from the army camps. The soldiers had been reduced to astrology for any signs of a victory. While Scipio retrained his warriors, he surveyed the territory of the Celtiberians. He observed that the town of Numantia in northern, central Spain was a key position and resolved to crush it.

Numantia was a formidable Celtic hill-fort. Set high on a mountain ridge, it was surrounded by dense forest and two fast-flowing rivers cutting through deep ravines. Behind its massive earthen ditches and ramparts, its wood and stone stockade, lay a town with paved streets, blocks of houses, and 8,000 warriors. It had withstood many sieges. In 153, the Romans had employed elephants in their assault. The animals had certainly frightened the Celtic warriors and their horses back into the town, but once the elephants approached the walls the defenders dropped rocks on them. A rock crashed onto the head of one elephant, driving him mad with fury. The great beast let out a terrible scream and turned round, trampling and gouging his own side. The rest of the elephants panicked and soon the Roman army was in tatters as the raging beasts were joined by the Numantines.

Scipio knew well the reputation of Numantia and confined his opening

manoeuvres to plundering the surrounding countryside. His troops harvested the fields, stored what was of immediate use and then burnt everything else. Their activities did not go unheeded and they were constantly ambushed. With losses mounting Scipio decided it was time to deal directly with Numantia. But, rather than attempting to scale its awesome natural and man-made defences, he erected seven forts around the town and linked them with a ditch and palisade. As the Romans laboured, they were joined by neighbouring Celtiberian tribesmen who valued their independence less than the destruction of a powerful rival. Scipio expected the Numantines to disrupt his siege preparations and organised special task forces. If a section of the earthworks was attacked, a red flag should be raised or a fire lit at night so reinforcements could come to their aid. When this first ring was completed another ditch was dug and a palisade built behind it upon an earthern mound eight feet wide and ten feet high. The Numantines, however, still managed to receive provisions from the river Duero. Scipio responded by building a tower each side of the river. To the towers he attached by rope heavy logs studded with knives and spearheads. The tree-trunks bobbed up and down in the furious mountain stream and prevented anyone sailing past. With ballistae and catapults mounted on the towers of his walls, Scipio now waited for starvation to do the rest.

Restless and frustrated, the Numantines led several forays against their besiegers. Emerging out of the night, they clambered over the palisades. They fought with spears and knives, but, above all, they wielded the *falcata*, a heavy cleaver-like cutlass used throughout Spain. According to Livy, the *falcata* could 'cut off arms at the shoulder and sever heads with one chop.' Carthaginian and Greek influences were strong amongst the Celtiberians and it seems likely that, in addition to simple shirts of mail, professional warriors may also have worn horsehair crested helmets and breastplates of strips or scales of metal and leather. They used massive oblong shields and small bucklers, and sometimes a round, concave shield called a *caetra*. In their night attacks, the Numantines probably also used javelins whose three-foot iron blades were tied with rags soaked in pitch. The rags were ignited and the spear flung at an enemy's shield.

These sorties proved unable to break the Roman ring and Rhetogenes, one of the leading Numantine warriors, decided to ride out for help. One cloudy night, with a few comrades and servants, he crossed the no-man's-land between the two earthworks. Carrying a folding scaling-ladder, the Celts scrambled up the first wall and silenced the guards. They then hauled up their horses and dashed along the palisade to freedom. They rode off to the hill-fort of the Arevaci, entreating them as blood relations to come to their aid. The Arevaci feared the retaliation of the Romans and refused. Rhetogenes rode onto a town called Lutia. There, the young men sympathised with the Numantines and prepared to join them. But older citizens doubted the wisdom of this and informed the Romans. Scipio reacted immediately. He surrounded Lutia the next day and demanded to see the

170

Model of a reconstructed Celtic chariot. Such chariots were mainly used for the spectacular arrival of chief warriors on the battlefield: intended to overawe the enemy.

young warriors. Under threat of attack, the young Celts emerged from the town. Scipio seized the 400 and had their hands cut off. That night he was back at Numantia.

As the weeks passed, hunger made the Numantines consider a negotiated surrender. Avarus, their leader, approached Scipio with terms of settlement. But Scipio was not interested. He would accept only absolute capitulation. The Numantines were furious and murdered Avarus and his envoys, thinking they may have made private terms for themselves with the Romans. Within the town, the situation became desperate. With no food at all, some citizens resorted to cannibalism. Finally, famine and disease broke their spirit. They surrendered, but many took their own lives. Appian, the Roman chronicler of these events, was moved by the valiant endurance of the Numantines. He wondered at how 8,000 Celtiberians could only be brought to heel by 60,000 Romans; and not even in a pitched battle, but through the prolonged agony of a siege. The survivors of the conflict were a strange and pathetic sight. 'Their bodies were foul, their hair and nails long, and they were smeared with dirt,' wrote Appian. 'In their eyes there was a fearful expression: an expression of anger, pain, weariness, and the awareness of having eaten human flesh.' Scipio was untouched by the spectacle. Having chosen fifty warriors for his triumph, he sold the rest of the Numantines into slavery and set fire to their town. Their territory was divided among neighbouring tribes, ensuring bitter feuds for years to come. The heartland of Celtiberian resistance had been devastated and 133 BC is generally accepted as the end of the Spanish war.

There were many rebellions, but essentially Celtiberian independence had been smothered by the Roman Empire. That said, there was no extensive Roman colonisation of Spain. Only a few legionary veterans settled around the prosperous coastal towns. Most of the Spanish interior remained under the direct control of Celtiberian warlords, even though they now did homage to Rome. Their culture continued strong, as did their warriors. At the end of the second century BC, when the wandering Germanic tribesmen of the Cimbri turned away from Italy and rode into Spain, it was Celtiberian warbands who confronted them. The Cimbri, allied with the Teutones, had already devastated three Roman armies. In Spain they met warriors of their own kind and after two years of raiding, their rough reception form the Celtiberians forced them back upon Italy. United again with the Teutones, who had received a similarly tough time from the Celts of northern France, they advanced to defeat at the hands of a reformed Roman army in 102.

It has been suggested that the Cimbri and Teutones were not Germans but Celts. Many ancient historians saw little difference between the two barbarian peoples and it is more than likely that this horde consisted of many Celtic freebooters from France and central Europe. Certainly, the plundering movements of these tribes were typical of the intertribal warfare that wracked non-Roman Europe. The immediate effect of these raiders in southern Europe was to stir up other Celtic tribes against the Romans. Only a decade earlier, the lands of Mediterranean Gaul had been annexed by the Romans. Now these tribesmen rebelled. In the Balkans, the Germans had been prevented from advancing any further by the Scordisci of Yugoslavia. Once they rolled back the Teutones, these tribesmen took advantage of Roman weakness and invaded their territory in Greece. Emboldened by their strength against the Cimbri, the Celtiberians again threw off Roman Imperialism. Eventually, after a disastrous start, the Romans took control of the situation, but it was a profound crisis that reminded them of the force of the Celts.

Realising that a successful military career was the best way to political power, the young Julius Caesar placed himself in the forefront of the border wars with the Celts. His first military experience was won against the Celtiberians. He then placed himself in command of the provinces of Cisalpine Gaul (northern Italy) and Provence. The ambition of this one man was to bring the Celtic warlords of France to their knees. But conquests are not won by brilliant leaders alone. As Caesar himself admitted: 'Fortune, which has great influence on affairs generally and especially in war, produces by a slight disturbance of balance important changes in human affairs.' In Gaul, the Roman's good fortune was to be the same that had dogged the independence of the Celtiberian chieftains. In this case, the threat of the Carthaginians was replaced by a German invasion of Gaul, but, as before, those Celtic chieftains who applied to the Romans for help were to find that they had played into the hands of a more ruthless master.

From 65 to 60 BC, a confederation of German tribes known as the Suebi were led by a dynamic warlord called Ariovistus. Recognising his power, Gallic chieftains employed the Suebi to defeat their Celtic rivals, but Ariovistus demanded in payment the land of his allies. Soon, Celtic warlords were asking the Romans to intervene against the German invaders. But the Senate did not like to back losers, entering into friendly relations with Ariovistus. One of the principal architects of this agreement was Caesar. The disarray of the Celtic tribes encouraged Caesar to move his legions westwards from Aquileia to the Rhone. He had planned to build a reputation for himself against the Dacians, but the inter-tribal conflict of the Gauls and their fear of the Germans seemed a golden opportunity. Events came to a head when the Helvetii of Switzerland wished to move out of the

Reverse of a British coin showing a horse and wheel of a chariot. Many Celtic coins were based on Greek or Roman prototypes, but on this one Celtic craftsmanship predominates and the chariot has been abstracted to its powerful essentials. Found in the south of England near Silchester, now in the British Museum, London.

Iron Celtiberian falcata, fourth to first century BC, now in the National Archaelogical Museum, Madrid. The iron scabbard frames of this sword remain to show how it was usually carried in a leather sheath hung from a baldric.

Hilt of an iron and damascened bronze Celtiberian falcata, fourth or third century BC, found near Cordoba, now in the National Archaeological Museum, Madrid. The total length of this sword, characteristic of the Spanish Celts, is 57 cm (22 in).

way of the Suebi and cross through the neighbouring Celtic territory of the Aedui to western France. The Aedui asked Caesar for assistance. With an army of Roman legionaries and Gallic cavalry he complied. The Helvetii gave him a tough time, using their wagon laager as a strong defensive position, but eventually they were subdued. Caesar massacred 6,000 of them and sent the rest back to Switzerland. Such ruthless strength clearly impressed the Celts and they redoubled their requests for his help against Ariovistus.

These facts we know from Caesar's own chronicle of the events. In his account he emphasises the Gallic fear of the Germans, their disunity, and their desperate plea for Roman assistance. The Celts are portrayed as a once mighty nation, now less brave than the Germans and in need of outside warriors to fight their battles. Such a view, of course, makes Caesar appear as the protector of the Gauls, whose entry into their territory is not an invasion, but in response to their repeated invitations. This begs cynicism. Celtic tribes had been determined and daring enough to defeat both Roman and Teutonic armies only fifty years earlier. And yet this is an eye-witness account: why should Caesar write of the Gauls with barely disguised contempt when it is in his own interest to make them seem a mighty, bold people, so as to make his own victory over them even greater? This he does do, but later in his account when describing their noble last-stand at Alesia. Caesar has his cake and eats it. In the meantime, Caesar reneged on Rome's friendship with Ariovistus and threw the Germans back across the Rhine. He now exploited his strong position in Gaul and annexed the land of the Aedui and the Sequani. Their weakness and supposed invitation is his excuse.

The Belgic tribes of northern France saw the error of their Celtic kinsmen and combined to confront Caesar's legions. The Belgae were a notoriously

173

Iberian dagger found near Cordoba, now in the National Archaelogical Museum, Madrid. The blade is 8 cm broad at the base and 19 cm ($7\frac{1}{2}$ in) long.

fierce confederation, hardened by years of border conflict with the Germans. They were part German themselves. On receiving this news, Caesar raised two more legions to add to his six already quartered in Gaul, and rapidly advanced on Belgic territory. His speed surprised the Remi, the nearest of the Belgic tribes, and they immediately caved in, offering him hostages and military intelligence. Caesar dispatched his Aeduan auxiliaries to plunder Belgic land, while he sat tight. The ferocious reputation of the Belgae discouraged Caesar from meeting them in a pitched battle, so he tested their stamina with numerous cavalry skirmishes. The main Roman army remained in a camp protected by marshes and entrenchments. The Belgae tried to entice the Romans into a full-scale confrontation, but Caesar's Gallic horsemen continued to keep them at a distance. As the skirmishing endured, the supplies of the Belgae began to run out. Like most barbarian armies, it appears they did not organise a proper supply train, so unless they gained sufficient food from their plundering their campaigns lacked staying power. When reports of Aeduan raids on their own territory added to their frustration, the Belgic horde retreated with the Gallo-Roman horsemen in hot pursuit. Thus the Belgic confederation was reduced tribe by tribe by a Romano-Gallic force in which the Celtic auxiliaries of Caesar played a vital part. Without doubt, the Celts could be their own worst enemy. And yet, to impose such concepts of a national identity on all Celts is misplaced, for the Belgae were as different and alien to the Celtic tribes to the south of them as they were to the Romans, even though they spoke a similar language. A shared culture never stopped the Romans or Greeks from ripping themselves to pieces.

A Gallic horseman proudly drawn by Alphonse de Neuville on the eve of the Franco-Prussian War. From Guizot's 1870 *L'Histoire de France*, it reflects a nationalistic pride in the Celtic roots of French culture.

174

Throughout the campaigns in Gaul, Diviciacus, chieftain of the Aedui, was constantly at Caesar's side, urging his Celtic confederates to submit peacefully to Roman domination. As the Roman war-machine rolled on, more and more Gallic warriors joined its legions. So far, in his march through Gaul, Caesar had had good excuses for his agression: the invitations of the Aedui, the attacks of the Belgae. But in 57 BC he sent a detachment under the command of a subordinate to the lands of the Atlantic coast. Their subsequent reduction of this peaceful area was unprovoked and patently revealed Caesar's intention to conquer the whole of Gaul. The next year, recovering from the shock of Roman occupation, the Celts of Brittany, led by the Veneti, took up arms. The Veneti were a maritime power, deriving much wealth from their shipping of British tin from Cornwall to Gallic traders. Their strongholds stood on headlands or islands in tidal estuaries which were cut off from the land for most of the time by the sea.

As the Romans approached the Atlantic coast, the Veneti strengthened their fleet and gathered fellow tribesmen, including many warriors from Britain. Caesar was secure in his excuse this time: the quelling of a tribe who had already submitted and the punishment of a terrorist kidnapping of Roman envoys. He again employed the assistance of friendly Celts who supplied him with Gallic ships built along the Loire. With his land forces he tried to capture the Breton strongholds. Using all the ingenuity of Roman siegecraft, he had huge dykes constructed to the island fortresses. But no sooner had these been completed than the defenders simply evacuated into awaiting ships and moved to another fortress. The lack of natural harbours and the rough ocean weather made Roman assaults by sea difficult. The considerable advantage of knowing the local seaways lay very much with the Veneti. But, as elsewhere, there was no shortage of Celts ready to assist the Romans.

Local Gauls presented the Romans with a rapidly-built fleet which cannot have been very different from that of the Veneti. 'They have flat bottoms.' wrote Caesar of the Gallic ships, 'which enables them to sail in shallow coastal water. Their high bows and sterns protect them from heavy seas and violent storms, as do their strong hulls made entirely from oak. The cross-timbers—beams a foot wide—are secured with iron nails as thick as a man's thumb. Their anchors are secured with chains not ropes, while their sails are made of raw hide or thin leather, so as to stand up to the violent Atlantic winds.'

When Caesar's fleet was ready, he confronted the Veneti in the Loire estuary. As the boats crashed into each other, legionaries and their Gallic allies watched the battle from the cliff-tops. The Romans in the boats—all land soldiers—were at a loss as to how to tackle the Gallic seamen. They improvised with scythes attached to long poles and used them to cut the Celtic rigging. With their sails fluttering uselessly and apparently no oars to assist them, the Celtic ships soon lost control. Several Roman boats then locked onto individual Celtic ships and boarded them. The Celtic sailors were overwhelmed by the armoured Romans and the fleet of the Veneti broke up. A fall in the wind prevented many from escaping and the majority of the Gallic force was captured. This seems a particularly miserable defeat for the Celts. A fleet of expert seamen shattered by landlubber Romans making do with scythes. Caesar's account doesn't ring true. It seems more likely that the fighting on the Roman side was conducted wholly by Gallic auxiliaries used to sailing. Whatever the actual details, this defeat of 56 BC was a crushing one for the Atlantic Gauls. Caesar had many of his prisoners executed and the rest sold as slaves to his legionaries and allied Celtic tribes.

Over the next couple of years, Caesar suppressed local rebellions in northern Gaul. An expedition was made to Britain on the pretext of quelling those tribes who had assisted the Veneti. At this time, south-east England had been overrun by Belgic immigrants. Their warlord Cassivellaunus was gradually extending his control over the native Celts. Again, it seemed as if Celtic dissension might aid Caesar, but on this occasion the Celts put up a stiff guerilla resistance and Britain remained an independent Celtic realm. Throughout his campaigns so far, Caesar had restricted himself to securing a ring of conquests around central Gaul without venturing into the interior. But as he consolidated this position, perhaps preparing for that next stage of his conquest, the Celts sprang out at Caesar with a vengeance.

The Celtic warriors were led by an Arvernian chieftain called Vercingetorix. A powerful personality, he instilled a strict discipline into his warrior retinue. Neighbouring tribes were asked to submit hostages to him and disaffection was punished with death. No waverers would be tolerated. Equally determined, Caesar plunged straight into the heartland of the Arverni. Initially successful, he was savaged by the Gauls at the hill-fort of Gergovia. At one stage, the Romans were surprised by the arrival of their own Gallic cavalry, for these auxiliaries were clad identically to other Celtic horsemen. According to Caesar, friendly troops usually 'left their right shoulders uncovered as an agreed sign.' With this defeat, Caesar's aura of invincibility was broken and Celtic tribes throughout Gaul joined the independence fighters. Even the Aedui threw in their lot with Vercingetorix. Caesar was shaken. He had to reinforce his cavalry with German horsemen.

The final confrontation was enacted at the siege of Alesia in 52 BC. It may have been that Vercingetorix hoped to hold Caesar outside the hill-fort until Gallic reinforcements arrived to crush the Romans between both forces. But Caesar employed Roman siegecraft to good effect and protected his rear with a second chain of earthworks. When the massive relief army arrived, the Roman force was strained to its limits but eventually fought them off. Alesia was then starved into surrender. With the capture of Vercingetorix, Gallic independence broke up and was eventually snuffed out. An overall peace was made and Caesar withdrew the majority of his troops from Gaul. Not only was the siege of Alesia the last major battle of the Gallic wars, it

Bronze anthropoid hilt of an iron sword from Salon in France, around the second century BC, now in the British Museum, London.

symbolized the extinction of Celtic liberty in Europe. Rebellions would come and go, but never again would a warlord independent of Rome rule a continental Celtic realm. Celtic independence remained only in Britain and Ireland.

This then is the story of Celtic defeat in Europe, an account based on the legends of Greece and Rome. For the chronicles describing these events are frequently the work of Romans and Greeks writing hundreds of years after the action they recount. Pausanias compiled his account of the Celtic invasion of Greece, the fullest we have, almost 500 years afterwards. It may have been based on earlier records but essentially it is a classical view of the Celts as inferior barbarians cowed by the civilization of Greece. Appian is a more realistic historian, cynical of his Empire's disgraceful conduct in Spain, but still his accounts of the Celtiberians are 400 years later and laced with hackneyed descriptions of noble but vanquished Celts. Caesar's memoirs are, of course, based on eye-witness experience but a calculating bias ensures that the inherent weakness of the Gauls is emphasised to excuse Roman intervention. This is the Mediterranean myth of the Celts. From now on, as Britain fights to maintain itself as the last Celtic bastion, we begin to see the struggle of the Celts through their own culture, through their own legends.

The Battle for Britain

Cuchulainn—ancient Irish warlord, Hound of Ulster—slept for three days. The men of Connacht had pushed a cattle raid deep into his territory. Short of warriors, he had had to restrain himself to brief, surprise attacks on the plunderers. Many of the enemy had been killed, but he was wounded and exhausted. In the delirium of his pain and fatigue, a heavenly phantom advised him to rest. After three days, Cuchulainn awoke. An excitement possessed him. Blood quickly pulsed through his body and his face turned red. He felt good. He felt fit for a feast, fit for fighting. He instructed a retainer to prepare his chariot.

The charioteer donned a tunic of supple stitched deers' leather. He wore an iron battle-cap and daubed a circle of yellow on his forehead to distinguish him from his master. Over his two horses he secured a harness studded with iron plates, spikes and barbs. Every surface of the chariot bristled with blades. Every inch had a ripping hook or a tearing nail. Finally the driver cast a protecting spell over the chariot and grabbed his iron-shod goad.

With the chariot ready, Cuchulainn prepared himself for battle. His followers strapped on his armour. A tunic of waxed skin plates, several layers thick, was tied securely with rope so it would not burst at the onset of his fighting rage. Over this, the warlord wore a thick, wide battle-belt of tanned leather from the choicest hides of his prize cattle. This covered him from his waist to his armpits. Around his stomach was a silk apron embroidered with gold, over which a battle apron of the darkest leather was

180

Roman horseman riding over northern British warriors. Detail of a second-century dedication slab from the eastern end of the Antonine Wall where it meets the Firth of Forth.

strapped. On his head was placed a crested helmet. Within the iron, his long battle cry echoed so as to cause the demons of the air and glen to scream back. Cuchulainn now reached for his weapons: an ivory hilted sword, several short swords, throwing and stabbing spears, a five-pronged trident, and a dark red curved shield. He held a shield stout enough to keep a wild boar in its hollow, with a rim so razor sharp that it could cut a single hair— a shield as deadly as his spear or sword.

Loaded and reinforced with all his battle gear, Cuchulainn began to work himself up into a fighting fury. A spasm tore through his body. It distorted him, made him a monstrous thing. Every bone and organ shook like a tree in a storm. His insides made a twist within his skin. His shins filled with the

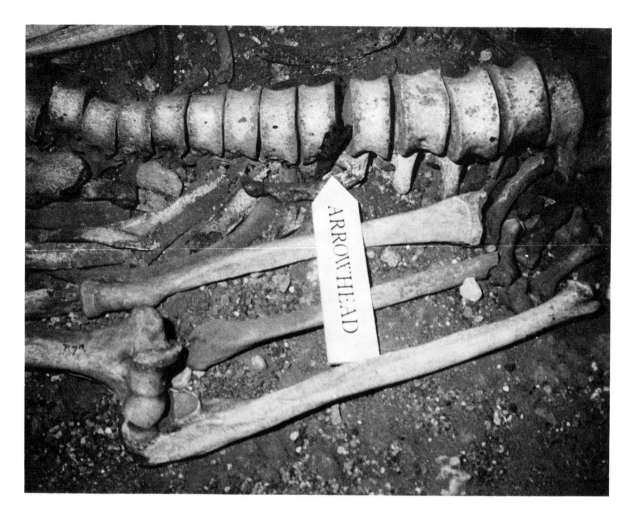

ARROWHEAD

bulging muscles of his calves. Balls of sinew as big as a warrior's fist pumped up his body. His head swelled and throbbed. Veins dilated. Suddenly, he gulped one eye deep into his head so not even a wild crane could pull it out from his skull. The skin of his cheeks then peeled back from his jaws to reveal the gristle and bone of his gullet. His jaws crashed together and foam oozed up out of his throat. His hair twisted and bristled like a red thornbush. Dazzling lights and thick black smoke rose above his head. A broad halo emerged over his brow. With the transformation completed, Cuchulainn leaped onto his chariot. He had no fear. He was a mad man. A hero.

Cuchulainn burst upon his enemies like a thunder storm. His chariot wheeled furiously in the mud: its iron tyres dug up earth tracks high enough for a fortress rampart. At the end of the day, the warlord had slain hundreds of his enemies. Nothing was too great or too insignificant to be spared Cuchulainn's blades. Chieftains and warriors, horses and dogs, women and children. All were slaughtered.

Roman ballista bolt-head lodged in the spine of a Celtic warrior. A victim of the assault on Maiden Castle by Vespasian in AD 43, his bones now lie in the Dorset County Museum, Dorchester.

The next morning, Cuchulainn arose to display himself to his followers. He paraded in front of his women and poets, reassuring them that his hideous battle form was now replaced by a handsome image, a youthful man whose hair was brown at its roots, rising through blood-red to a golden yellow at its tips. This hair fell luxuriantly in three coils over his shoulders. Around him was wrapped a purple cloak secured with a brooch of light gold and silver. Beneath he wore a fretted silk tunic and a warrior's apron of deep red royal silk. To his back was attached a gold-rimmed shield with five discs on a crimson background. From his belt hung a sword with a guard of ivory and gold. In his hands, he gripped nineteen human heads and shook them at his followers. All his people crowded forward to marvel at the hero.

This account of the Ulster warlord Cuchulainn comes from the *Tain Bo Cuailnge*: The Cattle Raid on Cuailnge. An Irish epic tale dated to the eighth century AD, it is believed to be centuries older, perhaps even pre-Christian. It is a terrifying vision of the ritual and glamour of violence. To his followers, this savage executioner is a hero of supernatural stature. For him, psychopathic aggression is physical strength. The epic tale is our deepest insight to the psychology of Celtic warriors: the importance of display and parade; the working up into a fighting rage. The belief in a hero's halo was widespread throughout the Celtic world and sometimes even exploited by non-Celtic adversaries. According to L. Annaeus Florus, around 130 AD, a Roman centurion struck terror into the Moesi by carrying a flaming brazier on his helmet. Other supernatural qualities ascribed to Celtic warriors in battle are elaborated in the Tain. Cuchulainn repeatedly leaps high in the air to come down heavily on his opponent's shield. Strange weapons are referred to, such as the legendary *gae bolga*, 'the lightning spear': a javelin that enters the body as one blade, but then bursts open into thirty barbs. Only by cutting away chunks of flesh could it be removed. The Tain also demonstrates that though there might be a sense of respect, even fair play, between two renowned warriors meeting in single combat, all other living things in a battle zone were vulnerable to brutal slaughter.

That such an epic tale as the Tain could be woven out of a relatively minor cattle raid should not be surprising. This is the stuff of Celtic warfare. Major campaigns against foreign enemies involving armies of united tribes—thousands of warriors strong—were rare. Most conflict was centred around the pursuit and prevention of plundering expeditions by a martial elite of warlords and their retainers, separate from the great body of tribesmen. However, to look upon the Tain as a war fought over the mere material gain of a few prize cattle is to miss the point. The rustling of cattle from an opponent's territory was simply an excuse to test that rival's strength. If a warlord allowed such a challenge to his authority without retaliation, he risked losing the respect of his own warriors as well as that of outsiders. This revelation of weakness could encourage an outsider to embark on a full-scale campaign in the belief that the victim was vulnerable. It might even encourage a coup d'état within the clan as a more able warlord arose to avenge the insult to his people. For Celtic warlords—as with all men of authority—a lack of respect means an actual lack of power. A cattle raid, therefore, had to be met with forceful retribution, otherwise worse could follow.

This endemic intertribal combat may have produced a hardened, highly experienced class of professional fighters but it also lay Celtic realms open to determined, strategically-wise foreigners. In 43 AD, the Atrebates of southern Britain fell back before the dominant Catuvellauni. The chieftain of the Atrebates asked the Romans for help and the Roman invasion began. Roman conquests in Britain were aided by further tribal dissension as well as friendly Celtic auxiliaries hoping for favours in the new regime. In just over fifty years, all England and most of Wales and Scotland had been absorbed into the Latin Empire. It is little wonder then that Gildas, a northern Briton, complained around 540 AD that 'It has always been true of this people that we are weak in beating off the weapons of the outside enemy but strong in fighting amongst each other.'

The plight of the Celts under Roman rule was not one of only abject slavery or bold revolts. More often than not, in the Roman provinces of Spain, France and Britain, Celtic chieftains continued to rule over their tribes and territory. These warlords might have Latin names, live in Roman villas, and fight alongside legionary armies, but they were still Celts. In a curious way, Roman Imperialism did not totally destroy Celtic power. It may even have strengthened it. Celtic warlords accepted the material luxuries, military sophistication, Christian religion and Latin literature of the Romans, but they still remained in control of their own land. Indeed, the military back-up of the Romans enabled them to keep their land free of Germanic raiders. Celtic chieftains would have to make tribute to their Imperial overlords, but essentially it was they who were there in the field to defend their own territory against all marauders. They maintained the Roman way of life because they liked it. But, beneath it all, it was Celtic tribal loyalties and customs that kept the ordinary man in order, not Roman citizenship. Thus, the Roman Empire in western Europe can be seen not so much as a defeated Celtic people under the yoke of Roman Imperialism, but a confederation of tribes held together by Romanized Celtic warlords paying feudal homage to a supreme, but absentee landlord.

This state of affairs became obvious when the agents of the Emperor, with their mercenary retinues, cleared out of Britain at the beginning of the fifth century to concentrate on the defence of Italy. Britain did not suddenly revert to a purely Celtic realm, naked without its Roman defenders. Of course, the warlords of Britain could always do with continental reinforcements, but they could also see to their own defence. For centuries they had dealt with Irish and German pirates and the plundering of the Picts. This was nothing new, but typical of old scores yet to be settled. Around the hard core of their retainers, the British warlords did as the Romans did. They supplemented their forces with mercenary

Northern ramparts and ditches of Maiden Castle, an Iron Age hillfort of the first century BC, near Dorchester, south-west Britain. The massive earth ramparts were originally surmounted by a wood palisade.

recruits from the coastal tribes of Germany. In the early years of the fifth century, it was Vortigern—overlord of the Romano-Celts in south-eastern England—who invited three shiploads of Saxons to assist him. Just like other provincial governors of Roman Europe, he settled these warriors along his borders as a buffer against raiders.

The Celts relished their inheritance of *romanitas*. In future centuries, they wrote about the Roman Empire as a time of greatness. In the Welsh saga of the *Mabinogion*—a fourteenth-century manuscript whose stories are much older—a Roman warlord Magnus Maximus is idealised. 'The ruler Maxen was Emperor of Rome,' it recalls, 'and he was handsomer and wiser and better suited to be an Emperor than any of his predecessors.' A senior officer in the Romano-Celtic army of Britain—probably stationed at Caerleon in South Wales—Magnus was a Spaniard, perhaps a Celtiberian. It may even have been the dream of establishing a truly Romano-Celtic Empire that excited his ambition. Whatever the spur, he was acclaimed Emperor by his followers in 383 AD. Leading a Romano-Celtic band of adventurers across

185

the Channel, he defeated the Emperor Gratian in Gaul and proclaimed himself lord of all the ancient Celtic realms of Britain, France and Spain. He had a precedent: a century earlier the Roman general Postumus had similarly ruled an *imperium Galliarum* for ten years. In events such as this, it is difficult to know whether to see Magnus as a rebel against the Roman Emperor, or simply one of many warlords pushing a little far the flexibility of Romano-Celtic command of western Europe. According to the tale in the *Mabinogion*, it is British warriors who storm the very walls of Rome and give the city to Magnus. Many of these Celtic warriors then settled in Brittany. In truth, Magnus never made it to Rome but was assassinated in Aquileia in 388. In Britain his legend lived on and many Welsh kings claimed him as their forefather.

Magnus was one of several Romano-Celtic warlords who assumed political as well as military control over their territories. Carausis was a Gaul from the coast of Belgium. Because of his profound sea-knowledge, he was given a naval command in the Channel with orders to crush the North Sea pirates. It was the late third century and Saxon raids on Britain and France were increasingly ferocious. From his bases in northern Gaul, Carausis successfully countered the freebooters; almost too successfully, for he was suspected of waiting for the priates to carry out their raids and only then, on their way back, would he pounce and confiscate their treasure for himself. But, before he could be arrested, he sailed to Britain and there proclaimed himself Emperor. Wild seas and the expertise of his Celtic fleet prevented the Romans from any immediate action.

For ten years Carausis prospered and built a string of forts along the coast of eastern England. These were massive fortifications, earthworks and stone walls, and intended as much to repel Roman invaders as Saxon raiders. But the Imperial Caesar Constantius was determined to end this Celtic break-

186

away state and set about blockading the Gaul's main continental base at Boulogne. While the French base succumbed to siege, Carausis was murdered by one of his retainers and in 296 a final assault brought eastern Britain back under direct Imperial control. During his reign, Carausis had done much to strengthen Britain's naval defences. In the next century, these were further improved by the introduction of camouflaged scouting craft. According to Vegetius, these boats had their sails and rigging dyed blue. With the sailors similarly disguised in blue tunics and painted faces, the craft acted as an early warning system against pirates.

The break-up of the western Roman Empire was not so much a sudden onslaught of Barbarian savages upon the Imperial frontiers as a gradual realisation among Germanic auxiliaries that it was they who wielded real power in the Romano-Celtic provinces. They arose from their frontier military settlements to assume political control. This happened in Britain. The Romano-Celtic overlord Vortigern had many problems. Irish and Pict raiders impinged on British land in Wales and northern England. Within Romano-British ranks, Vortigern contended with Ambrosius for the Emperorship of Britain. Added to this was the fear that Ambrosius might capitalise on continental Catholic fears of heresy in Britain and bring a Romano-Gallic army across the Channel. To strengthen his military position within and without, Vortigern invited Saxon mercenaries into his country and settled them on the island of Thanet in the river Thames. Initially they were welcome and proved useful, but the situation deteriorated.

Bronze helmet crest in the form of a wild boar. Found at Gaer Fawr, Welshpool, Powys, north-east Wales, now in the National Museum of Wales, Cardiff.

Hengist, the leading Saxon chieftain, was a shrewd warlord. He exploited Vortigern's weaknesses, his bitter rivalry with Ambrosius and other magnates. 'We are few,' he told the British overlord, 'but if you wish, we can send home for more men to fight for you and your people.' Across the Channel came nineteen more ships packed with Saxon adventurers. As Hengist amassed his warriors, tensions grew between them and the British. The Saxons complained that their monthly payments were inadequate. If they were to continue propping up Vortigern, then he would have to give them more supplies. Vortigern granted them land in Kent, but soon the Saxons were plundering further afield. By the 440s, the Saxons had openly turned against their paymasters and stormed several British towns.

'In this devastation by the pagans,' wrote the Romano-British Gildas, 'there was no burial to be had except in the ruins of houses or the bellies of beasts and birds.' But, as the Saxons consolidated their conquests in Kent and East Anglia, the British gathered their native troops and counter-attacked. Surprised perhaps by the strength of the Britons, the Saxons were shaken in two battles by Vortimer, son of Vortigern. On the banks of the river Darenth and again at Horseford or Aylesford, the Saxons suffered heavy losses. Horsa, one of their chieftains, was killed. In a third battle, according to the British chronicler Nennius, 'in the open country by the Inscribed Stone on the shore of the Gallic Sea, the barbarians were beaten. They fled to their ships and many were drowned as they clambered aboard them like women.' The Saxons fell back on their stronghold at Thanet where they were besieged three times.

Sending for reinforcements from the continent, the Saxons eventually broke out of Thanet and the war against the British ebbed and flowed, with the ordinary peasant Briton suffering most from the plundering of both sides. Upon the death of Vortimer, the Saxons resorted to negotiations to better their position. The ageing Vortigern could not maintain a state of war against the Saxons indefinitely without the political and financial support of all Britain's warlords. This was not forthcoming and old rivalries forced Vortigern to accept Hengist's suggestions of an armistice. The two sides agreed to meet, unarmed, to conclude a treaty. But Hengist ordered his men to hide their daggers in their boots. As the noblemen gathered, the Saxons sprang their trap and slaughtered 300 leading British aristocrats. Vortigern was spared his life on condition he handed over Essex and Sussex to the Germans. With Hengist now riding high, many more German warriors sailed to Britain. Over the next fifty years, Saxons, Angles and Jutes secured their hold over southern and eastern England.

The Anglo-Saxon wars in Britain were part of a broader conflict across north-west Europe. In France, the Romano-Gauls had long protected the coasts of Brittany against Saxon pirates with their river-mouth forts. During the fifth century, the Romano-Gallic warlords were joined by British immigrants. These were the cream of Romano-British aristocracy from Cornwall: some fleeing before Irish raiders, others hoping for closer

Iron spear heads from Llyn Cerrig Bach, Anglesey, north-west Wales, now in the National Museum of Wales, Cardiff.

associations with Imperial Roman culture. Allied sometimes with the Franks, it was this Romano-Gallo-British amalgam—the Bretons—who fought most ferociously against the Saxons of the North Sea and the Goths settled in central France. And then, in later centuries, when the Franks had established themselves as a separate kingdom, it was the Bretons who maintained Brittany as an independent Celtic state against the Merovingian and Carolingian dynasties. In the sixth century, Gregory of Tours records their damaging raids on the cities of Nantes and Rennes. Two hundred years later, the Bretons were still resisting and Charlemagne had to devote an entire campaign to their conquest. Even then this proved fragile and during his reign they were in constant rebellion.

Back in the fifth century, the security of the Bretons depended on the efforts of independent Romano-Gallic warlords like Ecdicius. With only his

'The Free Northern Britons surprising the Roman Wall between the Tyne and the Solway'. An engraving from a drawing by William B. Scott in the *Illustrated London News* of 1843. Chosen by the newspaper from a national competition of cartoons by history painters, it reveals a burgeoning British interest in their Celtic past.

private income to fund him and no assistance from other magnates, Ecdicius gathered together a small force of horse-warriors. He then set about ambushing the local plundering expeditions of the Goths of central France. So hard did the Gallic horsemen harass the Goth raiders that, according to the account of Sidonius, the bandits had no time to retrieve their dead. Instead, the raiders preferred to cut the heads off their comrades so that at least Ecdicius would not know how many Goths he had slain by the hairstyle of the corpses. When this private band of man-hunters relieved the town of Clermont from Goth bandits, Ecdicius was received rapturously by the townspeople. 'What tears and rejoicing greeted you!' wrote Sidonius, brother-in-law of Ecdicius. 'Some townspeople kissed away the dust that covered you. Others caught hold of your bridle, thick with blood and foam. When you wished to take off your helmet, the clamouring citizens unclasped the bands of iron. Some entangled themselves in the straps of your greaves. Some counted the dents along the edges of your sword blunted by slaughter. While others fingered the holes made by blade and point amid your shirt of mail. You bore all these stupidities of your welcome with good grace.'

These Gallic guerilla actions took place around 471 AD and may well have been inspired by stories of the successful resistance of the Britons led by Ambrosius Aurelianus. Ten years earlier, Ambrosius had commanded a similar task force of horse-warriors against the Saxons. Raised from the Romano-Celtic estates of the West Country and Wales, these swift-moving, professional, largely aristocratic horsemen hammered the Saxons in a series of confrontations. The Celtic warriors called each other *Combrogi*, 'fellow countrymen', a word probably derived from the Latin *cives*. It is the origin of *Cymry* and *Cumbri*, names still used by the Welsh and north-west British to denote their Celtic separateness from the Germanic English. For a hundred years, the British and Saxons fought their border wars. At sometime during the conflict Ambrosius died. He was replaced by an equally competent warlord, a major Romano-British land-owner and expert leader of horsemen: Arthur.

All we truly know about Arthur is a list of twelve battles he fought throughout Britain. Many of these have been traced to sites in northern England and may have been conflicts not with the Germans but against the Celtic warrior tribes of Scotland who were as much of a problem. Arthur probably commanded a flexible force of aristocratic young horse-warriors, riding from Roman fort to Roman fort across Celtic Britain. His stronghold in southern Wales may well have been Caerleon: a stalwart Roman fortress of earthwork ramparts and timber-laced stone walls, long in use after the last foreign Imperial garrison left. Was this Camelot? The British chronicler Nennius states that 'Arthur carried the image of the Holy Mary, the Everlasting Virgin, on his shield,' while the Welsh Annals declare that he wore 'the Cross of Our Lord Jesus Christ across his shoulders.' It seems likely that the Christian Romano-Britons considered their campaign against the pagan Saxons a Crusade and carried out their warfare with an outraged fervour: avenging the sight of their churches burnt and sacked by the Germanic barbarians.

At the end of the fifth century, Arthur's string of victories culminated in the battle of Badon Hill. Nennius describes the hot water that bubbled up at the natural springs of Badon as one of the wonders of Britain. It therefore seems likely that Badon was the Roman settlement of Bath and the battle took place on the hills overlooking its villas, temples, and hot-water bathing complex. It was a city worth fighting for and it was probably the Saxons of Wessex and Sussex who wished to claim it. The general conflict may have been a siege as Gildas describes it, for the Welsh Annals say that the battle lasted three days and three nights. But, in the event, it seems to have been decided by a grand cavalry charge in which Arthur slaughtered many of the enemy. So decisive was this victory that no other major battles are mentioned for two decades. Arthur appears to have successfully blocked the Saxon advance into the West Country.

Germanic desire proved relentless, however, and around 515 the British defence of the West was shattered. In the battle of Camlann, perhaps a siege of Caerleon, Arthur was killed. Nevertheless, Celtic resistance remained persistent enough to deny the Saxons part of the West Country for a further fifty years and most of Wales and Cornwall for centuries. In the wake of Germanic supremacy in Europe, it could be said that this part of Britain was the last independent Romano-Celtic province. But its defenders were not Roman legionaries but Celtic horsemen. It was these Celtic warriors who called the Saxons 'barbari' and preserved Latin culture. This is Arthur's success and the origin of his legend as the supreme Christian knight.

The conversion of the Anglo-Saxons to Christianity at the end of the sixth century brought no immediate softening of hostilities, but provided yet more causes for conflict. Around 603, St Augustine, the first Archbishop of Saxon Canterbury, set about bringing the British of the Celtic Church into line with Catholicism, altering their customs and rites in accordance with the Church of Rome. The Britons referred to their holy men and received the following advice. 'If Augustine is a humble man and rises as you approach, then he is a man of God and you may follow him. If he does not, but despises you, then you may despise him.' In the taut atmosphere of a synod on the Welsh border, the Celts approached Augustine. The saint remained in his seat. The Britons refused to join with the Catholic Church. Augustine was furious and threatened them with a prophecy that if they refused to worship as the English did, then they would fall victim to English swords.

Augustine's promise was fulfilled at the battle of Chester. As the Northumbrians prepared to assault the Romano-British city, their Anglo-Saxon warlord observed a large group of Celtic monks from a monastery in Bangor. The holy men had gathered to offer up prayers for the British warriors. They were guaranteed protection by a Welsh warrior called

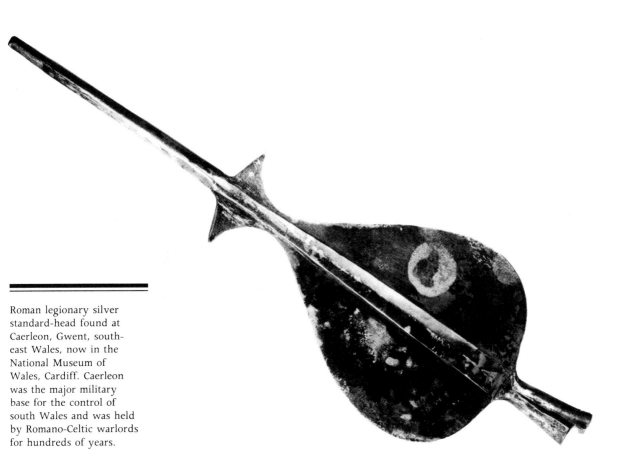

Roman legionary silver standard-head found at Caerleon, Gwent, south-east Wales, now in the National Museum of Wales, Cardiff. Caerleon was the major military base for the control of south Wales and was held by Romano-Celtic warlords for hundreds of years.

Brocmail. Their Celtic chants irritated the Northumbrians beyond endurance. 'Though they carry no arms,' the Angle warlord announced, 'those monks, by crying to their God, still fight against us.' Full of the righteous fury of a Catholic charging down a heretic, the Anglo-Saxons spurred on their horses and ploughed into the crowded monks. Brocmail had already fled at the sight of the onrushing Northumbrians. Twelve hundred holy men were massacred. 'Thus was fulfilled the prediction of the holy bishop Augustine,' concludes the Anglo-Saxon chronicler Bede.

Campaigns against the Anglo-Saxons in the sixth and seventh centuries were not the only battles the British had to fight. Romano-British warlords along the coasts of the West Country, Wales, and north-west England had to contend with the sea-borne raids of the Irish. These Celtic adventurers were called *Scotti*: a name probably derived from the Irish verb 'to plunder'. The kidnapping of St. Patrick was the most notable of their hit-and-run exploits. In earlier centuries, Roman forts had been raised against the pirates and much Roman bullion has been uncovered in Ireland. Some of it includes elaborate metalwork that has been chopped up, suggesting a booty divided to pay a marauding gang. However, it is just as likely that the Irish were such a problem that the Romans gave them silver and gold as a protection payment to keep them away from their coasts. Perhaps also Irish warbands were hired by Romano-British warlords as auxiliaries.

In later centuries, the Irish were settled on coastal territories by the British as a buffer against further raids. But, like the Saxons in eastern England, they exploited the agreement and expanded their authority over British land until in the fifth century there were strong Irish realms in south-west and north-west Wales. Some British legends report that Romano-British warlords were able to expel the Scots from Anglesey and Pembrokeshire at around the same time as Arthur battled against the Saxons. But Irish presence remained potent in south Wales for some time. In Llangors Lake at Brecon, there are remains of a lake-dwelling similar to those found throughout Ireland. These crannogs were fortified settlements built upon man-made islands in the middle of swamps and lakes. Nowhere, however, was the influence of the Irish stronger than in Scotland. There they settled the craggy north-west peninsulas and imposed their language and culture on the native Britons and Picts until the very land bore their name.

Facsimile drawings of Romano-Celtic soldiers illustrated in the fifth-century manuscript of Prudentius in the National Library of Paris. Warriors such as these defended the Romano-Celtic provinces of western Europe against the Germanic barbarians.

The Irish, like all coastal Celts, were excellent seamen. The Irish Sea was not so much a barrier as a great lake across which trading and raiding was effectively carried. Indeed, before the establishment of a road system in Britain, communications were more efficient across water than across land. The most characteristic Celtic boat is the curach. In its simplest form, this consists of a wicker framework over which hides are stretched. That these were sea-worthy is attested by Gildas, who writes of the Picts and Scots using them to raid southern Britain. Fleets of fifty curachs are also mentioned by ancient annals. In 891, the *Anglo-Saxon Chronicle* states that 'three Irishmen came to King Alfred in a boat without a rudder, from Ireland whence they had made their way secretly because they wished for the love of God to be in a foreign land. It was made of two and a half hides and they carried with them food for seven days. And after seven days they came to land in Cornwall and went immediately to King Alfred.' Such accounts probably exaggerate the fragility of Celtic voyages, as most Celtic sea-going boats would have been more sophisticated craft like those of the Bretons, furnished with sails and steering oars. For raiding, the Irish may also have employed narrow-beamed, oak clinker-built rowing boats similar to those of the North Sea pirates.

The Irish settlement in north west Scotland was called Dalriada. At first, it was ruled by kings living in northern Ireland, but then in the fifth century Ulster warlords sailed over to Dalriada and founded an independent line of Scots kings. These Irish warriors spoke Gaelic. Dunadd became a principal stronghold. Sited on a rocky outcrop and surrounded by bogland, it recalled the hillforts of ancient times. It consisted of an inner citadel, almost a keep, in which lived the Dalriadic warlords with their retainers. Outside, in a series of courtyards formed by the rock, sheltered the labourers, peasants and animals. For centuries, the Scots and Picts battled over the highlands, often employing Britons from the lowlands against each other. The Picts were an ancient race. They spoke a language combining Celtic with an older aboriginal tongue. Their name derives from the Latin meaning 'the painted people' and refers to their custom of daubing or tattooing their bodies with woad, a blue plant dye. By the fifth century, however, this custom appears to have been neglected. The Picts were the descendants of those Caledonian tribes defeated by the Roman governor Agricola at Mons Graupius in the first century. Nevertheless, after this show of strength, the Picts remained untamed enough to prevent the Romans ever again subduing them and the province of Britain never extended into highland Scotland. Their realm survived uncontested until the arrival of the Scots.

Though their literature remains largely indecipherable, there are many Pict remains demonstrating their military might. Inscribed stone monuments show that, like all Celts, they were keen horsemen. Battlefield encounters began with horse-warriors raining javelins upon each other. They then closed in with long stout lances. Foot-soldiers fought with spears

and square shields and one cross-slab in Angus suggests they countered horsemen with a kind of phalanx in which warriors holding pikes stood behind shield-carriers. Some of the formidable fortresses of the Picts have been uncovered. Early in their history, they probably made use of brochs, circular towers of dry stone-work. These brochs lacked any apertures apart from the entrance and were probably solely defensive refuges against Irish pirates and Romano-British slave-raiders who could not afford a long siege. More aggressive are the major Pict fortresses with timber-laced stone walls. These possessed defendable parapets and were centres of power from which raids could be led. Curiously, these stone and timber forts resulted in the vitrification of their silica-rich foundations. For whenever they were set alight by enemies the intense heat produced by the draught channels of the timber constructions turned the stone to glass. As these forts were used over and over again, the vitrified walls no doubt formed a strong part of the defences.

The border conflicts between the Picts and the Scots of Dalriada raged for centuries. Sometimes it was the Picts who were victorious. In 740, the *Annals of Ulster* shudder at a devastating attack on Dalriada by Angus mac Fergus. He captured their strongholds and drowned a Scots warlord in triumphant execution, forcing others to row back to Ireland. But then, under a fresh generation of warriors, the Scots struck back deep into Pictland. Hoping to exploit the dissension amongst the highland Celts, the Angles of north-east England pushed up past the Britons of Strathclyde. At Nechtansmere in 685, they were met by a Pict army and so soundly thrashed that the Angles never again ventured into the Celtic highlands. Eventually, however, it was the Scots who triumphed: partly in peace, partly in war. Ever since Angus mac Fergus plunged into Dalriada, it seems that Pictish noblemen were active in Scots circles and vice versa. There were Dalriadic kings with Pictish names in the late eighth century and through such aristocratic contacts and intermarriage, the Scots King Kenneth mac Alpin succeeded to the Pictish throne around 843. No doubt it was not wholly peaceful and one tradition maintains that it was a bloody coup d'état in which the Scots wiped out Pict warbands weakened by fighting against the Vikings. Whatever the truth, from this time on the two people were united, with the Scots predominating and the Picts becoming a people of the past.

In lowland Scotland, between the rambling remains of the Antonine Wall and Hadrian's Wall, lived the Britons of Strathclyde. In former times, when the Roman walls were patrolled by warriors from all over Europe, the native Celts were allowed to rule their own territory. Only partly subdued by the Romans, it was hoped they would absorb Pict raids before they touched any Roman citizens. With the breakdown of a centralized Roman military command, the defence of the walls and their many forts was assumed by tribal warlords who had served with the Romans and ruled the surrounding territory. Rival families controlled opposite ends of the walls. At the

beginning of the fifth century, it was a Romano-British warlord Coel Hen—
the Old King Cole of the nursery rhymes—who dominated the eastern end
of the walls down to York. Combating the ever more ambitious raids of the
Picts, Coel Hen followed Roman practice and employed Anglian warriors
from across the North Sea. Their military settlements probably pre-date
those of the Saxons. From this time on, it was not so much the crumbling
Roman walls that divided enemies, but the natural bulwark of the Pennines
that separated the major western and eastern powers of northern Britain. By
the late sixth century, the Angles had asserted themselves and challenged
the north-eastern Britons. One clash in this struggle is recorded in a Welsh
poem by Aneirin. It recalls the heroes of the Gododdin.

The Romano-British Gododdin controlled the eastern end of the Antonine
Wall and their power-base may have been at Edinburgh. At the time of
Aneirin's poem, around 600, they were ruled by a warlord called
Mynydogg. For a year before his campaign against the Angles, Mynydogg
feasted his followers on mead and wine. This probably refers to a time of
preparation and recruitment. For, throughout the poem, the fighting
services of his men are said to be given in payment for mead. The mead and
wine that a warrior received from his lord becomes a symbol of the material
bond and obligation between the two. 'The war-band of Mynydogg, famous
in battle,' proclaims Aneirin, 'they paid for their mead-feast with their
lives.' Later the poet recalls the action of one particular hero: 'In return for
mead in the hall and drink of wine, he hurled his spears between the
armies.' It may be that these warriors even drank a draught of mead before
battle, both to fortify themselves for conflict and to signify their loyalty to
their lord. Such drinking, however, may have affected their performance in
battle, as one translation suggests:

> To Nudd, the son of Ceido.
> I loved him who fell at the onset of battle,
> The result of mead in the hall and the beverage of wine.
> I loved him who blasphemed not upon the blade
> Before he was slain by Uffin.
> I loved to praise him who fed the bloodstains.
> He used his sword with animation.
> We do not speak of heroism before the Gododdin
> Without praising the son of Ceido, as one of the heroes
> of conflict.

Aneirin's poem is not a narrative but a series of panegyrics praising
individual heroes who fell at the battle of Cattraeth in Yorkshire. Mynydogg assembled three hundred horse-warriors from noble families throughout northern Britain and rode them south against the Angles of Northumbria. Some of the horsemen may even have been professional freelance
warriors from the highlands and north Wales. They were well equipped,
mail-clad, and wore gold torques around their necks. Wealthy as they were,

T·B·J·

each warrior would have been accompanied by several retainers on spare horses. The entire war-band was therefore considerably larger than the three hundred named warriors. Whatever its strength, however, it came to grief at the battle of Cattraeth. Virtually all the three hundred leading Celtic warriors were slaughtered.

With the Gododdin shattered, north-east England and lowland Scotland were absorbed into Northumbria. Across the Pennines, however, the Britons of Cumbria and Strathclyde proved stubborn, and bitterly contested any further conquests. Around Carlisle, in the territory of the Rheged, arose an Arthur of the north-west. Urien was a warlord of the sixth century and is featured in a cycle of Welsh poems. They tell of his fight against the Angles and culminate with his death in battle. The poet Llywarch Hen imagines himself a warrior carrying away Urien's head:

> A head I carry at my side:
> The head of Urien, a generous leader of his war-band.
> On his white chest now, a black raven is perched.
> A head I carry in my cloak:
> The head of Urien, generous ruler of his court.
> On his white chest ravens glut themselves.
> A head I carry in my hand:
> He was the shepherd of Erechwydd
> Noble in heart, a spender of spears.
> A head I carry on my thigh:
> He was a shield to his land, a wheel in battle.
> He was a pillar in conflict, a snare for the enemy.
> A head I carry from the land of Pennog:
> Far reaching was his fighting.
> The head of Urien, eloquent and famous.
> A head I carry from my arm:
> He made a pile of biers out of the Angles of Bernicia.
> A head I carry in my hand:
> The head of the pillar of Britain has been toppled.
> My arm has become numb.
> My breast beats.
> My heart has broken.
> I carry the head of one that supported me.
> A head I carry on my shoulder.
> Disgrace did not overawe me.
> But woe to my hand for striking the head off my lord.

The Celtic warrior had cut the head off his slain lord so as to prevent the Angles from mutilating it.

Carlisle was a Roman city near the western end of Hadrian's Wall. It remained an important centre of Romano-British culture and would have been a focus for much Celtic resistance. A seventh-century poem announ-

Part of a hoard of gold-alloy torques discovered in Ipswich, south-east England, now in the British Museum, London. Torques may have been the badge of the free-born male and were still being worn by Celtic warlords in the sixth century, according to Aneirin.

200

ced that its original walls were still standing and it boasted a marvellous Roman fountain. But this was recorded by an Anglo-Saxon and it was in this century that Anglo-Saxon expansion reached its zenith, impinging yet further on the border lands. Their conquests were strengthened by a series of dynamic kings and there was little hope of a Celtic counter-attack. But still the Britons held on. In the eighth century remained the Celtic realms of Cornwall, Wales, Cumbria, Strathclyde, and Scotland. Ireland was untouched. The battle for Britain had ended in stale-mate. Half the country belonged to Germanic warlords, the rest to Celtic warlords. That the Anglo-Saxons possessed the most desirable lowland territory is significant of their

upper hand in the conflict and aided the development of their culture. A lowland cereal-based output is capable of supporting a strong church, a money economy, and centralised royal authority. Amongst the herdsmen of the Celtic highlands—where a man's wealth was measured in cattle and sheep—tribal institutions prevailed. Had the Celts already lost the economic war? It certainly seems that the Anglo-Saxons were content with their conquests and under Offa, King of Mercia, the boundary with Wales was given physical permanence. He erected a great length of earthworks, longer than Hadrian's Wall, stretching from Treuddyn to Chepstow. Not so much a fortified wall, Offa's Dyke was intended more as a boundary marker and a discouragement to cattle raiders.

Behind the ramparts of Offa's Dyke, the warlords of Wales coalesced into several regions of power. In the north, incorporating the fecund island of Anglesey, emerged the land of Gwynedd, the dominant realm of Wales. Sometimes it allied with the Mercians against the Northumbrians and a victory of the Gwynedd warlord Cadwallon was remembered as one of the Three Pollutions of the Severn as the blood of the defeated Saxons reddened

Bronze penannular brooch, originally enamelled, sixth or seventh century. From Navan Fort, County Armagh, northern Ireland, now in the British Museum, London.

the river from source to estuary. In the north-east, on the border with Mercia, was Powys. Since the Saxons had conquered the land around Chester in the seventh century, direct links between the Welsh and the Welsh-speaking Britons of Cumbria had been broken. In the south of Wales there were several principalities, such as Gwent in the south-east and Dyfed in Pembroke, whose aristocratic families claimed descent from Magnus Maximus.

By the end of the eighth century, the British status quo was shaken. The Anglo-Saxon enjoyment of their conquests was cut short by the arrival of another sea-borne invader. This was a force that would absorb half the Anglo-Saxon kingdoms, ravage the Celtic realms of Britain, and achieve what no other continental power had so far managed: the invasion of Ireland. These warriors were the Vikings.

The Northern Menace

At first the pagan Vikings came as raiders. The *Annals of Ulster* chart their progress:

AD **793.** Devastation of all the islands of Britain by gentiles.

AD **794.** The burning of Rathlin by the gentiles. The Isle of Skye was pillaged and wasted.

AD **797.** The burning of the Isle of Man by gentiles. They carried off plunder from the district. The shrine of Dochonna was broken into and other great devastations were committed by them in Ireland and Scotland.

AD **801.** Iona was burnt by gentiles.

AD **805.** The monastic community of Iona slain by gentiles, that is, sixty eight monks.

AD **806.** The gentiles burn Inishmurray and invade Roscommon.

AD **810.** A slaughter of the gentiles by the men of Antrim and Down.

AD **811.** A slaughter of the men of Connemara by the gentiles. A slaughter of the gentiles by the men of Owles and Munster.

AD **812.** A slaughter of the men of Owles by the gentiles in which was slain the king of Owles.

AD **820.** Plundering of Howth by the gentiles. A great booty of women being taken.

AD **822.** The gentiles invade Bangor in County Down.

AD **823.** The plundering of Bangor by the Foreigners and the destruction of its places of worship. The relics of Comghall were shaken out of their shrine.

Etgal, monk of the Isle of Skellig, was carried off by the gentiles and died soon after of hunger and thirst.

AD **824.** Plundering of Downpatrick by the gentiles. Burning of Moville and its places of worship. A victory of the men of Antrim and Down over the gentiles in which a great many were slain. A victory over the men of Leinster by gentiles. The martyrdom of Blamacc, son of Flann, by gentiles.

AD **826.** The plundering and burning of Lusk. The destruction of Derry to Ochta-Ugan. The destruction of the camp of the Leinstermen by gentiles, where Conall, son of Cuchongult, king of the Forthuatha, and others innumerable, were slain. A royal meeting at Birr between the king of Munster and the high king of all Ireland.

. . . and so on, from raids on coastal islands to full-scale invasions of the mainland. With each new assault, the Vikings gained more knowledge of their victims' homeland and plunged ever deeper. When their longboats could travel no further along rivers or lochs, the sea-wolves took to horses to ravage the land. Ireland was the last Celtic realm to be invaded from the continent, the last to reel before the iron blades of professional warrior-pirates. As the Vikings grew bolder, so did the size of their expeditions, until vast invading armies—intent on permanent settlement—sailed into the Irish Sea.

'There were countless sea-vomitings of ships and boats,' wrote the chronicler of the Wars of the Gaedhil (the Irish) with the Gaill (the Vikings) in the early tenth century. 'Not one harbour or landing-port or fortress in all of Munster was without fleets of Danes and pirates. There came the fleet of Oiberd and the fleet of Oduinn, and the fleets of Griffin, Snuatgar, Lagmann, Erolf, Sitriuc, Buidnin, Birndin, Liagrislach, Toirberdach, Eoan Barun, Milid Buu, Suimin, Suainin, and lastly the fleet of the Inghen Ruaidh. All the evil Ireland had so far suffered was as nothing compared to the evil inflicted by these men. The whole of Munster was plundered. They built fortresses and landing-ports all over Ireland. They made spoil-land and sword-land. They ravaged Ireland's churches and sanctuaries and destroyed her reliquaries and books. They killed Ireland's kings and chieftains and champion warriors. They enslaved our blooming, lively women, taking them over the broad green sea.

Elsewhere in Celtic Britain, the Vikings proved equally rapacious. Scandinavian interest was first shown in the northern islands of Scotland. 'Picts and Gaelic priests were the original inhabitants of these islands,' wrote a Norwegian chronicler. 'The Picts were scarcely more than pygmies in stature, labouring strongly in the morning and evening at building their towns, but at midday they lost all their strength and out of sheer terror hid themselves in subterranean dwellings.' These dwellings may well have been the windowless stone brochs erected by Scottish natives against sea-raiders. By 800, the Norse were in firm control of the Orkneys and Shetland and sailing southwards. Though mainland Scotland was assaulted, it was largely

the Western Isles down to Man that were favoured as Viking haunts. Not all Norwegian settlement was violent and many Scandinavian farmer-fishermen lived alongside the native Celts. But, that said, it was the Vikings that dominated the Irish Sea. From their island bases, the Norse and the Danes ravaged north-west Britain and Wales. The Britons of Strathclyde and Cumbria were defeated and the Vikings tried to link their conquests around York to their bases in Ireland. On the north-west coast of England, a fierce combination of Norse and Irish set up the Viking kingdom of Galloway. In Wales, however, the Vikings bit off more than they could chew. Their raids in the 790s were repelled with heavy losses.

At this time, Wales was an assembly of little Celtic kingdoms, but it had the good fortune to be ruled by several effective warlords. In the north swelled the kingdom of Gwynedd. Its royal line claimed connections with Urien of Rheged and Coel Hen. Around the middle of the ninth century arose a warrior-lord the equal of his forefathers: Rhodri Mawr—Rhodri the Great. In 855 the Vikings made a powerful attack on the island of Anglesey, long admired as the granary of north Wales. This was to be no pushover. Rhodri responded with strength and assurance and threw the pirates out of Anglesey in a great battle. The Danish chieftain was killed. So momentus was this victory—the first major reversal of the Vikings in Britain—that it was recorded in the *Annals of Ulster* and celebrated in the court of the

'They made spoil-land and sword-land. They enslaved our blooming, lively women, taking them over the broad green sea.' A plundering expedition by Vikings. From Ward Lock's *Illustrated History of the World*, 1885.

Carolingians, also hard pressed by the Danes. Later though, Rhodri was savaged by the Vikings and fled to Ireland.

Welsh resistance remained defiant and there were no Scandinavian settlements in Wales. In the tenth century, Rhodri's grandson, Hywel Dda, maintained the family's dominance of Wales and emerged as its overlord. But, unlike Rhodri, Hywel was not anti-English. He knew strength derived from alliance. Thus, by doing homage to the Saxon Athelstan he kept his borderlands free of conflict and could concentrate on protecting the coastland. So successful was the Welsh defence that its general effect was to encourage the Vikings to swerve southwards and northwards to raid England. Asserting his authority over south Wales, Hywel then co-operated fully with the Anglo-Saxons of Wessex in their battle against the pagan pirates. This Christian unity seems to have worked, shielding south-west Britain from the terrible invasions that afflicted eastern England.

Scotland was similarly blessed with stout defenders and, though its islands fell completely to the Vikings, the majority of the Scottish mainland remained free of Scandinavian colonies. It was Ireland, the Celtic realm that had remained for so long free of invasion, that suffered the most. As in Anglo-Saxon England, the Viking presence was long and influential. They erected fortifications at river mouths and these developed into towns. Dublin, Waterford, Wexford, Cork and Limerick were the key Scandinavian settlements. From them, expeditions were led by land and water into the hinterland. Up until the ninth century, Ireland was roughly divided into four great spheres of power. Ulster in the north, Connacht in the west, Leinster in the east, and Munster in the south. Dominance shifted between these regions and men owed allegiances to a variety of clans within the provinces. The arrival of the ambitious Scandinavians added another element to the internecine warfare of the Celts. Irishmen allied with Danes to fight against Irishmen allied with the Norse. Throughout, the Vikings were regarded as the superior warriors. 'Not one of the champions of the Irish was able to deliver us from the tyranny of the foreign hordes,' wrote the Irish chronicler of the *Wars of the Gaedhil with the Gaill*. 'This is because of the excellence of the foreigners' polished, treble-plaited, heavy coats of mail, their hard, strong swords, their well-rivetted long spears, and because of the greatness of their bravery and ferocity and their hunger for the pure, sweet grassland of Ireland.'

That the Vikings did not conquer the whole of Ireland was probably due to the fact that it suited them just fine to extract tribute from the inland Irish through regular raiding campaigns rather than permanent conquest. The Vikings preferred to consolidate their hold on the coastline and build up their fortified ports, frequently using them to launch raids on England and Wales. Danish and Norwegian rivalry in Ireland was intense in the ninth and tenth centuries and often the only way the Irish could damage at least one of their conquerors. But, here again, as with the Romans, the Viking invasion was far from a complete disaster for the Celts. Irish

Viking broad-bladed battle axe of the tenth or eleventh century. The Irish are said to have adopted the axe as a primary weapon after the Scandinavian settlement.

warlords still ruled the interior and they gained much materially from the coastal settlements. Not least was a great improvement in trading and first-hand experience of Viking military craft. It was from this time that the Irish are supposed to have adopted the axe as a principal weapon. This was also adopted by the Scots and may have led to the development of the long-hafted battle-axe. In Ireland, Viking swords were copied, bought, and stolen. There were Irish resistance movements and one in 902 succeeded in throwing the Norse out of Dublin. But the Vikings returned and the Irish seemed content to use them in their own political intrigues, just as the Vikings employed the Irish against each other and against the kingdoms of Britain. Typical of this Celto-Scandinavian warfare was the battle of

Celtic raiders fall upon Greek guards at the pass of Thermopylae, 279 BC.

Celtiberian chieftain and warrior break through Roman siege-works surrounding their hill-fort. Numantia, northern Spain, 133 BC.

A Belgic chariot and horse-warrior harass Roman legionaries during Caesar's expedition to Britain. South-east England, 54 BC.

A sailing ship of the Veneti is boarded by Romano–Gallic auxiliaries from the Aedui. Morbihan Bay, the Atlantic coast of France, 56 BC.

Scots highlanders in a schiltron hold their ground against English knight Sir William Deyncourt. The battle of Bannockburn, 1314.

Edward Bruce attacked by Anglo-Irish warriors at Moiry Pass in Armagh, Ulster, 1315.

Pict horse-warriors chase an isolated Scot into a deserted broch. Dalriada, north-west Scotland, seventh century.

Murchad, the son of Brian Boru, High King of all Ireland, tackles a Viking at the battle of Clontarf, Dublin, 1014.

A Norman Breton landlord is ambushed by Welsh herdsmen. The Marches of northern Wales, late eleventh century.

Dermot MacMurrogh, warlord of Leinster, is backed up by a Norman Welsh knight and a Welsh archer. Ossory, south-east Ireland, 1169.

Cuchulainn of Ulster rides his legendary scythed chariot against Connacht raiders, described in the pre-Christian Irish saga *Tain Bo Cuailnge*.

An Arthurian Romano-British landlord clashes with a Saxon raider on the outskirts of Bath, Britain, in the late fifth century.

Owain Glyndwr and his Welsh followers are attacked by the English garrison of Caernarfon Castle, 1401.

James IV, King of Scotland, is cut down by English billmen, and longbowmen. The battle of Flodden, Northumberland, 1513.

A galloglas and his kern attendants await their Irish lord, Shane O'Neill, during his visit to the court of Elizabeth I, London, 1562.

Irish warriors of the army of Hugh O'Neill charge upon the English at the battle of the Yellow Ford, Ulster, 1598.

Clontarf at the beginning of the eleventh century—a campaign that made Brian Boru's reputation as one of the greatest warlords of Ireland.

As chieftain of the Dal Cais at the mouth of the river Shannon, Brian Boru established himself through a series of guerilla attacks on the Scandinavian settlers around Limerick. 'However small the injury he might be able to do to the foreigners,' wrote the chronicler of the Gaedhil, 'Brian preferred it to peace. From the forests and wastelands, he emerged to plunder and kill the foreigners. If he did not destroy them during the day, then he was sure to do so at night. Moreover, his followers set up temporary dwellings rather than settled camps as they moved through the woods and solitudes laying waste to northern Munster. The foreigners of Tratraighe raised great fortified banks around their settlements and prepared to conquer northern Munster. But Brian killed many of the foreigners of the garrison. Great were the hardships that Brian endured: bad food and bad bedding on the wet, knotty roots of his own country. It is said that the foreigners killed many of his followers so that only 15 survived.' But, with reinforcements from other Irish warlords, Brian continued his hammering of the Vikings.

At the age of 26, Brian Boru stormed the Viking city of Limerick. The campaign had begun with the battle of Sulcoit. There, the Vikings had assembled a force of Danes and Irish. The chronicler of the *Wars of the Gaedhil* says that these Irishmen were brought under tribute, and when some Munster chieftains refused to join the Danes they were murdered. In truth, many warlords of Munster were probably only too willing to side with the powerful Vikings against the upstart Brian. The Dal Cais and Brian's fellow chieftains were none too keen to confront the superior force in open conflict, but with the arrival of a renowned Irish champion, a freelance warrior with a hundred retainers all armed and bearing large shields, they decided to fight a 'manly battle on the open part of the plain.' The Vikings were mounted and wore mail. It is likely that Brian and his chief retainers were also so armed. This was, after all, a battle between professional warriors. Numbers were not large and few unarmoured peasants would have been involved. From sunrise to midday, the warriors struck and slaughtered each other. Finally, it was the Vikings who broke and were chased by the Dal Cais 'who killed and beheaded from that time until evening.'

Brian and his warriors overran Limerick, slaughtering and plundering. 'They carried off the foreigners' jewels and their best property: their saddles beautiful and foreign; their gold and silver; their satins and silken cloth, pleasing and variegated, both scarlet and green. They carried away their soft, youthful girls, their silk-clad women, and their large and well-formed boys. The fortress and the good town they reduced to a cloud of smoke and red fire. All the captives were assembled. Every one fit for war was killed and every one else enslaved.' It seems that many of the Danish women were then ritually raped. Brian's sack of Limerick, though barbaric, showed him as a man of power. He now consolidated his success. Local

Giant silver bossed Irish-Viking penannular brooch, late ninth or tenth century. Thought to be from Waterford, now in the British Museum, London. Almost a foot long, such ostentatiously large cloak pins were an Irish-Viking fashion.

opposing chieftains were slain. His warriors kept fit and fed by numerous cattle raids. He built a fleet upon the Shannon and sailed as far as Loch Ree where he plundered the territory of Connacht and Meath. With his hold over Munster secure, Brian then moved against the men of Leinster.

The lords of Leinster appreciated the benefits of Viking colonies on their land and allied with the Vikings of Dublin against Brian. The two forces met around the year 1000 and the men of Munster were triumphant. Dublin was ransacked and the Vikings forced to submit to Brian's authority. They were allowed back into their settlement on acknowledging Brian's overlordship and no doubt ensuring he received a goodly part of their trading profits. As lord of Munster, Leinster and the Viking communities, Brian's ambitions were now focused on the north. Mustering a war-band of Irish and Danes, he rode to Tara and challenged the high king of Ireland to battle. For centuries, the clans of the north had been the dominant force in Ireland.

The O'Neills had ruled Ulster and from them descended a line of high kings of all Ireland. Now, around the year 1002, Mael Sechnaill, lord of Meath and holder of the high kingship, sent requests to all the warlords of Ulster and Connacht to counter the usurper. But the head of the northern O'Neills recognised true power and replied to Mael Sechnaill: 'Whoever possesses Tara, let them defend its freedom. It is not right that one man should risk his life against the Dal Cais in defence of sovereignty for another man.'

Mael Sechnaill offered his crown to the O'Neills. 'I would rather give thee hostages,' he told them, 'than be dependent on Brian Boru.' But they refused. Even the men of Meath, Mael Sechnaill's homeland, would not take up arms to defend him. The overawed north chose a relatively peaceful submission rather than war. At Tara, Brian assumed the high kingship of all Ireland. He followed this up with raids on all the northern estates of Ulster and Connacht, principally to obtain noble hostages but also to fill his coffers and strengthen his army. As was becoming obvious, Brian Boru's conquest of Ireland was not a nationalistic battle of Celt against Viking. It was a personal struggle to supreme power in which Irishmen fought Irishmen with the Vikings helping as auxiliaries and hoping to hang on to their colonies. Despite regular rebellions, Brian ruled as overlord of Ireland for over a decade. He even sent expeditions across the Irish Sea to levy tributes from the Scots, Welsh and Anglo-Saxons.

As Brian grew older, so his grip on Ireland weakened. In 1013, the lords of Leinster and the Vikings of Dublin threw off their allegiance to him. After a series of probing raids on each other, Brian and his son led warriors from Munster and Connacht to Dublin and set siege to it. A lack of provisions forced Brian to retire, but in the next year he returned. Plundering through Leinster, he closed on Dublin. The Vikings sent messengers throughout their territories and across the Irish Sea to gather an army. On receiving the call, fleets of adventurers set sail. The Viking warlords of Orkney and the Isle of Man arrived with their followers. They were joined by Danish and Celtic Cumbrian mercenaries. The Irishmen of north Leinster were ready for the fight, but those of the south lost their nerve and backed away.

Brian's army relied principally on the men of Munster and the Dal Cais, the heartland of his support. There were some warriors from Connacht and Meath, but Brian knew these were not to be trusted, being likely to desert in the first onslaught. There were no men from Ulster. At the last moment, Brian was joined by a group of Vikings from the Isle of Man who had hastily converted to Christianity to assure him of their support. As his forces gathered beneath striped banners of red, green and yellow, Brian sent horsemen forward to plunder all round Dublin. He thanked the warlords who had brought him men and cursed those who did not.

To stop the Irish plundering, the men of Dublin rode out from their settlement, crossed the rivers Liffey and Tolka, and set upon Brian's warriors to the north of the town in an area called Clontarf. The Vikings were brilliantly garbed in mail-coats of iron decorated with brass rings. According to the chronicler of the *Wars of the Gaedhil*, these mail-coats were triple layered. The Danes opened the fighting with their bows and arrows. 'Poisoned arrows, covered in the blood of dragons, toads, and the water-snakes of hell.' They then set to with dark spears and stout swords. According to the chronicler of the *Wars of the Gaedhil*, the Irish warriors of Brian did not wear mail, but fought in long, many-coloured tunics with shields with bronze bosses. The chieftains wore crested helmets studded with precious stones, and sound like heroes from the *Tain Bo Cuailnge*. In reality, both sides probably looked very similar, clad in mail with swords, axes and spears. Brian placed his most dependable warriors of the Dal Cais in the forefront of the battle, led by his son Murchad. Behind these were the other men of Munster. On their flanks were Brian's Viking mercenaries and Irish auxiliaries. The men of Meath, led by Mael Sechnaill, were said to have made secret contact with the Vikings of Dublin and sat out the battle behind earthworks. The Vikings of Dublin, led by the warlord Sitric, and the warriors of Leinster, led by Maelmore, placed their Danish and Norwegian auxiliaries in the front of their army. The Vikings from Orkney were led by Sigurd and those from Man by Brodar.

'The two sides made a furious, smashing onset on each other. And there arose a frightful screaming and fluttering above their heads as birds and demons awaited their prey.' At first, Brian's flank of Irish auxiliaries clashed with the Leinstermen. The Leinstermen broke and were chased off by mail-clad horsemen. It was then that the Dal Cais and the Vikings hacked at each other with axe and sword. A strong wind hampered the throwing of spears. From their walls and towers, the inhabitants of Dublin watched the men of Connacht play a key role in bloodying the Vikings. But, above all, the battle of Clontarf was a combat of individuals. A fight in which warriors could make a name for themselves: become heroes recalled in epic poems. As the crowds surged—men flailing their limbs and weapons excited by fear and violence—the sagas isolated individual combats.

Murchad, son of Brian, wielded two swords, one in his right hand and one in his left: he had equal power in striking. Enraged by the Viking slaughter of his fellow Dal Cais, Murchad rushed at the Danes like a furious ox. He made a hero's breach in the enemy. Fifty foreigners fell to his right hand; fifty foreigners fell to his left hand. One blow was sufficient to kill them. Neither shield nor mail stood up to his blades. Murchad's retainers followed their master into the heart of the battle. Such feats cowed the Vikings: many turned and ran. But Sigurd of Orkney refused to flee. Slaughtering and mutilating the Dal Cais, no point or blade seemed to harm the Norseman. Murchad rushed upon him and dealt with his right hand a crushing blow to his neck that cut the mail and straps of his helmet. Murchad then brought his left-hand sword down on the Viking's exposed neck, felling the warrior with these two blows.

Still Murchad was not finished. Fury urged his body on and he charged

Welsh iron stirrups found in Glamorgan, south Wales, late tenth century, now in the National Museum of Wales, Cardiff. Welsh warriors kept Wales relatively free of the Vikings.

212

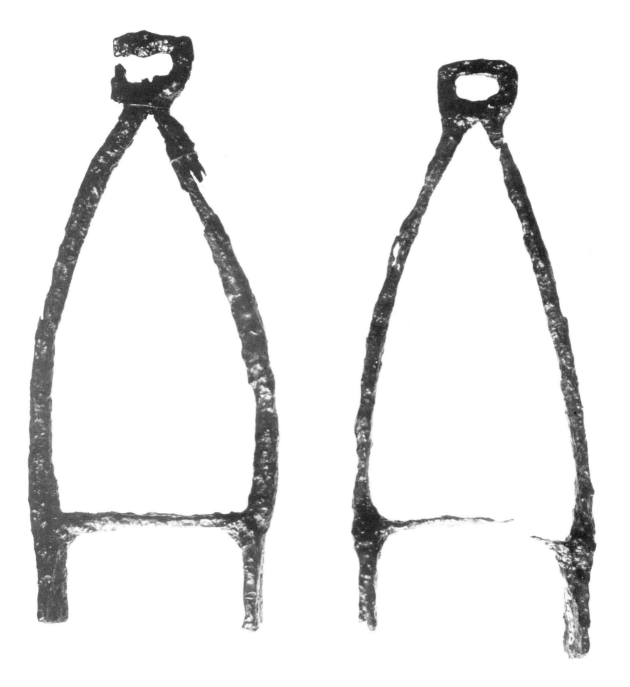

upon another Viking warlord. This time, the inlaid ornament of Murchad's sword began to melt with the heat of his striking. Throwing the burning blade away, the Irish hero gripped hold of the foreigner's armour and wrenched the mail over his head. The two warriors fell to the ground and wrestled. Murchad thrust the Viking's own sword into his ribs. But the foreigner drew his knife and ripped a gash in Murchad's guts. Exhaustion and pain overcame both warriors. They lay beside each other. But before he fainted, Murchad is said to have cut off the Viking's head. Murchad survived the night, but died the next day after taking communion and making his confession and will.

Throughout the battle, Brian took no active role in the fighting. He stayed at the rear protected by the shield-wall of his retainers, issuing orders and praying. It was there he received news of the eventual rout of the enemy and their desparate dash to the sea. But the victory was not clear-cut. Brian's army had lost many men, and in the chaos at the end of the day

Viking bands still roamed around the battlefield. One, led by Brodar of Man, rode through the relaxing Irish ranks toward Brian's camp. At the height of victory, Brodar's sudden attack was unexpected and the Viking succeeded in reaching Brian himself. Brian unsheathed his sword and gave the foreigner such a blow that he cut the Viking's leg off at the knee. The Viking then dealt Brian a stroke that cleft his head in half. Thus Brian died at the moment of his greatest victory.

For a victory, the battle of Clontarf seemed like a defeat. Ireland's greatest overlord was dead and his retinue devastated. In the aftermath, Ireland reverted to a disunity of warring clans. Nevertheless, it was a decisive defeat of the Vikings: keeping Ireland free of any further Scandinavian invasions. Of course, the Vikings of Dublin and Leinster continued to live in their coastal settlements, but they operated alongside the Irish and did not dominate them. They became Christians and intermarried with the Irish noble families. Vikings from abroad still harried the coasts in search of plunder but they could expect an equally ferocious reaction from the Irish. The Heimskringla Saga of the thirteenth century recalls raids by King Magnus of Norway on the Irish coast a century earlier. Sailing from Norway to the Orkneys to the Hebrides, Magnus then harried Ireland. Along the coast of Ulster, he demanded a shore-killing of cattle to provide his warriors with fresh meat. The Irish refused: Magnus and his followers disembarked. As they penetrated inland, they readied themselves for ambush. 'King Magnus wore his helm,' wrote the chronicler, 'and a red shield displaying a lion in gold. Strapped to his side was a sword called Leg-Biter: the best of weapons. Its hilt was of walrus tooth and the handle covered in gold. Over his shirt he wore a red silk jacket with a lion sewn in gold silk on its back and front. He carried a spear.'

Apparently, the Vikings found the slaughtered cattle, but as they returned through the coastal marshes, the Irish broke cover. In the confusion, the Vikings were separated and many fell to Irish arrows. Magnus ordered a shield-wall around his standard. The Viking retreat was hindered by a dyke. Magnus was wounded: stabbed with a spear through both legs beneath the knee. He grabbed the spear and broke it off, bellowing 'Here's how we break every spear shaft, my lads!' Some of his comrades clambered over the dyke in an attempt to cover the rest, but they panicked and ran for their ships. Magnus was wounded again: a mortal blow on the neck with an Irish axe. Around him his closest retainers fell. One, called Vidkunn, managed to escape the carnage, picking up his lord's sword and standard. The Vikings sailed immediately back to Norway. At home, Vidkunn managed to avoid the terrible disgrace of surviving his lord, by showing his many wounds and insisting that he had slain all Magnus' killers. Only then did the sons of Magnus receive him with love.

Although the Vikings established enduring colonies along the coast of Ireland and in the northern and western islands of Scotland, it remains a remarkable fact that mainland Ireland, Scotland, and Wales remained

215

relatively free of Scandinavian settlement, whereas a good half of Anglo-Saxon England was absorbed by the Danes and Norse. This may be due to the land of the Anglo-Saxons being richer and more attractive, but it must also attest to the fierce independence of the leading Celtic warlords. Such was the power of these Celtic warlords that Viking adventurers frequently found it more profitable to intervene on their side in the endless little wars of the Dark Ages. Macbeth, a Gaelic warrior from Moray, was assisted by the Vikings of Orkney in his assault upon Duncan, king of the Scots.

Macbeth has suffered badly from history. Shakespeare transformed him into an archetype of murderous medieval anarchy. In reality, it seems he was no worse and may have been better than other contemporary warlords. On seizing the crown of Scotland in 1040, he ruled the land for a prosperous 17 years. So settled was the country that he felt secure enough to leave and journey to Rome on a pilgrimage. As for Duncan: he had led his countrymen into a string of defeats. When Macbeth proclaimed himself king at Scone, few chroniclers protested. Indeed, later historians have even regarded his success as a highland Celtic reaction against the excessive English influence encouraged by Duncan. Besides, Macbeth, like Duncan, was a grandson of Malcolm II and had a legitimate claim to the throne. In Celtic clan law, election was the method of obtaining power. A more capable and popular warlord could legally oust an elder relative.

The Scotland that Macbeth ruled was a greatly extended country. In 1018, the Northumbrian Angles had been shattered at Carham by Malcolm II and he rode on to claim the lowlands as far as Hadrian's Wall. That same year, the king of the Britons of Strathclyde and Cumbria died without an heir and the triumphant Scots immediately placed Malcolm's grandson Duncan on their throne. In 1034, Duncan became King of Scotland. Six years later, he was killed by Macbeth in battle near Burghead on the Moray Firth. In that combat, Macbeth rode in an army of northern Gaelic clansmen allied with Norse warriors led by Thorfinn Sigurdsson, lord of Caithness and Orkney. It was the Vikings who took the lead in the battle, as it was they who Duncan had come to humble. Duncan fought alongside southern clansmen and Irish mercenaries. The *Orkneyinga Saga* evokes some of the conflict: 'After the crashing of spears, the Orkney warlord raised high his helmet. He exulted in battle and reddened spear point and sword edge with Irish blood. With stout arm, the gracious lord kinsman of Hlodver bore up his Welsh shield and rushed upon the enemy.' With his Irish auxiliaries routed, Duncan managed a counter-charge, but the Norse held firm and Duncan was slain amidst the fighting.

Duncan's son, Malcolm, lived as an exile in England and was brought up on that court's concepts of heredity. As Duncan's eldest son, he was convinced he was entitled to be king and not Macbeth. But Macbeth was strong and Malcolm had to bide his time. Malcolm's ambition and revenge suited the English just fine, for here was a man they could control. As soon as he reclaimed the throne, the Scottish monarchs would have to do homage

Welsh warrior with mace and dagger on the Cross of Briamail Fou. Cast of the restored tenth-century stone from Llandyfaelog Fach churchyard, Powys, north-east Wales.

to the Anglo-Saxon king and thus admit the feudal superiority of England over Scotland. It would also secure their northern borders. So, in 1054, backed up by an army of Anglo-Saxons and Danes, the 21-year-old Malcolm advanced on Scotland by land and by sea. His army was led by a Northumbrian-Danish warlord called Siward. The English met little resistance from the Scots in the lowlands and were confronted by Macbeth just outside Scone, the Scottish capital. This was the famous battle in which supposedly 'Birnam Wood do come to Dunsinane'. No doubt accompanied by his Norse allies—the lord of Orkney was his cousin—Macbeth put up a stiff fight. But the *Annals of Ulster* maintain that 3,000 Scots were killed and 1,500 English and Danes slain. Still, it was far from a victory and Siward had to withdraw his troops from Scotland, Malcolm having to be content with lordship over Cumbria.

The next year, Siward died and in 1057 Malcolm alone had to lead the battle against Macbeth. With the full support of the Northumbrians, Malcolm cornered the King of Scotland in his homeland of Moray. Macbeth and his retainers charged Malcolm's warriors but were overcome and killed. Even then, Malcolm did not immediately succeed to the throne but had to avoid the avenging highlanders and back off southwards to safety. The next year, Malcolm had to slaughter Macbeth's stepson, his legally elected successor, before the anglicised Malcolm could crown himself at Scone. With his accession came closer ties with England and a retreat in the influence of the Gaelic clansmen. Far from being a tyrant, Macbeth could be called the last of the truly Celtic kings of Scotland.

With the acceptance of Viking spheres of influence in the islands of Scotland and the cities of Ireland, there followed a short period of consolidation beneficial to both Celt and Scandinavian. This status quo was overturned at the end of the eleventh century with the arrival of another wave of North Men. This time, they did not come direct from Scandinavia, but were the French descendants of that aggressive colony of Vikings in north-west France: the Normans. In the years following their great victory of 1066, they successfully subdued the whole of England. It was not long before they then overran the borders of the British Celtic realms. In this adventure, the Normans were joined by other French warriors. Not least amongst them were the Celtic warlords of Brittany.

The Bretons had managed to hold on to their Celtic identity despite the power of the Franks. In the ninth century, they made large gains in Normandy and though beaten back, Rennes remained Breton. When Harold of England stayed with William of Normandy, he accompanied the Duke on expeditions against the Bretons. With the submission of several Breton warlords, William then included them as an important contingent in his invasion of England. At the battle of Hastings, they formed an entire flank. Highly regarded by the Normans and fighting in a similar manner, the Bretons did well out of the conquest and received extensive estates. Some were settled in the south-west and on the Welsh border where their Celtic language, similar to that of the Welsh, was of considerable help in dealing with the natives.

The Norman conquest of Wales was piecemeal. It took a long time and was never completed. Much of this difficulty has been ascribed to the rough Welsh countryside. The mountainous interior covered with forests. Heavy rainfall ensuring that the clay soil was marshy for much of the year. Above all, however, it was the quality of Welsh resistance. 'They make fine use of light arms, which do not impede their agility,' observed the twelve-century Welsh Norman writer, Giraldus Cambrensis. 'They wear short coats of mail, helmets and shields, and sometimes greaves plated with iron. They carry bundles of arrows and long spears. Their nobles ride into battle, but the majority fight on foot. In time of peace, young men learn to endure the fatigue of war by penetrating deep into the forests and climbing the mountains.' In short, the Welsh were excellent guerilla warriors. Giraldus, therefore, recommended that the Normans should also employ lightly armoured foot-soldiers, and when possible the Normans incorporated Welshmen into their own forces. But, before this, a conqueror of Wales must prepare his victim. Giraldus suggests the Normans divide the Welsh with bribes and treaties, then blockade the coasts and the English border so that few provisions reached them. In the event, the Normans chose their path of conquest carefully and exploited the Welsh geography by sticking to the wide coastal plains.

Led by adventurers hungry for land of their own, the Normans first settled Gwent in south Wales. Whenever possible, William preferred to admit the homage of native Welsh warlords, but the desire of his landless followers ensured that a slow advance began around the coasts of Wales. As always, foreign influence was aided by Celtic power-play and Welsh exiles from Ireland fought alongside the Norman knights. Bit by bit, the Norman lords of the Marches—a French word meaning frontier—encroached on Welsh territory. The Marcher lords were used by successive English kings as a means of creating buffer states between themselves and the Welsh. They were offered absolute power over any frontier land they could subdue. It was an offer the warrior families of the Fitzalans, Gilberts, Clares, Mortimers and Laceys could not refuse. At the head of their war-bands, supported by the border garrisons of Chester, Shrewsbury, Hereford and Bristol, they carved out private kingdoms where their word was law.

Fierce resistance rocked the invaders from the end of the eleventh century. Woodcutting pioneers had to advance before Norman war-bands, clearing away undergrowth that might hide Welsh guerillas. The Marcher lords managed to hold onto many of their conquests and even north-west Wales, the heartland of the powerful dynasty of Gwynedd, lay at times in their hands. But, recovering from the shock of the Norman war-machine, the Welsh had begun to fight back and much of northern and central Wales remained solidly Celtic. Two centuries of raid and counter-raid now followed: the borders becoming a wilderness of slaughter. In a constant

218

Celtic Bretons fought alongside the Normans at the battle of Hastings and gained much from the share-out. Hand-coloured engraving from Charles Stothard's *Bayeux Tapestry* published in 1819.

state of war, the Marcher lords grew in power and frequently had to be quelled by their own king. The Welsh in their turn became hardened and Gwynedd was re-established from Anglesey down the west coast. By 1137, Gwynedd was recognised by the Norman English as the chief Celtic realm of Wales, so Welshmen could proclaim: 'No other language but Welsh shall answer for this land on the day of Judgement.' The Welsh had defied the initial onslaught of the mighty Normans.

Scotland became the home for many English refugees of the Norman conquest. Malcolm III married the sister of Edgar Aetheling, the only surviving claimant to the Anglo-Saxon throne after Harold. Again, this brought increased anglicisation and the Celtic Church of Scotland fell in line with the Church of Rome. Malcolm was persuaded to support Saxon claims to the English throne and four times he invaded Northumbria. By 1072, William tired of this aggression and led an army north. He forced Malcolm to accept him as overlord. But, with William's death, the Scots again ravaged Northumbria. The Conqueror's son, William Rufus, countered swift and hard. In the fighting, he took Cumbria as far as Carlisle, thus establishing Scotland's frontier as it has remained ever after. It was in another raid across the border that Malcolm was killed by a Norman knight. His death encouraged a Gaelic backlash and a warlord from the Hebrides was elected king of Scotland at Scone. The English followers of Malcolm were expelled.

The Normans could not rest with such a state of affairs. Over the next stormy years, Norman-backed claimants proclaimed their crowning as an hereditary right against the old Celtic system of election. Eventually the Anglo-Norman kings triumphed and the Celtic way of life retreated to the highlands. Scots sympathetic to England and new Norman landlords infiltrated the lowlands. In peace, the Normans gained much more Scottish territory than they would have won from battle. Gaelic was still spoken by the common people of Scotland, especially the almost independent clan-lords of the north, but Norman-French became the dominant language of the Scottish aristocracy. Some refugees of the old regime fled to Ireland. There they joined with the Vikings of Dublin in raids against the west coasts of Britain. It may have been such conflict that encouraged certain Welsh Norman warlords to look across the Irish channel with ambition.

No one likes to commit to history the fact that his people have invaded another country out of sheer lust for conquest. Caesar justified his invasion of Celtic France as an intervention on behalf of the Gauls against the Germans. When Giraldus Cambrensis came to write his history of the Norman expedition to Ireland, he too opened his account with an invitation. The unity to be expected from the great victory at Clontarf in 1014 had come to nothing with the death of Brian. Ireland in the twelfth century was divided by bitter dynastic feuds. Leinster, always ready to do business with foreigners, was led by Dermot MacMurrough. Now Dermot had abducted the wife of Tiernan O'Rourke and in a revenge worthy of the Trojan War, O'Rourke and Rory O'Connor of Connacht, high king of Ireland, was coming to get him.

In 1166, Dermot sailed for help to the Norman court of Henry II. The king agreed to aid the Irishman as 'vassal and liegeman', but could not afford to send his own troops. Instead, Dermot was allowed permission to recruit the support of the Marcher lords of south Wales. Frustrated by the resurgence of the Welsh, many warriors were keen to join Dermot. They were led by the half-Norman, half-Welsh Robert FitzStephen who agreed to help Dermot in return for the town of Wexford as payment. By 1169, FitzStephen had disembarked at Bannow Bay in Leinster with thirty fully-armoured retainers, sixty half-armoured horsemen, and three hundred archers and foot-soldiers, all from south Wales. A force more Celtic than Norman, although the Annals of Tighernach say that the majority of soldiers were Flemish immigrants from settlements in Wales. Wishing to secure his promised land, FitzStephen wasted no time and made straight for Wexford. One of the major Viking settlements, Wexford was still ruled by Norse-Irish and considered itself independent from Leinster. The townsmen resolved to battle it out and advanced to meet the Norman army now joined by Irish warriors sent by Dermot. But the men of Wexford were overawed by the Norman horsemen and their armour, and retreated back into their town, burning all the outlying buildings.

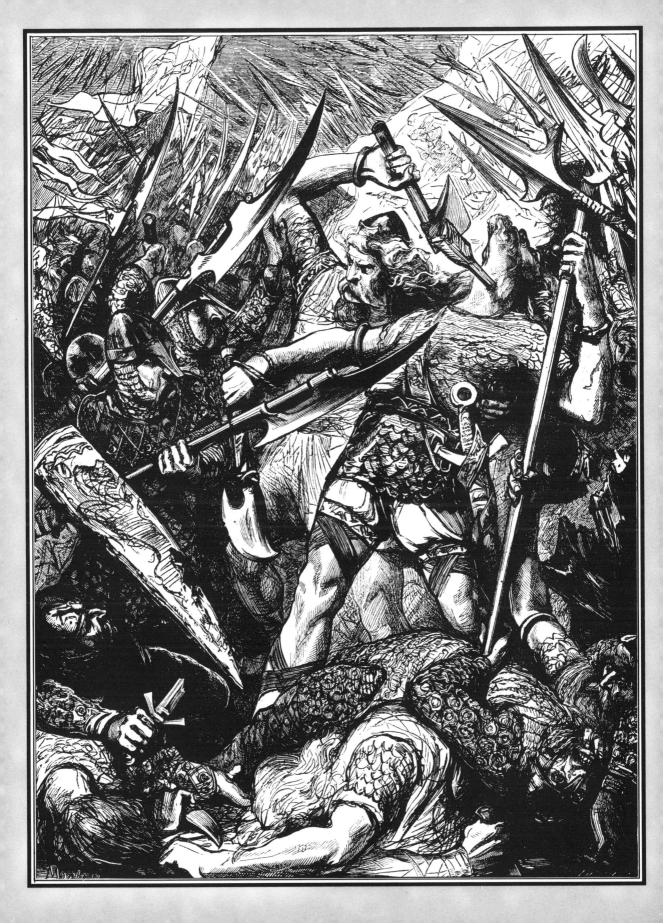

Throughout his account, Giraldus Cambrensis emphasises the military primitiveness of the Irish. 'They go to battle without armour,' he writes, 'considering it a burden and esteeming it brave to fight without it. They are armed with three kinds of weapons: short spears, light darts, and heavy battle-axes of iron, exceedingly well wrought and tempered. These they borrowed from the Norwegians. In striking with the battle-axe they use only one hand, instead of both. When all other weapons fail, they hurl stones against the enemy. In riding, they use neither saddles, nor boots, nor spurs, but carry only a rod in their hand with which they urge forward their horses.' Latin propaganda seems uppermost here, for in reality, the Irish nobility and certainly the Scandinavian Irish were as well equipped as the Normans and wore similar long coats of mail, iron helmets with nasal, and kite-shaped shields. And always, the Celtic Irish were excellent horsemen.

It is in Giraldus' contemptuous descriptions that we see the origin of the English prejudice against the Irish and their belief in the inferiority of Irish culture. 'Their clothes are made after a barbarous fashion,' he continues. 'Their custom is to wear small close-fitting hoods, hanging below the shoulders. Under this they use woollen rugs instead of cloaks, with breeches and hose of one piece, usually dyed. The Irish are a rude people, subsisting on the produce of their cattle only and living like beasts. This people, then, is truly barbarous, being not only barbarous in their dress, but suffering their hair and beards to grow enormously in an uncouth manner.'

FitzStephen lost no time in preparing for his assault on Wexford. His armoured warriors moved into the dry trenches around the city, while his archers covered them by raking the wall-towers. The Normans then heaved their siege ladders against the walls and clambered to the top with loud cries. The men of Wexford cast down large stones and wooden beams and managed to repulse the attack. With only a few hundred men under his command, FitzStephen called off the assault and withdrew to the harbour where he set fire to all the ships. Undeterred, the next morning, after celebrating mass, the Normans assaulted the walls again. This time, the townsmen despaired of holding the battlements and preferred to make a peaceful settlement. With bishops acting as mediators, the town did homage to Dermot and he in turn gave the town and its surrounding countryside to FitzStephen. The townsmen now joined the Normans and Leinstermen on their freebooting and ravaged the territory of Ossory. At the end of this raiding campaign, fought by horsemen amid woods and bogs, two hundred heads were laid at the feet of Dermot. He turned the heads one by one, raising his hands in joy as he recognised those of his enemies. 'Among them was one he hated above all others,' wrote Giraldus, 'and taking it up by the ears and hair, he tore the nostrils and lips with his teeth in a most savage and inhuman way.'

Receiving the homage of the lord of Ossory, Dermot was now perceived as a threat by Rory O'Connor, the high king. As the men of Connacht rode out against Dermot, he, under FitzStephen's direction, prepared a defensive position among the thick woods and bogs of Leinster. Trees were felled, underwood cut and woven into hedges, level ground broken up with holes and trenches, and secret passages cut through thickets. Hidden away thus, Dermot avoided a major conflict and instead offered to reassert his submission to Rory and give him hostages. The Normans would be sent away as soon as they helped Dermot secure Leinster. This apparently assured Rory and there was peace. But no sooner had the high king retreated than Maurice FitzGerald landed at Wexford with 140 Norman-Welsh warriors. While FitzStephen erected a fort of earth ramparts and wood stockade at Wexford, Dermot and FitzGerald marched on Dublin. They ravaged and burned the territory around Dublin so the Norse governors were compelled to accept Dermot's lordship. Dermot now sent

FitzStephen to the aid of the lord of Limerick and north Munster and they raided the land of Rory O'Connor. This was reckless indeed, but, with his Norman allies, Dermot now entertained thoughts of snatching the high kingship. On the advice of FitzStephen and FitzGerald, Dermot sent to England for more warriors. Above all, he requested the help of Richard FitzGilbert, a powerful Norman warlord of south Wales nicknamed Strongbow.

The special character of warfare in medieval Ireland is described fully by Giraldus Cambrensis. 'The Normans may be very good soldiers in their own country,' he wrote, 'expert in the use of arms and armour in the French manner, but every one knows how much that differs from the way of war in Ireland and Wales. In France, war is carried out across open plains; here, you find dense woods and mountainous terrain. In France, it is counted an honour to wear armour; here, it is a burden. There, victories are won by close fighting ranks; here, by the charges of lightly armed warriors. There, quarter is given and prisoners offered for ransom; here, heads are chopped off as trophies and no one escapes. Therefore, in all expeditions in Ireland and Wales, the Welshmen bred in the Marches make the best troops. They are good horsemen and light on foot. They can bear hunger and thirst well when provisions are not to be had. These are the men who took the lead in the conquest of Ireland and will be needed to complete it. For when you have to deal with a race naturally agile and whose haunts are in rocky places, you need lightly armed troops. In addition, in the Irish wars, particular care should be taken to include archers for they can counter the Irishmen who rush forward and throw stones at our heavily armoured warriors and then retreat.' It may be said that the Normans in England by the twelfth century should properly be called English for they were long descended from those Normans of 1066. This is true, but what is clear from Giraldus' passage above is that these warriors still considered themselves fighting in a Norman French manner different from that of the native Celts of Britain. Hence their dependence on Welsh auxiliaries.

In 1170, Strongbow arrived in Ireland. He brought with him 200 armoured horsemen and 1,000 Welsh archers and other soldiers. He had already sent an advance group of warriors and they had set up a beach-head near Waterford. The Viking-Irish townsmen savaged this advance guard and when Strongbow landed he made straight for them. Surveying the walls of Waterford, the Normans spotted a little wooden house on the outside attached to the stockade. This in turn was being supported by a single post. Under cover of their archers, armoured warriors rushed into the house and chopped down the pole. As the house collapsed, it brought with it part of the town wall. The Normans clambered over the wreckage and burst into the town. Some of the leading citizens held out in a tall stone tower but eventually they were overcome. Joined by Dermot, FitzStephen and FitzGerald, Strongbow now rode on Dublin. They descended unex-pectedly by a mountain track and the Viking lord of Dublin immediately entered into lengthy peace negotiations. While they talked, a group of Normans stormed the walls.

Heady with success, Dermot raided the territory of his greatest enemy: Tiernan O'Rourke. Rory O'Connor reminded Dermot of his peace agreement but not even the execution of his own son, kept hostage by Rory, could prevent Dermot's ambition and he now claimed the high kingship. But Dermot's luck had run out. A few months later he died, leaving Strongbow in command of Leinster and the Viking towns. This did not please king Henry II of England who feared a warlord grown too powerful. He ordered the Normans to return on penalty of losing their lands in England and refused to allow any ship to sail to Ireland. This loss of reinforcements and supplies fell hard on Strongbow but he held his conquered territories.

In the meantime, Haskulf, the Viking lord of Dublin, returned to his city with sixty ships full of Northmen from the Isle of Man and the Scottish Isles. 'They were under the command of John the Mad,' reported Giraldus. 'Some wore long breastplates, others shirts of mail. Their shields were round, coloured red, and bound with iron. They were lion-hearted and iron-armed men. A member of the garrison had his leg cut off by a single stroke of one of their battle-axes.' The Normans were bundled back into Dublin. They regrouped, however, and a contingent moved out unobserved and pounced upon the rear of the besieging Vikings. The Northmen were thrown into confusion and routed. In order to calm the still largely Scandinavian townspeople, Haskulf, though a prisoner, was brought back in triumph to Dublin. Before the Norman lord of the city, he did not thank him for his mercy but insisted: 'We came as a small band, but if my life is spared, we will follow up with a much more formidable assault.' Haskulf was beheaded.

Hoping to exploit Strongbow's isolated situation, the Irish now besieged Dublin. While a Viking fleet blockaded the port of the city, Rory O'Connor assembled his men of Connacht and Meath, and supporters from Leinster and Ulster. Even worse for Strongbow was the fact that FitzStephen was surrounded in his castle by the men of Wexford. For two months the siege of Dublin persisted. With food running low and no prospect of relief, the Normans decided to bring the struggle to a head. 'What are we waiting for?' asked FitzGerald of his comrades. 'Do we expect help from our homeland? No. Such is our situation that to the Irish, we are English, and to the English, we are Irish.' The Normans rode out in three groups. The first contingent of twenty knights, the second of thirty knights, and the last of forty knights led by FitzGerald and Strongbow. They were supported by other less well-armed horsemen, archers, and some of the Norse-Irish townsmen. The Normans charged upon the retainers of Rory O'Connor, hoping to discourage the rest of his army. Rory was surprised, and as his men collapsed before the Normans, he escaped just in time to lead the Irish retreat.

From Dublin, Strongbow rode to Wexford. It was too late. Thinking that

Line drawing of a warrior from a miniature in the Dialogues of Saint Gregory, from a manuscript in the National Library of France, Paris. The coat of mail and nasal helmet was an international style of war-gear worn by almost all European knights of the eleventh century, including Celts.

Dublin had fallen to the Irish, FitzStephen had agreed to sail back to England. As his retainers gave up their arms, the men of Wexford threw FitzStephen into their dungeon and threatened to cut his head off if Strongbow should advance against them. Receiving a summons from his king, Strongbow returned to Britain. In south Wales, he reaffirmed his loyalty to Henry II and agreed to give up the conquered towns of Ireland in return for keeping Leinster as a fief. From a Welsh-Norman adventure, the assault on Gaelic Ireland had now developed into an Anglo-Norman invasion headed by the king of England.

Landing at Waterford with 500 knights and many more archers and light horsemen, Henry was greeted by the men of Wexford. Hoping to curry favour with the king, they offered him FitzStephen so he could be punished for invading Ireland without royal licence. This Henry did and FitzStephen was kept in chains as a royal prisoner until it was felt safe to pardon him. Henry paraded throughout Leinster. The lords of Cork, Limerick and many other southern Irish estates all did homage to him. They gave him hostages and agreed to pay a yearly tribute. At Dublin, Henry received the submission of Rory O'Connor and all the northern Irish lords except those of Ulster. He then convoked a synod of all the clergy of Ireland and tried to bring them in line with the English church. It seemed that the conquest of Ireland had been achieved with ease and only trouble at home forced Henry back to England. He was not to return to Ireland.

The submission of Rory O'Connor, lord of Connacht and high king of all Ireland, though attested by Giraldus, is not recorded by any other chronicler. With Henry gone and only Dublin and Leinster ruled by his governors, the north and west of Ireland remained Gaelic. Strongbow reasserted his hold over Leinster and led an attack against Munster. His first raid was successful, but his second met with complete defeat and he was pushed back to Waterford. Rory O'Connor led a force across the Shannon and ravaged the Normans in Meath. Strongbow struck back and by 1175 Meath was under Norman control. It was then that O'Connor made a formal submission to Henry II. It was acknowledged that Dublin, Meath and Leinster were to be ruled directly by the Normans, while the other Irish lords could rule their own lands in return for a yearly tribute of one hide for every ten animals slain. O'Connor remained Irish overlord. A year later, Strongbow was dead. His lands were held by the king and then divided among trusted vassals.

According to Giraldus, it would seem that the Celts of Ireland had been dealt a profound blow. Behind a rough diagonal from Cork and southern Munster to the eastern coast of Ulster, the Normans ruled from their stone-built castles. But how did the Irish see this invasion? Throughout the period described by Giraldus, the *Annals of Ulster* are very much concerned with the wars of the Celtic clans. The Normans—called Saxons in the *Annals*—are hardly mentioned and only then as a minor back-up force to Dermot MacMurrough: sometimes successful, sometimes not. 'They inflicted

In 1169, 30 Norman knights, 60 men-at-arms, and 300 archers landed at Bannow Bay in Leinster. A drawing by Alphonse de Neuville for Guizot's *L'Histoire de France*, 1870.

slaughter upon the Vikings of Dublin and Waterford and, on the other
hand, many slaughters were inflicted upon themselves.' But, all the time, it
is the Irish who are in control: conducting their own politics, their own
wars. The only occasion the English are seen as a superior force is when
King Henry lands with 240 ships. The Irish do homage to him, but the king
soon leaves and the Irish lords continue their feuding. In the *Annals of
Ulster*, the English—on the few occasions they are considered worthy of
mention—are quickly absorbed into the Celtic world of raid and counter-
raid.

To encounter such a perspective of the Normans in Ireland after reading
that of Giraldus, encourages the view that Giraldus was engaged in the
business of legend-making. His chronicle of the Normans in Ireland is a saga
full of bold personalities and daring exploits. We are shown the Norman

228

invasion from the point of view of a handful of conquistadors, cutting their way into virgin territory held only by easily outwitted natives. Of course, this is how the English wished to view their first assault on the Irish. To them it was a heroic tale. Little did they realise, however, that the Irish considered the 'invasion' little more than a pinprick. The power-play of the Irish warlords remained, with the Normans now playing that role of opportunist auxiliaries formerly fulfilled by the Vikings. In time, both the Vikings and Normans were to be absorbed in the Irish way of war. Against the English, the North Men may have gained significant victories, but against Celtic warriors it had been a far longer, harder struggle: with no victors.

Celtic Counter-attack

WELSH
AND SCOTS
AGAINST THE
EDWARDIAN
KINGS
1200–1450

'To his most excellent lord, Philip, the illustrious king of the French . . .'. Llywelyn, lord of north Wales, supervised the composition of a letter of alliance. 'How am I to repay the excellence of your nobility,' the scribes continued, 'for the singular honour and priceless gift of sending me your knight with letter sealed in gold in testimony of the treaty between the kingdom of the French and the principality of north Wales. This letter I will keep in the church as if it were a sacred relic. An inviolable witness that I and my heirs will be friends to your friends and enemies to your enemies.'

There was more: the demand. 'Having summoned the council of my chief men and having obtained the common assent of all the princes of Wales, I promise that I will be faithful to you for ever. From the time I received your highness's letter, I have made neither truce nor peace with the English. By God's Grace, I and all the princes of Wales have manfully resisted our, and your, enemies. With God's Help we have by force of arms recovered from their tyranny a large part of the land and strong defended castles which by fraud they have occupied. Therefore, all the princes of Wales request that you make no truce with the English without us, knowing that we will not for any terms bind ourselves to them without your approval.'

When Llywelyn ab Iorwerth sent this treaty of alliance to the King of France in 1212, Celtic Wales was in a far stronger position than it had ever been since the Normans first surged into their land. In the previous century, the Welsh had made the most of crises in the English monarchy: the civil war of Stephen's reign; the unpopularity following Henry II's assassination of Thomas à Becket; the absence of Richard I on crusade in the Holy Land. Re-establishing themselves, the Welsh also adopted the castle-building of the Normans.

By the early thirteenth century, Llywelyn ab Iorwerth—Llywelyn the Great—had built a string of castles around Gwynedd. At Dolbadarn, dominating the mountain pass to Conwy, is a fully developed, strongly-fortified round stone keep, the match of any fortress built by the Marcher lords. In the heartland of the mountains of central Wales, stands Castell-y-Bere. Founded in 1221, the castle follows the shape of its base rock. Towers command each angle with the entrance protected by another tower and ditches cut in the rock. The towers are of the D-shaped type characteristic of Welsh castle-building. One served as the keep, while another was decorated with sculpture and probably contained a chapel. The high standard of stonework suggests this was one of Llywelyn's principal strongholds.

It was at the age of 21 in 1194 that Llywelyn claimed the throne of Gwynedd. He married the daughter of King John of England and gained a useful insight to the English way of power. He observed that a greater degree of centralisation was important to the maintenance of strength. Subsequently he cut across the native rivalry of the Welsh clans. Improvements in administration were coupled with the annexation of neighbouring Welsh estates. He did not lack for enemies among his own people. But, when King John set about cutting him down to size, it was Llywelyn's strength that encouraged the other Celtic warlords to join in his successful defence of Gwynedd. By 1215, baronial discord had undermined John's plans for Wales and the *Magna Carta* recognised that Celtic Wales, the Marches and English land in Wales were each ruled independently by the law of their own lords. Following hard on this victory, Llywelyn rode into south Wales at the head of a powerful array of united Welsh chieftains, leaving the English with few remaining footholds. Llywelyn was now overlord of Wales. He never actually called himself Prince of Wales, but preferred to honour himself as Prince of Aberffraw and Lord of Snowdon, to whom all other Welsh lords did homage. Even the Marcher lords were cowed.

Aside from their political strength, the Welsh were notably hardy fighters. 'In a certain part of this island, there is a people called the Welsh,' wrote King Henry II to the Emperor of Constantinople. 'They are so bold and so ferocious that even when unarmed, they do not fear to confront an armed force. Ready to shed their blood in defence of their country and to sacrifice their lives for renown. Even when the beasts of that land became calmed, these desperate men remained untamed.' Such hyperbole was probably intended as an excuse for Henry's lack of military success against the Welsh. But it is supported by Giraldus Cambrensis' description of their fighting spirit. 'The English fight in order to expel the natural inhabitants from the island and secure it all for themselves. The Welsh, who have for so

Drawing of a Welsh archer from the famous Register, Liber 'A', which includes the text of the Treaty of Montgomery, 1267, agreed between Llywelyn ap Gruffydd and Henry III. Correctly, the archer does not carry a 'longbow', supposedly characteristic of the Welsh, but an ordinary wooden bow probably more suited to the close-range archery praised by Giraldus Cambrensis.

long been sovereign over their land, maintain the conflict so that they may at least find a hiding place in the worst corner of it, among woods and marshes. The English fight for power, the Welsh for liberty. The English fight for money, the Welsh for their country.'

The Welsh warlords and their retainers were armed very much like their Norman-English enemies. They were mail-clad horse-warriors wielding sword and lance. It was their foot-soldiers, however, the common tribes-men, who seem to have contributed a particular Welshness to border warfare. 'The men of Gwent,' remarked Giraldus, 'are more used to war, more famous for their courage, and more expert in archery, than those of any other part of Wales. In an assault on the castle of Abergavenny, for example, two knights were passing over a bridge to take refuge in a tower built on a mound of earth. The Welsh, taking them in the rear, fired arrows that penetrated the oak door of the tower to a depth of four fingers. In memory of that feat, the arrows were preserved in the gate. William de Braose also testifies that one of his warriors was wounded by a Welsh arrow which passed through his mail clad thigh, his saddle, and penetrated his horse. Another knight had his armoured hip pierced by an arrow to the saddle. When he turned round, he received another arrow through his leg which fixed him to his horse. Yet the bows used by the Welsh are not made of horn, ivory, or yew, but of wild elm. They are unpolished and rough, yet stout. They are not intended to shoot an arrow at a great distance, but to inflict severe wounds in close fighting.'

It is generally assumed that it was amongst these talented Welsh archers that the celebrated longbow developed. In truth, there was no such weapon as the 'longbow' in the middle ages. It was referred to only as a 'bow', and the simple wooden bow used by the Welsh was common throughout Europe. What is significant, however, is that the English were so impressed by the forceful use of the bow by Welsh woodsmen, that they rapidly learned to employ large contingents of Welsh archers in their battles against the Irish, the Scots and each other. It was this deployment of large bodies of archers on the battlefield that was novel for the period. From this, of course, derived the tradition of massed Anglo-Welsh bowmen set against cavalry, culminating in the legendary archery triumphs of the Hundred Years War. What is surprising is that according to Giraldus the Welsh did not use their bows as the English were to—as a long-range shock weapon against organised formations of horsemen or foot-soldiers—but employed it as a precise close-range weapon in their guerilla wars of ambush.

Llywelyn ap Gruffyd maintained the strong, independent Wales that his grandfather, Llywelyn the Great, had built up. He exploited English weakness. The civil war between Henry III and his barons encouraged Llywelyn, under the guise of supporting Simon de Montfort, to attack the royalist Marcher lords. In 1265, this opportunism was transformed into a formal alliance. Simon recognised Llywelyn as Prince of Wales. Later that year, the wheel of fortune revolved, and Simon was killed at the battle of

Evesham by King Henry's son, Edward. In the fighting, the defeated Welsh auxiliaries of Simon were treated ruthlessly. They fled to a church for sanctuary. Undaunted, Edward and his warriors set about slaughtering the Welshmen, both inside and outside the church. Llywelyn now stood alone against the royalists, but his power was such that the war could only be brought to an end by treaty. In 1267, Henry III signed the Treaty of Montgomery, confirming Llywelyn as Prince of Wales and giving him the homage of all other Welsh chieftains. Llywelyn ap Gruffyd was riding high.

With King Henry's death in 1272, Edward claimed the throne. He was to be a formidable, unforgiving monarch. Llywelyn misjudged his character and immediately relations between the two warriors broke down. Although Edward's overlordship was never in doubt, Llywelyn nevertheless refused to attend the king's coronation. He refused to pay tribute and he refused to do homage. It now seemed as if Wales might break away completely as a separate state. In 1273, Edward sent a letter to Llywelyn, forbidding him to build a castle at Abermule near Montgomery. 'We have received a letter written in the king's name,' replied Llywelyn ironically. 'It forbids us to build a castle on our own land. We are sure it was not written with your

Welsh warrior with spear and sword, also illustrated in the Liber 'A' manuscript now in the Public Record Office, London. Alongside Welsh archers, Giraldus noted the fighting skill of the spearmen from north Wales. It has been suggested the one foot left naked was to enable a better grip on soggy terrain.

233

Welsh arrow-heads of various types from the castles of Caerleon, Cardiff, Castell-y-bere, and Dyserth, twelfth to fourteenth centuries, now in the National Museum of Wales, Cardiff.

234

knowledge and would not have been sent if you had been in the country, for you know well that the rights of our principality are totally separate from the rights of your kingdom. We and our ancestors have long had the power within our boundaries to build castles without prohibition by any one.' Today the walls of Dorforwyn castle near Abermule still stand.

Edward harboured Llywelyn's disrespect until he was secure in his new crown. As for Llywelyn, it was not wholly his proud independence that repeatedly prevented him from paying homage. Many of Llywelyn's fiercest Welsh enemies had fled to the English court and the Welsh prince would be risking his life to ignore their presence. In 1276, Edward's patience snapped. He was an exceptionally able warlord and personally commanded all his armies. For the first two years of his reign he had fought in the Holy Land and defeated the Saracens at Haifa. For his first royal campaign on British soil, he assembled a powerful army of his own retainers and those of the Marcher lords. Overawed by Llywelyn, the Marcher lords were keen to reinstate their power. They spear-headed the invasion with two strikes against central Wales. In 1277, Edward took the field and advanced into northern Wales.

Llywelyn was unused to such English unity. He believed they were still divided by the split loyalties of the Barons' War. Instead, it was the Welsh who cracked up. Llywelyn's former Welsh allies broke away and marched alongside the English. Unprepared for such a rapid collapse of his power structure, there was little the Welsh prince could do. Literally cutting a path through the Welsh forests, Edward rode through the north of Wales, initiating the construction of a castle wherever he camped. Employing ships from the Cinque Ports, Edward cut off Llywelyn's supply lines from the grain-rich island of Anglesey. With only his faithful men of Gwynedd to protect him, Llywelyn was forced through hunger and the sheer size of Edward's campaign to admit a humiliating defeat. Llywelyn now not only paid homage to Edward, but lost much of the land he had conquered over the previous years. He lost also the homage of all his former Welsh vassals. He remained Prince of Wales, but this was now a meaningless title.

Retreating to his mountain castles, Llywelyn waited for events to overtake him. The English victory bit deep, and in 1282 it was Llywelyn's brother David who expressed Welsh resentment. Llywelyn had learned his lesson and repeated his homage to Edward, but, seeing his brother burn and loot English settlements, vengeance overcame caution. The rapidity of the uprising surprised Edward. Throughout Wales, Celtic warlords joined in an assault on the castles of the Marcher lords. Edward felt he had been generous in the first conflict, allowing the Welsh chieftains to keep their lands. Now he resolved to crush them. Gathering an army of feudal retainers and paid companies of crossbowmen and archers, he repeated his many-pronged campaign. Loyal Marcher lords rode into southern and central Wales, while the king's major force advanced from Chester. Edward again utilised ships to capture Anglesey. But this time, rather than waiting to starve out Llywelyn, one of his vassals, Luke de Tany, constructed a pontoon bridge across the Menai Strait to Bangor. Thus, Edward hoped to draw the net tight on Llywelyn and his followers in the mountains of Snowdon.

Carefully and efficiently, Edward captured castles on the mainland. But Luke was impatient. His warriors charged over the bridge. Ambushed by the Welsh, they rushed back to Anglesey. In the panic many were drowned. This victory temporarily bolstered the Welsh, who believed it a sign that, according to the prophecy of the legendary Merlin, Llywelyn would soon receive the crown of the Britons. The Welsh prince left his mountain lair to David and rode south. In a skirmish near Orewin bridge where the river Yrfor joins the Wye, he was confonted by the Marcher lord Roger Lestrange. Archers pelted the Welsh and then the mail-clad knights charged. In the fighting, Llywelyn was run through. His head was cut off and sent to Edward in north Wales. He in turn sent it to his warriors in Anglesey and then had it conveyed to London where it was stuck upon a spear and displayed at the Tower of London.

The Welsh were shattered. His own countrymen handed David over to the English. Wales was now under direct English control for the first time in its history. The Celtic heartland of Gwynedd became English crown lands. Edward's son, born at Caernarfon, was proclaimed Prince of Wales. A crown supposedly belonging to the legendary King Arthur was fortuitously uncovered and presented to Edward. He had become King of the Britons. This meant much to Edward: the Anglo-Normans had adopted Arthur as the leading hero of their cycle of chivalric tales. For had not Arthur defeated Saxons, just as the Normans had done? The Celts were furious that their national hero had been taken up by their enemies. Welsh propaganda maintained that Arthur was still alive in the mountains of Wales, awaiting his time to triumph over the enemies of his people. The English responded by uncovering the bones of the dead Arthur on English soil at Glastonbury. During his fighting in Wales, Edward deemed it important to interrupt his campaign to witness the disinterring of what were believed to be Arthur's bones and their reburial in a grander English tomb. Not only had the English taken the land of the Celts, they had stolen their legends.

The collapse of Celtic Wales cannot be wholly blamed on Llywelyn's over-confidence. It was Welsh misfortune to choose a fight with one of England's most powerful and effective rulers. Like other medieval kings, Edward had problems to settle in France, but throughout his reign these were overruled by his determination to increase English influence in Britain. Such a focus of attention, backed up by high military expertise, was bad news for the island's Celtic realms. For, after Wales, Edward set his sights on Scotland. In 1286, Alexander III, king of the Scots, went for a midnight ramble. 'Neither storm nor floods nor rocky cliffs, would prevent him from visiting matrons and nuns, virgins and widows, by day or by night as the fancy seized him.' On one of these adventures, Alexander

Gruffydd, son of Llywelyn the Great and father of Llywelyn the Last, tries to escape from the Tower of London. The rope snaps and he breaks his neck. After a drawing by Matthew Paris in his *Chronica Majora* of the thirteenth century in Corpus Christi College, Cambridge.

plunged over a cliff and was found with a broken neck. His only direct heir was his grand-daughter. Edward proposed a marriage between her and his son, the Prince of Wales. But she too met an untimely death. The competition for the Scots throne was now flung wide open.

Acknowledging his feudal and military superiority, the Scots regents allowed Edward to decide who should rule Scotland. The front runners were John Balliol and Robert the Bruce the Elder. Both these lords were descendants of the knights of William the Conqueror. For, by this time, Scotland, especially the lowlands, was dominated by Anglo-Norman landowners ruling estates throughout the realm. John Balliol ran vast estates in France; Robert the Bruce the Younger owned land in Essex. This conquest of Celtic Scotland had been achieved through court politics, intermarriage, and peaceful settlement. In the north, there were some Scots landowners and clansmen who were of direct Celtic descent, but increasingly the politics of the day was handled by warlords of Norman blood. The ensuing Anglo-Scots war can therefore be more clearly seen as a power struggle between Anglo-Norman dynasties and not an international war of Scots versus English or Celts against Normans, as was more true in Wales and Ireland. That said, the common people of Scotland and many of the lower aristocracy, the clansmen, were Celtic and still spoke Gaelic. It was these people, rallying to the cause of their Scots Norman masters, who may have envisaged their battle against the English invader as a national or Celtic struggle for independence.

Edward wanted to dominate Scotland. If he could not become its king, then he would choose the most malleable contender. He selected John Balliol as his puppet monarch. The elderly Robert the Bruce passed his family's claim onto his son, also called Robert the Bruce. They refused to do homage to the new king. Tiring of his humiliating role as frontman for Edward's ambitions, John Balliol renounced his allegiance to the English king and prepared for war. Robert the Bruce ignored his call to arms. Loyal to king Edward, it seemed now that Balliol might be displaced in favour of the Bruce claim.

Although embroiled in war in France and Wales, king Edward rode north with an army of English knights and Welsh archers. It may, incidentally, be thought remarkable that the Welsh should form such a major part of Edward's army so soon after their own defeat at his hands. But the defeat was against the Welsh Celtic nobility, whereas the ordinary Welshman was happy to fight for money and food on any side. For many of the Celtic nobility, however, Wales had ceased to be their homeland and several served abroad as mercenaries. Froissart, for instance, mentions an Owen of Wales who offered his services to the King of France during the Hundred Years War.

Berwick at once fell to Edward. His lieutenant, John de Warenne, shattered the Scots at Dunbar. Parading in triumph through Scotland, Edward demanded the abdication of Balliol. At Montrose, the two kings

237

confronted each other. In front of both English and Scots courtiers, Balliol's coat of arms was ripped from him and thrown on the floor. His humiliation was complete. But Edward's arrogance had further heights to reach. Through fear alone, he received the homage of the Scots magnates. At Perth, he commanded that the sacred stone of Scone—upon which generations of Scots kings had been crowned—be removed and delivered to Westminster Abbey. Ignoring the Bruce claim, Edward appointed an English viceroy over the Scots. Scotland it seemed was now part of an English Empire. As Edward returned over the border, a chronicler recorded his concluding remarks on the campaign: 'It is a good job to be shot of shit.'

Recovering from Edward's blitzkrieg, a few Scots warlords set about reclaiming their dignity. Foremost among these was the Gaelic-speaking William Wallace. A man of low status and called by some a bandit, it may have been that Wallace was used by more powerful Scots aristocrats as a cover for their rebellion so they would be seen not to break their feudal vows of homage to Edward. In the *Lanercost Chronicle*, Wallace is called 'Willelmus Wallensis'—Welsh William—perhaps a reference to his Celtic tongue or his descent from the Britons of Strathclyde. Harassed by English tax collectors and hiding in the forest of Selkirk, Wallace gathered around him a band of outlaw warriors. One evening, he made a dash to see his lover. Surprised by an English patrol, he retreated into his woman's house and disappeared out the back door. The frustrated Englishmen set fire to the house and slaughtered Wallace's lover and family. The tall, angry Scotsman vowed vengeance. He had little time to wait. He and his retainers caught up with the English patrol and cut them to pieces.

This blow against the English encouraged several Scots aristocrats to raise their banners in rebellion. Among them were Sir William Douglas, the former commander of Berwick, and James Stewart, a major Scots land-owner. King Edward hoped to settle the insurrection with his Scots allies and sent Robert Bruce from his base in Carlisle to capture the Douglas castle. But Robert was none too sure of the righteousness of his order. His mother was Celtic and his deep feelings for the country of Scotland ran contrary to his family's political friendship. Besides, the Bruces had been used before with the promise of kingship and Edward had failed to deliver. At the castle of Douglas, Robert made the vital decision. He would fight with his countrymen, not against them.

In the meanwhile, William Wallace fought in the name of the deposed king, John Balliol. He readied his followers for a decisive clash with the English invaders. Committed to continental politics in 1297, king Edward sent John de Warenne to sort out the Scots. Wallace positioned his men in the hills around a bridge crossing the river Forth north of Sterling. Not all the Scots felt confident about the confrontation. James Stewart approached the English warlord with an offer of peace. Warenne refused and his knights began to advance across the bridge. With half the English over the river, it was then that Wallace pounced. Half his warriors fell upon the leading English, while the rest set about chopping down the bridge. The English knights across the bridge floundered in the waterlogged fields of the river-bank. Scots spearmen pierced and prodded them off their horses. Scots axes rent the rings of English mail. With the bridge destroyed, the English vanguard was isolated. Their comrades on the south side of the river could only watch as the Scots wiped out the beleaguered knights. Among the dead was Hugh de Cressingham, chief tax collector of Edward's

The mighty four-towered gatehouse of Harlech Castle. Built by Edward I between 1283 and 1290 to prevent Snowdonia from ever becoming a region of stiff Welsh resistance.

regime in Scotland. His body was flayed and Wallace had a broad strip of his skin from head to heel made into a baldric for his sword. John de Warenne and the rest of the English fled back to Berwick. James Stewart captured their baggage train on the way.

In the forest of Selkirk, William Wallace was proclaimed Guardian of the Kingdom of Scotland and knighted by Robert Bruce. The Earl of Carrick, Bruce had himself roused the men of his own estate and Galloway to the

Reconstruction of the seal of king Edward I, showing the scourge of the Celts in full knightly panoply.

common cause, but had yet to meet the English in battle. Throughout the rest of 1297, Wallace ravaged the border land of England for corn and cattle. Such a turn of events wrenched Edward back from his adventuring in Europe. He transferred his headquarters to York. Now he would hammer the Scots. Feudal dues were called upon. Gascon crossbowmen and Welsh archers were recruited. A vast supply train of wagons and ships was assembled. By the summer of 1298, 2,500 horse-warriors and 12,000 foot-soldiers marched into Scotland. The Scots retreated before the mighty army. But the further the English advanced, the more their supplies began to break down. Their ships brought no food, only wine. Fighting broke out between the Welsh and the English. With his expedition on the brink of collapse, Edward suddenly caught wind of the Scots. The action would take place on hills near Falkirk.

William Wallace feared the greater numbers of the English horsemen. To counter them, he positioned his spear-carrying foot-soldiers behind boggy land, with woodland and rough terrain guarding their flanks. The spears of the Scots were long pikes and they stood in crowded phalanx formations—schiltrons—presenting the enemy with a forest of iron points. In front of the spearmen, stakes were hammered into the ground with ropes joining them. Groups of archers gathered between the schiltrons. The few Scots horsemen waited in reserve, hoping to exploit any break in the enemy. King Edward realised his superiority in horse-warriors and sent his knights in on the first wave of the attack. Galloping into the marshland, the horses slowed down. The majority of the English horsemen then wheeled to the left and right and rode round the swamp, hitting the Scots in the rear.

The shock of battle scattered the Scots horsemen and the English now plunged amid their foot-soldiers. The bows of the Scots had little penetrating power against the mail of the English and soon they too had joined the routed horsemen. But the Scots spearmen held firm. Their rope and stake entanglements tripped up the English horses: knights crashed to the ground. The English men at arms could not break the relentless rows of pikes. The Master of the Templars rushed too recklessly on the spear forest, flailing madly with his sword, hoping to break it with his animal strength. He and his five retainers were impaled. By this time, Edward and his foot-soldiers had caught up with his knights and called off their rash attacks. With no enemy horse or archers to harry him, Edward gathered his Welsh bowmen in front of the Scots schiltrons. They fired hail after hail into the standing targets. The stalwart Scots could only take so much. Men fell and gaps appeared in the once formidable spear wall. It was then that Edward sent his knights in among the broken formations. With war hammer, mace and sword, the horse-warriors hacked at the Gaelic underlings. William Wallace escaped the slaughter, but his power perished with his army.

Edward's victory at Falkirk was not complete. The countryside remained hostile and he was desperately short of supplies, forcing him to retreat to the border. In Carlisle, he sent out summonses for warriors for yet further

campaigns. His obsession turned the lowlands into a devastated killing ground. Among the Scots, William Wallace returned to his raiding: there would be no key role for him. In 1305, he was betrayed by demoralised countrymen, dragged through the streets of London, half hanged and then dismembered. The next year, Robert Bruce eliminated his only serious rival to the Scots throne and had himself crowned Robert I. The English fell upon him with a vengeance. His retainers were smashed at the battle of Methven. Members of his family were executed. His lover and sister held like animals in cages on the battlements of Berwick and Roxburghe castles. Robert was reduced to the life of a fugitive, hunted by Scotsmen eager for the bounty placed on his head by Edward.

When Robert emerged from hiding in 1307, the harsh retribution of the English had provided Bruce with many fresh supporters. But his greatest break was yet to come. As the elderly king Edward prepared to launch another assault, the veteran warrior died. The aura of inevitable victory that seemed always to follow the English when led by Edward was at last at

Caernarfon Castle, begun in 1283 and built by Edward I to command the entrance of the Menai Strait. These castles are still regarded by many Welshmen as unacceptable symbols of English domination.

an end. But Edward's determination to subdue the Scots lived on. He had extracted from his son two promises: first, that the Prince of Wales should carry on the fight against Bruce; and, second, that Edward's coffin be carried ahead of his army into Scotland.

Edward II could not hope to be the supreme warlord his father had been. It was not until 1310 that this king of England crossed the border. In the meantime, Robert's guerilla warfare had undermined his enemies in Scotland and he had regained his leadership of the Scots. In 1308, it is said, he held a parliament at St Modan's Priory, Ardchattan, at which the business was conducted in Gaelic: perhaps an acknowledgement to the loyal support of the clansmen and the lower Scots classes. Eventually, Edward II did march against Bruce. But Robert avoided confrontation, devastated the land before him, and the English had to turn back. Robert now took the war across the border and ravaged Northumberland. In Scotland, he reduced resistant castles one by one, until only Sterling held out. The revival of Robert's power was remarkable. From a fugitive to chief Scots warlord in just over two years: a clear sign of his popular support.

In 1314, Edward II gathered a great army outside Berwick to raise the siege of Sterling: 500 knights accompanied by 2,000 mounted retainers;

Battle axe discovered in the Thames, thirteenth or fourteenth century, now in the London Museum. The breadth of the cutting edge is 17 cm (7 in).

3,000 Welsh archers and 15,000 foot-soldiers armed with spear, pole-axe, dagger and shield. In his eagerness to finish off Bruce, Edward marched his men into the ground. By the time they reached a little stream called Bannock, north of Falkirk, they were exhausted. It was then that Robert brought his men out of his lair in the forest of Torwood and confronted the English. His army was around a quarter of the numbers of Edward's. His warriors came from all over Scotland. His 5,000 massed spearmen consisted of lowlanders and highlanders, with some soldiers coming from the Western Isles. Bruce himself commanded a phalanx of Gaelic clans. These were led into battle by their own clan chieftains. The following claim to have been represented: Cameron, Campbell, Chisholm, Fraser, Gordon, Grant, Gunn, MacKay, MacIntosh, Macpherson, Macquarrie, Maclean, MacDonald, MacFarlane, MacGregor, MacKenzie, Menzies, Munro, Robertson, Ross, Sinclair and Sutherland. Among the bristling schiltrons, there were a few archers and about 500 lightly clad horsemen. This was the same battle formation that had been devastated at Falkirk.

Although short in numbers, Robert hoped to make up for this deficiency by training his men hard. The Scots knew how to wield their 12-foot spears, stand tight in their formations, and resist the temptation to run wildly into the conflict. Bruce prepared the ground around the burn of Bannock carefully. Pits were dug and then covered with brushwood. Tree trunks were built into barricades across forest paths. The time of combat was getting nearer. Robert dispatched his camp followers to a nearby valley.

On the morning of the battle, the Scots celebrated mass. By midday, the English had ridden into view. The first warriors on the field were the vanguard of English knights. They expected to overawe the Scots with their brilliant armour and streaming pennons. In the open ground between the two armies they came across a few Scots scouting out the land. Among them was Robert Bruce. One of the leading English knights, Sir Humphry de Bohun, recognized the Scots king, couched his lance, and spurred his horse into a gallop. Seeing the English knight powering towards him, the sensible reaction for Robert would have been to fall back. His death would mean the end of the battle. But to turn now, in front of his own men, would be equally disastrous. Besides, Robert had a particular loathing for the knight de Bohun. When he had been on the run, Edward I had handed his estates in Annandale and Carrick over to the de Bohuns. Later, Edward II gave the Bruce's estates in Essex to the same family. Robert urged his grey palfrey on towards the duel. Henry de Bohun's lance charge was deflected. Robert stood in his stirrups, raised his battleaxe high and brought it crashing down on the knight's helmet, splitting it and breaking open his head, shattering the axe shaft. A great cry went up from the highlanders. They clambered over their earthworks and ran on towards the English horsemen. Thrown into a panic by the hidden pits and charging Celts, the English backed off.

Elsewhere on the battlefield, another group of English knights rode upon the Scots. This time they were confronted by a schiltron of spearmen. Of the

The abbot of Inchaffray
blesses the Scots
highlanders of the
schiltron before the battle
of Bannockburn, 1314.
From Cassell's *Illustrated
Universal History*, 1884.

two leading English knights, one was killed immediately, the other captured, his horse being impaled on the pikes. The rest rode more cautiously around the circle of spears. Out of desperation, some threw their knives, lances and maces at the Scots. The spearmen thrust at the horses. Eventually, the intense summer heat proved decisive, and the humbled, sweating Englishmen rode off. That night, the Scots were convinced they had done enough to claim victory and were ready to decamp. Certainly, across the battleground, panic had swept through the English ranks; so much so that king Edward had to send heralds around his camp to assure the men that the conflicts so far had been mere skirmishes, the main battle was yet to come. In the meanwhile, English deserters reassured Robert of his success and encouraged him to stay with the promise of an absolute victory the next day.

During that short summer night, the English knights had taken the best ground around Bannockburn for their brief rest. Their archers and foot-soldiers had been forced to lie on the soggy, marshy land near the stream. In the dawn light, the English knights impatiently mounted their horses, keen to avenge the humiliation they had suffered the previous day. They expected Robert to remain in his defensive position, awaiting their attack. Instead, the Scots took the offensive, rolling down the hillside in three densely-packed schiltrons. Foot-soldiers daring to attack horsemen! The English could not believe their luck. The Earl of Gloucester was among the first of the knights to charge upon the Scots. Spears cracked and splintered, but the Scots held firm. No matter how many knights hurled themselves on the forest of points, the schiltrons rolled on.

With their knights already immersed in the fighting, the Welsh and English archers had little opportunity to break the Scots with their arrow storm. The battle was now a hand-to-hand struggle. Axe against sword. Spears thrust through visors. The lightly-armoured Scots leaped among the fallen mail-clad knights, hammering them mercilessly. The Scots crushed the English towards the marshy river bank. Despite the chaos of the crowded

Robert Bruce commanding his Highland warriors at the Battle of Bannockburn. After having routed an enemy, warriors of the schiltron would often jump on horses and thus drive home their victory. From Cassell's *History of England*, 1905.

fighting, English arrows still fell hard and these Robert feared most. He therefore ordered his small band of 500 horsemen forward against the archers, cutting them down. The schiltrons pressed on. Robert sent in his reserves. Scotsmen leaned on their comrades in front, pushing and heaving forward. English knights trampled their fellow warriors into the mud in desperation to escape. Horses and men fell into the stream, drowning. Realising the battle was over, English noblemen grabbed the reins of their king and led him away. With victory safe, the Scots camp followers, women and children, joined in the final struggle, looting and slaughtering. With their make-shift banners held high, it appeared to the English that a second Scots army had arrived and their rout was completed.

Bannockburn was a devastating defeat for the English. The Earl of Gloucester, thirty-four barons, and two hundred knights were among the dead. Nearly a hundred other knights had been captured, to be ransomed over the next year. Robert Bruce was undisputed king of Scotland. In the aftermath, the Scots paid back the English for all those years of invasion. They swept south and raided northern England as far as Durham and Richmond in Yorkshire. They drove back herds of cattle and wagons of loot. The English dared not confront the Scots and Northumberland was left to fend for itself. But the victory of Bannockburn also allowed Robert to consider a grander strategy. He sent his brother, Edward, to Ireland. Some said this was merely an excuse to rid Scotland of a strong rival to Robert's throne, providing Edward with the chance to win a crown of his own. However, it also made good strategic sense. The English estates in Ireland had been a source of warriors and supplies for the armies of both Edward I and Edward II. It was also part of a general Scots determination to master the Irish Sea. For, as soon as Edward had landed in Ireland, his fleet was returned to Robert who used it to secure the homage of the Norse-Scots lords of the Western Isles.

In Ireland, Robert Bruce hoped to arouse a sense of Celtic brotherhood. He sent before Edward a remarkable letter addressed to all the Irish chieftains. 'We and our people and you and your people,' he proclaimed, 'free since ancient times, share the same national ancestry and are urged to come together more eagerly and joyfully in friendship by a common language and by common custom. We have sent to you our beloved kinsman, the bearer of this letter, to negotiate with you in our name about permanently maintaining and strengthening the special friendship between us and you, so that with God's will your nation may be able to recover her ancient liberty.' Clearly, the medieval Scots were aware of their Irish ancestry and now wished to call upon that valued Gaelic aspect of their nationhood to overthrow the Norman-Saxon English. In the wake of Bannockburn, the Irish were indeed tempted by the successful independence of the Scots. The O'Neills of Ulster were particularly keen to hit back at the English and offered Edward Bruce their kingship.

Donal O'Neill called upon fellow Irishmen to support Edward against the 'sacrilegious and accursed English who, worse than the inhuman Danes, are busy heaping injuries of every kind upon the inhabitants of this country.' He noted that their past disunity had made the Irish vulnerable: 'we, being weakened by wounding one another, have easily yielded ourselves a prey to them. Hence it is that we owe to ourselves the miseries with which we are afflicted, manifestly unworthy of our ancestors, by whose valour and splendid deeds the Irish race in all past ages has retained its liberty.'

Landing at Lough Larne in Ulster, Edward Bruce led an army of 6,000. A small force, it nevertheless comprised veteran warriors of the war of independence and soon defeated the local Anglo-Irish barons. A few Irish chieftains immediately allied themselves with Bruce, but others had to be beaten into submission. Despite a call for Celtic unity, this would become a campaign as much against the native Irish as against the English. The Scots' progress through the country sent out ripples of mayhem. An army from Connacht arose to confront him, but was split by Edward playing off one clan against another so that Connacht was itself plunged into civil war. In 1316, in Dundalk, Edward Bruce was crowned High King of all Ireland. He now invited his brother to survey his newly conquered territory. Robert Bruce arrived with a powerful force of galloglas, notoriously ferocious Norse Gaelic mercenaries from the Hebrides. So far, Robert's masterplan had worked well. With Edward in Ireland, the Western Isles under Robert's control, rumours soon spread that the Bruces were to land in Wales and restore their ancient liberty. An all-Celtic movement seemed imminent, unifying the Celts against Edwardian England. Encouraged by such thoughts, the Welsh rose in revolt under Llywelyn Bren. Edward II could not even trust his Welsh archers and all ideas of a counter-attack against Scotland had to be forgotten as he defended his lands in Wales and Ireland.

In Ireland, it was customary that a High King parade all round the country to secure his homage and respect. Early in 1317, Edward Bruce set out with his brother on just such an expedition. They received a rough welcome. The earl of Ulster set an ambush. Allowing Edward's vanguard to proceed through forestland, he then set his archers on Robert's rear. Robert was not provoked and maintained his warriors in good order—except for his nephew Sir Colin Campbell: he spurred his horse on towards the Irish despite the likelihood of a trap. Robert dashed after him and stunned him with a blunt weapon before he could be surrounded. At that moment, more warriors emerged from the forest and a fierce struggle ensued. Only the discipline and military expertise of the Scots saved them from the superior numbers of the Irish.

The people of Dublin, fearing that Edward would march on them next, demolished and set fire to the suburban buildings outside their walls so as to deprive the Scot's army of any cover. It was a decision they were later to regret, for they destroyed many important buildings in their panic, including the king of England's Irish manor. And, anyway, Edward had little time for a siege and had decided to bypass the stout defences of the

Robert Bruce kills the English knight Sir Humphry Bohun with a single blow in the first day of the battle of Bannockburn. From Cassell's *British Battles on Land and Sea*.

city. The Bruces advanced into Munster, for here Irish clansmen promised that the entire countryside would rise to their side. But mutual suspicions overrode these ambitious plans and famine prevented any successful campaigning. Edward was forced to turn back and consolidate his base in Ulster. After such an anti-climax, Robert returned to Scotland. The shock-waves of Bannockburn had begun to recede and Edward II was able to act with more confidence in the support of his barons. A small force of Genoese crossbowmen was sent to Ireland to encourage the cause of the English. Through a generous attitude to enemies and a consolidation of feudal privileges, king Edward managed to increase his influence among the Anglo-Irish. A royal mission to the Pope had also brought benefits. Archiepiscopal vacancies in Ireland were filled by men favourable to king Edward and all supporters of both Bruces were excommunicated. It appeared that Edward II was far more astute at politics than warfare.

Donal O'Neill, self-styled king of Ulster and 'true heir by hereditary right of all Ireland', wrote to Pope John XXII with the Irish point of view. He detailed how the English dominated his land and treated the Irish as inferior beings. He recorded the fact that the English said it was no worse to kill an Irishman than a dog. But there were few other Irish who saw the Bruce invasion as a welcome blow against the English. Many Irish viewed Edward as yet another alien adventurer and preferred to do business with the English simply because they had been longer established. A chronicler of Connacht summed up Bruce's army as: 'Scottish foreigners less noble than our own foreigners.' As for the ideal that both Irish and Scots should unite under a common Gaelic banner, this seems to have been soon forgotten by both sides in the powerplay that followed invasion. Among the remote tribesmen of the Irish mountains who did join Edward Bruce, the prospect may have appealed of fighting alongside warriors speaking a similar Celtic language. But, by 1318, Edward Bruce still only had the support of a few Ulster opportunists. The action of English privateers in the Irish Sea had broken the dominance of the Scots and reinforcements from Scotland could not be depended on. Nevertheless, Edward Bruce was a potent political force and, supported by the de Lacy family, he rode southwards at the head

250

of an Irish-Scots army over two thousand strong. An Anglo-Irish force under Richard Clare, Lord Lieutenant of Ireland, met him at Faughart, just north of Dundalk.

Bruce was heavily outnumbered and his senior knights advised him to wait for reinforcements. But Bruce was impatient for a victory that would give him greater political control. His Irish allies refused to join in the foolhardiness and suggested they harry the English with raids while Bruce awaited the extra men that were expected. Again Edward ignored this sound advice and sent his warriors into battle. The vanguard and mainguard became spread out, their thin numbers annihilated piecemeal by the Anglo-Irish. Loyal to death, Edward's knightly retainers charged alongside their leader as the rearguard rumbled forward. Having belated thoughts of mortality, Edward exchanged his conspicuous royal armour for the plainer garb of a lowly knight. The Scots fought bravely, but inevitably were overwhelmed. According to legend, the English found the body of the lowly knight clad in royal armour and presumed it to be Edward Bruce. His head was cut off, salted in a bucket, and sent to Edward II. But the Bruce

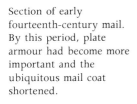

Section of early fourteenth-century mail. By this period, plate armour had become more important and the ubiquitous mail coat shortened.

had not escaped the slaughter. His body lay elsewhere on the battlefield. As the Gaelic prisoners were led away, a Scots knight Sir Philip Mowbray regained consciousness and broke away with other captives. They carried the heavy news of Edward Bruce's death to Scotland.

In that second decade of the fourteenth century, it seemed as if the Celtic realms of Britain and Ireland might rise together and throw back the descendants of the Normans and Saxons. In the event such a dream did not come true, and the English held onto many of their Celtic possessions. But the struggle had not been in vain. In Ireland, English control had been further weakened. Irish chieftains contested the land as strongly as the Anglo-Irish barons. Although some admitted the overlordship of the English king, all were united in their determination not to be ruled by a middle strata of Anglo-Irish adventurers.

Norman dynasties were bundled out of several Irish estates. A Gaelic revival was under way that would eventually reduce the power of the English to the Pale—the royal territory around Dublin. The authority of the great Irish lordships emerged intact from the Celtic highlands. Already, in 1258, an attempt had been made to restore the high kingship of all Ireland. In 1327, Leinster—the heartland of Anglo-Irish support—had thrown itself behind the MacMurroughs and elected one of them king of Leinster, the first since the Norman conquest. Military victories were paralleled by a resurgence of Gaelic culture that engulfed the Anglo-Irish and ensured that the Celtic tongue and law were dominant in Ireland until the coming of the Tudors.

In Scotland, the struggle had been decisive. The Scots had powerfully secured their border. No Englishman dared set foot on Scots land in the years following Bannockburn. In battle, Gaelic-speaking, spear-wielding common foot-soldiers had shown they were the equal of any lance-carrying, knightly horse-warrior. Above all, the Scots had a king from their own country. Robert Bruce was an intelligent and ingenious warlord and repelled all attacks on his kingdom by Edward II until the unpopular English monarch was murdered in 1327. In 1328, the young Edward III acknowledged at last Robert's title of king and a 13-year truce was agreed. A year later the Bruce was dead. Hostilities recommenced, but a legend of Scots independence had been established.

In Wales, the mere rumour of a Bruce invasion had been enough to encourage the Welsh to rebel. Throughout the rest of the fourteenth century, the English managed to control the principality, but such Celtic anger could not be stemmed forever. When it burst in 1400, it was not in the form of a nationalist uprising; there were very few such movements in the Middle Ages. It broke as a feud between Marcher lords. That it then developed into a popular strike for independence is a tribute to the charisma of its leader: Owain Glyndwr. Here was a Welsh warlord who satisfied both the English and the Celtic qualifications of leadership. Descended from the royal family of Llywelyn, he could rightfully claim to be

Scots footsoldier armed with pike and sword as he might have fought in the famed schiltron. From the thirteenth-century Liber 'A' manuscript now in the Public Record Office, London.

252

Reconstruction of the seal
of Robert Bruce, king of
Scotland, now in the
National Library of France,
Paris.

253

Prince of North Wales. But he also satisfied the older Celtic tradition of a warrior accepted by his peers as chieftain because of his military prowess and because he was the most competent figure to fill the role.

Although of Welsh blood, Glyndwr was a perfect English knight. He fought loyally and bravely for the king of England against the Scots and was a respected member of the English court. In 1400, he was a middle-aged man when he returned to his family estate in north Wales. He probably considered himself to be in retirement. He was an unlikely hero of what was to follow. When a border dispute with his neighbour, Lord Grey of Ruthin, irritated him beyond endurance, he did not immediately take to arms, but chose to settle the argument through the English parliament. The mood at Westminster was far from sympathetic to the Welsh. A civil war had rent the kingdom. Henry IV had defeated Richard II. The Welsh had supported Richard's claim. Eager to demonstrate their loyalty to the new king, English lords were far from keen to support the cause of a Welshman. Owain's case was dismissed. He accepted the decision, but events would not leave him alone.

The siege of Carlisle by the Scots in 1315. Line drawing of the initial letter from the charter granted to the city by Edward II in recognition of their successful defence. The Scots' siege engines were not used to good effect in the assault.

Irish footsoldier of the time Edward Bruce landed in Ireland. A drawing from the Liber 'A' manuscript now in the Public Record Office, London.

Lord Grey, as chief Marcher lord, was entrusted by king Henry to raise warriors in north Wales for a campaign against the Scots. He sent notice to all the king's subjects, demanding their presence in the royal retinue. If subjects did not respond to this duty then their lands could be taken away from them, for they received them only on condition of their service to the king. Whether by chance or ploy, the summons to arms arrived too late at the estate of Owain for him to gather his forces and join the king. His absence was noticed, and in the ensuing defeat at the hands of the Scots a furious king empowered Lord Grey to arrest Glyndwr. According to tradition, Glyndwr escaped from the trap set by Grey and began raising forces against the Marcher chief. On the banks of the Dee at Carrog, he was crowned Prince of Wales. Bards spread it far and wide that the stream in which the decapitated head of Llywelyn the Last had been washed now ran with blood.

Glyndwr's followers struck back at Ruthin, Grey's town. They then raided Denbigh, Flint, Hawarden, Holt, Rhuddlan, Oswestry and Welshpool. Glyndwr was declared an outlaw and his estates confiscated. In turn, he set up a mountain stronghold in Snowdonia on the shores of Lake Peris. Support was growing for Glyndwr, but his immediate military power was undercut by royal pardons issued to all Welsh rebels apart from their leader. The Marcher lords required sterner measures to protect their interests. A state of emergency was declared which effectively took all power of administration and law away from native Welshmen and handed it over to the English. Even the Welsh students ensconced in English universities were outraged and there were skirmishes with the citizens of Oxford. The situation deteriorated into open warfare. In 1401, the Tudor brothers from Anglesey captured the castle at Conwy. A year later, the rumour that the deposed king Richard was still alive stiffened opposition to Henry IV.

Avoiding confrontation, Glyndwr's warriors spread the rebellion from the north of Wales to the south. In a mountain glen in the Hyddgen valley, near Llanidloes, Glyndwr's guerilla band of 400 men was surrounded by 1500 Flemish immigrants and merchants of south Wales, fiercely determined to protect their newly-established colonies. For Owain, it was death or surrender. But the Welsh rebels were hardened fighters and they savaged the Flemish civilians. It was Glyndwr's first victory in a pitched battle and it increased his following overnight. Such a force, however, could not hope to survive the mighty army that Henry IV now assembled to finish off the Welsh. In desperation, Glyndwr wrote to both the kings of Ireland and Scotland. 'So long as we shall wage manfully this war on our borders,' he told the Gaelic high king of Ireland, 'so you and all other chieftains of your parts of Ireland will in the meantime have welcome peace and quiet repose.' Unfortunately, both letters were intercepted by king Henry. There would be no union of the Celtic realms.

Henry's army burned and ransacked monasteries and villages. It took

255

Irishmen fighting with axes. After the illustrations in Giraldus Cambrensis' early thirteenth-century *Topographia Hibernica & Expugnatio Hiberniae*, now in the National Library of Ireland, Dublin.

prisoner the children of suspected rebels. But it came nowhere near to ending Welsh independence. Glyndwr emerged from his mountain lair to capture Lord Grey of Ruthin. By 1404, he was at the height of his power. He summoned a national Welsh parliament which all the leading Welsh magnates attended. His unity was greater even than that of Llywelyn, for Powys had always remained aloof: now Powys did homage to Glyndwr. He planned to establish a separate Welsh church and university. He made individual treaties with France and Scotland. It seemed that Welsh independence would again become reality.

In 1405, the French invaded Britain. Almost 3,000 French warriors landed at Milford Haven. They were met by an army of 10,000 Welshmen. Together they would smash the English. At Caerleon, the French marvelled at the Roman amphitheatre. They were told it was the original Round Table of the Arthurian knights and that, of course, Arthur was the warrior hero of the Celtic Britons and not the English. Worcester, the first major English town in their path, was devastated. At Woodbury Hill, they set up camp.

Kidney daggers, fourteenth to fifteenth centuries, now in the London Museum. Commonly a civilian weapon, but also carried by archers in battle.

Scots knights charge English archers at the battle of Homildon Hill, 1402. The Scots were defeated, however, and later one of their leaders, the Earl of Douglas, made a pact to aid Owain Glyndwr against Henry IV. From Cassell's *History of England*, 1905.

They were confronted by an English army led by king Henry's son, the future Henry V. Apparently, with their minds full of Arthurian legend, the Franco-Welsh challenged the English not to battle but to a tournament. For eight days, knights of both sides hurtled towards each other with lance and sword. Two hundred died in the sporting combat. Eventually Prince Henry tired of the game. He retired to Worcester and then turned on the retreating French, harrying their rearguard. Some French sailed home, others stayed with the Welsh. The ambitious expedition had run out of steam and the tide now turned for Glyndwr.

From 1406 onwards, Prince Henry and the English tightened the ring around Glyndwr's principality. The Marches were won back slowly and the Welsh retreated to the mountains of central Wales. As always, the superior economic and logistical back-up of the English was beginning to dominate the struggle. But the Glyndwr was far from finished. In 1415, Henry V sent an envoy to offer a pardon to the Welshman. Owain refused. It was then that Glyndwr became swathed in legend. His whereabouts were unknown. The chronicles are silent. The date and site of his death are a mystery. Many Welshmen were convinced that like Arthur, Glyndwr was asleep in a cave in the heart of Wales awaiting the right time to lead his people to freedom. The inspiration of Celtic liberty remained. But increasingly, despite the action of heroic warlords, the future of all the Celtic realms of Britain and Ireland was haunted by the English. In the next century, Celtic warriors would face the final challenge to their independence. It came from a dynasty of Celtic ancestry: the Tudors.

The Final Challenge

For two hundred years, English influence in Ireland declined. From the invasion of Edward Bruce to the rise of the Tudor dynasty, the power of the English crown had been so reduced that in 1465 the Pale included only the four home counties of Dublin, Kildare, Meath and Louth: a frontier of not even 150 miles. Civil war and continental conflict had undermined English control, but it was also the independent Celtic spirit of the Irish warlords. The majority of Anglo-Irish lords, descendants of the Normans, had gone native. Their language, appearance and law was Gaelic. Militarily, the Irish were no longer cowed by English or Welsh mercenaries. They had fierce mercenaries of their own. Emerging from the ancient relationship between Ulster and the Scots Isles and Western Highlands, a potent military force had developed over the two centuries since Edward Bruce. Scots adventurers and families of professional warriors sailed to Ireland intent on hiring themselves out to the highest bidder. These were the galloglas, a fiery mixture of Scots, Irish and Norse.

Galloglas means 'foreign young warrior' and probably refers to their Viking blood. But, essentially, these warriors were Gaelic in tongue and custom. Some had accompanied Edward Bruce and many fought for the Ulster chieftains. As their notoriety grew, they were hired by other Irish warlords. Such business enabled generations of galloglas families to prosper from Gaelic feuds. The principal mercenary dynasties were the MacDonalds, MacSwineys, MacSheehys, MacDowells, MacRorys and MacCabes. It was only a matter of time before the English felt the need to employ them as well. In between bouts of fighting, the galloglas set up their own settlements on Irish territory. By the sixteenth century they had become an institution and were the elite of every Irish army. John Dymmok in the late sixteenth century captured their basic image: 'The galloglas are picked and select men of great and mighty bodies, cruel without compassion. The greatest force of the battle consisteth in them, choosing rather to die than to yield, so that when it cometh to bandy blows, they are quickly slain or win the field.' Such a description of the short bursts of fighting energy of Celtic warriors could have come from the pens of Latin writers of the first centuries AD. Perhaps the English saw themselves as the new Romans and so inflicted such classical imagery on their Celtic opponents. 'They are armed with a shirt of mail, a skull [*close-fitting iron helmet*], and a skean [*long knife*],' continued Dymmok. 'The weapon which they most use is a battle-axe or halberd, six foot long, the blade whereof is somewhat like a shoemaker's knife, but broader and longer without pike [*that is, spike*], the stroke whereof is deadly where it lighteth. And being thus armed, reckoning to him a man for his harness bearer, and a boy to carry his provisions, he is named a spare [*spear? or 'sparre' meaning a long-handled axe*] of his weapon so called, 80 of which spares make a battle of galloglas.' Although frequently from noble families and regarded as gentlemen soldiers by the English, the galloglas did not fight on horseback, but assembled in bodies of heavily-armoured foot-soldiers.

On an equal ranking were Irish horse-warriors. 'Their horsemen are all gentlemen (I mean of great septs or names, how base soever otherwise),' noted Fynes Moryson in 1600 with a pertinent afterthought. Like the galloglas, many were professional soldiers of fortune. 'These horsemen,' wrote Rochard Stanihurst in 1577, 'when they have no stay of their own [*that is, are not retained by any lord*], gad and range from house to house like errant knights of the Round Table, and they never dismount until they ride into the hall and as far as the table.' They were highly respected as light cavalry by the English. Sir Anthony St Leger remarked on them in a letter to Henry VIII in 1543: 'I think for their feat of war, which is for light scourers, there are no properer horsemen in Christian ground, nor more hardy, nor yet that can better endure hardness.' Later in the century, Edmund Spenser concurred: 'I have heard some great warriors say that in all the services which they had seen abroad in foreign countries they never saw a more comely horseman than the Irishman, nor that cometh on more bravely in his charge.'

It seems the high skill of Celtic horsemanship had not deserted the Irish. And yet, in other descriptions of Irish cavalry we have a clear picture of a military primitivism that is supposed to have been characteristic of Irish warfare. 'The horsemen are armed with head-pieces, shirts of mail or jacks [*leather quilted coats sometimes plated with iron*], a sword, a skein, and a spear. They ride upon pads [*stuffed saddles*] or pillons without stirrups, and in this differ from ours; that in joining with the enemy, they bear not their

An Irish kern and old man with two women in old English dress. From a water-colour drawing by Lucas de Heere, c. 1575, after a lost drawing by an anonymous artist showing Irishmen from earlier in the century.

staves or lances under arm, and so put it to rest, but taking it by the middle, bear it above arm, and so encounter.' Contemporary engravings reinforce this image of stirrupless riders, while Edmund Spenser states that among the Irish 'the stirrup was called so in scorn as it were a stair to get up'. It is baffling that, alone among all Europe's horse-warriors, the Irish chose to ride without stirrups or good saddles. It seems more likely that such primitivism was an invention of the English to play up their barbarity. Yet it is mentioned and illustrated by several sources, not all of them wholly uncomplimentary to the Irish. There seems little point either to focus on this detail when the general character of the Irish was found sufficient by the English to condemn them. In an earlier time, a French manuscript of the fourteenth century shows an Irish noble horseman clad in archaic coat of mail with no stirrups and bare feet. That Irish cavalry held their spears overarm rather than couched underarm is also a primitive military custom, reminiscent of ancient Celtic horsemen hurling spears before their initial contact. This, however, is the most effective tactic of light cavalrymen determined to harass and avoid confrontation.

In battle, records John Dymmok, 'every horseman hath two or three horses, and to every horse a knave; his horse of service is always led spare, and his knave, which carrieth his harness [*armour*] and spear [*presumably spears*], rideth upon the other, or else upon a hackney.' The lowest in status of the three main contingents of Irish armies was the kern. 'The kern is a kind of footman, slightly armed with a sword, a target of wood [*shield*], or a bow and sheaf of arrows with barbed heads, or else three darts [*javelins*], which they cast with wonderful facility and nearness, a weapon more noisome to the enemy, especially horsemen, than it is deadly; within these few years they have practised the musket and caliver, and are grown good and ready shot.' Earlier, Sir Anthony St Leger described these light foot-soldiers as 'naked men, but only for their shirts and small coats. And they have darts and short bows; which sort of people be both hardy and active to search woods or morasses, in the which be hard to be beaten.'

The ferocity of the kerns left deep impressions on many veterans of the Irish wars. In 1600, Gervase Markham wrote a poem in which he imagined the town of Kerne as an Irish Sodom. Because of the licentious behaviour of its inhabitants, it is drowned beneath the waters of Lough Erne and the citizens transformed into wolves.

> The kerns sprung thus from this prodigious brood
> Are still as lewd as when their city stood.
> Fraught with all vice, replete with villainy,
> They still rebel and that most treacherously.
> Like brutish Indians these wild Irish live;
> Their quiet neighbours they delight to grieve.
> Cruel and bloody, barbarous and rude,
> Dire vengeance at their heels hath them pursued.
> They are the savagest of all the nation;
> Amongst them out I made my peregrination,
> Where many wicked customs I did see
> Such as all honest hearts I hope will flee.

From the verse above, it can be seen that by the sixteenth century the gulf in understanding between Irish and English cultures had become irreconcilable. The disdain of Giraldus had been succeeded by the invective of Tudor conquest.

The Irish of the sixteenth century were as adept at guerilla warfare as their forefathers. 'Because they are only trained to skirmish upon bogs and difficult passes or passages of woods,' observed Fynes Moryson in 1600, 'and not to stand or fight in a firm body upon the plains, they think it no shame to fly or run off from fighting, as they advantage.' 'A flying enemy,' is how Edmund Spencer chose to describe the Irish warrior's tactics. 'Hiding himself in woods and bogs, from whence he will not draw forth but into some strait passage or perilous ford where he knows the army [*of the enemy*] must needs pass, there will he lie in wait, and if he find advantage fit, will dangerously hazard the troubled soldier.' Right into the sixteenth century, the Irish maintained a particularly Celtic manner of warfare: light cavalry and guerilla tactics. It was to prove relentless and costly for the English.

Gaelic culture was predominant among the native Irish and the Anglo-Irish, more so than in any other Celtic realm. The language was spoken throughout the land and even in the Pale, while Gaelic law was still an institution difficult for the English to comprehend. 'For whereas by the just and honourable law of England, murder, manslaughter, rape, robbery, and theft are punished with death, by the Irish custom, or Brehon Law, the highest of these offences was punished only by fine, which they called an ericke.' Such humanity was not appreciated by the English and featured little in their savage dealings with the Irish in war. Leading Irishmen continued to elect their leaders in the time-honoured Celtic manner. 'It is a custom amongst all the Irish that presently after the death of any of their chief Lords or Captains, they do presently assemble themselves to a place generally appointed and known unto them, to choose another in his stead: where they do nominate and elect for the most part not the eldest son nor any of the children of their Lord deceased, but the next to him of blood that is the eldest and worthiest.' Again, such good sense was not appreciated by the English who had fought many wars over the rights of the elder son to claim his father's throne.

Once the English had reconstructed royal authority after the Wars of the Roses, the Tudor dynasty set about curbing the prevailing Gaelic culture of Ireland. In 1494, Henry VII issued Poyning's Law which dictated that the Irish Parliament could only pass bills approved by the Privy Council in London. It ensured a subordinate, colonial role for the Irish government and was only repealed in 1782. Next was an attack on Irish customs. Henry VIII struck at the very heart of Gaelic identity when he recommended a ban on native appearance. 'No person or persons shall be shorn, or shaven above the ears, or use the wearing of hair called glibes [*a thick fringe of hair on the forehead that frequently covered the eyes and was characteristic of Irish warriors*], or have to use any hair growing upon their upper lips, called or named a crommeal [*an attack on the moustache, the quintessence of Celtic manhood for so long*], or to use or wear any shirt, kerchief, of linen cap, coloured or dyed with saffron [*the traditional colour of Irish noblemen*], nor yet to use or wear in any of their shirts or smocks above 7 yards of cloth. Be it enacted that every person or persons, the King's true subjects, in habiting this land of Ireland, of what estate, condition or degree he or they be, or shall be, to the uttermost of their power, cunning, and knowledge, shall use and speak commonly the English tongue and language.'

The prohibition of Irish manners and customs was made law in the reign of Queen Elizabeth in 1571. 'The sons of all husbandmen and ploughmen shall follow the same occupation as their fathers. If the son of a husbandman or ploughman will become a kern, galloglas, or horseboy, or will take any other idle trade of life, he shall be imprisoned for a twelve month and fined.' Private armies were banned. 'For avoiding of robberies and idleness, no lords or any others shall keep more horsemen or footmen than they are able to maintain upon their own costs. They shall present the names of such men as they keep in a book to the justices of the peace in the country where they dwell.' Failure to do so brought death. 'All Irish law called the Brehon Law to be of no force, and all persons taking upon them to adjudge causes according to the said law, to have a twelve months' imprisonment and to forfeit all their goods and chattels.' The wearing of Irish clothes and the Gaelic hairstyle known as the glib was to be punished with a £100 fine. Such measures may seem silly or impossible to maintain, but it was a law against Irishness and meant that every Irishman had been declared an outlaw. This was a convenient weapon against rebels, if no other crime could be proved.

Gaelic discontent with the Tudor anglicisation of Ireland was strongest in western Ulster. Beyond the river Bann and Lough Neagh was a land ringed by mountains and deep cut waterways, a land the Normans had never penetrated. Gaelic clans ruled the territory as they had for centuries and the

An Irish lord, probably a MacSwiney of a galloglas dynasty, prepares to set out on a cattle-raid. From a woodcut, probably by John Derricke, for his book *The Image of Irelande*, published in London in 1581.

O'Neills were, as always, the dominant family. But, even there, the foreign policy of Henry VIII cracked open splits in the Celtic society. The head of the O'Donnels of Donegal submitted to the English king and he was followed by Con O'Neill who pledged the loyalty of Tyrone, forsook the title of The O'Neill, and agreed to pursue English customs and language. Such submission meant that Con O'Neill's eldest son, Matthew, was his successor according to the English law of primogeniture. This was too much for another of Con O'Neill's sons, Shane. He had been elected successor by the senior members of the clan according to Brehon law and the principle of tanistry. He set about proving he was the more effective man. Matthew was proclaimed a bastard son, ambushed and murdered. Con O'Neill was thrown out of Tyrone, dying shortly after in the Pale. Fifteen thousand Scots mercenaries were invited over from Kintyre and Islay: the Campbells, McLeans, MacLeods and McKays. In addition, Shane broke with the tradition that only freemen could carry weapons: all the peasants on his estates were armed. The Anglo-Irish army in the Pale barely numbered 2,000 and were clearly over-awed, preferring to sit tight and observe Shane consolidate his power.

In 1561, Shane O'Neill moved against his biggest rivals in Ulster. Calvach O'Donnel was betrayed by his wife to Shane. He kept O'Donnel in chains and his woman as a mistress. All of Ulster was now under his direct control. The Earl of Sussex, Lord Lieutenant of Ireland, had to act. But Shane was in no need of a confrontation. Sussex advanced to Armagh in south east Ulster and Shane's lightly armed warriors kept out of his way. The English army paraded on through Tyrone to Lough Foyle. They captured 4,000 cattle but not even this traditional challenge could bring O'Neill into the field. Eventually, achieving nothing, the English force wearied of the guerilla response and backed off to Newry. Tyrone had been ravaged but the hearts and minds of the Ulstermen were with O'Neill. In order to put his case fairly to Queen Elizabeth, Shane accepted an offer of safe conduct and travelled to London.

To the English, Ireland was one of the frontiers of Europe, a land on the edge of their world, full of barbarians. It is little surprising then that the courtiers of Elizabethan London observed O'Neill's retainers with 'as much wonder as if they had come from China or America,' according to a contemporary chronicler. Indeed, the Celtic party, headed by The O'Neill, presented a fantastic sight. In defiance of previous Tudor legislation, his warriors were wholly Gaelic in appearance. Their hair was long: fringes hanging down to cover their eyes. They wore shirts with large sleeves dyed with saffron, short tunics and shaggy cloaks. Some walked with bare feet, others wore leather sandals. The galloglas carried battle-axes and wore long coats of mail. O'Neill was himself a man of fearsome reputation. He could not abide anything English. He is said to have hanged a warrior for eating an English biscuit and called a stronghold 'Fuath-na-Gall', 'hatred of the Englishmen'.

Though bold and confident, O'Neill was not foolish. In front of Elizabeth, he begged for forgiveness for his alleged rebellion and explained his case. Matthew O'Neill had been a mere bastard, so, according to both English and Celtic laws of succession, Shane was entitled to be The O'Neill. Above all, the O'Neills had run Ulster as long as anyone could remember. But Shane was willing to admit Elizabeth's overlordship and help her in any way possible. The Queen held back her anger and invited him to clear eastern Ulster of the 'robbers of Hebrides': the military Scots families who had settled in Antrim. Thus, O'Neill returned to Ireland with his status enhanced, his position recognised, and carte blanche to acquire further territory in north-east Ireland.

The MacDonalds were the chief galloglas family of Antrim. They were the sons of the Lord of Islay and Kintyre and great-great-grandsons of John MacDonald of the Isles. Arming his warriors with matchlock handguns, O'Neill saw no need to employ the hit-and-run tactics he had against the English, but chose confrontation. The MacDonalds in their turn raised the alarm for reinforcements from the Western Isles by lighting beacons on the coastal cliffs of Antrim. They clashed a few miles south of Ballycastle. The battle was ferocious and long. By nightfall, it was clear that the O'Neills were victorious. The leading MacDonalds were made prisoner and thirteen clan banners captured. Queen Elizabeth rejoiced at the breaking of the Scots foothold in Ireland, but now she faced an independent Irish warlord of even greater strength. O'Neill followed up his military victories with political strategy. He wrote to the king of France requesting 6,000 troops 'to assist in expelling the English'. O'Neill was under no illusions. He played along with Elizabeth's efforts to set one Gaelic faction against another, but he knew that in the end it was the English who were his greatest enemy.

In 1566, Sir Henry Sidney, a new English Lord Deputy of Ireland, set about curbing the power of The O'Neill. 'Lucifer was never more puffed up with pride and ambition than O'Neill is,' he wrote to Elizabeth. 'He continually keepeth six hundred armed men about him and is able to bring into the field one thousand horsemen and four thousand foot. He is the only strong man of Ireland.' Marching to the mouth of the river Blackwater, Sidney captured O'Neill's Coney Island stronghold in Lough Neagh. A stone tower 30 feet high and surrounded by sharpened stakes, a thick hedge, ditch, and stone rampart, it was the Ulsterman's treasury. Sidney then progressed through Tyrone, again demonstrating English power, and again being avoided by O'Neill's men who had reverted to their guerilla tactics. Such a parade of strength, however, had damaged Shane's pride and purse and restored the O'Donnells in Donegal. With little money to pay his followers and a dent in his control of the land, O'Neill had to act decisively or he would lose the support of his warriors. He decided to regain his reputation as a winner by attacking the O'Donnells.

In the spring of 1567, the O'Neills rode into view of the O'Donnells at Farsetmore, a sandy ford across the river Swilly. At first, the horsemen of both vanguards exchanged blows. Spears were thrown over-arm in the traditional Celtic manner. But the clatter of javelins was joined by the crack of gun-fire as the arquebusiers of each side joined in. The O'Donnells were pushed back to their prepared positions on boggy ground. Reinforced by galloglas of the clan MacSwiney, they then counter-attacked. Galloglas of the MacDonalds fought alongside the O'Neills. 'Fierce and desperate were the grim and terrible looks that each cast at the other out of their starlike eyes,' recorded the *Annals of the Four Masters*. 'They raised the battle-cry aloud and their united shouting when rushing together was sufficient to strike with dismay and turn to flight the feeble and unwarlike. They proceeded to strike and cut down one another for a long time, so that men were soon laid low, youths slain, and robust heroes mangled in the slaughter.' The galloglas of both sides, axes swinging, were engaged in a struggle fuelled not by the animosity of their pay-masters but by deeply inbred clan rivalry. Exhaustion brought the battle to its crisis and the O'Neills were the first to break. Many tried to cross the river Swilly, but the waters had risen since they first crossed and many were drowned.

Shane O'Neill's forces were routed and with them disappeared his power. His judgement shaken by the defeat, Shane sought shelter among the MacDonalds of Antrim. Although politics had united them while Shane was riding high, the Scots clan could not forget the damage he had done to their people on behalf of Elizabeth. Initially, they welcomed him and helped him forget his sorrows with a drinking party. But, whether it was the drink or a prepared trap, fighting broke out. Shane and his bodyguard were cut to pieces. A few days later, O'Neill's head was presented to Sir Henry Sidney. Where the English had failed, Celtic warriors had succeeded in destroying the one Irish warlord who could have kept at least one part of Ireland wholly Gaelic. In 1569, the title of O'Neill and the sovereignty of the dynasty was abolished. The Elizabethan conquest had begun in earnest.

Frontier warfare brings out the worst in its warriors. Both sides consider each other alien and inhuman, so savagery prevails. Beyond the Pale, English conquistadors suspended any humanity they possessed and treated the Irish as they would the Indians of America: natives to be dispossessed and exterminated. The Irish responded with equal ferocity. The English spearheaded their campaigns with warlords of barbaric renown. In 1570, Humphrey Gilbert was made commander of the English army of Munster. Any visitor to his camp was compelled to walk between two lines of severed Irish heads leading to his tent. Largely due to the efforts of Gilbert, resistance in Munster was crushed and the land divided into English plantations. Similar ruthlessness ensured the English conquest of Connacht. Only Ulster remained a Celtic realm. And yet its leading Gaelic heir of The O'Neill had been educated in England as a potential weapon against the Irish.

Hugh O'Neill was the son of Matthew, the son of Con O'Neill. After the

Homage by the citizens of Dublin to Sir Henry Sidney, Lord Deputy of Ireland, after he returns from a victory over the Gaelic Irish in 1575. From John Derricke's *The Image of Irelande.*

O Sydney worthy of tryple re-
nowne,
For plagyng the traytours that
troubled the crowne. 1581.

269

murder of his father by Shane O'Neill, Hugh was brought up in England as a royal ward. Attached to the household of the Earl of Leicester, he learned lessons in England, both political and military, which were to prove highly useful. Returning to Ireland in the year after Shane O'Neill's death, he served with the government forces. He was considered safe enough to be rewarded with the title of Earl of Tyrone. The English now had a puppet ruler of Ulster through whom they could further exploit the country; or so they thought. Once settled in his homeland, Hugh's Gaelic blood rose. He consolidated his native power base. 'All men of rank within the province are become his men,' it was observed, 'they receive his wages and promise him service according to the usual manner of that country.' In 1593, Hugh O'Neill was elected by his clan to the title of The O'Neill. It was a slap in the face of English law. Drawn between both the role of an English peer and that of a Gaelic chieftain, it was to the latter that Hugh finally dedicated his life. Such a turn of events was encouraged by the presence of Red Hugh O'Donnell. Having dramatically escaped from Dublin castle, O'Donnell gathered his forces, including 3,000 Scots mercenaries, and took his revenge on the English colonists in Connacht: 'sparing no male between fifteen and sixty years old who was unable to speak Irish.'

O'Neill was ordered to attack O'Donnell, which he did, but he also dragged his feet. Observing the English hard-pressed, he continued to build up his own forces. Queen Elizabeth had permitted him 600 troops, trained by English captains. These were then used to train further recruits: Irish

Spanish morion helmet of around 1580. The Irish obtained much arms and armour from abroad, usually smuggled through English ports and sometimes direct from Spain.

and Scots mercenaries called bonaghts. The institution of the galloglas had declined since the heroic days of the early sixteenth century. Many of the Scots adventurer families had long since become a part of the Irish community. They were landowners and no longer needed to fight for their living. Effective English fleets in the Irish Sea prevented any frequent forays from the Western Isles. Besides, the traditional arms of the galloglas, the sword and pole-axe, had been supplanted by the pike and musket as the universal instruments of death. Those Scots warriors who now fought with the Irish mainly served under the name of bonaghts and wielded pike or musket. Organised in companies of 100 men and armed with the latest weapons imported from Scotland and Spain, or smuggled from English ports, there was little to distinguish them from their English adversaries, apart from the drone of the bagpipe that urged them on into battle.

By 1595, O'Neill had recruited and trained some 1,000 pikemen, 4,000 musketeers, and 1,000 cavalry. He was strong enough to declare his Gaelic interests and was forthwith proclaimed a traitor. An English policing force was mauled at Clontibret. The O'Donnells captured Sligo, thus securing the south-west approach to Ulster against English reinforcements. But, before all-out war could break, a truce was called. In the meantime, O'Neill asked for assistance from England's arch enemy—Spain. In his correspondence, he allied the survival of Gaelic Ireland with the re-establishing of the Catholic religion against the Protestant regime of Elizabeth. He received a friendly ear but effective military aid was not forthcoming. No agreement was reached between O'Neill and the English and, in 1597, a three-pronged campaign was launched against Ulster. Each element was repulsed and O'Neill and O'Donnell were forced ever closer in the common defence of their land.

In 1598, Sir Henry Bagenal of Newry was instructed to relieve an English fortress on the banks of the river Blackwater besieged by the Ulstermen. He commanded an army of around 4,000 foot and 300 horse. Almost 2,000 of these were raw recruits, barely a couple of months in Ireland and poorly equipped. 'The want of the men's apparel is such,' wrote Captain Francis Stafford, 'that if they be not speedily relieved, many will march without shoes or stockings.' Irish clothing was recommended for the English soldiers as being cheaper and more durable than the clothing imported from England, but Lord Burgh, Lord Deputy of Ireland, could not accept this because such clothing was made by the Irish who would thus receive 'her Majesty's good coin, wherewith they buy out of Denmark, Scotland and other parts, powder and munition to maintain their rebellion.' The rest of Bagenal's army, however, were veterans of the Irish war, half of which were probably native Irishmen, including many cavalry.

The English force marched from Armagh to the Blackwater across 'hard and hilly ground, within caliver shot of wood and bog on both sides, which was wholly possessed by the enemy continually playing upon us.' Charles Montague, Lieutenant-General of the English, was correct in this account.

O'Neill and O'Donnell had invested some 5,000 warriors in the densely-forested countryside. The English marched in battle order, returning the skirmishing fire, but inevitably the advancing line became strung out and soon it was to be every man for himself. The English pressed on; the fort on the Blackwater was now nearer than Armagh. But O'Neill had carefully prepared the territory. Brushwood and undergrowth had been weaved together to create living fences. Pits had been dug to ensnare the unweary and impede cavalry action. Finally, boggy land was linked by a trench some five feet deep and four feet over, with a thorny hedge on the other side.

The English tried to break through. Their formations were scattered. The first half of the English vanguard was isolated beyond the trench, within sight of the beleaguered garrison of the Blackwater. The garrison threw up their caps in joy and dashed out to meet the English relief force. But O'Neill was well in command of the situation and pulled the noose tight. His skirmishers pummelled the English ranks further. Then horsemen surged forward and foot-soldiers armed with sword and shield. This was not a time for orthodox pike and shot tactics. Irish blades cut in among the English. The recent recruits broke before the Irish war cries. The vanguard was cut to pieces.

Realising the danger of his vanguard, Bagenal rode forward to support them. At the trench, he raised the visor of his helmet to gain a better view. Gun shot shattered his face and killed him instantly. The other English commanders decided on retreat, but this was easier said than done. A loud explosion ripped through the chaos. An English musketeer had gone to replenish his powder-flask: his lighted match carelessly sparked over the open powder barrels and the contents blew up, throwing a black cloud over the disintegrating army. Confusion tore the English apart. Some had not received the orders of retreat and pressed on to the killing ground of the trench. Others threw down their arms and deserted into the woods. At the end of the day, a shocked and bewildered English army reached Armagh. O'Neill had won a great victory. He did not follow it up: the remnants of the English army were allowed to escape. But Ulster remained resolutely Gaelic until the end of the century.

The strength of Hugh O'Neill's military leadership lay in his combination of professional training and the latest weapons with a traditional Celtic talent for guerilla warfare. In his victory he showed that Gaelic warriors, given the arms and training, were more than a match for any contemporary army. This is worth stressing, as much has been written about the archaic nature of Irish warfare and Celtic warfare in general. Certainly, it was a hard fact realised by English officers at the time. 'The Irish are most ready, well disciplined,' said one, 'and as good marksmen as France, Flanders, or Spain can show.' The Elizabethan invasion of Ireland was not so much an act of colonial discipline as a full-blown continental war, and one in which the Gaelic Irish won much success.

In the next century, the Irish were joined by Spanish soldiers landed at

Kinsale. Drawn out of their strong defensive situation in Ulster, the Gaelic Irish advanced to support the Spanish on the soutern coast of Munster. The English were besieging Kinsale, and O'Neill hoped to crush them against the Spanish. Advancing in the most contemporary tactical formations—the *tercio* of pike and shot—O'Neill led a formidable force. But his Celtic warriors were far away from familiar territory and were now being drawn into a confrontation on open ground. Confusion and panic broke the army. The Spanish and Irish did not act together. The English triumphed and O'Neill dismally dragged his forces back to Ulster. The Spanish capitulated and sailed home. A great opportunity had been lost. The Gaelic Irish had taken the offensive in what could have been a final shattering blow to English occupation. Instead, it proved the downfall of the Gaelic regime.

The English pressed hard on O'Neill and a harsh winter in 1603 finally compelled the Celtic warlord to surrender. Queen Elizabeth was dead but James I continued the anglicization of Ireland. O'Neill was allowed to return to his Ulster estates, but it was no longer a Celtic realm. English law predominated. Gaelic laws and customs were illegal. English government effectively reduced the power of the Gaelic chieftains; so much so that O'Neill and O'Donnell felt the land had now become alien and they preferred to sail into exile. O'Neill died in Rome in 1616. There would be further uprisings against the English and the O'Neill dynasty was far from finished, but essentially Gaelic power had been broken. The culture remained, but the military potential of Celtic warriors to maintain an independent realm was over. The same was true of other Celtic regions.

In Wales, the fiery independence of the Celtic Welsh was paradoxically undermined by the victory of one of its warlords. In 1485, Henry Tudor, a

Caricatured Irish soldiers in the service of Gustavus Aldolphus, 1631. From a contemporary German Broadside now in the British Museum, London. After the Elizabethan conquest, many Irish warriors sort a better life abroad.

In folchem Habit Gehen die 800 In Stettin angekommen Irrlander oder Irren.

member of the Anglesey dynasty, sailed to England under the red dragon standard. He advanced with a Welsh army to the battle of Bosworth. There, he smashed an English army, killed an English king, and assumed the English crown. At the time, a Venetian ambassador proclaimed that the Welsh had at last regained their liberty. But, in reality, this was not a Welsh victory, it was a Tudor triumph. The Tudor dynasty could not afford to tolerate any independent powers that might threaten its security. So Wales was incorporated into a union under the English crown. The old tripartite Wales of Celtic, Marcher and Royal estates was reorganised as English counties. The Welsh language was banned from public life. It was relegated to the language of the common people: no longer spoken by ambitious intelligentsia or the ruling classes. That this Celtic cultural defeat was delivered by an English monarch with Welsh blood in his veins seems to have softened the blow, for there were no more armed uprisings. Perhaps the Welsh felt they could claim with satisfaction that they were now ruled by a Welshman. Certainly, the Tudors rewarded their Welsh followers and could depend on their support.

In Scotland, English was also the language of the rulers, with Celtic the tongue of the ruled. However, after centuries of fighting the English for their independence, Scots aristocrats were far from happy to be told they were speaking the language of their enemy. Therefore, in the fifteenth century, the northern English spoken by the Scots ruling class became known as Scots, while the previously Scots Gaelic language was termed Irish. A wedge was again hammered between the anglicized Scots and the Gaelic Scots during the Reformation. Scots rulers accepted Protestant ideas and were urged to crush old Gaelic affinities to the Catholic faith, thus further lessening the presence of Celtic culture in Scotland. By 1521, the divide between the Gaelic Highlands and the Scots of the Lowlands was crystallised in a characterisation that has lingered on ever since.

'Just as among the Scots we find two distinct tongues,' wrote John Major in his *History of Greater Britain*,' so we likewise find two different ways of life and conduct. For some are born in the forests and mountains of the north, and these we call men of the Highland, but the others men of the Lowland. By foreigners the former are called Wild Scots, the latter householding Scots. One half of Scotland speaks Irish and all of these as well as the Islanders we reckon to belong to the Wild Scots. In dress, in the manner of their outward life, and in good morals, for example, these come behind the householding Scots—yet they are not less, but rather much more, prompt to fight. It is, however, with the householding Scots that the government and direction of the kingdom is to be found. One part of the Wild Scots have a wealth of cattle, sheep, and horses, and these with a thought for the possible loss of their possessions yield more willing obedience to the courts of law and the king. The other part of these people delight in the chase and a life of indolence. Their chieftains eagerly follow bad men if only they may not have the need to labour. They are full of mutual dissensions and war rather than peace is their normal condition. The Scottish kings have with difficulty been able to withstand the inroads of these men. These men hate our householding Scots, on account of their differing speech, as much as they do the English.'

Although this description of the Gaelic Scots by an outsider is a typical example of anti-Celtic propaganda, it nevertheless demonstrates the independent lifestyle maintained by the Gaelic clans and their clashes with Lowland kings. For, throughout the fifteenth century, the Gaelic lords of the Western Isles and Highlands were as much a danger to the kings of Scotland as the English. Indeed, many of the island chieftains used alliances with English factions to pursue their clan ambitions. The leading dynasty throughout this period was the MacDonalds. All other island clans did homage to them: the MacLeans of Mull, the MacLeods of Skye, the MacNeils of Barra, the MacIntoshes and the MacKinnons. In 1411, Donald, Lord of the Isles, led a formidable army to within a few miles of Aberdeen. In 1429, Alexander, Lord of the Isles, sacked Inverness. In 1451, John, Lord of the Isles, seized the royal castles of Urquhart, Inverness and Ruthven, and ravaged the islands in the Firth of Clyde. In 1491, Alexander, a nephew of the Lord of the Isles, invaded Ross and destroyed the castle of Inverness. It is little wonder, then, that when James IV ascended the throne in 1488 his immediate attention was directed towards the Islands and Highlands.

'The king is of noble stature, neither tall nor short, and as handsome in complexion and shape as a man can be.' So wrote Don Pedro de Ayala, Spanish ambassador, of James IV. 'He speaks the following foreign languages: Latin very well; French, German, Flemish, Italian, and Spanish. The king speaks besides, the language of the savages who live in some parts of Scotland and on the islands. He is courageous, even more so than a king should be. I have seen him often undertake most dangerous things in the last wars. He is not a good captain, because he begins to fight before he has given his orders.' Armed thus with both an aggressive nature and a working knowledge of Gaelic, James sailed to the island strongholds of the clans and commanded their respect. James was the last monarch to speak Gaelic and he used it to good effect. He treated the Highland chieftains with friendship and granted them land. In return, the clansmen acknowledged his overlordship. James even extended his influence over the Irish Sea, receiving the submission of Hugh O'Donnell of western Ulster.

The Celtic warriors confronted by James on his expeditions to the Western Isles have been described by John Major. 'From the mid-leg to the foot, they go uncovered. Their dress, for an over-garment, is a loose plaid and a shirt dyed with saffron. They are armed with bow and arrows, a broadsword, and a small halberd. They always carry in their belt a stout dagger, single-edged, but of the sharpest. In time of war they cover the whole body with a coat of mail, made of iron rings, and in it they fight. The common folk among the Wild Scots go out to battle with the whole body clad in a linen garment sewed together in patchwork, well daubed with wax or with pitch, and with an over-coat of deerskin.' After a few years of settlement, it was inevitable that the clansmen should kick against royal authority.

At the age of 25, James revoked all the charters he had granted the lords of the Isles. It was a constitutional act, but it now meant that the clansmen were tenants at the king's pleasure. To secure this relationship he appointed several deputies over the region once ruled by the Lord of the Isles. Displeased by this increased supervision of their traditional spheres of power, the clansmen became restless; particularly so when one of the king's deputies, the Earl of Argyll, was noted to grant favours to his own clan members. In the tenseness of the situation, James imprisoned Donald Owre, the generally acknowledged successor to the last Lord of the Isles. Later, James relented and released him. It was to be a costly generosity. At once, Donald set about claiming his true right of lordship. Many disaffected chieftains joined his banner, including MacLean of Lochbuie, MacLean of Duart, and Ewen Allanson of Lochiel. Supporters of the king in the Isles were killed and clansmen ravaged Bute.

In retaliation, the Scots parliament enacted several laws against the independent Celtic warriors. The king's muscle was supplied by one of his deputies, the Earl of Huntly, who assaulted clan strongholds on the mainland, and the king's ships which sailed for the remote castle of Cairn na Burgh to the west of Mull. Little is known of the action in this confrontation, but it is clear the Highlanders were not quelled. Further ships were equipped with cannons and German gunners from Edinburgh Castle and these patrolled the Western Isles. By 1507, however, the last rebel stronghold was besieged by the royal fleet and Donald Owre had been captured. Relationships between the clansmen and the king became more friendly, but the extent of James' trust of the Highlanders is demonstrated by his strengthening of several castles at strategic points throughout the Highlands. It might seem that James had maintained his authority, but in reality little had been achieved against the Gaelic Scots. The clansmen remained semi-independent warlords ready to prove a major threat to Scots kings in the future.

By 1511, James had other enemies to consider. Scotland was enmeshed in continental affairs. Her Auld Alliance with the king of France was tested as the Pope, the king of Spain, the Doge, the Emperor, and the king of England all prepared to divide France. The Scots stood by their traditional ally and in 1513 James demanded Henry VIII withdraw from his invasion of France. Henry refused, adding that he was 'the very owner of Scotland' which James 'held of him by homage', thus evoking the claims of English kings before the war of Independence. Outraged, James responded by recruiting a great army and marching across the Tweed. Raiders rode ahead, clashing with the border landlords and their retinues. In the main body of the army, seventeen cannon were dragged forward by four hundred oxen. Three

English castles fell to James, but many Scotsmen had already lost the stomach for fighting and desertion plagued the king's army. To march on York was now considered foolhardy and unnecessary. The invasion slowed down. An English army was reported to be advancing northwards. Led by the Earl of Surrey, it numbered about 20,000. The Scots army cannot have differed greatly in strength as neither side was daunted by the numbers of the other. James prepared a secure position on Flodden Hill and awaited confrontation.

The rain rushed down the hillsides around Flodden, overflowing streams and transforming fields into swamps. James felt content with the situation. If the English attacked, his cannon and schiltrons would hurl them back down the slippery slopes of Flodden Hill. If they did not, then he could retreat to the frontier and reinforce his army for whatever move he considered prudent. Surrey tried to draw James off the hill with a challenge to come down from his fortress-like position and fight on the plain of Milfield. But, though a lover of the tournament and the chivalric duel, James refused: 'Show to the Earl of Surrey that it beseemeth him not, being an Earl, so largely to attempt a great prince. His Grace will take and hold his ground at his own pleasure.' James was a cooler general than Ayala had credited him for. Surrey, however, was no fool either. He commanded his troops to march northwards and then wheel round so as to stand between the Scots and Scotland. The next day, James awoke to this danger. He had to get to Branxton Hill, to the north-west of Flodden, before the English, otherwise they would possess a similarly impregnable position. The alarm was sounded. The camp was stripped down and burnt: a great cloud of smoke hung over the land. Teams of oxen heaved the Scots' cannon across to Branxton Hill. Battle was approaching and the Scots assembled in their familiar schiltrons. Four massive squares took shape: the king commanded the right centre while the majority of Gaelic warriors in the army—the Highlanders and Islanders—formed the right wing. A further body of soldiers were placed in reserve. They now all looked down the muddy slopes of Branxton Hill at the advancing English.

The Earl of Surrey felt distinctly uneasy. The Scots had moved quicker than anticipated, leaving the English vanguard in the deadground at the base of the hill awaiting the rest of the army. If the Scots had attacked then, they could have destroyed the English piecemeal. Instead, time passed, and the English rearguard joined its fellow soldiers. At last, the Scots' cannon opened fire, hurling balls of stone among the enemy. The English replied with their guns. Apparently, the English gunners were more accurate and their shot crashed into James' division, mowing down his armour-plated comrades. It was then that James' bold recklessness finally took over from his strategic prudence and he led his warriors forward. Before the advancing schiltrons, the English right flank just ran away. But the English counter-attacked and both backed off. The king of Scotland's division surged on towards the Earl of Surrey. It was in this combat in the centre that the battle was won and lost. Thomas Ruthall, the bishop of Durham, described the crucial conflict only a few weeks later. 'The Scots were so surely harnessed that the shot of arrows did them no harm and when it came to hand strokes of bills and halberds, they were so mighty that they would not fall when struck by four or five bills all at once. But our bills did us more good that day than bows for they soon disappointed the Scots of their long spears. And when they came to hand strike, the Scots fought valiantly with their swords yet were unable to resist the bills which alighted on them so thickly.' From contemporary accounts, it appears the English soldiers armed with 8-foot bills, a kind of pole-arm, were at an advantage in close combat as the Scots' 15-foot spears were too unwieldly to be effective. Yet when the Scots threw them down and drew their swords, they were outreached by the bills.

In the struggling crowd, James also threw aside his pike, slashing and hacking at the English with his sword. He got within a spear's length of Surrey, but a series of bill blows cut him down. It might be thought that the death of a commander would go unnoticed in the chaos of fighting, but unless he is always on show, urging his warriors forward, the loss is soon clear and the fight drains from soldiers only there because of him. At the foot of Branxton Hill, the death of James broke his army. A further surprise appearance of an English force around the hillside shattered the Highlanders who had yet to prove themselves but saw little reason for standing in the dusk with no king to note their loyalty. In the fading light, the surviving Scots made their way home, pursued relentlessly by the victorious English.

The death of James IV, the last Gaelic-speaking monarch, did not particularly harm the Celtic cause in Scotland. Indeed, his death initiated a century of uncertainty and weakness for the Scots monarchy that allowed the Highland warlords to increase their power and liberty. Again they allied themselves with the Tudors, but in the end victory for the English could mean only ultimate defeat for all Scots. For with the increasing influence of English Protestantism on Scotland and its eventual success, the Catholic-orientated culture of Gaelic Scotland was dealt a severe blow. Yet, in 1603, it was the Scots' king James VI who became James I of England and succeeded Elizabeth, that scourge of Celtic society. Like the Welsh, over a century earlier, all Scots could at least claim that Britain was ruled by one of their own. But here again, as with the Tudors, dynastic survival overcame national loyalty and James VI came down hard on the clans.

In the year of James I's accession, a bloody incident at Glenfruin encouraged a stern anti-Gaelic stance. In a pitched battle between the Macgregors and the Colquhouns of Luss, two hundred of the Colquhouns and several spectating citizens from Dumbarton were slaughtered, Immediately, James passed an act outlawing the entire Macgregor clan. A few years later in 1609, James enacted further statutes against the Highlanders intended to bring them in line with the Lowlanders. One of the statutes

prohibited the importation of whisky, known as *aqua vitae*, to the Western Isles. It was claimed that 'one of the special causes of the great poverty of the Isles and of the great cruelty and inhuman barbarity which has been practised by sundry of the inhabitants upon their natural friends and neighbours has been their extraordinary drinking of strong wines and aqua vitae brought in among them, partly by merchants of the mainland and partly by traffickers among themselves.' Another statute hit harder at Gaelic identity. 'The Irish language which is one of the chief and principal causes of the continuance of barbarity and incivility among the inhabitants of the Isles and Highlands may be abolished and removed.' It was decreed that every gentleman must send his eldest son or daughter to the Lowlands to learn to speak, read and write English. It was clear the English and Lowland government were intent on extinguishing the Gaelic culture of Scotland as far as it could be seen to be a political threat.

The importance of language to the identity of a people cannot be overestimated. In the ancient world, it was only the common Celtic tongue that gave unity to an otherwise varied and often divided people. The Celt existed through his language. Without it, he ceased to be truly Celtic. Thus, by ensuring Celtic was spoken only by the common people and not by their leaders, it effectively struck away at Celtic power. The destruction of their language was the greatest blow Celtic warriors could ever receive. It denied their very existence.

Bibliography

THIS IS, OF NECESSITY, A SELECT BIBLIOGRAPHY OF
BOTH PRIMARY AND SECONDARY REFERENCES

PRIMARY SOURCES

ALL THESE TEXTS ARE AVAILABLE IN ENGLISH TRANSLATIONS IN SEVERAL EDITIONS.

Annals of Ulster: Medieval Irish history from the earliest times.

Appian, *Roman History*: principal source for Roman conquest of Spain by a Graeco-Roman of the second century AD.

John Barbour, *The Bruce*: fourteenth-century poem about Robert Bruce written by the Archdeacon of Aberdeen.

Brut Y Tywysogion—Chronicle of the Princes: Welsh history of Wales from the seventh to thirteenth centuries. There are two other versions of this chronicle, *The Red Book of Hergest* and *The Kings of the Saxons*.

Caesar, *The Gallic War*: first century BC autobiography of campaigns against the Celts of France.

Four Ancient Books of Wales: nineteenth-century compilation of the major early medieval British sagas, including the Urien cycle.

Wars of the Gaedhil with the Gaill: twelfth-century Irish account of the invasion of Ireland by the Vikings.

Gildas, *The Ruin of Britain*: sixth-century chronicle of the Anglo-Saxon wars by a Romano-Briton from the northern kingdom of Clyde.

Giraldus Cambrensis, *Historical Works*, including a geography of Wales and Ireland and an account of the Norman invasion of Ireland: twelfth-century chronicles by a Norman-Welsh ecclesiastic in touch with eye-witnesses of the events he describes.

The Gododdin: sixth-century poem attributed to Aneirin, a northern Briton, recounting war against the Angles.

Lanercost Chronicle: fourteenth-century chronicle by an anonymous English historian at Lanercost near Carlisle.

The Mabinogion: thirteenth-century compilation of Welsh tales and history of ancient times.

Nennius, *The History of the British*: ninth-century chronicle by a Briton.

Pausanias, *Description of Greece*: principal source for Celtic invasion of Greece by a Greek geographer of the second century AD.

Scalacronica: fourteenth-century history of the Edwardian wars in Scotland by Sir Thomas Gray, an English knight held prisoner in Edinburgh castle during the wars of Edward III.

Edmund Spenser, *A View of the Present State of Ireland*: first published in 1633, but written at the end of the sixteenth century by a Tudor Englishman.

Tain Bo Cuailnge: Irish epic tale dated to the eighth century but believed to be centuries older, perhaps pre-Christian.

SECONDARY WORKS

Alcock, L., *Arthur's Britain*, London, 1971.

Arribas, A., *The Iberians*, London, 1964.

Bannerman, J., *Studies In The History of Dalriada*, Edinburgh, 1974.

Canny, N.P., *The Elizabethan Conquest of Ireland*, Hassocks, Sussex, 1976.

Carr, A.D., 'Welshmen and the Hundred Years War', *The Welsh History Review*, Vol. 4, p.21, Cardiff, 1968.

Chadwick, H.M., *Early Scotland*, Cambridge, 1949.

Chadwick, N.K., *Early Brittany*, Cardiff, 1969.

Chadwick, N.K., *The British Heroic Age*, Cardiff, 1976.

Davies, W., *Wales In The Early Middle Ages*, Leicester, 1982.

Drinkwater, J.F., *Roman Gaul*, London, 1983.

Edwards, O.D. (editor), *Celtic Nationalism*, London, 1968.

Ellis, P.B., *Macbeth*, London, 1980.

Falls, C., *Elizabeth's Irish Wars*, London, 1950.

Filip, J., *Celtic Civilization and Its Heritage*, Prague, 1977.

Frame, R., 'The Bruces In Ireland', *Irish Historical Studies*, Vol. 19, p. 3, Dublin, 1975.

Harding, D. (editor), *Hillforts*, London, 1976.

Hatt, J-J., *Celts and Gallo-Romans*, Geneva, 1970.

Hayes-McCoy, G.A., *Irish Battles*, London, 1969.

Hogan, J., 'Shane O'Neill comes to the court of Elizabeth', *Essays and Studies presented to Professor Tadhg Ua Donnchadha*, Cork, 1947.

Hogg, A.H.A., *Hillforts of Britain*, London, 1976.

Laing, L., *The Archaeology of Late Celtic Britain and Ireland*, London, 1975.

Loyn, H.R., *The Vikings In Britain*, London, 1977.

Lydon, J., *The Lordship of Ireland In The Middle Ages*, Dublin, 1972.

Lydon, J., and MacCurtain, M., (editors), *The Gill History of Ireland* (several volumes), Dublin, 1972.

Mackie, R.L., *James IV of Scotland*, Edinburgh, 1958.

Maxwell, C., (editor), *Irish History From Contemporary Sources*, London, 1923.

McKerral, A., 'West Highland Mercenaries in Ireland', *Scottish Historical Review*, Vol. 30 p. 1, Edinburgh.

Morris, J., *The Age of Arthur*, London, 1973.

Myers, J.P. (editor), *Elizabethan Ireland: A Selection of Writings by Elizabethan Writers*, Connecticut, 1983.

Nicholson, R., *Edward III and the Scots*, Oxford, 1965.

Otway-Ruthven, A.J., *A History of Medieval Ireland*, London, 1968.

Pine, L.G., *The Highland Clans*, Newton Abbot, 1972.

Powell, T.G.E., *The Celts*, London, 1958.

Quinn, D.B., *The Elizabethans and the Irish*, Ithaca, 1966.

Rees, W., *South Wales and the March 1280–1415*, Oxford, 1924.

Sandars, H., 'The Weapons of the Iberians', *Archaeologia*, Vol. 64 p. 205, Oxford, 1913.

Scott, R.M., *Robert the Bruce*, London, 1982.

Shetelig, H., (editor) *Viking Antiquities in Great Britain and Ireland*, Oslo, 1940.

Thompson, E.A., *Saint Germanus of Auxerre and the End of Roman Britain*, Woodbridge, 1984.

Wheeler, M. and Richardson, K.M., *Hillforts of Northern France*, Oxford, 1957.

Wightman, E.M., *Gallia Belgica*, London, 1985.

Williams, A.H., *The History of Wales: The Middle Ages*, Cardiff, 1948.

King Arthur of Britain by
Walter Crane.

Early wheeled cannon employed against a castle; detail from a mid-fifteenth-century manuscript.

Right: The Battle of Crécy, 1346, from Froissart's *Chronicles*. The English longbowmen are here seen in action with the French crossbowmen.

287

MEDIEVAL WARLORDS

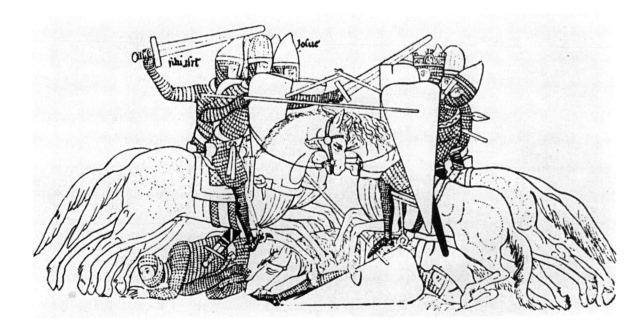

Combat between knights
using lance and sword;
from a twelfth-century
miniature.

The Battle of Poitiers, 1356, from Froissart's *Chronicles*, showing the English long-bowmen in action.

Medieval Warlords

In the court of a warlord, fear prevails. Fear to make your stomach churn. Fear to make any ordinary person want to run far away and be thankful to have escaped unscathed. It is the fear of physical violence. The warlord maintains his power through the threat of destruction and death. On anyone at anytime. He has no fear of inflicting violence. He is used to it and well practised in it. His is the rawest kind of power. To survive and succeed in the court of a warlord is to compete in an arena of perpetual terror. It takes an extraordinary person. Some are clever, some are tough, some are mad.

Dracula, prince of Wallachia; 15th century woodcut based upon a near contemporary oil painting.

FLAVIUS AETIUS

In the court of Alaric, Flavius Aetius grew strong in the skills of battle and politics. The Barbarian King of the Visigoths had demanded two hostages of noble background. They were the human guarantee in a treaty extracted from the Romans. Of the two teenagers delivered to his camp in northern Yugoslavia, Alaric took a liking to Aetius. It may have been that his father, Gaudentius, was a soldier of Barbarian blood that caused favour. Gaudentius had come from Scythia to rise in the Imperial army to the rank of Master of the Horse before being struck down by mutinous Gallic warriors. Now the boy looked to Alaric for fatherly guidance. His mother was an Italian of good family and vast wealth. It was from her that Aetius derived his hostage status. In the court of Alaric, however, it was the character of Aetius that impressed his hosts most of all. Alaric gave him weapons – sword, spear, and quiver – and encouraged him in the exercise of combat. Aetius grew fit and strong in muscle. And all the time, he watched and noted the ways of Alaric: learning the qualities that made a man a lord of warriors.

In AD 410, Alaric had had enough of Roman intrigue. He marched on Rome. The full facts of his entry into the Eternal City are unknown. Pagan chroniclers blame the catastrophe on the Christian neglect of the ancient temples and gods that had protected the capital for 800 years. Christians blamed the corrupt ways of their fellow men and saw the fall of Rome as a punishment of God. For the Romans in the city, they seem to have come to some compromise with the Barbarians as there was no great siege or bloody

assault. The gates of Rome were opened to Alaric and his gang of followers. Collectively known as the Visigoths, they were a force of Germanic and Eurasian freebooters, bandits, and runaway slaves. They were probably as closely related to their original tribal homeland beyond the Black Sea as the Romans. Travel weary, brutalised, and starved, these warriors were hungry for their slice of the greatest prize of all. Alaric was highly conscious of this: his power relied on their contented support. And yet he did not want to see Rome destroyed. He allowed his troops to satiate their wish for pillage, but he ensured the protection of the city's great buildings and holy places. After three days, strict order was restored. The reasoning behind this is obscure. Perhaps by showing his restraint and preserving the city, Alaric could use it as a bargaining point to gain a responsible position within the Imperial hierarchy. What Aetius did during these momentous events, we do not know. But we can be sure the young man observed with fascination the way Alaric maintained control of the situation, how he handled the politics, and how he exerted his authority over his warriors.

A crisis in food supply urged Alaric to quit Rome shortly after its conquest. The Visigoths rode south. At the toe of the Italian peninsula, they planned to sail to Sicily and then on to Africa. But Alaric grew ill and died. His warriors grieved. So that no one should know where their mighty leader lay, they buried Alaric beneath a dammed river and then let its waters flow over the grave and obscure it forever. Demoralised, hungry, and desperate for a legitimate place to settle, the Visigoths elected a warrior who could lead them towards compromise with the Romans. Athaulf was the chosen politician. He led his people into alliance with the Empire and married a Roman princess called Placidia. As part of the new spirit of friendship, the Visigoths returned their Roman hostages, among them Aetius.

At this stage, Aetius must have been aged about 20. He was a vigorous young man, but due to the death of his father, he may have lacked the patronage to gain him entry into a military career. Subsequently, and because of his brilliant track-record among the Visigoths, he was soon submitted as an Imperial hostage to another Barbarian people. This time it was the Huns. Dwelling beyond the Danube, and never having settled on Imperial territory, the Huns had not been Romanised to the degree of the Visigoths. The court into which Aetius was delivered was far removed from the Mediterranean palaces enjoyed by Alaric. Aetius could no longer expect such fine food or surroundings. The weather was harsh. One cannot help wondering whether Aetius had been involved in this onerous duty by an Imperial official who perceived in the competent and ambitious young man a possible threat. Perhaps it was hoped Aetius would never return.

The Huns were an essentially Turkish confederation of tribes. They fought in the manner of all Eurasian horsemen, placing a special emphasis and value on archery. To Aetius, this would not necessarily have been so alien as it was to other Romans or Germans. His father had come from Scythia and maybe it was Sarmatian and not Germanic Barbarian blood that pumped through his body. In the company of Hun horse-archers, he developed a fine sense of horsemanship and handled both lance and bow expertly. Later chroniclers remarked specifically on these skills acquired among the Huns. 'His intelligence was keen and he was full of energy,' wrote Renatus Frigeridus, 'a superb horseman, a fine shot with an arrow and tireless with the lance.' On the plains of Hungary, Aetius learned also the ability to withstand hardship. 'He bore adversity with great patience and was ready for any exacting enterprise,' continued Frigeridus, 'he scorned danger and was able to endure hunger, thirst and loss of sleep.' Aetius' hardship among the Huns earned him a reputation for toughness that gained him the respect of common soldiers. He was building himself up.

In the second decade of the 5th century, the Huns were ruled by a King known as Charaton. It was at his court that Aetius became acquainted with the leading warriors of the horde. During feasts, Hun noblemen were fascinated to hear him recount his experiences with Alaric and during the sack of Rome. On hunting expeditions, Aetius may even have exchanged words with a similarly ambitious young man called Attila. It was Aetius' association with the older members of the horde, however, that were to prove invaluable in the future. He was securing a friendship with the Huns that would provide him with real military power. The Huns held no fear for him. Supposedly the most terrible of all the Barbarians, Aetius knew them as drinking partners. He knew how they thought and how they fought. This too was to be precious information in the future. Far from pining away in the wastes of the Barbaricum, Aetius emerged from the experience even stronger in character, connections, and knowledge. It was now time to direct his talents within the Imperial hierarchy.

The Empire that Aetius rejoined some time in the late years of the second decade was ruled by two Emperors. In the East, at Constantinople, the more vigorous and senior throne belonged to Theodosius II. In the West sat Honorius, constantly playing Barbarian against Barbarian, Barbarian against Roman, Roman against Roman. In 421, the elderly Honorius held his Emperorship jointly with his chief warlord, Constantius. Constantius had begun his career as an ordinary soldier and now, married to Placidia, the sister of Honorius, he had reached the peak of his ambition. It would not last long. For seven months, he enjoyed a life he had always dreamed of. He extorted great wealth from the most noble families of Italy. He constantly marvelled at the fortune and hard work that had brought him from frontier warfare in Dacia to an Imperial palace in Ravenna. Aetius may have been bored by such self-congratulation over lavish dinners in Ravenna and wondered whether he too possessed the ability to pursue this wild ambition. The sudden death of Constantius came as no surprise, but it aroused a sense of scandal in court circles, particularly regarding Placidia, who had never wanted to marry the soldier. 'So great had grown the affection of Honorius for his own sister,' rumoured Olympiodorus, 'that their immoderate passion and their continuous kissing on the mouth brought them under a shameful suspicion in the eyes of many people.' But politics soon brought an end to that. Fighting broke out in the streets of Ravenna between the Barbarian body-guard of Placidia and the Imperial guard of Honorius. Honorius banished Placidia and her son, Valentinian, to Constantinople in 423. A few months later, Honorius was dead.

The death of the Western Emperor was an irresistible opportunity for

An Emperor's *bucellarii*, his elite bodyguard. Usually Germanic warriors, they wore their hair long and wore torcs around their necks. Detail of a 6th century mosaic of Justinian from the church of St Vitale, Ravenna.

anyone bold enough to snatch it. With Placidia and her son in Constantinople and no other member of the Theodosian dynasty at hand, the Emperorship was wide open. Surprisingly, the throne was not seized by a military man, but a civilian. Nevertheless, John, chief secretary in the Imperial household, was backed by Castinus, Master of the Soldiers. He was supported also by Aetius, who had risen to the post of *cura palatii*, Governor of the Palace. It seems likely that Aetius achieved this rank through marrying the daughter of Carpilio, one time Head of the Imperial Household. Aetius had no wish to lose his job and for this reason may have felt compelled to throw in his lot with John.

In Constantinople, the death of Honorius meant that Theodosius was sole ruler of the Empire. He was loathe to give this up to Placidia. She insisted that her four-year-old son, Valentinian, was the true heir to the Western Empire. The usurpation of John, however, urged action. In addition, Placidia was not without power and influence of her own. Before her marriage to Constantius, she had been the wife of the Visigoth Athaulf. She admired the Germans and trusted her protection to a private army of Visigoth warriors. This gave her independence, and with all her connections built up over years in royal courts, she now called upon one of her most powerful friends. In north Africa, the warlord Boniface threatened to block grain shipments to Italy unless Valentinian was recognised as Emperor. Theodosius was forced to raise a Romano-Barbarian army led by the Alan officer Ardabur and his son Aspar. Alongside them rode Placidia with her gang of Visigoth retainers. Numbering as many as a few thousand, they were called *bucellarii*. The name refers to the dried bread which these hardy worriors received as rations. They were of high status: valued retainers, elite soldiers. They wore a kind of torc around their neck which perhaps symbolised their status and close relationship to their master. Like most Germanic warriors of the time, they wore their hair long, carried large oval shields and long spears.

Hearing of this force advancing towards Italy, Castinus set about adding troops to the court *bucellarii* of John. Seizing upon Aetius' contacts among the Huns, he sent the young man with a great sum of gold to their tribal leaders in Pannonia, now western Hungary. Aetius was to recruit the Huns and descend upon the rear of the Eastern Imperial army as it entered northern Italy. Castinus would then engage its vanguard. It was the chance Aetius had been waiting for: a demonstration of his worth and the military power he could call upon. On the Hungarian plains, he reawakened old friendships. The Huns gathered their horsemen for his gold. But events were moving too fast. John's troops had already captured Ardabur. Despite an apparent friendship between the two, the Alan general succeeded in undermining John's support from within to the extent that his army disintegrated and he was handed over to Placidia. While her son fidgeted beneath the robes of a Caesar, the Imperial mother watched with satisfaction as the usurper John was brought into the arena at Aquileia for execution.

Byzantine torc of gold on a bronze core, 6th century. Perhaps worn by a warrior of the *bucellarii*. Now in the British Museum, London.

Three days after John's execution, Aetius arrived in Italy with a force of Huns reputedly 60,000 strong.

It is possible that Aetius had not heard the news of John's death. But it would equally have been understandable if Aetius had realised the strength of the Eastern Imperial army and saw no point in identifying himself too strongly with the losing side, thus arriving too late. Nevertheless, in the new regime that would follow, Aetius had to prove from the start his strength. Therefore, he maintained his Hun army and confronted the Easterners. It seems unlikely that much blood was shed. Aetius did not wish

303

to waste his good relations with the Huns by losing them in a futile bloodbath. Instead, within weeks and after much negotiation, Aetius was reconciled with Placidia and the Huns were sent back to Hungary with a handsome payment. Aetius had successfully demonstrated his military potential. He was rewarded with the rank of *comes* – loosely 'count' – and command of Imperial forces in France. Castinus, who had supported John from the beginning, could not expect such generous forgiveness. He immediately escaped into exile.

Over the next four years, Aetius strengthened his ties with the Huns. He sent his own son among them as a hostage to learn the lessons he had. He successfully used Hun contingents to defeat the Visigoths in the south of France and the Franks in the north. The clash with the Franks was a typical case of maurauding Germans from beyond the Rhine border being driven back by the Empire. The struggle with the Visigoths, however, was an act of policing and serves as a useful introduction to explain exactly what Aetius' function was in France.

After the death of Alaric and the succession of Athaulf, the Visigoth leadership had sought to reach an agreement with the Romans. But there was dissension among the Goths and Constantius came down hard on them, expelling them from the prosperous cities of southern France. For a few years, they fought on behalf of the Empire in Spain against less acceptable Barbarians. In 418, Constantius recalled the Visigoths to southern France. He had another task for them. He signed a peace treaty with their leaders and settled them in Aquitaine around the city of Toulouse. It is interesting to note that such a move was not the wild roving of independent Barbarian warbands, but on the orders of a Roman with whom they were eager to deal. The military strength of the Visigoths was clearly inferior to that of the Romans. So why should Constantius invite the Goths back into France and give them the prime land of Aquitaine, for years the major source of grain for the Imperial army on the Rhine frontier? The fact that this territory was such a key agricultural area for the Empire holds the answer to Constantius' strategy. It is explained also by the fact that Aquitaine was not a borderland, but in the heart of France. The Goths had been settled there not to defend the frontiers of the Empire against outside Barbarians, as other tribes were. Aquitaine had to be protected from its own people: the discontented farmers and peasants of Roman France – the *Bacaudae*.

In 407, the *Bacaudae* of Armorica, now Brittany, had set upon their tyrannical land owners. They had taken their estates and thrown out Imperial governors. They set up an independent state and ruled the land for 10 years free of Imperial law and order. The organisation of the revolt, coinciding with a major Barbarian invasion, and its vast scale, demonstrated that this was no simple peasant revolt. Like other uprisings of the *Bacaudae* in the past, it may have begun with a mob of runaway slaves, army deserters, and bandits overthrowing several estates, but eventually it became a movement joined by small land owners and middle classes who had suffered under the oppressive and corrupt wealthy estate owners and government officials. The revolt of 407 was the longest and most successful of all Bacaudic uprisings and profoundly terrified neighbouring landowners south of the Loire in Aquitaine. Campaigns against the *Bacaudae* were not easy. Like the Barbarians, the rebels avoided major confrontations, preferring to split up into a myriad of tight, controllable raiding parties: ravaging the enemy with relentless skirmishing and ambush and always gathering food and booty.

Slowly, Imperial forces managed to quell the most outrageous of the *Bacaudae* by 417. But to secure the estates of neighbouring territory, Constantius employed Barbarian auxiliaries. In 418, he installed the Visigoths south of the Loire around Toulouse. He bound the interests of the Barbarians to the settled business of land ownership by giving their chieftains their own estates. Thus the Visigoths had common cause with Roman aristocrats against the rebels. Generally, this proved successful and for many years the Goths kept the natives of Armorica in check. Sometimes there would be friction among the new allies: a rogue Visigoth ignoring the treaty of his lords, or, as in 425, the Visigoths taking advantage of the usurpation of John to attack Arles. On these occasions, Aetius had to intervene to keep the Visigoths in line. But on the whole, Theoderic, King of the Visigoths, and Aetius were united in the same task: the suppression of the Gallo-Roman lower classes. The defence of the Imperial frontier was, of course, still of vital importance. But frequently, it would be undertaken simply to secure Barbarians in the service of the Romans against the potential rebellion of the *Bacaudae*. This was the job of Aetius in France.

Such was his initial success as defender and policeman in the late 420s that Aetius was given the highest military rank of all: *magister militum*. Only Boniface, Count of north Africa, now possessed military power in the Western Empire to rival Aetius. But Boniface had problems of his own. He was a hard man, and in the late 420s, he was having a hard time. The Moors and African Barbarians he had successfully controlled for so long were beyond his authority. In 427, Boniface was recalled to Ravenna to explain his failures. He refused. A Western Imperial army was sent to bring him back. It was defeated and absorbed by Boniface. A second army of Goths was also subdued and Placidia agreed a peace. But events would not leave Boniface alone. In 429, the Vandals invaded Africa and Boniface proved unable to stop them. The time had come for the warlord to clear out and seek the grace of his patron Placidia. The Empress mother received Boniface with pleasure. Their dispute forgotten, she needed him to counter-balance the overwhelming presence of Aetius. Barbarian ambassadors were ignoring her and dealing straight away with Aetius. So powerful was he, that the Senate, the court, and reluctantly Placidia, had to acknowledge him as consul.

While Aetius campaigned in France, Placidia entertained Boniface and invested him with the office of *magister militum*. Aetius was furious, cut short his plans, and rushed back to Italy. Just south of Ravenna, at the 5th milestone beyond Rimini, the two warlords clashed. The word *pugna* used in one description of the battle suggests a minor combat, almost a duel. It was probably fought between the *bucellarii* of both men. In the struggle, Boniface was wounded but victorious, forcing Aetius to go into hiding, reputedly among the Huns. A few days later, Boniface died from his wounds. Aetius re-emerged with a contingent of Huns and defeated Boniface's son-in-law Sebastian. Aetius was now undisputed overlord of the entire Western Roman Empire. Placidia could do nothing but hope to earn his protection. A year later, Aetius was elevated to the honourable rank of patrician.

Having risen so far by the age of 40, Aetius contented himself with consolidating his power in France. Although happy to enjoy the high life of Ravenna and Rome, his heartland was most certainly in France. Policing the Visigoths and the *Bacaudae* consumed much time and effort. In 437, however, Aetius set his sight on controlling another potential threat. The Burgundians were a Germanic tribe settled in the southern Rhine region. 20 years earlier they had supported the Romano-Gallic usurper Jovinus. It may be that Aetius had intelligence suggesting they were involved in another attempted coup. Whatever the reason, Aetius and his lieutenant Litorius recruited a large number of Huns. They then hammered the Burgundians so devastatingly that the slaughter passed into Germanic legend. Gundahar, King of the Burgundians, his family, and 20,000 followers were all slain. Such was the devastation and terror wrought by the Huns that the incident formed the kernel from which the medieval German epic tale of the *Nibelungenlied* is derived. In the legend, the Huns were said to have been led by Attila and not Aetius. This is probably a mistake as chroniclers all name Aetius, while Attila only became leader of the Huns in 445. But it does suggest that the Burgundians may have been annihilated as a favour to the Huns who lived directly to their east, rather than specifically for Aetius.

For six years, the smashed Burgundians disappear from history. Then in 443, Aetius calls upon the survivors and settles them in the region of Savoy in South-east France. As with the Visigoths, the Burgundians were set up on prime Roman soil not to protect frontiers, but to secure the valuable Rhone Valley estates against the notorious *Bacaudae* among the western foothills of the Alps. In a similar endeavour in the early 440s, Aetius settled one group of Eurasian Alans in the Rhone Valley around Valence and another around Orleans as a buffer against unrest in Armorica. The Alans were regarded as particularly ferocious by their contemporaries. 'Aetius the Magnificent has been so enraged by the insolence of the proud Armoricans' wrote a contemporary 'that he punishes them for daring to rebel by giving Goar, the savage King of the Alans, permission to subdue them. Goar with a Barbarian's greed thirsts for Armorica's wealth.'

Between 437 and 439, Aetius had to contend with a major outbreak of Visigoth violence in southern France. Busy elsewhere, Aetius entrusted the

Byzantine Empress of the 5th century. Placidia was a powerful woman and made her son Emperor of the West.

command of a Hun contingent to Litorius. Liberating Narbonne from a Goth siege, Litorius went on to further victories. 'At Snake Mountain,' recorded Flavius Merobaudes, 'he surprised the enemy, as is his custom, and killed a great many of them. Once the crowds of foot soldiers were routed, he himself followed hard on the scattering horsemen and overwhelmed those standing fast with his might and those fleeing with his eager rapidity.' There is some confusion about who this passage actually refers to and it may indeed describe Aetius in action. Initial Imperial victories were lost in a morass of guerilla fighting. Outside Toulouse, Litorius and his Huns were savaged by the Visigoths. Litorius died shortly after from his wounds. Aetius took charge of the situation. From the scant source material available, it appears the warlord either besieged the Goths in Toulouse or attacked their fortified camps outside the city. Merobaudes takes up the story.

'Barricades protected them, as did towers and ramparts piled on high ground. There was a horde mixing Barbarian roughness with Roman military ways. Warriors stood fortified with shields, brandishing spears and swords and causing harm with arrows. On the one side there was the height, impassable and bristling with defenders and ramparts. On the other side, there was the bravery of our leader, destined to overcome war by skill. And so, growling savagely with united strength, the warriors prepared to fight. They cut down wood by the column. Fir was joined with fir to make siege towers and when it was ordered to overtop the walls, it frightened the opposing battlements with its height. At that time, there was no day without war and every night was spent in arms. Warlike arrows, destined to bring slaughter, found concealment throughout the dark shadows.' In this evocative though unclear passage, it appears Aetius finally led a night assault on the Goth defences. He triumphed and immediately concluded a treaty with Theoderic that reaffirmed the terms of the Visigoth settlement initiated by Constantius.

By the early 440s, Aetius was established as the chief defender of the Western Roman Empire, his power almost equal to the Emperor. Valentinian III was now of age to assume his Imperial responsibilities, but his mother Placidia still dominated the court and had found little way to curb Aetius' power. Aetius strengthened his position by surrounding himself with brilliant followers. Flavius Merobaudes, the author of many pretentious and obscure panegyrics to Aetius, took care of his master's propaganda in Rome and Ravenna. He probably wrote the inscription for the statue of Aetius erected by the Senate in the Atrium of Liberty at Rome. It proclaimed his important victories so far as those over the Burgundians and the Goths. The poet was rewarded with the rank of *patricius*. It seems to have gone to his head and brought out the most melodramatic myth-building when describing Aetius' childhood in the northern *Barbaricum*: 'scarcely had he planted his first steps in the snow over which he crawled than his hands sought a missile. He played with frozen rain and made a javelin out of ice.'

Other important followers of Aetius are described in the poems of Sidonius. There was the loyal Domninus: 'a renowned man who was content to the end with a single high office in the Imperial service just so long as he might follow one friend and cling to him in times of jeopardy. Not once but several times, the Imperial court strove with offers of the consulship to steal him from Aetius, but he stood firm – a greater man than those who received these dignities. A loyalty which no price could tempt came to be held more precious.' Aetius entrusted this loyal retainer with his treasury. Avitus followed Aetius because 'he had learned many a lesson from Scythian warfare,' that is, the warlord was experienced in Hun tactics. Avitus gained renown as a remarkable warrior: 'the Herulian found in him a match in fleetness, the Hun in javelin-throwing, the Frank in swimming, the Sauromatian in use of the shield, the Salian in marching, the Gelomian in wielding the scimitar. In the bearing of wounds, Avitus surpassed any mourning Barbarian to whom wailing means the tearing of cheeks with steel and the gouging of red traces of scars on his threatening face.' Avitus would become Emperor one day, but under Aetius he was content to serve as an envoy and lieutenant. By surrounding himself with such competent retainers, Aetius maintained his power as supreme warlord of the west.

In 445, Attila murdered his brother Bleda to become King of the Huns. Aetius was now over 50 and losing his old friends among the horde. He sent his eldest son, Carpilio, and other skilled ambassadors to make treaties with the new Barbarian ruler. The meetings were tense. Attila was no longer content for his people to be the sword and bow of Aetius. He had ambitions of his own. 'He fancied himself about to grasp the Empire of the world,' remembered one envoy. An old friendship could not be counted upon. In 448, Eudoxius, leader of the *Bacaudae*, found sanctuary among the Huns. Aetius asked for his extradition. It was not granted. But the two warlords did hold much respect for each other. They did business together. Above all, Attila seemed more interested in ravaging the Eastern Empire. The reputation of Aetius appears to have persuaded the Hun onto softer targets.

In 450, Theodosius, Emperor of the East, was dead. The succession was smooth and the new Eastern Emperor, Marcian, made it clear that no more tribute money would be paid to the Hun unless peace could be guaranteed. He did not fear Attila and would be happy to prove the point in battle. In the West, in that same year, the King of the Franks lay dead also. His succession was far from agreed. The King's younger son – a boy adopted by Aetius – went to the warlord for help. The elder son, not wishing to face

Sarmation horse-warrior. The Alans settled in France by Aetius wore similar scale armour. Marble stele found at Tanais in the Ukraine, now in the Hermitage, Leningrad.

Aetius alone, rode out of France to the court of Attila. An opportunity to crack open the West was welcomed. In the Imperial court at Ravenna, there was much diplomatic activity as well. Placidia was an old lady and would not last out the year, but before she died she witnessed one more attempt to break Aetius' power. According to the chroniclers, Honoria, sister of Valentinian and daughter of Placidia, sent her ring to Attila and pledged herself in marriage to him. The ridiculous though important offer had arisen out of a family squabble in which Honoria would give herself to Attila if he used his power to avenge an arranged marriage forced upon her. But was the real purpose behind this affair an attempt by Placidia and her son to recruit Attila as a new *magister militum*, the only hard man strong enough to oppose Aetius? In his correspondence with the Imperial court, Attila proclaimed he would advance into France on behalf of the Empire against the Visigoths, just as Aetius had done. Was Attila proposing himself as a new Defender of the West in return for the hand of Honoria and the possibility of inheriting the Imperial throne?

The new strength of the Eastern Empire, the Frank succession crisis, and the political offers of the Imperial court at Ravenna, all enticed Attila westwards. Throughout the remaining months of 450, the Huns prepared for a major campaign Attila called upon subject Eurasian and Germanic tribes that owed him service. The harvest was gathered and booty stored. Attila put pressure on the Imperial court. He demanded half of the Western Empire as his dowry on marriage to Honoria. Placidia had now died and Valentinian was left alone to decide what next. Attila's demands frightened him; he knew he could not handle the Hun. He caved in and begged Aetius for help. Aetius was well aware of the growing crisis and the threat of invasion. He mobilised his own forces. These were normally sufficient to quell any internal insurrection, but against a major external threat he was less well prepared. He had relied for so long on the Huns as his prime source of warriors, that he was now somewhat at a loss facing them as enemies. Who could he turn to?

The forces that Aetius eventually gathered all had a common stake in the defence of Imperial France. Essentially Barbarian, they had all been settled on Imperial territory in accordance with Roman treaties and now enjoyed their lives as Romano-Barbarian landowners. Aside from his own *bucellarii* and the private armies of Imperial magnates, Aetius was joined by the Visigoths, Burgundians, Alans, and Franks loyal to Aetius' adopted son. Curiously, the Armoricans are mentioned among the Western forces as well. Presumably, they refer to the *Bacaudae*. Perhaps the rebels realised their safety depended also on a concerted defence against Attila. In recognition of their service, Aetius acknowledged their presence as an independent contingent – a precedent they could call upon in future dealings with the Empire.

In the spring of 451, Attila and his horde crossed the Rhine into northern France. They rode for Metz and captured it. Then they cut through

Champagne until they struck Orleans with their battering rams. With this direct attack on his homeland, Sangiban, King of the Alans, lost his nerve and offered the city to the Huns. Just in time, Aetius and his allies arrived to prevent the loss. Outside the city walls, they set up earthworks and forced the Huns to withdraw. The Huns probably regrouped on the plains of Champagne, grassland admirably suited to their horsemanship and the confrontation they now anticipated. The scene was set for a battle whose exact location has forever remained a mystery. Generally called either the battle of *locus Mauriacus* or the battle of Chalons, it has most recently been accepted as taking place somewhere near the city of Troyes. Throughout the centuries, the battle at this location has been viewed as one of the decisive conflicts of history: Attila poised with a mighty army to crush the Western Empire in one final blow. It is little wonder the man standing in his way should have been called 'one of the last Romans', even though he was himself half Barbarian. It would be Aetius' greatest test.

On the eve of the titanic battle, Attila consulted his shaman for good omens. The man of magic examined the cracked shoulder blades of a sheep. The cracks did not augur well. The next day, Attila postponed the conflict until the afternoon, knowing that any disastrous withdrawal could be covered by night. The battlefield was a plain rising by a sharp slope to a ridge. When fighting eventually broke out, both sides sought to gain the advantage of this position. Horse-warriors from both sides rode up the slopes of the ridge. Aetius' horse-archers clad in mail and scale armour dashed forward. Joined by Visigoth nobles and their retainers, wielding lance and sword, they captured one side. Along the other slope charged the Huns with subject German tribes. A great struggle ensued for the crest of the hill. Archers let fly from afar while Germanic warriors thrust and hacked at each other. Theoderic commanded the Visigoths on the right wing of the allied Western army, while Aetius held the left. In the centre were the suspect Alans led by Sangiban. 'For he who has difficulties placed in the way of his flight,' wrote the chronicler Jordanes, 'readily submits to the necessity of fighting.' Attila positioned himself alongside his bravest warriors in the centre, with Ostrogoths and other Germans on his flanks. As the fight for the hill-top intensified, foot-soldiers joined the flailing crowd. Those Franks allied with Aetius hurled their famed *francisca* axes at the enemy before running into close combat.

Eventually, Aetius and the Visigoths gained the upper hand and threw the Huns back down the hill. Attila rode into the action and rallied his men with words of strength. 'Let the wounded exact in vengeance the death of his foe,' he bellowed. 'Let those without wounds revel in the slaughter of the enemy! No spear shall harm those who are sure to live. And those who are sure to die, Fate overtakes anyway in peace!' Warriors hammered each other until exhaustion or pain overcame them. Theoderic, the old and venerable chieftain, encouraged his Visigoths against their rival kinsmen, the Ostrogoths. They fought furiously and in the crush Theoderic was

thrown from his horse. Trampled in the chaos, he did not rise again. Enraged by such a loss, the Visigoths pushed back their adversaries and fell upon the majority of the Huns. Many Huns and their allies now took flight while Attila and the body of his army retreated behind the bulky wagons of their encampment. As dusk drew on, fighting became confused in the half-light, gradually ceasing as weary, wounded warriors stumbled back to their camps. During the night, it was claimed, the ghosts of the fallen continued the battle.

The next day, each side awoke to the dreadful spectacle of a battlefield heaped with the slain and wounded. Acccording to Jordanes, 165,000 warriors lay dead. Aetius and his followers felt certain they had won a great victory. But Attila still remained in the battle zone within his wagon fortress. 'He was like a lion pierced by hunting spears, who paces to and fro before the mouth of his den and dares not spring, but ceases not to terrify the surroundings with his roaring.' Aetius and his Germanic commanders decided to besiege the Hun camp. Attila had no great supply of food and according to Jordanes could make no successful counterattack as Aetius maintained a large number of archers within his camp. The Visigoths burned to avenge their dead chieftain. Attila prepared for a last stand. Determined not to be taken alive, he piled saddles within his wagons to form a fire upon which he would fling himself. But as the Visigoths grieved for their king and the Western army prepared itself for a final assault, Aetius had second thoughts. Why finish off the Huns? In the past, they had proved his most effective means of controlling the ambitions of the Germans in France. Attila would not rule the Huns forever and it seemed foolish to wipe out totally any possible renewal of the working alliance in the future. Besides, if the Visigoths were allowed to deliver the final blow, Aetius could not imagine restraining their demands for more land as a reward. Therefore, Aetius advised the son of Theoderic that others might sieze power in his homeland if he suffered badly in the forthcoming fight. Accepting this counsel, the Visigoths left immediately for Toulouse. Aetius used a similar argument to recommend the withdrawal of the Franks. Attila and his mauled forces were allowed to retreat westwards.

Aetius had won the greatest victory of his career. His reputation and power could stand no higher. He was truly Defender of the Western Empire. But was his judgement correct in letting Attila go? The discontent among his followers after such a defeat did not overthrow Attila. The Hun's grip on his warriors was too firm. Aetius had got it wrong. Attila considered his defeat a mere insult that determined him on a second assault on the West. In the spring of 452, the Huns descended on northern Italy, devastating Roman cities from Aquileia to Milan. The role of Aetius in this conflict is obscure. Strategically, he could not call upon the Romano-Barbarian forces he depended on in France. It seems likely he sacrificed the northern Italian cities in order to draw a line of defence north of Ravenna and south of the river Po. Throughout the summer, Aetius' horsemen harassed the plundering gangs of Huns. The previous year, the Po Valley had been ravaged by a terrible famine. The activities of the Huns did little to encourage the recovery of what paltry crops remained. Malnutrition struck Italians, Huns, and animals alike. Inevitably, disease broke out and Attila's horde could barely consider keeping hold of present conquests, let alone riding on to Rome or Ravenna. Attila's army collapsed as war bands began to make their way home. It was then that Aetius struck. Not with force, but with negotiation. The result was that Attila returned homewards beyond the Danube.

Attila's wagons may have been loaded with loot, but his second assault on the Western Empire had been a failure. He had not compelled the Romans to agree to any favourable treaty. They would not pay him tribute. They would not appoint him *magister militum*. The horde was devastated. And above all, Aetius remained the most powerful warlord in the Western Empire. A year later, Attila was dead and the Hun kingdom broke up. Contrary to legend, it may be that Attila was murdered by Hun chieftains outraged at their leader's costly failures. Perhaps Aetius had been right

The fury of the Huns. A savage drawing by Alphonse de Neuville for Guizot's *L'Histoire de France*, 1870.

about the Huns after all. It had taken two hard victories, however, not one.

To the followers of Aetius, it seemed remarkable that their lord should not wish to assume the Western Emperorship for himself. Valentinian was weak and posed no opposition. Instead, Aetius seemed content to rule as overlord of his pleasant estates in France. Besides, he knew from his youth the complications of usurpation, the possibility of provoking a vigorous Eastern Emperor. It didn't seem worth it. Anyway, everyone already acknowledged him as the most powerful man in the West. The conclusion of the war against Attila must also have worn out the warlord. He probably contemplated retirement. Such thoughts do not seem to have reassured

Attila the Hun. A demonic 16th century portrait at Certosa di Pavia. The Italians never forgave Attila for his destruction of their northern towns.

316

Valentinian. Without his mother and the removal of Attila, he could call upon no one to counter the power of Aetius. Suspicion irritated the Emperor beyond endurance. Eventually he could stand it no longer.

In September 454, Aetius was in Rome. He spoke with the Emperor. If Aetius had no Imperial aspirations for himself, he appears to have possessed them for his son, Gaudentius. Repeatedly, Aetius pressed a marriage between the young man and a daughter of Valentinian. The anxious Emperor could not bear the subject. He suddenly leapt up and cast wild accusations at the amazed warlord. All the resentment and fear Valentinian felt for the success of Aetius spurted out. 'Your desire for power will not end until you rule the Eastern Empire as well as the West.' Aetius tried to calm the nervous anger of the Emperor, but in the excitement Valentinian drew his dagger. He stabbed Aetius. The Emperor's chamberlain also drew a blade and cut the warlord down. Boetius, a close friend of Aetius, tried to prevent the tragedy, but was stabbed before he could save his master's life. To prevent the news of Aetius' death arousing the fury of the warlord's *bucellarii*, Valentinian blamed the murder on others and had them executed immediately. In the words of a shocked court minister, the Emperor had 'cut off his right hand with his left'.

The truth of this foolish, mad act did not remain long hidden from Aetius' most ardent followers. A few months later, one of the warlord's most loyal *bucellarii* completed the revenge. His name was Optila and fittingly he was a Hun. One morning, Valentinian rode into the Campus Martius to practise archery. As he helped the Emperor dismount, Optila plunged a knife into Valentinian's temple. When he staggered round to view his striker, Optila dealt him a second blow to the face that brought him down. Members of the Emperor's bodyguard stood by and watched. No one raised a hand to defend him. The assassination was an execution. The murder of a mighty warlord by a mediocre Emperor should end like this. Valentinian would not be missed. But the loss of Aetius was profound. He alone had maintained Imperial control over France, giving reality to the concept of a Western Empire. Without him, the individual Germanic settlements would soon rise to replace the old Roman province with a fragmentation of German kingdoms. And yet, despite the great military and political success of Aetius, there had been one warlord at the edge of his realm who had consistently defied him. Although the western provinces of north Africa were technically considered part of the Western Empire, Aetius seems hardly to have concerned himself with regaining Roman control over these regions. He led no campaign against the Vandals who now ruled them. Did Aetius' lack of interest in Africa reflect a sensible concentration of power or was he simply afraid? The answer may lie in the fact that the man who ruled the Vandals was Gaiseric: the other great warlord of the 5th century.

GAISERIC

Gaiseric was very clever. Everyone thought so. 'He was a man of deep thought and few words,' wrote Jordanes, 'holding luxury in disdain, furious in his anger, greedy for gain, shrewd in winning over the Barbarians and skilled in sowing the seeds of discord among his enemies.' As a young man just turned 20, his wit was already keen. He had won a following among the young aristocrats who hunted and raided alongside his father, King of the Vandals. But Gaiseric was a bastard, his mother anonymous among the King's concubines.

C.400−477

When the King lay dead, it was announced he had wished his eldest legitimate son, Gontharis, to succeed to his power. It was sensible to proclaim this. An eldest son, in any eyes, did have a strong claim to inheritance. To pass him over could cause considerable resentment and even split the tribe in bitter rivalry. 'But Gontharis was still a child,' wrote Procopius, 'and not of very energetic temper, whereas Gaiseric had been excellently trained in warfare and was the cleverest of all men.' Many agreed with this and sometime before AD 429, the boy Gontharis was removed. Gaiseric was undisputed King of the Vandals. 'The Germans choose their kings by birth,' wrote Tacitus, 'their generals by merit.' The tribal chieftains recognised the importance of a skilled warlord as their leader. They were preparing for a great adventure.

A more prosaic account of Gaiseric's kingship is given by Hydatius who simply states that Gaiseric assumed the throne after the death of his brother. Procopius' description is enriched by his own experience of court intrigue and murder a century later. Little changes, he says. One agrees. The Vandals were a Germanic confederation of tribes from beyond the Danube. In 406, their warbands in alliance with Alans and Suevei rode west, crossed the Rhine, and invaded France. It was not an entire people on the move. It was a lean, hard army of young men, leaving their homeland and families behind, searching for wealth, excitement, and a new life. After a few years of marauding, they crossed the Pyrenees into Spain in 409.

Clearly, the Roman Empire wasn't interested in hiring them as a useful buffer against peasant revolts. The Empire saw them for what they were: gangs of freebooters little interested in constructive settlement. In Spain, they grew up. The Empire employed Visigoths to harry and hunt them. Between battling with Romano-Hispanic landlords and rival Barbarian tribes, and then being hammered by the Visigoth Imperial Enforcers, the leading Vandals began to desire a land in which they could settle free from attack and free to raise a farm and family. They had grown tired of war, but war would not leave them alone.

Gaiseric understood the desires of his older comrades. Those raw, young men that had ridden into Spain 20 years ago now had the wealth they wanted – the comfortable Roman way of life they had dreamed of. And yet every year, they saw their brothers and the sons of their Spanish wives die in relentless feuding and raiding. Other Barbarians were hard on them all the time. The Vandals had never been and never would be invited to serve on behalf of the Empire. Their presence in Spain would not be tolerated and as long as other Barbarians were ambitious for Imperial employment, the Vandals would remain a target for every Imperial-backed marauder. Among Gaiseric's young contemporaries, the mood was different. They were hungry for triumph in war, hungry for adventure. Somehow, Gaiseric had to compromise the weary wishes of the older chieftains for settlement and the ambition of his young warriors for a new challenge.

At the beginning of the 420s, the Vandals had won a great victory against a Romano-Goth army led by Castinus. It had given them the confidence to establish their power in the ports of southern Spain, formerly Roman strongholds. There, they employed native ship-builders and practised the craft of seamanship. Soon, Vandal boats were riding the waves towards the Balaeric Islands of Majorca and Minorca, and the north African coast of the Roman province of Mauretania. Such seaborne raiding may have appealed especially to Gaiseric. At some stage, he had suffered a severe fall from his horse which left him permanently lame. Ever after, riding could not have been a favourite activity. On board ship, however, he could satisfy his need for the excitement of the raid. In lightly-built, oar and sail driven ships, Gaiseric speeded towards foreign coasts. While his retainers ensured his share of the booty, the young Vandal warlord gathered valuable in-formation. He already knew, as everyone knew in the Roman world, that the north African provinces were the chief suppliers of grain and oil to the Empire, especially Italy. But he also learned the strength and nature of the defences of this Imperial bread-basket. As king of the Vandals in 429, it seemed this was the direction his people should take. A final savage combat with the Suevi convinced him that the Vandals should cross the narrow strait of water into Africa.

Bearing in mind the situation in Spain, the seaborne success of the Vandals in the late 420s, and the accession of their first new King since 406, it seemed more than likely that the Vandals would move on to Africa. That said, many chroniclers insist that Gaiseric was invited into Africa by Boniface, chief Imperial warlord of the entire region. As *comes Africae*, Boniface had established his great power in Africa through force of arms and the patronage of Placidia, mother of the Western Emperor Valentinian III. 'Boniface was a heroic man,' wrote the contemporary Olympiodorus. 'He fought valiantly against the Barbarians, sometimes attacking with a few troops, sometimes with many, and occasionally even engaging in single combat.' He was a warlord with no fear of physical involvement in a fight. Olympiodorus records his willingness to bloody his hands. A landowner came to Boniface complaining that his lovely young wife was being seduced by one of the warlord's Barbarian followers. He bewailed the disgrace to his name and beseeched Boniface to set it right. In an action fitting of a young 'Godfather', Boniface made his way personally to the field in which the acts of seduction took place. He then surprised the Barbarian with the estate owner's wife and cut off his head. The next day, the landowner was called before Boniface and the decapitated head revealed. The man was shocked and amazed and forever in debt to Boniface. Thus, the warlord extended his power.

Throughout the early 420s, Boniface maintained a firm grip on the Roman province of north Africa, defending it against the incursions of the powerful Moorish tribesmen. By the middle of the decade, the situation was proving increasingly difficult. St Augustine, a friend and adviser, wrote to the warlord wondering at his lack of command. 'Who would ever have believed that Boniface, after becoming a Count of the Empire and Africa and with so large an army and so great authority, that the same man who formerly kept all these Barbarian tribes in peace by storming their strongholds and menacing them with his small band of followers, should now have suffered the Barbarians to be so bold, to destroy and plunder so much, and to turn into desert such vast regions once densely peopled?'

At the root of Boniface's military decline was a spiritual crisis. The death of this first wife affected Boniface profoundly. He had always wished to lead a more Christian life and now believed he was being punished for his violent career. In another letter from St Augustine, the bishop reassured Boniface that it was possible to be engaged in military service and please God. 'Some of us, in praying for you, fight against your invisible enemies. You, in fighting for us, contend against the Barbarians, our visible enemies. Think then, when you are arming for battle, that even your bodily strength is a gift of God. War is waged in order that peace may be obtained.' St

Roman galley with oars and sails. Such ships enabled Gaiseric to spread his power throughout the Mediterranean. Detail of a mosaic now in the Sousse Museum, Tunisia.

320

Augustine maintained that although it was acceptable for a warrior to fight, he must 'let the manner of his life be adorned by chastity, sobriety, and moderation. For it is disgraceful that lust should subdue him who man finds invincible and that wine should overpower him who the sword assails in vain.' It is the credo of the Crusader.

The common sense of St Augustine seems to have had little effect. At one time Boniface considered becoming a monk. But then, returning to earthly ways, he remarried. His wife was a Christian of the Arian faith, a heresy in Catholic eyes which believed that Christ was not of the same divine substance as God. The marriage shocked the Catholic Augustine. It also appears to have done little to prevent Boniface's continued military decline. 'What can I say of the devastation of Africa at this hour by hordes of African Barbarians,' Augustine exclaimed, 'to whom no resistance is offered, while you are engrossed with embarassments in your own circumstances and are taking no measures for averting this calamity?' He ends by saying he should not have dissuaded Boniface from the monastic life and he should now 'withdraw yourself so far as might be possible without prejudice to the public welfare from the labours of military service, and take to yourself the leisure you desired for a life in the society of saints in which the soldiers of Christ battle in silence, not to kill men, but to wrestle against the powers of spiritual wickedness, the devil and his angels'.

St Augustine was not the only Roman concerned with the breakdown in mind and performance of Boniface. In 427, he was recalled to the Imperial court at Ravenna to explain his failure. He refused and two armies were sent to get him. Surprisingly, considering the reason for which he was under attack, Boniface emerged triumphant from the assault. But at what cost? Prosper, Jordanes, Procopius, and John of Antioch all maintain that in his desperation, Boniface invited the Vandals into Africa to assist him against the Imperial forces from Italy. It was they who won him a respite from a displeased Emperor. And yet, almost as soon as Boniface had beaten off this immediate threat, there begins a war between him and the Vandals. Certainly both sides in this Roman civil war may have requested mercenaries from the Vandals, and Boniface through his wife may have had special connections with the Arian Germans. But it seems foolish of Boniface to invite Gaiseric and his followers into Africa without some formal treaty. What seems more likely is that Gaiseric was fully aware of the weakness of Boniface. When the Imperial forces came to battle with the rebel warlord, Gaiseric took advantage of the chaos and went ahead with his planned invasion. A fleet was constructed and while uncertainty dominated the Roman province, the Vandal King landed with followers reputedly 80,000 strong.

If the arrival of the Vandals in Africa was a mixed blessing for Boniface, depending on which story you believe, it was most definitely a catastrophe for the Catholic communities of Mauretania. The bishop Possidius described the dread felt by Catholics: 'They poured into Africa from across the sea in ships from Spain, a huge host of savage enemies arrived with every kind of weapon and trained in war. There were Vandals and Alans, mixed with one of the Gothic peoples, and individuals of various nations. They overran the country, spreading all over Mauretania and passing on to our other provinces and territories. There was no limit to their savage atrocities and cruelties. Everything they could reach they laid waste, with their looting, murders, tortures of all kinds, burnings, and countless other unspeakable crimes. They spared neither sex nor age, nor the very priests and ministers of God, nor the ornaments and vessels of the churches, nor the buildings.' It is from these outraged Catholic accounts that our concept of the Vandals as wild, wanton destroyers is derived. It was the fierce partisanship between Catholic and Arian that made the ensuing war in north Africa so bitter. One can compare it to the religious conflict of later centuries between Catholic and Protestant. Once when Gaiseric was embarking on a piratical expedition, the ship's pilot asked him where he was going. 'Against all who have incurred the wrath of God,' he boomed.

Soon after Gaiseric landed at Julia Traducta, now Tarifa, Boniface clashed with the pirate horde. As Possidius suggests, the Vandals included adventurers from other Germanic tribes as well as Spanish and Moorish marauders. The core of Boniface's army was his *bucellarii* – his private army. Their ranks thinned by fighting the Italian Imperialists, any gaps would have been filled by prisoners from the defeated Romano-Goths. To this may be added auxiliary forces of native tribesmen. Despite this array, Boniface was overwhelmed and the countryside lay open to Gaiseric. Boniface fell back to the fortified coastal town of Hippo Regius, now Bona. The Roman warlord probably felt compelled to draw his line of defence here as St Augustine was bishop of the community. Unable to capture the town in a direct assault, Gaiseric settled for a siege. Refugees from all around crowded into the walled town. Each day, they saw the Vandal siegeworks grow longer and stronger, depriving them even of their sea links. Catholic priests joined together in prayers for a hasty release, strengthening the resolve of the citizens against the Arians.

Three months into the siege of Hippo Regius, Augustine fell ill. The immediate presence of the Arians cannot have helped his state of mind. Within days, he was dead. The blow to the morale of the garrison was tremendous. Boniface probably felt directly responsible for the death of his venerable adviser. Eventually, messengers broke through the Vandal lines and after several months, a relief army was dispatched from Constantinople to Carthage under the leadership of Aspar. After 14 months, hunger and disease were ravaging the Vandals as much as the besieged inhabitants of Hippo. With the news of Aspar at Carthage and skirmishing along the coastline between the two cities, Gaiseric decided to relax the siege and enter into negotiations. Gaiseric still maintained the upper hand and wanted a good settlement. Boniface was allowed out of Hippo with his bodyguard, but having failed to stop the Vandals, his power in Africa was handed to Aspar and he sailed to Italy to be reconciled with his Emperor. Aspar established better relations with Gaiseric. He was an Alan by birth and Gaiseric's official title was 'King of the Vandals and Alans'. The two warlords exchanged gifts and ambassadors. Gaiseric was now established in Hippo, while Aspar maintained Imperial authority in Carthage. This division of the coastline was officially acknowledged in 435. Gaiseric obtained what every Barbarian chieftain desired: a treaty with the Empire legally accepting Barbarian claims. Using the face-saving convention of proclaiming the Vandals *foederati*, they were granted all regions west of Carthage. In reality, the Vandals would no sooner fight on the behalf of the Empire than anyone else. Gaiseric had won for his people an independent kingdom in north Africa, the first and only assault on this rich province by Germanic Barbarians.

The regime of Gaiseric was rigorously Arian. Catholic communities were disrupted and any priests refusing to perform the Arian service were banished or enslaved. It was also determinedly piratical. As in Spain, the

Moorish horsemen. The Moors were ferocious natives of north Africa, but just as the Romans had employed them, Gaiseric recruited the tribesmen into his armies. Segment from Trajan's Column, 2nd century.

Vandals augmented legitimate trading wealth with raids on prosperous neighbours. Hippo was an excellent port for such expeditions, all raiders paying a proportion of their booty to Gaiseric. In 437, the coasts of Sicily were plundered, pointing the way for future action. The presence, however, of Imperial forces in Carthage proved inhibiting. In 439, Gaiseric launched a surprise attack on Carthage. According to Hydatius, he captured it by trickery. Aspar had returned to Constantinople in 434 and the defences appear to have been soft. The shipyards of Carthage were a great prize for the Vandals. It enabled them to equip a fleet the equal of any navy possessed by the Romans or Byzantines. How the Empire ever allowed this catastrophe to occur must be one of the most monumental blunders of its history. In the hands of Gaiseric, Carthage once more rose as a great enemy of Rome. To celebrate the achievement, the Vandals made 439 the first year of a new calendar.

The ships the Vandals possessed in Carthage were the same as those employed by the Empire throughout the Mediterranean. The general trend at this time was for fast, light ships. The massive, several banked galleys of previous centuries had been replaced by *dromon* type craft. The name meant 'racer' and was applied to galleys of one bank of oars with each rower working one oar. It was only later in the Byzantine navy of the 10th century that *dromon* applied to more massive warships. In Procopius' 6th century descriptions of *dromon*-type ships, they emerge as galleys of the cataphract kind, that is, they have high parapets or a raised deck overhead from which hung a screen covering the oar-ports. Thus, the rowers were protected against arrows and other missile weapons. Cataphract means 'totally fenced in'. This was vital as an average crew of 30 to 35 men functioned as both rowers and warriors. A naval historian has estimated that such ships were 50 feet long, had a 17 tons' displacement, 22 oars, and a maximum speed of 6.3 knots. This may be an underestimate of size, but clearly they were light, fast ships which suited very well the sudden piratical attacks of the Vandals. To increase speed when not under attack, a *dromon* possessed mast and sail. The earliest evidence of the lateen sail – the triangular sail with the whole of its leading edge attached to a yard – is vague, but it was pioneered in north Africa by the Arabs in the 7th century and it seems likely it was known among Moorish sailors of previous centuries. Bigger warships were present in the Imperial navy, but on the whole, there appears to have been little need for large standing navies of multi-banked galleys. The *dromon* was the fighting ship of the 5th century.

Already by the spring of 440, a vast fleet manned by Vandals, Alans, Goths, Romano-Barbarians, and Moors set out from Carthage for Sicily. With the loss of Africa, this island had become a principal supplier of oil and grain to Italy. Now its coastal towns were looted, Palermo besieged, and swollen ships returned to the court of Gaiseric. The Eastern Empire responded by sailing a powerful fleet into Sicilian waters in 441 under the command of the Romano-Goth Areobindus. But a major invasion of the

Balkans by the Huns, and the threat of a Persian attack, forced the ships homeward before they could achieve anything. As a result, the Western Emperor thought it more astute to prevent any further assaults with a treaty. In 442, there was no face-saving. Gaiseric was acknowledged as an independent ruler. He was granted control of the most valuable land around Carthage and Hippo, as well as the land far to the west that dominated the straits of Gibraltar. Egypt and eastern North Africa remained part of the Eastern Empire and beyond Vandal ambitions.

Within his kingdom, Gaiseric settled his foremost retainers on the rich villa estates around Carthage, thus keeping a close eye on them. The transformation of the region from Roman to Vandal only affected the upper classes of society. The great Imperial estate holders were dispossessed, if they had not already fled, while everyone else – traders, farmers, and peasants – continued their lives as before, resenting the corruption and exploitation of their Vandal rulers only as much as they had that of the ruling Romans. The exception to this continuity was, of course, the Catholic priesthood. They suffered terribly.

With his powerbase acknowledged and secure, Gaiseric emerged as a statesman as well as a warlord. 'The occupier of Libya has dared to tear down the seat of Dido's kingdom and has filled the Carthaginian citadel with northern hordes,' announced the Imperial poet Merobaudes. 'But since then, he has taken off the garb of the enemy and desired ardently to bind fast the Roman faith by more personal agreements, to court the Romans as relatives of himself, and to join his and their offspring in matrimonial alliance.' It was true. A marriage was proposed between Eudocia, daughter of the Western Emperor, and Huneric, son of Gaiseric. It was a great honour for a Barbarian leader. But whose idea was it? It seems possible that Aetius, chief defender of the Western Empire, realised the impossibility of defeating the Vandals in battle. His forces were committed to France and he saw the betrothal as the best hope for peace. From another point of view, it could be that the Emperor Valentinian desired a powerful alliance with a Barbarian force that would counter-balance the considerable power of Aetius with his Huns and Goths. Whose ever idea it was, the political result must have pleased them both for it led to Gaiseric's first major political blunder.

Huneric was already married to a Visigoth princess when the Imperial offer of marriage arrived. Gaiseric had to make his son free again. They contrived that the poor Visigoth girl should be accused of trying to poison the Vandal king. As a punishment for the fictional crime, her ears and nose were cut off and the disfigured girl was sent back to her father in Toulouse. This savagery enraged the king of the Visigoths. He swore revenge. From then on, the Vandals and Visigoths were the bitterest of enemies. Needless to say, the proposed marriage between Vandal and Roman fell through and Gaiseric was left only with the addition of a major enemy. Nevertheless, Gaiseric seems to have been assured of Roman friendship and the remaining decade saw little serious conflict between them. Gaiseric sat back and enjoyed the considerable fruits of his African estates. He was in his middle 40s and may have felt he had attained all he wished. 'He is sunk in indolence,' wrote Sidonius of Gaiseric. 'And thanks to untold gold, no longer knows aught of steel. A drunkard's heaviness afflicts him, pallid flabbiness possesses him, and his stomach, loaded with continual gluttony, cannot rid itself of the sour wind.' Certainly, Gaiseric was enjoying himself, but he was far from slowing down. The events of 455 would demonstrate this only too clearly.

In 454, Aetius was murdered by a suspicious Emperor. The next year, Valentinian was stabbed to death by avenging *bucellarii*. The story goes that Eudoxia, the widow of the Emperor, was then forced to marry Maximus, usurper of the vacant throne and involved in her husband's assassination. To revenge herself against Maximus, Eudoxia wrote to Gaiseric, inviting him to take possession of Rome. No such invitation was needed. Gaiseric's peace treaty had been with Aetius and Valentinian. They were now dead, so was the treaty. Vandal agents reported the weakness of a new regime trying to establish itself. Gaiseric was angered by the news that Maximus had hurriedly married his son to Eudocia, for so long promised to Huneric. For over 10 years, the Vandal fleet had been built up, awaiting a major expedition. It was now cut loose.

As the Vandal fleet sailed along the coast of Italy in 455, none challenged it. Maximus could not rely on the support of the army and by the time the Vandal sails came in view of the port of Rome, he was on the road to Ravenna. An angry Roman crowd recognized him and stoned him to death. Unopposed, Gaiseric entered Rome. He was met by Pope Leo I who persuaded the Vandal King from fire and slaughter, to content himself solely with plunder. For two weeks, Gaiseric stayed in the Imperial palace. The Empress Eudoxia, her two daughters, Eudocia and Placidia, and Gaudentius, the son of Aetius, all became his prize prisoners. To this was added all the treasures and Imperial insignia of the palace, loaded on his ships to adorn his palace in Carthage. Part of the gilded roof of the Temple of Jupiter Capitolinus was removed. The invaluable vessels of Solomon's Temple, taken by Titus from Jerusalem, passed on to the Vandals. Gaiseric was master of the Western Mediterranean. He could have seized the Emperorship but probably considered it more trouble than it was worth. Instead, he finally had the satisfaction of seeing his son married to the daughter of a Roman Emperor. After their brief stay, Gaiseric and the Vandals sailed back to their stronghold in Carthage.

Gaiseric's position among his own people was unassailable. His overwhelming success encouraged autocratic power. As did a conspiracy among some Vandal lords which was bloodily suppressed. In response, Gaiseric favoured a government in which the old tribal aristocracy was replaced by officials who owed their position to his patronage and not their birth. This allowed Gaiseric to employ the talents of Romans and non-

Vandals. Later, he passed a law in which succession to his throne was restricted to the royal family and not subject to the ancient Germanic custom of election. Such was his authority that Gaiseric's will was accepted with little struggle. According to Procopius, Gaiseric organized his warriors into 80 companies commanded by captains called *chiliarchs*, which means 'leaders of 1000'. This force included all Gaiseric's Vandal and Alan supporters, but increasingly, as time passed and many Germans retired to the good life, the largest proportion consisted of black Moorish tribesmen. These were either paid recruits or warriors delivered as tribute by subject chieftains. If Gaiseric could assert his control over half the Roman Empire, then one can assume the majority of Moorish kingdoms gave him few problems. 'Now Gaiseric arms mine own flesh against me,' bemoans the personification of Africa in a poem by Sidonius. 'I am being cruelly torn under his authority by the prowess of mine own. Naught does he perform with his own arms. Gaetulians, Numidians, Garamantians, Autololi, Arzuges, Marmaridae, Psylli, Nasamones – it is these that make him feared.' These Moorish tribes – real and imagined – had indeed become the key strength of Gaiseric's army. They accompanied him to Rome and they fought in every succeeding campaign.

In the years following the sack of Rome, the Vandals relentlessly plundered Sicily and the coasts of southern Italy. Avitus, a new Emperor of the West, applied to Constantinople for help. But there, Aspar was dominant and his old relations with Gaiseric, as an Alan and an Arian, discouraged him from taking any direct action against the Vandals. Avitus turned to his chief warlord Ricimer. The half Suevian, half Goth Ricimer had a couple of successes against the Vandals, but on the whole they proved elusive. 'Unconquerable Ricimer,' wrote Sidonius, 'to whom the destiny of our nation looks for safety, does barely drive back with his own unaided force the pirate that ranges over our lands, that ever avoids battle and plays a conqueror's part by flight.' Sidonius goes on to describe one of the few Roman victories against a Vandal raid. He recalls a skirmish in Campania in southern Italy, sometime in 458 at the beginning of the reign of another new Emperor, Majorian.

'A savage foe was roaming at his ease over the unguarded sea. Under

Germanic gilt-bronze belt fitting inlaid with garnet and glass, 5th or 6th century. Possibly Vandal, found in the Near East, now in the British Museum, London.

southerly breezes he invaded the Campanian soil and with his Moorish soldiery attacked herdsmen when they dreamed not of danger. The fleshy Vandals on their oarsman's benches waited for the spoil, brought to them by their Moorish captives. Suddenly, the warriors of Majorian had thrown themselves between the two enemy hosts on the plain separating the sea from the hills. The plunderers fled towards the mountains and cut off from their ships became the prey of their prey. Then the Vandal pirates were aroused and massed their forces for battle. Some landed their well-trained horses in light rowing boats, some donned meshed mail as black as themselves, some readied their bows and arrows made to carry poison on the iron point and wound doubly with a single shot. The dragon standard sped hither and thither in both armies, its throat swelling as the zephyrs dashed against it. The trumpet's deep note sounded with a terrific blast and was greeted with shouts. From everywhere a shower of steel came down. A hurtling javelin struck one man down in the dust. Another man was sent spinning by the thrust of a spear. One gashed by a blade, another by a lance, fell headlong from his horse. A warrior swept off part of a foeman's brain and part of his helmet together, cleaving the hapless skull with a two-edged sword wielded by a strong arm. As the Vandals began to turn and flee, carnage took the place of battle. In their panic, the horsemen plunged into the water and swam back in disgrace to their boats from the open sea.'

After this minor victory, swollen by the hyperbole of Sidonius, Majorian initiated the building of a great fleet and the recruiting of a mighty army. In France, he obtained recognition from the Visigoths and Burgundians, many of whom joined the Suevi, Huns, Alans, and other Barbarians forming his army. In 460, Majorian moved swiftly into Spain and on to Africa. Apparently, the Imperial force was so strong that immediately Gaiseric thought it more prudent to suggest a treaty. Majorian refused. Gaiseric instructed his Moorish warriors to lay waste Mauretania and poison the wells in order to hinder the Roman advance. Then, through a combination of treachery and the action of his most able buccaneers, several of Majorian's ships were captured in their port. With both advance on land and sea devastated, Majorian was forced into peace talks. He left the continent a failure, the defeat bringing a speedy end to his reign.

The accession of a new Western Emperor in 461 gave Gaiseric the excuse to break all previous treaties and resume his raiding on Sicily and Italy. 'They did not lightly attack the cities in which there chanced to be a military force of Italians,' wrote Priscus, 'but seized the places in which there was not a rival force. The Italians could not bring assistance to all parts accessible to the Vandals, being overpowered by their numbers and not having a naval force.' Every year, the Vandals grew ever more daring and ever more rapacious. Sardinia, Corsica, and the Balearic Islands all came under their control. In 467, Gaiseric went too far. It may not have been his fault – more the greedy action of a rogue Vandal pirate. Territory of the Eastern Empire was violated by a raid on southern Greece. The Eastern

Vandals clash with Romans. Although portrayed as northmen, it seems the majority of Vandal armies in the mid 5th century were composed of black Moorish warriors. From Ward Lock's *Illustrated History of the World*, 1885.

Emperor Leo was outraged. Despite the reluctance of Aspar, Leo urged retaliation and sought closer links with the Western government. Leo obtained the Western Emperorship for his candidate, Anthemius, with the backing of Ricimer. At last, it seemed as if both halves of the Empire would move against the Vandal King. In response, Gaiseric declared his treaty with the East void and allowed his ships to attack Yugoslavia and Greece. Even Alexandria in Egypt was not safe.

Sixty five thousand pounds of gold and 700 pounds of silver were poured into the equipping of 11,000 ships and 100,000 warriors. It was the most ambitious fleet ever sent against the Vandals and brought Leo near to bankruptcy. In 468, the fleet sailed from Constantinople. The Byzantine commander was Basiliscus. Not the most competent of generals, his appointment may have been urged by Aspar who still favoured good relations with the Vandals. The Byzantines were joined by the Italian fleet of Marcellinus. Together, they designed a common strategy: a three-pronged attack. Basiliscus took the major part of the Eastern fleet direct to Carthage. Heracleius, a Byzantine general, obtained auxiliaries in Egypt and then sailed for Tripoli where he would disembark and march by land to Carthage. Marcellinus, in the meantime, used his Italian fleet against the Vandals in Sardinia. Sailing into Sicilian waters, Basiliscus confronted a Vandal fleet and sent 340 enemy galleys to the bottom of the sea.

Set sea battles were rare in the 5th century and something the Vandals avoided whenever possible. The classic ram and board warfare of the ancient Mediterranean still pertained. But greater emphasis was placed on fire-power, as the proliferation of cataphract-type ships suggests. A hail of archery preceded any encounter. To this was added the shot of catapults and *ballistae*: their stones and iron weights were intended to hole a galley.

Vandal horseman lassooing a stag. The majority of Vandals in north Africa became a ruling elite over the native population. Mosaic from Carthage, c.500, now in the British Museum, London.

Vandal nobleman hunting with hound. His horse is branded with an Arian cross. Mosaic from the Vandal capital at Carthage, c.500.

Greek Fire was a feared weapon of the Byzantine navy, but it is uncertain whether this was widespread in the 5th century. Other bizarre missiles were claypots filled with quicklime or serpents and scorpions. The Byzantines also invented a device for filling an enemy ship with water.

Marcellinus had success in Sardinia and regained control of the island with no great difficulty. Heracleius landed with a considerable force in Tripoli, confronting a Vandal army along the Libyan coast. The battle between the two land forces probably took the form of later Vandal conflicts described by Procopius. The true Vandal warriors, by this time assuming an elite rank in Gaiseric's armies, were all horsemen. Like most warriors of Germanic blood and culture, they maintained a prejudice against horse archery, believing it more manly to enter into close combat as soon as possible with sword and spear. Under the command of their *chiliarchs*, the Vandal horsemen usually gathered on the flanks of an army. In the centre were the Moors. They travelled on camel back and if the fighting was to be an aggressive, skirmishing attack, they remained in the saddle. If they were to face a professional, regular army, they may have taken a more defensive stance. On these occasions, they dismounted and incorporated their camels into a phalanx in which they stood with spears, javelins, and shields amid the legs of their animals. Horsemen unfamiliar with the sight and smell of Moorish camels could be thrown into disorder. Against Heracleius, however, they had little effect. The Moorish javelin shower, the camel phalanx, and the elan of the Vandal horsemen failed to break the Imperial force. The Byzantines counterattacked, delivering a cracking punch with their hordes of Barbarian horse-archers, among them many Huns. Following this victory, Heracleius captured several towns and marched confidently towards Carthage. With all three forces of the Empire closing in on him, Gaiseric must have feared for his survival. Now was the time for his famous intelligence.

Basiliscus and his fleet anchored at the Promontorium Mercurii, now Cape Bon, not far from Carthage. The Vandal capital lay vulnerable. Immediately, Gaiseric sent ambassadors to the Imperial warlord to gain a little more time. His envoys promised Basiliscus great wealth and according to some chroniclers this may have purchased an armistice. While the Byzantines discussed when to finish off the Vandal menace, Gaiseric ordered a fleet of old galleys and filled them with brushwood and pots of oil. When the wind rose and the moon was obscured by cloud, the hulks were towed towards the Imperial mooring. Against the black sky, Byzantine guards observed Moorish sailors darting to and fro with blazing torches on the boards of the old ships. Too late the alarm was sounded to the accompaniment of an explosion of flames. The ocean wind pushed the fireships further towards the Imperial fleet. The fire leapt from galley to galley. By morning, Basiliscus had lost the campaign. His burnt-out fleet drifted back to Sicily, harassed by Moorish pirates.

In Sicily, it was hoped Marcellinus would save the situation. But an assassin, perhaps a Vandal agent, killed him. Any further expeditions against Africa were abandoned. Heracleius heard the news just in time to retrace his steps eastwards. Basiliscus returned to Constantinople but public outrage was so intense he was forced to seek sanctuary in St Sophia. For the Eastern Emperor, the failure was a crisis politically and economically. For Gaiseric, it was a remarkable victory. The combined might of both Empires had been thrown against him and he had emerged triumphant. His followers regarded the old man with awe. He was the strong man of the Mediterranean.

Gaiseric maintained pressure on the Empire through diplomatic channels as well as war. In France, Imperial authority had retreated to the extent that the Franks, Burgundians, and Visigoths all governed independent kingdoms. Gaiseric capitalised on this. By the time a new King rose to the Visigoth throne, previous antagonism between the two peoples appears to have been overlooked in the pursuit of political expediency. 'Eurich, King of the Visigoths, beheld the tottering Roman Empire and reduced Arelate and Massilia [in southern France] to his own sway,' recorded Jordanes. 'Gaiseric enticed him by gifts to do these things, so as to hinder plots which the Emperors Leo and Zeno had contrived against him. Gaiseric also stirred the Ostrogoths to lay waste the Eastern Empire and the Visigoths the Western, so that while his foes were battling in both Empires, he might reign peacefully in Africa.' Gaiseric funded and patronised terrorism throughout the Mediterranean. Jordanes even alleges the Vandal was behind Attila's invasion of France in 451. 'When Gaiseric learned that Attila was bent on devastation of the world, he incited Attila by many gifts to make war on the Visigoths, because he was afraid that Theoderic, their king, would avenge the injury done to his daughter.'

Germanic gilt-bronze disc brooch with glass inlay, Vandal, 5th century. Found in Bone, Algeria.

334

The early 470s saw some major changes within the Imperial hierarchy. In 471, Aspar was murdered by the Emperor Leo. In 472, Ricimer died. In 474, Leo died. All these events encouraged major assaults on Italian and Greek coasts. The butchering of Aspar and his family particularly angered Gaiseric, revealing the special relationship they enjoyed. The new Eastern Emperor Zeno tried to bring a negotiated end to the raids. His embassy to Carthage met with surprising success. It may have been the incorruptible quality of Severus, the leading ambassador, that so impressed Gaiseric. Used to buying the services of Imperial agents, the Vandal king presented him with rich gifts and money, but Severus refused. 'In place of such things, the reward most worth while for an ambassador is the redemption of prisoners.' In reply, Malchus records that Gaiseric acquiesced. 'Whatever prisoners I, along with my sons, have obtained, I hand over to you. As for the rest who have been portioned out to my followers, you are at liberty to buy them back from each owner, but even I would be unable to compel their captors to do this against their will.'

In addition to the freedom of prisoners, Severus obtained a truce in the Vandal persecution of Catholics. In his old age, Gaiseric appears to have wanted to impress the rest of the Mediterranean with his tolerance and civilisation. In return, the Eastern Emperor recognised the full extent of the Vandal kingdom, including all of western Africa, the Balearic Islands, Corsica, Sardinia, and Sicily. Gaiseric was content with peace. Gazing out from his palace across the Mediterranean, he considered his life. He had observed the Western Roman Empire break up into numerous Germanic kingdoms. He had humbled a dizzying succession of Emperors, both West and East. He had outlived all the great warlords: Aetius, Attila, Theoderic, Ricimer, and Aspar. In 476, he witnessed the deposition of the last Emperor of the Western Roman Empire. The next year, Gaiseric was dead.

In an age of relentless assassination, it is significant of Gaiseric's stature among his own people that he was allowed to die a natural death. In his will, he proclaimed his eldest son, Huneric, as successor. But no one could hope to continue the success of Gaiseric. Within a few years, the Moors revolted and the great kingdom began to crumble. No one could command the respect Gaiseric had won. Just over 50 years later, the Vandal kingdom was crushed by the Byzantines and the last Vandal King taken as prisoner to Constantinople. The Vandal kingdom of north Africa was the creation of Gaiseric, the personal realm of a warlord.

AN LU-SHAN

C.703–757

The smell of sweating folds of flesh was overwhelming. The giggles of the harem girls became strained under the weight of the fat man's massive bulk. They carried him on through corridors in the Imperial Palace. Finally, before the Emperor's consort, Yang Kuei-fei, they slammed down their ridiculous burden. Yang screeched with laughter. Tears ran down her face. The fat man bubbled with laughter too. The obese warlord An Lu-shan was dressed in nothing but a huge baby's diaper. When the amusement subsided, An was lifted nearer Yang. She would adopt the fat man as her son. Against a background of sniggering, the ceremony proceeded. Everyone knew it was only a game, not an official adoption, but everyone also knew the joking meant that An Lu-shan had the intimate friendship of the most powerful heads of the Chinese Empire. Not bad for a half-breed Barbarian. The fat man was laughing indeed.

An Lu-shan was half Turk, half Iranian. Such people, like all nomadic tribesmen beyond their frontier, were considered Barbarians by the Chinese. He was born around AD 703 in the region of Bukhara in Sogdiana, present day Uzbekistan, Soviet central Asia. He came from a good family. His mother was descended from a noble Turkic clan. Some say she was a shaman and told fortunes. His father died while he was still a child. He may have been a warrior: Lu-shan is believed to be a Turkic word meaning 'warfare'. His mother continued to mix with the Turkic military elite and eventually remarried the brother of a warlord.

In previous centuries, the Turks of central Asia were famous as metal-

336

workers. They were employed by the Juan-Juan, making the blades that made this tribe so terrible to the Chinese of the Han dynasty. Around the middle of the 6th century, the Turks rebelled against Juan-Juan overlordship. Bumin, their leader, asked for a Juan-Juan princess in marriage. The overlords replied that no princess could marry a blacksmith slave. In alliance with Chinese warriors, the Turks smashed the arrogant Juan-Juan and Bumin became warlord of the steppes. His descendents expanded Turkic rule both east and west. Raiding campaigns cowed the Chinese. But clever Chinese diplomacy and internal disputes eventually split the Turks into eastern and western Khanates. The Turks revived in the early 7th century when rebellion in China produced the T'ang dynasty. Yet the strength of the early T'ang Emperors meant an inevitable end to the eastern Turks. By the beginning of the 8th century, the Turks had fought back and were again prime enemies of the Chinese Empire along its western and northern borders. Their eastern Khan Qapaghan had even been accepted by many western Turks as their leader, so in theory the Turks were once more united. Such a powerful alliance could not be maintained. In 716, Qapaghan was lured into a trap by rival Turkic tribesmen. His head was presented to the Chinese. The chaos following his assassination convulsed the Turks. Their lordship of the steppes was saved by a coup. A bloody purge of Qapaghan's supporters followed. Many Turks fled across the Chinese border, among them the An tribe and the teenage Lu-shan.

The fugitives were received by the son of a friendly Turkic warlord, a deputy commander of a Chinese frontier post. The banishment had been traumatic. In the aftermath, Lu-shan and other members of the An clan swore to become brothers. They had helped each other escape and would help each other in the future. Lu-shan formally took the surname of An. The An fugitives had arrived with little wealth and were forced to seek various means of income. One chronicler maintains that An Lu-shan became a notorious bandit. Another account is more prosaic. Because of his knowledge of several Barbarian languages, he made a living as a middleman, a broker, in the frontier markets set up by the Chinese government for trading with the Barbarians. Apparently Lu-shan's income was not enough. He was caught stealing sheep. The trembling 20-year-old was brought before Chang Shou-kuei, the military governor of Fan-yang on the north-east border. Lu-shan was forced to kneel. The executioner raised his club. Lu-shan screamed: 'Does the great lord wish to destroy the Barbarians? Why kill a brave warrior?' Shou-kuei stopped the execution. Lu-shan was a stout, strong young man with extensive knowledge of the Barbarians. He could be useful. Shou-kuei employed him as a scout.

On the north-east Chinese frontier, beyond the Great Wall, Khitan and Hsi Mongolian tribesmen were causing great trouble with their raiding. In the spring of 733, they defeated a Chinese army and killed its leader. Shou-kuei took command and Lu-shan soon found himself involved in cavalry skirmishes with the enemy. He proved adept at such fast-moving

operations, confirming Shou-kuei's faith in him. He became Shou-kuei's chief lieutenant and a successful battlefield commander. Warfare at this time consisted simply of raid and counter-raid, terrorism and counter-terrorism. Gangs of horse-archers on both sides fought to maintain the authority of their masters over the borderland. Ordinary people suffered from both sides, while the warriors grew rich in booty and reputation. The Chinese recruited great numbers of Barbarian horsemen for their frontier armies. They were called the 'claws and teeth' of the Empire. As was true in most nomadic armies, the horsemen were organised in units of multiples of 10. The Chinese believed the high martial skills and fervour of such warriors could only be aroused by charismatic leadership. Lu-shan appears to have possessed this quality. Chang Shou-kuei adopted him as his son.

Relations between An and Chang were not always friendly. Lu-shan's tough stoutness was already beginning to turn to flab and Shou-kuei frequently berated him for his fatness. Lu-shan feared Shou-kuei as much as admired him and in his presence he was careful not to gorge himself, even though he might be feeling ill with hunger. More serious problems also rocked Lu-shan's ambitious career. In 736, the Hsi and Khitan tribesmen rebelled against Chinese overlordship. Shou-kuei was away visiting the capital. Lu-shan had to face the raiders alone. He suffered a severe defeat with many casualties. Shou-kuei was furious. He accused Lu-shan of inadequate preparation and overconfidence. He requested permission from the Emperor for his lieutenant's execution. It was granted. But the anger subsided. The bad sense of killing a major commander saved Lu-shan's life. He was temporarily reduced to civilian status. By the end of the year, he was back in the saddle.

China in the early 8th century was still a vast unified Empire. But hair-line cracks were beginning to open. In the previous century, the T'ang military system had been based on the *fu-ping* organisation. This depended on an army of militia men. Serving in rotation, they spent some time at a frontier post, some time guarding the Emperor at the capital, and some time tending to their farm work. Because the militia men were committed to military service until the age of 60, many came from the privileged classes. A high standard of professionalism and loyalty could be expected from them. The organisation also meant that the armed forces tended to be divided between a large number of small units scattered around the country, moving around every three years, and a concentration of Imperial guards at the capital. The political advantages of centralised control of the army are obvious. The part-time nature, however, of the militia meant that it was best suited to planned campaigns, so that the men need not be away from their farms for too long, rather than sustained, static frontier defence.

Continued Barbarian pressure and a relaxation of T'ang offensive dynamism urged a change in military organisation by the middle of the 8th century. The status of militia service at the Imperial palace had declined in favour of specially raised elite units permanently entrusted to guarding the

Emperor. The praetorian tendency for such forces to be involved in palace intrigue was well understood by the Emperor Hsuan-tsung. In one attempted coup, the Northern Army guardsmen had to be put down by the Flying Dragon Palace Army, a corps under the direct command of the palace eunuchs. Increasingly, the Emperor cut the number of soldiers in his capital by sending them to the frontiers. One chronicler writes that Hsuan-tsung discouraged military preparation of any kind within the capital: 'The Emperor had spear and arrow points melted down in order to weaken his Imperial warriors. Anyone who carried warlike arms was punished and anyone who practised archery committed a crime. When worthless youths became soldiers their elders repudiated them and would not associate with them. Only in the frontier districts were large bodies of warriors maintained.'

On the frontier, the military situation was certainly different. Defence expenditure was stepped up by 50 per cent. By 737, no less than 85 per cent of the Empire's troops were under the control of regional military governors. Central government could not call upon a comparable force. In the same year, an edict ordered frontier troops to be permanently engaged in their region. Veterans were offered tax exemptions, land, and houses in order to settle on the frontier. No longer would seasoned troops be replaced by inexperienced militia recruits every three years. Military colonies of professional warriors were established on the frontiers and the militia ran down. The cost was high. Regional commanders demanded increased rewards if they were to bear the brunt of T'ang military policy. A greater degree of independence meant also that these military governors frequently added Barbarians to their forces. The rise of Barbarian officers within the provincial armies loosened their ties with central government. Loyalty resided with individual warlords, not with the Emperor. Had Hsuan-tsung's palace fears made the Empire vulnerable to an even greater danger?

It was on this wave of military change that An Lu-shan rode to high office. In 742, he became military governor of the P'ing-lu frontier district in the extreme north-east of the Empire. It was a peak position and entitled him to report regularly to the Emperor at the capital Ch'ang-an, in northern central China. It is said Lu-shan bribed government ministers to speak well of him at court to obtain advancement. This seems unnecessary. His military strength, political sense, and good humour made him a favourite at the Imperial palace. At this time, the Emperor was infatuated with a noted beauty, Yang Kuei-fei. She was installed in the Emperor's harem and adopted her name which means 'precious consort'. Once recognised as the Emperor's senior female confidant, she dominated the palace and became a key political figure. An Lu-shan enjoyed a close relationship with the consort. He bowed to her before doing homage to the Emperor. 'Why do you do this?' wondered Hsuan-tsung. 'My lord,' he replied, 'your subject is a mere Barbarian. A Barbarian puts his mother first and father afterwards.' In truth, Lu-shan realised the influence wielded by the beautiful woman.

Turkic painted stucco figure of a horse with decorated saddle. Naturally, An Lu-shan was an excellent rider. From Astana Cemetery in Xinjiang, north western China, late 6th to early 8th century.

Ferocious head of a
bearded Turk. From Ming-
oi, 8th century, now in
the British Museum,
London.

Court gossip inevitably surrounded the warlord's friendship with Yang
Kuei-fei. He had free access to the palace and spent many occasions in
delicious debauchery in the harem. But between the warlord and the
consort there appears to have been no impropriety. It was essentially an
amusing friendship of mutual political advantage. Certainly the Emperor
did not condemn it. He encouraged Lu-shan's advancement. In 744, he was
awarded command of the Fan-yang frontier district next to P'ing-lu. In 750,
he received a civil post in the Ho-pei province to the south of the Great Wall
and the next year he added military governorship of the Ho-tung frontier
district to his other two.

It was most unusual for one man to hold several governorships
simultaneously, but the development was in line with the Emperor's wish
to withdraw from active leadership and let the frontier look after itself. As
the single most powerful man in north-east China, An Lu-shan set about
consolidating his position there. In the north of Fan-yang, he built the
fortress of Hsiung-wu. He declared it a key garrison against Barbarian
bandits. Within it, he stored grain, livestock, weapons and 15,000 war
horses. He attracted many important warrior chiefs to his standard and
trained over 8,000 Tongra, Hsi, and Khitan warriors who had surrendered
to him. To prove his loyalty to the Emperor, he sent a regular tribute of
camels, horses, falcons, and dogs. He also demonstrated his fighting
efficiency by sending bags of heads belonging to Khitan chieftains. But
these were said to have been gained by deception rather than martial
prowess. Khitan chieftains had been invited to join Lu-shan at a banquet.
Their wine was drugged with the herb *scopolia japonica*. When the Khitan
became intoxicated, their heads were struck off. 'None were aware of their
deaths,' wrote the chronicler. Not all Lu-shan's assaults on the Barbarians
were successful.

In 751, An Lu-shan led an army reputedly 50,000 strong against the
Khitan. He was joined by Hsi horsemen. They rode north-eastwards beyond
P'ing-lu to the land of the Khitan. The journey was long and the Hsi
chieftain demanded a rest. Lu-shan's retainers assassinated him. The Hsi
promptly deserted, warning the Khitan. Beyond the Lao river, the heartland
of the Khitan, Lu-shan's army was ambushed. Heavy rain hampered the
Chinese archery. Exhaustion lowered their strength. The Mongolian
tribesmen surrounded them. An Lu-shan came under personal attack. An
arrow shattered his jade hair-pin. He only just managed to escape back to
P'ing-lu with the remnants of his army. Scapegoats were seized upon.
Surviving subordinate officers were executed. Other more sensible
commanders waited in the mountains for Lu-shan's anger to subside before
reappearing.

In the capital, the Emperor had left policy-making completely to his chief
minister, Li Lin-fu. Throughout the 740s and early 750s, Lin-fu acted as
dictator. He fended off many conspiracies but in the end could not cheat
death. In 752, his rivals emerged to battle for his position. Chief among

Painted earthenware figure of a tomb guardian, T'ang dynasty, early 8th century. The Imperial bodyguard of Hsuan-tsung wore similar, elaborate armour of decorated leather. Now in the British Museum, London.

Glazed earthenware model of a horse, early 8th century. In the T'ang dynasty, horses were used in greater force than ever before and celebrated in art. A reflection of the influence of steppe warfare on Chinese culture.

Glazed earthenware camel with dragon mouth saddle, T'ang dynasty, early 8th century. Camels were sent as tribute to the Emperor by central Asian chieftains. An Lu-shan probably incorporated camels into his army for carrying baggage.

these was Yang Kuo-chung, a cousin of Yang Kuei-fei. He assumed the title of Chief Minister and at once set about slandering the regime of Lin-fu. An Lu-shan would not accept these insults. He had no respect for the newcomer. Yang Kuo-chung did not trust the Barbarian warlord at all. He warned the Emperor that Lu-shan would rebel. Hsuan-tsung sent a eunuch to spy on the warlord. Lu-shan bribed the eunuch and he returned to the Emperor with glowing reports of his loyalty. Hsuan-tsung was assured of the warlord's allegiance and awarded him further Imperial posts, among them Commissioner of Horse Pastures, Stables, and Flocks. Lu-shan used the position to gather the finest animals for his warriors. If anyone advised the Emperor that An Lu-shan would rebel, Hsuan-tsung had them bound and sent to the warlord. In 755, this trust was ruptured.

Hsuan-tsung summoned An Lu-shan to his court. This time the warlord felt court politics were too dangerous. He said he was too ill to make the journey. The Emperor then presented a bride to Lu-shan's son and ordered him to attend the wedding. An Lu-shan refused. He had a strong military base. The 8,000 Barbarian soldiers he had trained formed the elite corps of an army said to number 100,000. The 8,000 were called 'sons', the most faithful of his warriors. Equipped with the finest horses and stock-piled weapons, Lu-shan decided the moment was right for his move. Before the government could mobilise forces against him, he ordered his warriors into the interior. He covered the raising of warriors by pretending to have received Imperial requests to counter a gang of bandits. In truth it was a rebellion against the Emperor and his Chief Minister. Travelling by night and eating at day-break, Lu-shan's Barbarian horde rode swiftly towards the capital. The cuts in the number of military garrisons in the interior meant the rebel army encountered little resistance.

In the winter of 755, An Lu-shan crossed the Yellow River. The ice would not hold his warriors so they hurled uprooted trees into the river to break it up. Their boats were pulled through the freezing waters and the next day the river froze again. An Lu-shan was in his early 50s and grotesquely fat. He had to be supported by two advisers when walking. On campaign he travelled in an iron palanquin. On top of his obesity, the warlord developed an irritating skin disease and his eyesight failed to the point that he could hardly see. The rigours of a winter campaign and the decay of his body made An Lu-shan intensely ill-tempered. He was quick to order execution and destruction. When he took a city, many of its inhabitants were slaughtered. Lu-shan had little interest in restraining the excesses of his Barbarian warriors. He simply urged them on to the capital with the promise of more plunder.

In January 756, the rebel army attacked the Imperial second capital of Lo-yang. The defenders burned the bridges leading to the city. They ripped down walls and trees in the Imperial gardens to build barricades. At the last moment, their nerve left them and they fled. Lu-shan angrily entered the ruined city. He proclaimed himself Emperor of a new dynasty: the Yen regime. He chose the title of 'Heroically Martial Emperor'. His Barbarian troops were jubilant. They were in the heart of an Empire that could become their own. An Lu-shan's coronation celebrations gave the Imperial army time to gather its forces. There were loyalist uprisings in areas under An Lu-shan's dominion. Weakening his rear guard, it prevented advance westwards. As he remained in Lo-yang, Imperial forces drew a line of defence at T'ung-kuan Pass on the road to the capital. The two armies faced each other in a stalemate.

An Lu-shan was reluctant to attack. The arrival of fresh Imperial troops in his old regions stiffened the loyalist revolts. Valuable P'ing-lu frontier units broke away and joined the Imperial army. Suddenly, Lu-shan's conquests seemed to be disappearing from behind him. To Yang Kuo-chung at the Imperial court in the capital, the opportunity seemed right for a major counterattack to clear the rebel army at T'ung-kuan Pass. A massive army of 80,000 horsemen and footsoldiers assembled. In July, the Imperial army attacked the rebels west of Ling-pao. The details of the battle are vague, but the confrontation of two major Chinese armies must have been a spectacle. The high proportion of Turkic and Mongolian horse-warriors on both sides ensured a monumental cavalry battle. Whistling arrows were shot high in the air, opening the combat. Horse-archers dashed forward on their steppe ponies, the smooth drumming canter of these small animals being ideal for the shooting of composite bows. Catching the bamboo shafts and steel tips on their mail and leather armour, the more heavily armed horsemen awaited the attack.

Armour was highly valued by the Chinese. To prevent it reaching the Barbarians, the Chinese punished the unauthorised transport and possession of armour and weapons with long prison sentences and exile. But An Lu-shan had purposely gathered the finest arms for his followers. Old forms of armour made from the leather of wild animals, including rhinoceros, buffalo, and shark, were widely available. Metal plate from Korea and scale armour from Tibet were accompanied by mail, recently introduced into China from central Asia. In the battle for the T'ung-kuan Pass, the heavily armoured cavalry of both sides weathered the arrow storm. Contingents of footsoldiers ventured onto the battlefield possessing crossbows and long bladed polearms, but on the whole they were restricted to guarding the baggage trains and forming a rear guard. Once the light cavalry had exhausted themselves and exploitable gaps could be observed, the first units of heavily armoured horsemen thundered forward. They rode bigger, handsome Arab chargers. As warriors clashed and broke, sabres and single-edged daggers were unsheathed. With slashing and cutting the battle would be determined. The Imperial commanders needed a victory. They sent in the Imperial Guard. Magnificently clad in embroidered leather breastplates, shoulder pads, tassets, and greaves, they were the elite forces. It was not enough. The Barbarians were far from overawed. They held and smashed the Imperial resolve. The Imperial army was completely defeated.

Turkic warrior in scale armour. Many such horsemen rode in An Lushan's army. From Mingoi, north west China, 8th century, now in the British Museum, London.

A. WARRIOR IN SCALE ARMOUR
MINGOI. c. 8ᵀᴴ–10ᵀᴴ CENTURY.
'Serindia'. Plate CXXXV. Mi.xii. 0010, 0015, 0017.

It fled to the capital, leaving the T'ung-kuan Pass wide open.

The Emperor was advised to evacuate the capital. On the way south-west to safety, demoralised and defeated Imperial soldiers seized the caravan of Yang Kuo-chung. He was dragged from his wagon and killed. The soldiers then demanded the execution of the Emperor's favourite. Reluctantly, the Emperor consented to the strangling of Yang Kuei-fei in order to save his own life. The Heir Apparent, Su-tsung, gathered all remaining Imperial troops and made for the north-west frontier. A few days

Earthenware figure of a rider and horse clad in cloth or leather armour. An Lu-shan's heavy cavalry probably wore similar protection against the archery of their adversaries. Six Dynasties Period, 7th century.

later he proclaimed himself Emperor. With the capital deserted, rebel warriors entered Ch'ang-an. Two Imperialist assaults on the capital were beaten off. The loyalist rebellion in P'ing-lu was finally subdued. An Lu-shan was at the peak of his career. But the warlord was suffering. His skin disease and blindness enraged him. He treated his officers harshly, dismembering anyone found guilty of even minor crimes with axes and halberds. In this atmosphere, Lu-shan's subordinates began to doubt the longevity of their lord as an effective leader. Loyalty had turned to fear. Conspiracy grew.

Yen Chuang, one of Lu-shan's foremost advisers, was flogged. He spoke to his master's principal heir, An Ch'ung-hsu. The two agreed Lu-shan could no longer lead them. On the evening of 29 January 757, An Ch'ung-hsu stood outside the door to his father's tent in Lo-yang. Chuang entered with a Khitan eunuch called Li Chu-erh. As Lu-shan lay dozing, Chu-erh pierced his massive bulk with a sword. Many years ago, it had been Lu-shan who had severed Chu-erh's sexual organs and made him a eunuch. Lu-shan had favoured Chu-erh greatly, allowing him the intimacy of dressing him, lifting his great stomach to secure his loose clothes. Now, the eunuch aimed all his frustration at the belly of the blind warlord. Lu-shan awoke. He groped for the sword that always lay at the head of his bed. It was gone. He grabbed the curtains around his bed and cried: 'There is a thief in my house.' The eunuch plunged the blade again and again into Lu-shan's thick stomach. Finally the warlord's words ceased. Chuang ordered the huge carcass wrapped in a carpet. A hole was dug beneath Lu-shan's bed and the corpse rolled into it. Outside the tent, Chuang announced that Lu-shan had died suddenly from his illness and Ch'ung-hsu was the new rebel leader.

The rebellion begun by An Lu-shan did not end with his death. A desperate guerrilla war waged back and forth for six more years. An Ch'ung-hsu proved an incompetent commander. Within months, the Emperor Su-tsung had re-captured the capital with the help of 3,000 Uighur Turkic tribesmen. Lo-yang soon after fell and the rebels fell back to Ho-pei. There, Ch'ung-hsu was deposed from his leadership and condemned for the murder of his father. He was strangled. Eventually, Imperial forces triumphed in 763. But such was the state of the country that the T'ang dynasty could no longer exert absolute control over its provinces. The action of An Lu-shan had shattered the ancient unity of China and introduced the country to the power and devastation of the warlord. To the Barbarian warriors on the north-east frontier, he became a cult figure – the realisation of all their ambitions.

OWEN OF WALES

C.1335–1378

Before the King of France, Owen explained himself. He claimed he was the grandson of a Celtic prince of Wales. King Edward I of England had conquered Wales, and slain Owen's grandfather along with his brother, Llywelyn, the last true ruler of Wales. All Owen's inheritance had been given to Edward's son, falsely named Prince of Wales, a mere puppet of English tyranny. Owen's father was the next to suffer. Slaughtered by the English King, he too had all his land taken. Owen fled from the English simply to save his life. Would the great and just King of France accept Owen into his service so he could one day avenge his family and claim his estates in Wales? The King was uncertain. Many adventurers came to his court, boasting of an illustrious background now lost, and seeking lucrative employment. Was this mysterious Welsh warrior speaking the truth?

Ever since Owen appeared at the court of Philip VI of France, historians have tried to prove the Welshman's royal lineage. Among those who have traced his career, respect is high. 'He is probably the greatest military genius that Wales has produced,' enthuses one historian, while a near contemporary chronicler claims that Owain Glyndwr was inspired by the exploits of his earlier namesake. From what little evidence remains, it seems that Owen was in fact the grandson of Rhodri ap Gruffydd, brother of Llywelyn. But far from being a valiant Celtic supporter of the last Welsh prince of Wales, documents reveal that Rhodri had been settled upon an English estate by Edward I and was quite happy to serve the English King. In 1278, Rhodri entered into a bitter dispute with his brother

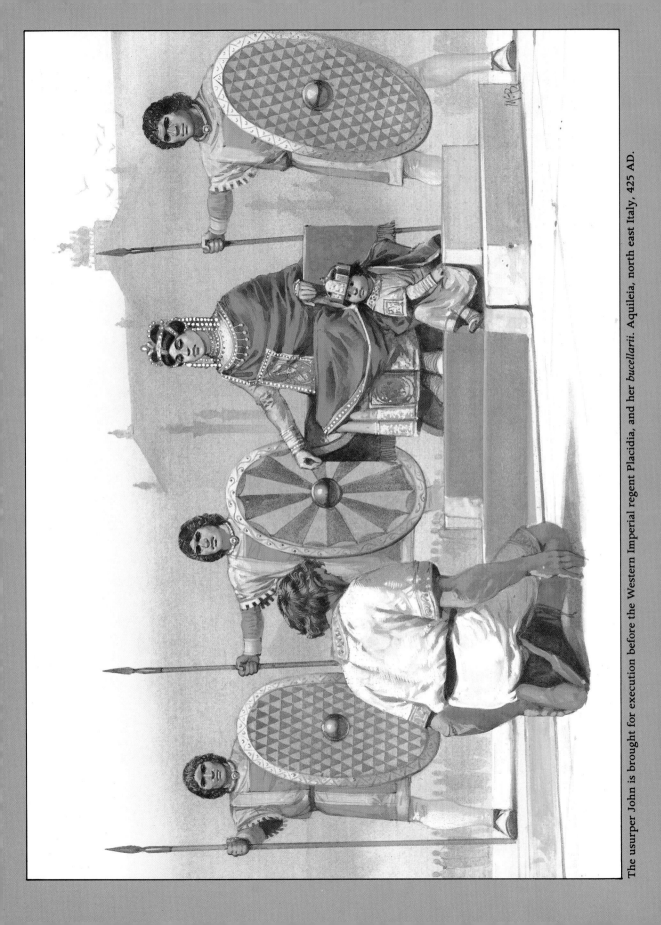

The usurper John is brought for execution before the Western Imperial regent Placidia, and her *bucellarii*. Aquileia, north east Italy, 425 AD.

Alan horseman of Orleans, on the orders of Aetius, clashes with *bacaudae* on an estate in eastern Brittany, 440s.

The Warlord Aetius and a Burgundian retainer attacked by a Hun at the battle of *locus Mauriacus*, north west France, 451.

Vandal and Moorish pirates flee to their ship after an ambush set by *bucellarii* of the Western Emperor Majorian. Campania, south west Italy, c.458.

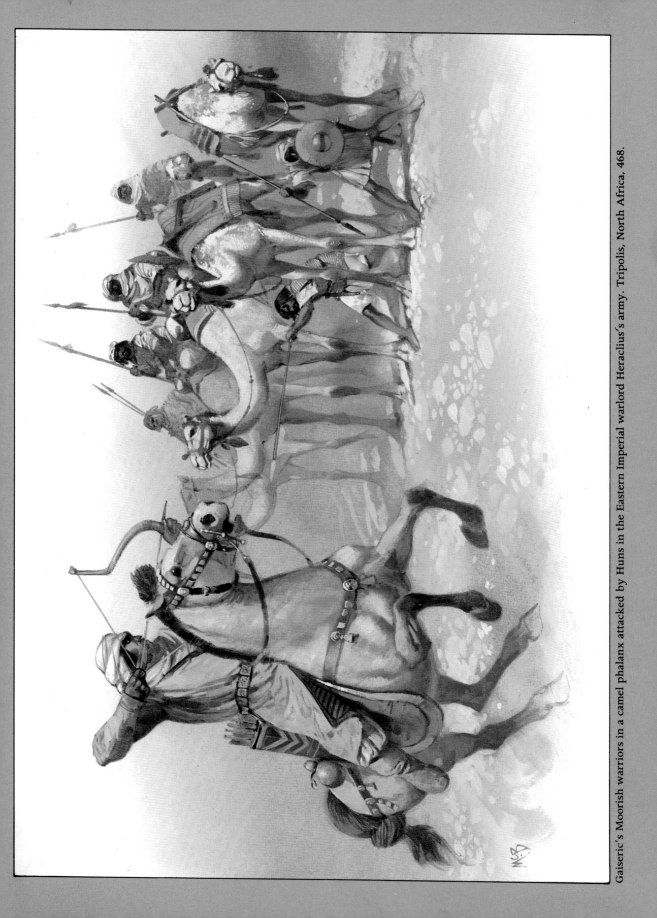

Gaiseric's Moorish warriors in a camel phalanx attacked by Huns in the Eastern Imperial warlord Heraclius's army. Tripolis, North Africa, 468.

An Lu-shan pursues a Khitan Mongol beyond the Great Wall on the north-east Chinese border, 735.

Yang Kuei-fei – the Emperor's consort – and the Imperial Guard prepare to leave Ch'ang-an before the army of An Lu-shan, 756.

Spanish galley collides with English cog at the battle of Rochelle, French coast, 1372.

Owen of Wales is pursued by halberdiers from Berne at Buttisholz, Switzerland, 1375.

Bertrand du Guesclin and his retainers surprise men-at-arms of Sir Hugh Calverly on the road to Montmuran, Brittany, 1354.

Sir John Chandos is harassed by Moorish genitors in the army of Henry of Castile at the battle of Najera, northern Spain, 1367.

Teutonic knight attacked by Lithuanian horse-archers at the battle of Tannenberg, 1410.

Taborite war wagons await the attack of Sigismund's Hungarian horsemen. Outside Kutna Hora, 1421, eastern Bohemia.

Jan Zizka enters Prague with his Orebite warriors, 1423.

Dracula supervises the execution of prisoners after a raid on a German settlement in southern Transylvania, 1460.

Wallachian horsemen surprise janissaries crossing the Danube, southern Romanian border, 1462.

Llywelyn. In an English court, Rhodri argued that land belonging to his uncle in north Wales was being withheld by Llywelyn. Eventually, it was agreed that Rhodri should forgo his claims to the Welsh land and settle for 950 marks paid by Llywelyn. In 1282, Llywelyn was killed by the English. Rhodri lived on comfortably in England receiving a pension from the English treasury.

The only son of Rhodri's second wife was called Thomas. He lived as an English gentlemen on his Tatsfield estate in Surrey. He sold family land in Cheshire and bought a small manor in Gloucester. Like his father, Thomas was always keen to exploit his Welsh connection in the pursuit of land. He bought a small estate in north Wales and made an unsuccessful attempt to claim some of the patrimony of his ancestors. Thomas bought the Welsh manor of Dinas from John de Cherleton in 1333. Cherleton was an active knight in the King's service in Ireland. Relations between Cherleton and Thomas were not good. Five years later, Cherleton and his retainers seized Dinas. Thomas sought redress through the courts and received money from Cherleton but not his manor. Thomas spent the remainder of his life on his English estates. This is the true background of Owen, son of Thomas, son of Rhodri. His family had a history of collaboration with the English. They sought conflict only through the courts. Neither his father nor his grandfather died violently at the hands of the Edwardian conquerors.

At the age of 20 Owen stood before Philip VI and elaborated his life. The French King was impressed by his hatred of the English. Whatever his true background, Philip employed the imaginative Welshman at his court. In time, Owen became a favourite of the Valois court and after the death of Philip, in 1350, he continued to serve under King John. In 1356, Owen fought on the French side at the battle of Poitiers. The combat was a disaster. The French army was shattered and King John captured. French fortunes could not have been lower. A humiliating treaty in 1360 ensured English presence in France. There was continued raiding throughout the country and civil war in Brittany. Owen saw no reason to remain in France. He had lost his patron. With a group of adventuring knights, he rode into northern Italy seeking employment.

Owen's father died in 1363. The news took time to reach Owen. He had been away from England for many years and probably no longer considered it his home. His relationship with his father appears not to have been close and may account for his fantasy background. Certainly, the officials dealing with the disposal of Thomas' estate knew of no heir. Sometime in 1365, Owen appeared in England. Just like his forefathers, he sought justice through the court of the King of England. He was successful, obtaining both Dinas and his English estates with few problems. But retirement on a minor landholding in an alien country did not suit Owen. He continued with his fictional tales of woe. He left England and travelled to several European courts. Each time, the story of his lost inheritance became more tragic. He began to conceive of himself as the rightful heir to the entire principality of

Wales. Welsh retainers in his company fuelled the fantasy and encouraged his story-telling before European monarchs.

War broke out again between France and England in 1369. Owen presented himself to the new King of France, Charles V. He was placed in charge of a fleet and several thousand soldiers at the port of Harfleur. Charles was excited by the prospect of a sea-war against the English. A treaty allowed him to call upon the powerful Spanish fleet of King Henry of Castile. In the spring of 1372, Spanish and French naval strength was demonstrated before the port of Rochelle. The town was besieged by the French and the English hoped to relieve it. An English fleet under the command of the Earl of Pembroke sailed from Southampton. His navy included big, deep draught ships with single square sails and stern rudders. These were a medieval innovation, called cogs. Clinker-built galleys, powered by 100 oars, and with an oar-shaped rudder hanging over the side, were still common in northern waters. In addition to these fighting ships were smaller oar-driven barges mainly used for the transportation of troops.

As the English sailed into view of Rochelle, they sighted a large Spanish fleet of over 50 sailing ships and galleys blocking their way. The English were outnumbered, but committed to the relief of Rochelle. Battle stations were ordered. Archers assembled in the wooden castles on the bows. The Spanish ships were bigger than the English, with taller towers and ramparts. While the English prepared for the clash, the Spanish took the offensive. They caught the wind and bore down hard full sail. The castles of their ships were crammed with cannon and armoured soldiers shooting crossbows and handguns. The noise was terrific. Stone and iron cannonballs crashed through the English planking. The Spanish craft closed in. From their higher decks, iron and lead bars were flung down, ripping great holes in the hulls of the English cogs and galleys. A hail of bolts and arrows swept the decks.

The battle of Sluys, 1340. The English savaged the French, sinking the majority of their ships. The French were avenged under Owen of Wales.

355

Despite the inferior size of their ships, the English put up a brave fight. Their spears tipped Spanish men-at-arms into the waves. All the time, they expected the English garrison at Rochelle to sail out and join the battle. The English knights within the castle of Rochelle were indeed trying to raise assistance from the townsmen to reinforce their comrades. But the townsmen were essentially French and had little sympathy for the English cause. The battle in the harbour came to an end with nightfall. Aside from numerous casualties, the English had had two barges sunk containing provisions. The next day, the Spanish weighed anchor and resumed battle order. Under a blast of trumpets, drums, and cannon, the Spanish ships formed a line, hoping to surround the English huddled together. But the English too broke open into a line, placing their archers in barges as a vanguard. The Spanish sailed close to the English. They flung grappling hooks with chains of iron, lashing themselves to the English in fierce hand-to-hand combat. Again, the larger, higher vessels had the advantage. Iron and lead bars smashed the wooden structures. Several prominent English knights were slain. Their ships were boarded. The Earl of Pembroke was captured. With great victory and booty to match, the Spaniards set sail and left Rochelle to the French.

Whether Owen was present at this battle, or just viewed it from the shore, its outcome greatly influenced his life. Charles V committed him to a career of seamanship. In May 1372, from the port of Harfleur, Owen issued a proclamation of thanks and debt to the King of France. He began his declaration with an account of his royal Welsh lineage, the slaughter and exile of his family, and the claim that Wales was his by right of descent. He then thanked Charles for recognising his plight and providing funds for the restoration of his inheritance. He had received 300,000 francs of gold and command of 4,000 men-at-arms, archers, crossbowmen, and sailors. He promised to repay the sum in his own lifetime or through his successors. Finally, he ensured an alliance between France and his own country, Wales. In this declaration, he styled himself Yvan de Galles: Owen of Wales. This is the name by which the French knew him throughout his campaigns against the English.

In the summer of 1372, Owen's French fleet sailed from Harfleur. His declaration of May suggests it was an invasion fleet intent on reaching Wales. Whether by design or chance, it actually landed on the coast of the island of Guernsey, not far off the coast of Normandy. Edmund Rose was captain of the English garrison at Guernsey. An alarm resounded throughout the island and 800 men gathered. Somewhere near St Peter Port, the English and French clashed. It was a savage encounter. Over 400 Englishmen are said to have been slain. Rose's army broke, making for Castle Cornet on an island in the harbour of St Peter Port. Owen rallied his men and tried to take the castle by assault. The castle was strong and well provided with weapons and cannon. Owen settled for a siege.

After the battle of Rochelle, the Spanish fleet had returned to Castile. But

Seal of the port of Poole,
1325, illustrating a typical
English clinker-built cog
with single sail, rear
rudder and castles.

357

Charles V was so highly pleased with their performance that he wanted to continue the seaborne campaign against the English. Hearing that Owen was bogged down on the island of Guernsey, he ordered the Welshman to forget the siege and sail to Spain. There, he was to invite the King of Castile, his admiral, and all available ships to lay siege to Rochelle and finally take the stubborn English castle. Contrary winds had slowed the return of the Spanish fleet and Owen caught up with them along the coast of Galicia in north-west Spain. At the port of Santander, the Spaniards disembarked. Their prisoners were taken in chains to the port's castle. Owen was told of the presence of the Earl of Pembroke among them. He made for the chamber in which Pembroke was held. He had never met the Welsh Earl before. Pembroke was surprised to hear an English voice.

'Who are you, that you speak my language?'

'I am Owen, son of a true prince of Wales, whom your King put to death and disinherited. But with the help of my dear lord, the King of France, I shall remedy that. Let it be known that if I ever cross you again I shall fight you and reveal the wrong you have done me and my father.'

At this, one of Pembroke's knights stepped forward.

'Owen, if any wrong has been done to you by my lord, and if you maintain he should do homage to you or any of your ancestors, throw down your gauntlet. I shall pick it up.'

'You are a prisoner,' replied Owen. 'No honour can be won from you. When you are free, we shall talk about this matter, for it cannot rest.'

The English knight angrily dragged his chains forward. Spanish knights intervened and separated Owen from his challenger.

Aside from his impotent meeting with Pembroke, Owen's mission to Spain was a complete success. He arrived before Rochelle with the Spanish admiral, Don Ruy Diaz de Rojas, 40 great ships, and 8 galleys full of soldiers. The fleet blockaded the port. The civilian townsmen of Rochelle sent envoys to Owen and the Spanish admiral agreeing not to assist the English garrison so long as the fleet left them alone. The secret truce was accepted. Owen sent scouts into the surrounding countryside to gather information. In the meanwhile, the Constable of France, Bertrand du Guesclin, had sent 300 lances under the Lord of Pons to capture the nearby castle of Soubise. At the mouth of the river Charente, it was only a few miles from Rochelle. The Lady of the castle had few warriors and sent for help from Jean de Grailly, commander of English forces in Aquitaine. Owen also realised the strategic value of this river-mouth castle. All three forces converged on Soubise.

Owen decided on an approach by sea. He filled three barges with 400 men. Neither the French Lord of Pons nor Jean de Grailly knew of Owen's presence. Grailly expected little conflict and reduced his force by 100 lances. At night, he surprised the French in a fierce skirmish. The Lord of Pons and 60 men-at-arms were captured. Owen heard the struggle. He ordered his men to light torches and plunged into the dark. With 400 men, he descended upon the English and Gascon warriors. Grailly had thought

French 14th century cog alongside a smaller, oar-driven galley or barge, both filled with men-at-arms. From Froissart's Chronicles in the Bibliotheque Nationale, Paris.

victory was his and allowed his men to split up in pursuit of booty and prisoners. They were easily overcome. By the light of the flaming torches, an English knight recognised Owen and called him a traitor to the King of England. Owen struck him down with his battle-axe. The next day, the rescued Lord of Pons joined Owen in an assault upon Soubise. The Lady of the castle resisted strongly but in the end admitted defeat.

As town after town fell to the French, Rochelle became isolated. Its townsmen were keen for the siege to end, but could do nothing while their castle remained in English hands. The Town Mayor, Jean Caudourier, assembled those sympathetic to the French and suggested a plan. He told them that Philip Mansell, the English captain of the castle, was not a man of great intelligence. He proposed to pretend to receive an order from the King of England commanding the assessment of all armed men in Rochelle. Over dinner, he told Mansell of the letter. A manuscript bearing King Edward's seal was shown to the captain. The words referred to a matter many months old, but Mansell could not read. The Mayor had the desired meaning read out. All the townsmen were to be armed and assembled before the castle. Likewise, Mansell's garrison was to parade outside the walls. The Mayor could then assure King Edward of Rochelle's ability to resist the French. He added also that the King commanded him to pay the garrison out of his own funds. Mansell agreed.

The next morning, the Mayor assembled 2,000 men near the castle wall. The watch bell sounded and Mansell proceeded across the drawbridge with 60 men-at-arms. As they assembled keenly before the Mayor, awaiting their pay, the townsmen surrounded them. Thus the port of Rochelle fell into French hands. Out in the bay, Owen heard he was not to be allowed the honour of entering the town. The people of Rochelle carried out careful negotiations with the French King before opening their gates to any troops. In the end, the port pledged its loyalty in return for permission to mint its own coins. It was left to Bertrand du Guesclin to receive the official welcome and homage of the townsmen.

After Rochelle, Owen joined the company of Bertrand du Guesclin. He became involved in the civil war in Brittany. But he also retained his reputation as a powerful naval commander with Spanish connections. In 1373, the King of England feared Owen was planning an invasion with 6,000 men. An English fleet of 60 ships and 2,000 men-at-arms sailed from Cornwall to confront it. Nothing happened, but it appears Owen was still very much in control of French coastal waters, indulging in profitable piracy and raiding. In 1375, a year's truce was declared. To maintain his income and keep his followers together, Owen sought service with mercenary companies in Switzerland. The Hapsburgs frequently sent punitive expeditions against the rebellious Swiss cantons. In December, Owen and his Austrian commander were confronted by Swiss troops at Buttisholz. Pike and halberd phalanxes from Lucerne, Entelbuch, and Unterwalden repulsed the mercenary horsemen. The Swiss were angry at

their persistent looting and destruction. Other Swiss soldiers from Berne and Fribourg pursued the foreign companies, inflicting two more defeats on them. It must have been with great relief that Owen heard of the resumption of hostilities in France.

In 1377, Owen was employed alongside Bertrand du Guesclin by the Duke of Anjou on a campaign against Gascony, a region sympathetic to England. They laid siege to the town of Bergerac. Skirmishing outside the walls proved indecisive and the Duke sent for a war engine: a massive device that cast rocks and carried 100 men within it towards the wall. Apparently, the pieces for the machine could only be obtained from the nearby town of La Reole. 300 French lances rode out. Information was then received of a sighting of 400 English lances from Bordeaux in the vicinity. A rearguard of 200 lances, including Owen, was sent after the Frenchmen. All three forces met near Ymet. The skirmish was fought on horseback with lances couched. Froissart described the initial encounter as a joust. But then a French squire was struck in the throat, slicing his jugular vein. Several more knights died. When their lances were broken, swords were drawn. Finally, the French were triumphant. The sight of the great siege engine outside Bergerac soon convinced the town to yield. Owen's part in this campaign reveals that though he might be a notorious privateer, on land he was a minor warlord and still expected to fight in the field.

Throughout the summer of 1377, the Duke of Anjou took a succession of Gascon towns. Eventually he tired and wished to return home to Toulouse. He garrisoned his conquests and ordered his followers to continue the campaign. Owen was given 500 lances of Bretons, Angevins, and other Frenchmen. He must lay siege to the castle of Mortaigne, at the mouth of the river Garonne. He must not leave the siege for any other lord, not even the King, until he had taken it. Owen agreed. He knew that whatever the Duke ordered had the permission of the King and his funding. A great many notable knights rode under his command. Owen was now regarded as an independent warlord. Perhaps his earlier action at Bergerac impressed the Duke.

At Mortaigne, Owen ordered the digging of earthworks to cut it off from sea and land. It was a strong castle and Owen did not favour an assault. As the wood and earth barricades were erected around the castle, young knights of both sides skirmished with each other. It was the only chance they had to achieve feats of arms. The grim, slow business of siege was too dull for these young men, offering them no opportunity to display their martial skills and win personal advancement. As the knights passed the time in deadly jousts, news came through of the death of Edward III. It made little difference. The siege dragged on for 18 months. The war continued. In Bordeaux, the English commanders were becoming tired of the gradual reduction of their possessions. Town after town, castle after castle fell under French dominion. Plans were devised to halt the French advance. A hit-list of primary French warlords was drawn up.

A Welshman called John Lamb joined Owen's camp at Mortaigne sometime in 1378. This was nothing unusual. Owen always had a warm welcome for Celtic exiles. He loved to hear the language of his forefathers and news of Wales. Lamb spoke Welsh fluently and eagerly, telling Owen that his reputation was high among his countrymen. They all desired the warlord to return and lead the Welsh against the English. Owen was overjoyed to hear these words and made Lamb his personal servant. Every morning, Owen sat before the castle of Mortaigne and prepared himself for the day. Lamb accompanied him, combing his hair. One such morning, it had been a hot night and Owen rose early. As everyone slept, he proceeded to sit before the fortress and ponder his fate. He felt confident the castle would soon fall. He asked Lamb to fetch his comb. Lamb went away and returned with a comb. In addition, he carried a short Spanish javelin with a long blade of steel. As Owen sat on the grass, Lamb plunged the spear into his master's·back. Owen rolled forward. Lamb left the spear in the body and quickly departed, making his way through the earthworks and entering the castle.

The captain of Mortaigne, the Lord Letrau, was far from pleased. Although desperate, he knew a code existed between knights in which their mutual safe-keeping was assured whatever happened to them. Captured knights were always well treated. The murder of a great knight such as Owen by a treacherous nobody like Lamb would not reflect well on Letrau's chivalric reputation. These things mattered. 'We shall have blame rather than praise for this,' he concluded. Besides, Owen's army would be angry and likely to order the assault of the castle with no quarter given. In Owen's camp, there was much grieving. His body was carried to the graveyard of the local church of Saint Leger and buried near one of the earthworks he had erected. All the noble knights swore to avenge his death and take the castle at once. This was not to be.

Falchion of the mid 14th century, a heavy slashing sword.

A large force of English and Gascon troops sailed down the river Garonne to relieve Mortaigne. Despite the great investment of time and their vows, the majority of French knights quickly withdrew. Only Owen's closest Breton and Welsh retainers would not give up so easily. They gathered all their weapons and missiles into the church of Saint Leger. Within sight of their dead lord, they made their last stand. The English arrived in barges. Men-at-arms with crossbows crept up on the church. A fierce skirmish lasted for three hours. The church was built upon a great rock and not easily approached. With many men hurt, the English retreated. Owen's followers spent the night with Saint Leger. At daybreak the English knights ordered a major assault. Trumpets were sounded and the English advanced. Arrows and crossbow bolts shattered the stained-glass windows. Owen's followers huddled among the pews and before the altar. Chunks of decoration fell to the floor beneath the barrage. Plaster and wood splintered. The English battered against the substantial church doors. The French retaliated. The English were beaten back. The siege earthworks were proving the greatest obstacle to a clear attack. The English began to fill in the ditches and tear down the barricades. As the Bretons and Welsh observed the magnitude of the forces gathering against them, their nerve finally left them. Heralds were sent out and a truce accepted. The followers of Owen were granted safe passage out of Saint Leger on account of their defence of their dead lord's honour.

Despite the lord of Mortaigne's chilvaric conceit, the English were highly pleased with Owen's assassination. Lamb received a payment of £20 from the court in England and a sum of 522 livres 10 sous from the English government in Bordeaux. Charles V was greatly saddened by Owen's death. The war was far from won. He needed more such warlords to support the efforts of Bertrand du Guesclin. The Welsh missed him too. Although they never knew his rule and Owen's claims to Welsh leadership were laced with fantasy, the humbled principality was happy to celebrate any hero of Welsh blood. Even better if that man was a notorious batterer of the English. Welsh poets created myths around his life. He was called Owen Lawgoch: Owen of the Red Hand, or Owen the Outlaw. He was not dead in France. They believed he slept with his followers in a cave in south Wales awaiting the bell of destiny to lead him forth to conquer the English and win back the land of his forefathers. In Welsh minds, Owen became another Arthur.

BERTRAND DU GUESCLIN

'Perceval was a huntsman,' recalled the poet. 'He rode into the forest with his javelins. As he practised the throwing of spears, he heard a clattering of wood against iron. Perceval was frightened. His mother had told him that devils make the most terrible noise. He crossed himself and gripped his javelins. Out of the wood came the most beautiful sight. Figures wearing sparkling metal clothing, carrying long spears with red and green banners, rounded pieces of metal bearing gold and silver.

'My God, these are not devils,' said Perceval, 'but angels.' Before the beautiful creatures, he threw himself upon the ground. One of the figures rode forward.

'Be not afraid, young man,' he said.

'But you are angels?'

'No, we are knights.'

The adolescent Bertrand du Guesclin listened with wonder. Beyond the walls of La Motte-Broons, he imagined the encounter in the thick Celtic forest of Brittany. An awkward forestboy, wishing above all else to be a knight, Bertrand knew this was the only way for him to transcend his unhappy circumstances. By all accounts, he was an ugly, violent boy: disliked even by his parents. He could not count upon friendship or good looks to win him respect. But fighting would. He had little fear of physical violence or pain. When not the victim of beatings, he beat the young aristocrats and servants around him. At one time, he had to be locked in his father's dungeon. He was a bully and a thug. The warlord had already emerged.

C.1320-1380

366

At the age of around 21 in 1341, Bertrand du Guesclin was a muscular, stocky young man. In his presence, other men felt anxious: intimidated by his fearless pursuit of physical action. He wrestled as well as he jousted. He was a warrior in need of a war. In that same year, French politics provided it. John, Duke of Brittany, died without children. His niece, Jeanne de Penthièvre, was married to Charles, Count of Blois, nephew of Philip of Valois, the King of France. Valois saw at last an opportunity to bring the semi-independent Duchy of Brittany closer to his crown. But Valois and Blois were blocked by another claimant, the Count of Montfort, half brother of the dead Duke. Montfort acted quickly and seized both Rennes and Nantes, the chief cities of the Duchy. He proclaimed himself Duke of Brittany. Valois took Montfort to court and transferred the title to Blois. Montfort escaped back to Brittany and called upon Edward III, King of England, to assist him. Edward had already claimed the crown of France and so civil war in Brittany merged into the opening rounds of the Hundred Years War. Bertrand du Guesclin and his Breton family favoured the cause of the Count of Blois and the French King.

The fighting in Brittany was typical of medieval warfare: bands of marauders surprising each other in short-lived skirmishes. Such warfare could and would last for years. It was an environment of relentless hostility in which Guesclin thrived. He learned his trade in the forests of Brittany and built up a reputation as a man who succeeded in whichever way was required. In 1350, he disguised 60 of his followers as wood-cutters. They burst into the castle of Fougeray while its English commander was away plundering. As the English returned, Guesclin ambushed them. In the skirmishing that followed, Guesclin captured the nobleman Baron de la Poole. The English knight bore the insignia of a hen, so ever after Guesclin joked that the Breton eagle – the black two-headed eagle on his shield – had plucked the English hen.

In 1354, another demonstration of Guesclin's early military prowess was recorded. The English had occupied several towns in Brittany and Sir Hugh Calverly wished to capture the castle of Montmuran. Knights did not receive a regular wage from their commanders and had to pursue their own raiding campaigns to ensure an income and a following. The Lady of Montmuran had organised a grand banquet for several leading French warlords. Word reached her of the advancing English. Guesclin, one of her lesser guests, at once led forth 30 mounted archers and placed himself along the trail travelled by Calverly. As the English raiders rode past, Guesclin sprang his ambush and cut them down, carefully preserving Calverly however for profitable ransom. For this action Guesclin was knighted. The ambush is characteristic of the small-scale raid and counter-raid that constituted much of the Hundred Years War. It was such guerrilla conflict that made war economically viable.

In 1346 and 1356 at the battles of Crecy and Poitiers, the French forces of Philip and then John, Kings of France, were devastated. These famous

English victories have long been ascribed to the power of their archers. Over the centuries, the English longbowman has been heroised. Through association with these triumphs, his bow has been regarded as the supreme missile weapon of the Middle Ages. In reality, the so-called English longbow was a very ordinary weapon of no great power, considerably inferior to other contemporary continental bows of a more sophisticated design as well as the much maligned crossbow.

To begin with, the word 'longbow' did not exist in medieval vocabulary, it was simply called a bow. What is today identified as a 'longbow' is based in design upon the Victorian sporting bow which received its legendary name from manufacturers who saw it as a good selling point. The typical 14th century English bow, as far as it can be reconstructed, was a simple, thick, often inefficient wooden weapon. Bow design on the continent was far more sophisticated. Lighter, reflexed, composite bows were available. Superior to all, was the crossbow: the most powerful missile weapon in western Europe. Often made with a composite bow of sinew, wood, and horn, it could hurl a bolt 300 yards and further, beyond an average range of 200 yards for the 'longbow'. At this long range, the crossbow was not shouldered to aim, but held at a 45 degree angle so as to deliver its steel-tipped bolts as an artillery barrage. As for the much repeated criticism that it was slow to use, practical research and medieval illustrations reveal the rapid way to shoot crossbows.

In the illuminated manuscript of Froissart's Chronicles in the Bibliotheque Nationale, Paris, one crossbowman is depicted loading his weapon, while another shoots his. Historians have assumed that each bowman was in charge of both loading and shooting his own weapon. But one of the crossbowmen in the painting wears a box of quarrels around his waist and the other does not. From practical research, it is possible for two men to shoot two crossbows in rapid succession if one man specialises in drawing the strings of the bows and then hands them to a shooter who concentrates on aiming them. Thus a team of two men can keep up a hail of crossbow bolts long after the muscle fatigue of the solitary 'longbowman' has begun to slow his rate of shooting. At Jaffa, during the Third Crusade, it is recorded that Richard I's crossbowmen were employed in pairs: one to load, one to shoot.

The outcome of both Poitiers and Crecy was not due to the superior bows and bowmanship of the English, but a host of other reasons: principally, French incompetence. The most effective aspect of the English archers was that they were organised in massed formations in strong defensive positions, thus delivering an artillery shock to the French who had allowed themselves to be provoked into attacking at a disadvantage. These truths Bertrand du Guesclin knew. His warrior brigands were armed with both fine reflexed bows and crossbows. The individual English archer held no fear for him. It was the folly of confronting massed archers in strong defensive positions that he wished to avoid.

In his freelance guerrilla war in Brittany, Guesclin had become master of his own swift-moving retinue. In 1356, the Duke of Lancaster, in support of the Montfort claim, besieged Rennes. Guesclin maintained the pressure on the English through a series of raids on the area, but Lancaster was resolved to take the city. 'By the blood of Christ and by the Virgin His Mother,' he had sworn, 'I will not raise the siege until I have placed my banner on those walls.' In response, Guesclin became bolder. He attacked the English camp. Lancaster tried to speed up the siege. He ordered sappers to undermine the city walls. To discover the routes of these mines, the ever-resourceful citizens of Rennes hung copper pots with lead balls in the cellars nearest the walls. When the vibrations of the subterranean attackers shook the balls in the pots, the citizens knew they were underneath. Counter-mines were dug and noxious, smoking materials flung down at the English sappers. But ingenuity could not feed stomachs. Famine threatened to achieve what Lancaster could not.

Charles of Blois directed two armies to the relief of Rennes. One was defeated by Lancaster, but the other, commanded by Thibaud de Rochefort, made for Dinan. There he was joined by Guesclin. The two continued to ravage the English. Lancaster assaulted Dinan. He failed, but Guesclin realised the garrison could not hold out for long and agreed upon a truce. If, at the end of the truce, Dinan had not been relieved, then it would surrender. As Guesclin waited, his brother was captured by an English knight, Thomas of Canterbury. Guesclin was outraged at the violation of the truce. He rode to Lancaster's camp. Guesclin stated the trangression and the English knights agreed that honour should be satisfied. A combat was arranged in Dinan between Guesclin and Canterbury. The English knight John Chandos lent Guesclin his own horse and armour as the Breton's equipment was not fine enough for such a contest.

On the day of the duel, Guesclin and Canterbury rode into the market square of Dinan. As ever, Guesclin had little fear of physical combat. It was a carelessness others dreaded. Canterbury had second thoughts about the duel and offered to return Guesclin's brother without a ransom. 'If he will not fight,' replied the Breton, 'let him surrender to my mercy and present his sword to me, holding it by the point.'. This Canterbury would not do. The two knights urged their horses forward and smashed at each other. Sparks cracked beneath their blows. Neither could be cut beneath the armour. Like the Breton wrestlers of his childhood, Guesclin sheathed his sword and grabbed the English knight around the chest, trying to wrench him off his horse. Canterbury's sword fell to the ground. Guesclin dismounted, picked up the sword and threw it into the crowd. He then threw his own after it. The crowd screamed and applauded. Canterbury was still mounted and charged at the Breton, hoping to trample him beneath his animal's hooves. The English horse reared, Guesclin lunged at its belly with his dagger. The horse crashed to the ground with Canterbury beneath it.

Guesclin rushed over to the knight, ripped open his visor and battered the stunned Englishman with his armoured fists.

Seeing the combat was over, English knights jumped into the arena and begged Guesclin to spare Canterbury his life. Intoxicated with adrenalin, Guesclin reluctantly agreed. Lancaster admitted that Guesclin had fought with honour. 'Your brother shall be restored to you,' he declared, 'and I will bestow upon him 1,000 florins. The arms, armour, and horse of the dishonourable knight now belong to you. He shall never be present at my court.' Throughout this account, Jean Cuvelier, the chronicler, repeatedly points out that Guesclin was poorly equipped. Later, when an English herald wishes to see the Breton, Guesclin is mistaken for a brigand rather than a knight, being clad in a plain black tunic with an axe suspended around his neck. Through legendary encounters such as the duel at Dinan and his conduct at the siege of Rennes, the fame of Guesclin grew ever greater. His status as a man of honour was not incompatible with his military role as a guerrilla leader.

Through further deception and craft, Guesclin renewed his attacks on Lancaster's camp. On one occasion, while Lancaster pursued false reports of a relief army, Guesclin invaded his camp, stole all his provisions, and entered Rennes. Lancaster retaliated by erecting a siege tower to bring his costly campaign against Rennes to an end. Sappers began to fill the city moat to allow the tower to be rolled forward against the walls. Before this could be completed, Guesclin led 500 crossbowmen against the tower, setting fire to the great wooden engine. The siege seemed endless. Eventually, Lancaster received news that a truce had been signed between the Kings of England and France. Lancaster was ordered to leave the siege. But the English knight had sworn to take Rennes and he would not break a vow. Word of this reached Guesclin. He understood. It was agreed that Lancaster be allowed within Rennes with 10 knights and place his banner on the battlements. The ludicrous concession was enacted, but as soon as Lancaster had crossed the drawbridge, a triumphant townsman tore down the flag and threw it at his heels.

Rennes made Guesclin's reputation. Charles of Blois personally congratulated Guesclin on his defence of the city. He gave him lordship over La Roche-Derrien and made him a knight banneret. This meant he could replace the swallow-tailed pennon of a knight bachelor for a square flag. Guesclin's name was spoken in the right circles. It came to the attention of the Dauphin Charles. In 1357, the Dauphin granted 'an annual income and pension of 200 pounds of Tours from the revenue of the castle and town of Saint-James-de-Beuvron, to Sir Bertrand du Guesclin, for his loyalty and courage in the defence of Rennes during a long siege.' The Dauphin had assumed French rule in the absence of his father, the French King, captured by the English. As Duke of Normandy also, he was currently battling against Charles the Bad, King of Navarre, owner of vast estates in Normandy, and claimant to the French crown.

To combat Navarre, the Dauphin made Guesclin captain of Pòntorson, a frontier town between Normandy and Brittany. The Breton, along with 60 men-at-arms and 60 archers, was to be paid out of royal French coffers. Bouciquaut, the Duke of Normandy's marshal, rode with Guesclin. Together, through cunning, they captured Mantes and Melun, key castles on the Seine. At Melun, Guesclin could not solely rely on craft. While the Dauphin watched at a safe distance, Guesclin despaired of his warriors' tardiness and himself placed a ladder against the castle wall. Bellowing his famous war cry, 'Notre Dame Guesclin', he clambered up the ladder beneath a hail of arrows and stones. Some way up the ladder, a barrel of rocks was tipped over the battlements. The ladder snapped and Guesclin plummeted into the castle moat. He was carried away unconscious, but his bravery made a lasting impression on the Dauphin.

In 1360, the treaty of Bretigny was signed between the Dauphin and the Prince of Wales. The King of England received the vast territory of Aquitaine and Gascony in south-west France, as well as Calais and Ponthieu, a district around the mouth of the Somme. The King of France was released on ransom of three million gold crowns. Later, because one of the agreed hostages broke parole, the King returned to the court of England, thankful to leave the problems of France to his son. It was very much a one-sided treaty, but with the aggression of the King of Navarre, the Dauphin needed the break. Truce, however, did not mean security from English forces. They were left unemployed in France. Consisting of English, Gascon, Navarrese, German, Spanish, and Flemish mercenaries, these companies now acted as independent armies. Terrorising, pillaging, kidnapping, and murdering their way across Normandy, Champagne, Burgundy, and Languedoc, they were posing a greater problem than if they had been under the control of the English King. In Normandy, Guesclin was employed to hunt the rogue companies and did so with much success. In 1362, Guesclin was made *capitaine souverain*, supreme commander of the Duchy of Normandy.

Early in 1364, news arrived of the death of the King of France in England. The Dauphin was crowned Charles V. He made Guesclin *chambellan du roi*. On the eve of Charles' coronation, the King of Navarre concentrated his troops at Evreux in Normandy. They were recruited from the free companies and commanded by Jean de Grailly, captain of the town of Buch. Froissart described his soldiers as 'archers and brigands'. They numbered 700 lances, 300 archers, and 500 other soldiers. Among them were several knights, a banneret from Navarre, and an English knight, Sir John Jouel, who led the largest personal contingent of men-at-arms and archers within the army. Before this main army, Grailly sent out a knight to gather information and conduct frontier war against the French. The reports he received did not please him. A force of 1,500 soldiers was spotted, the majority of them being Bretons led by Bertrand du Guesclin. Alongside him rode knights from Auxerre, Beaumont, Chalon, Beaujeu, the Master of the Crossbows, Baudouin of Annequin, and many warriors from Gascony. 'By

English bowmen at the battle of Crecy, 1346. Such simple wooden bows were not exclusive to the English but common among the French as well. They were inferior in both power and range to the crossbow. From the Chronicles of Froissart in the Bibliotheque Nationale, Paris.

the head of Saint Anthony,' swore Grailly, 'Gascon against Gascon.' He had many Gascon mercenaries in his army and did not relish testing their loyalty.

A few days later, the Navarrese crossed the river Eure and made camp on the hill of Cocherel. After resting, they drew up in their order of battle. Sir John Jouel formed the first battle, surrounded by his English men-at-arms and archers. The second battle was led by Grailly and numbered 400 fighting men including the knight of Navarre. The third battle consisted of 400 warriors led by three French knights. Grailly's banner was placed upon a bush of thorns and guarded by 60 men. The Navarrese waited for the French to attack them. They arrived late on the battlefield. Realising they had already lost the advantage of territory, the French nevertheless prepared for battle in a swampy field with the river behind them. Guesclin and his Bretons formed the first battle. The second was led by the Count of Auxerre and included warriors from Normandy and Picardy. The third battle of Burgundians was led by the Archpriest Arnaud of Cervole. A rearguard was formed by the Gascons. They wished to be allowed to

The taking of Valonges. Guesclin watches one of his warriors carry his standard up to the battlements. Note the so-called longbows used by the French men-at-arms. One of a series of illustrations from a life of Guesclin made about 1400, in the library of Henry Yates Thompson.

374

concentrate on the taking of Grailly's standard, suggesting a snatch-group of 30 horsemen be organised to capture the enemy commander and bring a quick end to the battle. It was agreed. The French knights then debated who should be commander for the day and what battle-cry they should adopt. The Count of Auxerre was the most senior in rank but he declined, saying there were others more experienced than him. Finally, they agreed that Guesclin was the most competent and he should be obeyed throughout the day's combat.

Having established authority, the French faced the problem of the Navarrese firmly positioned on a hill. It was a very hot day; they were short on provisions. As the French discussed what to do, some prisoners were freed from the Navarrese army. They told the French that Grailly would soon be reinforced and should attack at once. But the French were reluctant to assault such a strong position. The next day, Guesclin suggested an acceptable strategy. 'Let us make preparations to withdraw. Our people are troubled by the heat. The servants and spare horses should be sent back to our camp. If the enemy are impatient to fight then they will come down the hill and we can turn and fight them on more equal terms.' The French knights drew up their standards and the baggage train proceeded to retreat over the river Eure. Guesclin had judged the mood of the Navarrese correctly. Sir John Jouel was tired of waiting. When he saw the French withdrawal, he feared he would be denied a battle altogether. His soldiers had to be paid and he would not let their prize disappear. Grailly was not so impetuous. He suspected a trick. But Jouel could not stand the sight and shouted to his men: 'By Saint George, whosoever loves me, let them join me in my fight with the enemy!' Jouel and his Englishmen dashed down the hill. Grailly would not see his army defeated piecemeal and ordered a general advance.

The French were triumphant. They turned and cried 'Notre Dame Guesclin!' Seeing the ordered French lines, the Navarrese recoiled. Their archers ran to the front. At close range, the arrows were deadly, but the French were largely on foot and protected by warriors carrying large shields. The battle broke into crowds of knights and footsoldiers in fierce hand-to-hand combat. Shortened lances, axes, and swords hacked and tore. When possible, knights were isolated and captured for ransom. But the fighting was bitter and many prominent knights were slaughtered, among them the Master of the Crossbows and the banneret of Navarre. The Archpriest Arnaud had withdrawn to the bridge over the Eure at the beginning of the battle on the pretence of some tactical manoeuvre. In truth he was waiting to see who would triumph. In the meanwhile, Sir John Jouel charged straight at the Bretons and Guesclin. He fought remarkably, was wounded several times, fainted under his wounds, and was taken prisoner, later to die. The Gascons remained committed to their assault on Grailly. The 30 horsemen lunged forward. Grailly defended himself with a great axe. The horsemen pushed into the crowd and finally plucked him from among his men. The Gascons then surged on to his standard. The banner was ripped to pieces. The battle was over. Several knights were captured, but the majority of ordinary Navarrese were slaughtered. It was good news for Charles V on the eve of his coronation. And all thanks to Guesclin. The Breton was made Count of Longueville in northern Normandy, a former property of the King of Navarre.

Guesclin was now 44 and it might be thought he had done enough to deserve retirement, but the warlord's tasks were never over. Constantly in the field against ravaging bands of soldiers in Normandy, there was still the problem of the succession of Brittany to be settled. Since 1343, John, the Montfort heir, had been kept at Edward III's court. In 1362, he was released under heavy obligation to seek his fortune in Brittany. He endeavoured to strike a peace with Charles of Blois, but his wife refused. In the late summer of 1364, the town of Auray, loyal to the Blois cause, was besieged by Montfort. Blois asked Guesclin for help. The Breton, ever faithful to his first master, immediately left Normandy with his victorious army of Cocherel. Blois assembled 2,500 lances. Guesclin was the chief military adviser. Outside Auray, they formed three battles with a rearguard. As usual, Guesclin and his Breton followers formed the first battle, the Count of Auxerre led the second and Blois the third. Each battle consisted of 1,000 fighting men. Montfort's army numbered many Englishmen. The active commander was Sir John Chandos. He organised three battles, each containing 500 men-at-arms and 400 archers. A rearguard of 500 men was placed on the wing to reinforce any group that faltered. Hewe Caurell, the knight placed in charge of this wing, felt ashamed to command reinforcements, preferring to be among the first to fight. Chandos reassured him it was not because he was a bad knight, but because he was wise and was needed to lead such a crucial group. Otherwise Chandos would have to do it himself. The knight accepted the task.

On a plain before Auray, the two armies waited. Last-minute Breton negotiations tried for peace, but Chandos' English soldiers told him they had spent all their money and needed a battle to replenish their resources. Chandos promised not to accept a truce. The two forces closed for battle. The French were dismounted in close order, their shortened lances and spears held by a phalanx of foot soldiers. The English struck the first blow. Their shot did little damage to Frenchmen well protected by shields and armour. The archers cast away their bows and broke into Guesclin's battle, fighting with axes. Blois clashed with Montfort. The English suffered badly but were reinforced by the wing of Hewe Caurell. This proved a turning point. Sir John Chandos hammered the Count of Auxerre. Auxerre's battle crumbled, many fled, he was wounded and captured. Seeing Montfort's warriors in good order, many Frenchmen mounted their horses and left the carnage. But still the Bretons around Guesclin kept fighting. Chandos concentrated on them. Axes swung and bascinets were ripped open. Guesclin was overwhelmed and taken prisoner. The entire French army broke. A valiant few fought a last stand around Charles of Blois. The Blois standard was torn down and the Breton leader slain. The English had agreed beforehand not to spare him for ransom: the civil war had to end. Similarly, the French had agreed not to spare Montfort. The Breton succession had to be settled. On that day it was. Charles V concluded a peace in Brittany and acknowledged Montfort as Duke. In default of male heirs, however, the duchy was to revert to the children of Charles of Blois, thus revealing the French King's true sympathies.

The mercenary companies were again unemployed. They plagued the land, ravaged its resources, threatening to set up independent realms. As many of them were English or foreign with anti-French interests, the problem very much belonged to Charles V. Pope Urban V suggested the best way to rid the land of these parasites was to send them on a crusade. The King of Hungary was keen for help against the Turks. But such a trek involved travel through Germany and the Emperor would not tolerate their presence on his territory. Just then, a crisis developed in Spain. The ruler of Castile was Don Peter, called the Cruel. In his court, his wife had died in mysterious circumstances. She was Charles' sister-in-law. The personal insult was compounded by the political situation. Don Peter was in conflict with the King of Aragon, but Peter had a rival to his crown, Don Henry, who could rely on the support of Aragon and now invited Charles V to his assistance. Finally, the Pope recognised the presence of Jews and Muslims among the supporters of Don Peter and declared the enterprise a crusade. White crosses were sewn over the hauberks of the myriad freebooters in France. They became the White Company. Such a vicious gang of marauders needed a strong leader and Charles could see no one more competent for this post than Bertrand du Guesclin. The Breton was ransomed for 40,000 florins from Sir John Chandos. It is a token of the comfortable respect shown by these two warlords for each other, that Guesclin immediately invited Chandos to join him on the profitable endeavour. Realising the long-term political consequences of this campaign, Chandos declined.

The kind of freelance warrior that rode in Guesclin's army has been recorded by Froissart. One evening, in front of a roaring fire at the court of the Count of Foix, the chronicler listened to the reminiscences of the Bascot de Mauleon. He was not a knight, called a squire by Froissart, but he had arrived like a baron with many followers and several pack animals. His men ate off silver plates. Mauleon was a Gascon of about 55. At the time of Guesclin's expedition to Spain in 1365, he would have been 32. He remembered his career before this. He fought his first battle in his early 20s at Poitiers. He had the good fortune to take prisoner a knight and two squires. This set him up materially, bringing in 3,000 francs of ransom. He next fought in Prussia under Jean de Grailly in the usual sport of warlords, known as the crusade against the Baltic pagans. On their return to France, they rescued noblewomen from the rebellious peasants of the Jacquerie, slaughtering some 6,000: 'They never rebelled again.' From there, Mauleon joined Grailly in the Navarrese war. They pursued a campaign of plunder. 'We became masters of the farmlands and the rivers. We and our friends won a great deal of wealth. But then a truce was made and Mauleon had to leave his captured castles.

'Some of our leaders held a conference about where we should go. We had to live somewhere. We went to Burgundy and had captains of all nationalities: English, Gascon, Spanish, Navarrese, German, Scots. I was there as a captain. There were more than 12,000 of us there along the Loire and in Burgundy. Of that assembly, between 3,000 and 4,000 were really fine soldiers, as trained and skilled in war as any could be. Wonderful men at planning a battle and seizing the advantage. At scaling and assaulting towns and castles. And didn't we show it at the battle of Brignais when we smashed the Constable of France with a good 2,000 lances of knights and squires. This battle was much needed. Before, our men had been poor, now they were rich through prisoners and the towns they took in the archbishopric of Lyons and along the river Rhone.' The mercenary companies caused such aggravation in that area that war broke out between them and the Papacy in Avignon. The Pope invited a Lombard warlord to deal with them. He simply hired the majority of the companies, including the captain Sir John Hawkwood, and took them to Lombardy for his war against the Lord of Milan. A few stayed in France. Mauleon was among them. They made a good living out of ransacking town after town. Then came the campaign of Cocherel and Mauleon rejoined Grailly with a force of 12 lances, attaching himself to the company of John Jouel. Mauleon was taken prisoner but released on ransom, being captured by a cousin. His gang of marauders then suffered badly when ambushed on a raid by the count of Sancerre.

After these set-backs, Mauleon was thankful to join Guesclin's expedition to Spain. He had been present at Auray under the command of Sir Hugh Calverly and now served under him with 10 lances. This was the same Calverly who had been a bitter enemy of Guesclin, but such was the material common interest of knights in the 14th century that both Calverly and Mauleon were happy to accept Guesclin as their leader. Jean de Bourbon, a cousin to Don Peter's dead wife, was figurehead of the French expedition, giving it some legitimacy, but Guesclin was the supreme military commander. The army numbered some 30,000. It marched on Avignon. The Pope gave the expedition his blessing, excommunicated Don Peter, and was compelled to give large sums of money to the ravenous horde. As they disappeared over the Pyrenees, Frenchmen breathed a sigh of relief. The campaign in Castile was fierce and quick. Within a couple of months, several towns had been captured, many Jews slaughtered, and Don Henry crowned king. Don Peter had expediently retreated to Seville. He went in search of powerful allies. In Aquitaine, he secured the support of the Black Prince and through him the King of England. The King of Navarre

The siege of Melun. On the left, Guesclin parleys with the garrison, while on the right, his sappers are undermining the wall. Guesclin's career consisted of many such actions.

lent tacit support by opening the passes of the Pyrenees to the troops of the Black Prince riding with Don Peter to claim back his crown.

At the end of their campaign, the army of Guesclin disintegrated into a rabble of marauders. The Spaniards wanted them no more than the French. Many of the free companies pillaged their way back to France under constant attack from the local Spanish. Guesclin had been rewarded with vast estates in Spain and was in no hurry to leave. In his advance southwards, the Black Prince was accompanied by John Chandos and the King of Majorca who had business to settle with Aragon. Many of the soldiers previously in Guesclin's army were re-hired to fight against him. Guesclin and King Henry advanced into Aragon to meet the invaders.

The Black Prince camped on the border of Navarre and Aragon. Before him rode Sir Thomas Felton, gathering intelligence. He crossed the river Ebro and lodged in the town of Najera. A skirmish between Felton and King Henry's troops encouraged Henry to advance on the Black Prince. The Prince rose to the challenge and had his trumpets call for battle order. He created 300 new knights. Anticipation gave way to evasion. Once Henry

knew the full strength of the Prince's army he decided to wait for Guesclin, who arrived with 3,000 French and Aragonese troops. Skirmishing between scouting parties grew more ferocious. In one encounter Felton and his followers were slain. Food shortages and bad weather wore the Prince down. He moved his army across the Ebro and lodged at Logrono. Henry moved his troops back into the town of Najera. His army had grown considerably, numbering 3,000 barded horses, 7,000 genitors (lightly armed horsemen), 10,000 crossbowmen, several thousand footsoldiers armed with javelins, spears and lances, and 20,000 men-at-arms from Castile, Galicia, Portugal, Cordova, and Seville. Guesclin urged battle. Again, there was more manoeuvring, but finally, outside Najera, Henry prepared his men.

At midnight, on the eve of 3 April 1367, King Henry's soldiers were ordered into the battles they would fight in the next day. The first battle consisted of all the freebooters from France, Provence, and Aragon. They were led by Guesclin and a host of foreign knights and amounted to some 4,000 men-at-arms, well armed and dressed in the French manner. The second battle was led by Henry's brother, Don Tello, and included the genitors, some of them Muslim, and 15,000 horsemen and footsoldiers. They were placed to the left behind the first battle. The third battle was King

The clash of arms at the battle of Auray, 1364. The two leading knights both wear the arms of Brittany, representing their struggle for succession. Guesclin fought alongside Charles of Blois.

380

Henry's with 7,000 horsemen and several thousand footsoldiers armed with crossbows. In these formations, the men spent the night.

The next day at dawn, banners were unrolled and the Black Prince advanced across hilly scrubland to Najera. John Chandos requested permission to unfurl his own banner: silver field, a sharp pile gules. It was granted and flew alongside the cross of St George. As was the practice of the day, the English and Gascon men-at-arms dismounted. The Black Prince made a short prayer and then proclaimed: 'Advance banners in the name of God and Saint George.' The first battle was led by Chandos and the Duke of Lancaster and clashed with Guesclin's company. Spears and shields broke upon each other. The Black Prince and Don Peter led the second battle against the Spanish. The Spanish company under Don Tello broke immediately. The Black Prince crashed onto the battle of King Henry. Many Spanish were armed with slings and their stones caused serious injuries. The English archers retaliated. On the wings of Henry's battle, the Spanish light horsemen kept good order, dashing in among any gaps, hurling their javelins. As the fighting wore on, many of the ordinary Spanish gave way. The longest held combat was between Guesclin and Chandos. The old rivalry struggled on. Chandos pushed so far into the fray that he was surrounded. Suddenly, a Spaniard leapt upon him. Underneath the big man, Chandos twisted to reach the dagger strapped to his chest. He plunged it into the side and back of the Spaniard until he was free. The English pressed on. With the rout of Don Tello's second battle, King Henry three times rallied his warriors. Eventually, the tide of battle had been determined, King Henry withdrew with his warriors to Najera. Several English and Gascons took to their horses to pursue the Spaniards, breaking into the town and pillaging King Henry's treasure. Guesclin remained on the field and was made a prisoner by Chandos.

The Black Prince was celebrated as the greatest knight in Christendom. Najera joined Crecy and Poitiers as a trinity of historic English victories. But his men were hungry and without pay. Don Peter refused to reward them, insisting that the rabble leave Spain straight away. Most of the French and Spanish prisoners were ransomed for immediate cash, but while the Prince remained in Spain, Guesclin was considered too dangerous to free. The deposed Don Henry gathered support in Aragon and southern France. He raided the territory of the Black Prince. In 1368, with the Prince back in Aquitaine, Guesclin's ransom was set at the huge sum of 100,000 francs. Amazingly, within the month, the sum was paid by the King of France and the Duke of Anjou. Such was the value of this warlord. Guesclin's captivity had been far from harsh. He enjoyed the company of Chandos. He called him 'the most renowned knight of the world'. He recognised him as the true victor of Najera.

The Spanish campaign had cost the Black Prince dearly. He returned to Aquitaine in need of money. He proceeded to raise a tax. Several lords, especially those of Gascony, rejected the tax and gathered at the court of the

King of France. In Aragon, Don Henry thought it timely to reattempt an assault on Castile. He captured the town of Leon and then laid siege to Toledo. Guesclin heard news of the resurgence and took leave from Anjou to join Henry. Popular Spanish support lay with Henry and Don Peter had to request the kings of Portugal and Granada for help. 20,000 Saracen horsemen rode to his banner at Seville and from there Don Peter made for Toledo to raise the siege. Guesclin advised Henry to surprise Peter. Henry took his best men and descended on the castle of Montiel in southern Castile where Peter had spent the night. Peter's forces outnumbered Henry, but the surprise gained him an advantage. With cries of 'Castile for King Henry' and 'Notre Dame Guesclin', Henry crushed Peter's vanguard. Because of the

Edward, the Black Prince, a leading adversary of Guesclin. Detail of the latten effigy in Canterbury Cathedral of around 1376.

great number of Muslims among the enemy, Guesclin had given orders that no prisoners were to be taken. Don Peter rallied and ordered the rest of his men forward. A great battle developed. The Saracens proved particularly fierce, shooting bows and hurling javelins. But Don Peter's army began to break and he was urged to withdraw to the castle of Montiel.

Having obtained the victory, Don Henry laid siege to Montiel. The castle was tough but the surprise of the assault meant it was poorly provisioned. One night, Don Peter crept out of the fortress. The Begue of Villains was on guard and claimed the fugitives as his prisoners. Peter agreed and was taken to his quarters. The news brought Don Henry to the Begue's lodgings. 'Where is that son of a whore and Jew that calls himself the King of Castile?' he bellowed. Out of the gloom, Peter replied: 'No, you are the whoreson and I am the son of King Alphonso of Castile.' He grabbed Henry by the arms and threw him over a bench. He drew a dagger and was about to slay him, when the viscount Rocaberti caught Peter by the leg and tripped him. Henry drew his long knife and plunged it into his brother. Two English knights tried to defend Peter but were cut down. The Don lay dead. The war of the Castilian succession had ended. Guesclin was made constable of Castile and given further estates in Molina and Soria, worth 20,000 francs a year. Henry even tried to entice Guesclin on further adventures by proclaiming him King of Granada. But he was destined not to carry this crusade against the infidels, or even enjoy a warlord's retirement in Spain, In 1370, Charles V recalled Guesclin to France.

Charles V had used the troubled peace since the treaty of Bretigny to strengthen his forces for the war he knew would come. The French crown could not tolerate vast stretches of French land in foreign hands. With the burden of King John's ransom removed, taxes were diverted towards the equipping of a royal army. A powerful artillery train was built up. Paris was surrounded by new walls; a royal navy created. Statutes were passed: they encouraged the practice of archery and crossbow shooting; the organisation of an army into companies under captains led by lieutenants or the constable; and a regular inspection and repairing of important castles. Aside from military organisation, Charles was adept at diplomacy. A marriage ensured friendly relations with Flanders, for so long allied to England, while Charles' support of Don Henry maintained an important Spanish ally. By 1369, over 800 towns and districts in Aquitaine had declared an allegiance to the French crown. In the north, Ponthieu rejected English dominance. The time for war had arrived.

With the retirement of Moreau de Fiennes, Charles V needed a new Constable, a supreme commander of French forces. The victorious activities of Guesclin made him the most obvious candidate. But there was the problem of Guesclin's lowly social status. He himself admitted this when summoned to Paris. 'My lord and noble King,' he explained. 'I am of too low blood to accept the great office of Constable of France. Whoever accepts it must command the most noble men as well as the ordinary. How could I be

The battle of Najera, 1367. According to this illustration, Muslim warriors fought on both sides. The English and French men-at-arms dismounted for the battle.

so bold to order these lords here, your cousins and relations? Envy should be so great that I would fear it. Is there not some other office I could fulfil?' The King would not accept this. 'Sir Bertrand,' he replied, 'there is neither a brother nor cousin, nor count nor baron in my realm who shall disobey you. And if they do, they shall receive my greatest anger. Take the position I offer you. We need you.' Guesclin was invested with the office of Constable. In order to strengthen his authority, the King placed him next to him at his dinner table and showed him great friendship. In addition, Guesclin and his heirs were given many estates. According to Froissart, the Duke of Anjou was influential in securing Guesclin this position.

In his 50s, Guesclin's energy was no less than it had been in his youth. He conquered the area of Poitou in English-held Aquitaine and captured the town of Poitiers. The port of Rochelle opened its gates to him. In Brittany, Duke Montfort declared for England, but the timing was wrong. The majority of Breton lords favoured the French King. Montfort was forced to flee to England and Guesclin occupied the most important Breton towns. Guesclin's success was partly facilitated by the death of his arch rival Sir John Chandos in 1369 in a skirmish. The weight of victory, however, lay in Guesclin's experience of commanding men and handling the logistical and

Muslim horsemen confront 14th century knights. In Guesclin's Spanish campaigns, Muslim light horsemen called genitors were particularly feared. From the *Histoire du Voyage et Conquete de Jerusalem*, 1337, now in the Bibliotheque Nationale, Paris.

strategical problems of campaigning. In 1373, Edward III sent an army to Calais. It was confronted by the characteristic guerrilla tactics of Guesclin. According to Froissart, this strategic evasion may have owed much to Charles V, despite Guesclin's experience in such warfare. The King of France specifically forbade his men to engage the English in battle. Instead, he set 600 lances to follow and harass the English army. Sometimes, it was claimed, the two forces rode so close that English knights spoke to French knights riding at their flank. 'It's a fine day for hawking,' said one frustrated English knight happening upon a Frenchman. 'Why don't you fly for a kill since you've got wings?' 'That's true,' replied the French knight. 'If it depended on me, we would fly out after you.' But the King of France would not be drawn into a major battle.

Charles' advisers backed him totally: 'Let the English ride on. They cannot rob you of your inheritance. They will grow tired and crumble away to nothing. Sometimes a storm cloud appears over the country, but later it passes on and disperses. So will it be with the English soldiers.' This strategy was clarified and confirmed at a conference in Paris. 'I do not say that the English should not be fought,' advised Guesclin,' but I want it to be executed from a position of advantage. That is what the English did at

385

Poitiers and Crecy.' Oliver de Clisson, a lieutenant to Guesclin, had spent much time with the English and agreed with his commander: 'The English have won so many major victories that they have come to believe they cannot lose. In battle, they are the most confident nation in the world. In my humble opinion, it would be inadvisable to fight them unless they can be taken at a disadvantage.' The King of France then asked his brother, the Duke of Anjou, for his thoughts. 'Anyone who gives you different advice to what has been said betrays our interests. When the English expect to find us in one part of the country, we shall be in another, and we shall take from them when it best suits us the few pieces of territory they still hold.' Charles V was pleased with this advice. 'Indeed, I have no intention of marching out and hazarding my knights and my kingdom in one encounter for a piece of farmland. I entrust the whole responsibility of my realm to my Constable and his associates.' The intelligence and concordance of French military leadership ensured a victorious campaign.

The Dukes of Lancaster and Brittany plundered their way across France. Several times they sent their heralds to demand battle from the French. Guesclin refused. Frequently the English were forced to camp in open country, while the French tailing them lodged comfortably in friendly castles. The land they passed through had been devastated by marauding companies before them. The English suffered from a lack of food, but they dared not go out foraging. The French had grown to 3,000 lances and would annihilate any raiding parties. The English baggage train, when not ambushed, was ravaged by illness and bad weather. By the time the English army reached Aquitaine, it was useless. Like many of his knights, the English commander contracted a sickness and passed away. At the end of this dismal campaign, Guesclin counter-attacked and captured yet more English territory.

In 1375, a truce was agreed at Bruges. In 1376, the Black Prince died. A year later, he was followed by his father, Edward III. With the principal antagonists out of the way, Charles V surged on with his counter-attack, even taking the fighting against the English coast. Charles the Bad of Navarre remained a source of anti-French conspiracy and the French King moved against him. Guesclin was sent to Normandy to occupy his remaining estates, while King Henry of Castile seized his land in Spain. From there, Charles turned his attention to Brittany. He deposed the Duke of Brittany and annexed the entire country to his royal domain. Such a move was politically insensitive. The Bretons had always considered themselves an independent people and many of Charles', most loyal retainers were Breton, not least of them being Guesclin.

Although Guesclin had sworn to obey the French King, his ultimate loyalty lay with a Brittany independent of both English and French control. But he had vowed to serve the King and he could see the political sense of making Brittany French rather than letting it fall into the hands of the English. As ordered, he rode to Rennes at the heart of his homeland. There

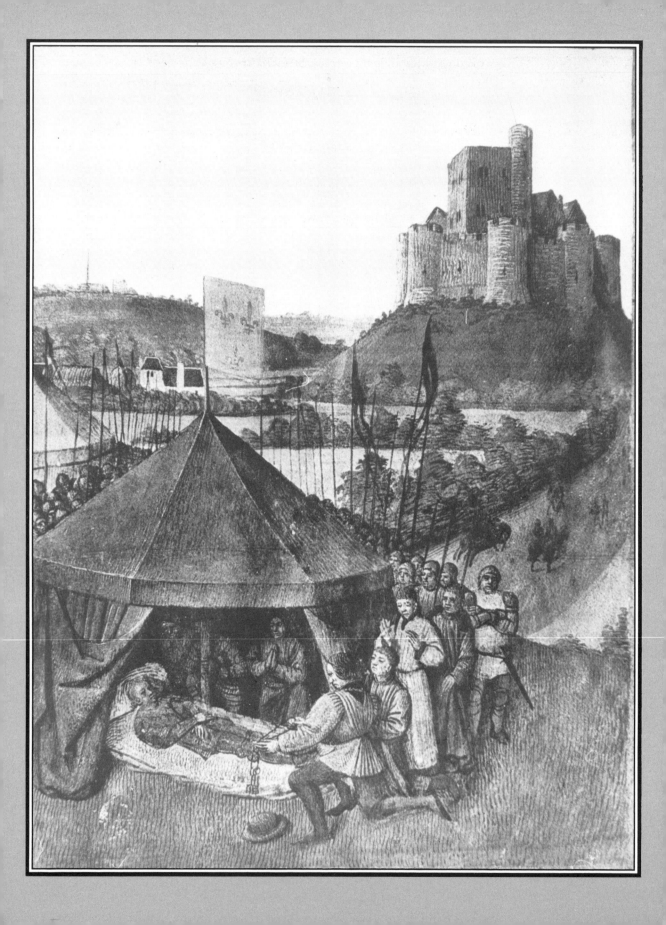

was no fighting. He repeatedly asked the Duke of Anjou to arrange a truce with Brittany. He wanted negotiation. He would not fight his own people. But in the minds of many Bretons, Guesclin had already become a traitor. He had entered Brittany with an army of conquest. He served the King before Brittany. In Paris, the royal court noted the reluctance of Guesclin. They suggested to Charles that Guesclin could no longer be trusted. In order to prove otherwise, and maybe because the King realised Guesclin's dilemma, the Breton was sent to Auvergne in south-east France to quell some marauding soldiers.

At nearly 60, this was a dismal finale to the splendid career of Bertrand du Guesclin. The suspicion of his royal master and the conflict with his homeland must have profoundly saddened Guesclin, loosening his interest in life. In Auvergne, he faced the brigand armies he had fought so many times before. Would they never cease? At last, campaigning tired him. Before the town of Chateauneuf de Randon, Guesclin fell ill. On 13 July 1380, he died. The same day, the castle surrendered. Its keys were placed at the dead warlord's feet. Guesclin's body was taken back to Paris and buried at Saint Denis in a tomb near to that prepared for Charles V. Despite their final disagreement over Brittany, Charles realised his kingdom owed a great debt to Guesclin. The King believed it not wise to broadcast the death of such a powerful man, but at the quiet funeral service words were spoken 'as though he had been the King's son'. A few months later, Charles himself was dead.

The legend of Guesclin grew stronger as the Hundred Years War slowly turned against the French once more. During the reign of Charles VI, nine years after Guesclin's death, a spectacular memorial service was held in his honour. It is believed to have contained the first funeral oration for a layman other than a king or prince. The text took the biblical theme *Nominatus est usque ad extrema terrae*: 'His name is known to the ends of the earth.' Four men, armoured and mounted on fine chargers, entered the church representing the dead warlord as he was when alive. Throughout French court art and literature, Guesclin was added to the list of chivalric heroes known as the Nine Worthies. He was ranked alongside Alexander, Caesar, Arthur, and Charlemagne. In the early 15th century, when the French began their final counter-attack against the English, a gold ring belonging to Guesclin is said to have been given to Joan of Arc. In death, the Breton warlord continued to serve the French kingdom as successfully as he had during his life.

JAN ZIZKA

Jan Zizka had little to lose. The small freehold estate his father had left him could not keep him out of debt. The contract he had signed, confirming the debt, promised hard retribution from the lord of the region, Peter of Rosenberg, the greatest of Bohemian magnates. In 1380, at the age of 20, Zizka sold his land in Trocnov, southern Bohemia, and made for the court of King Wenceslas IV at Prague. He was a pugnacious young man. In a boyhood fight he had lost an eye. Zizka is thought to mean 'one-eyed' and was his name alone in his family.

By 1392, Zizka's tough character had earned him the position of Royal Hunter amid the forestland of Zahorany, just south of Prague. The job kept him fit and alert, but above all it enabled him to rub shoulders with the King and principal Bohemian aristocrats. In the blood and bluster of the chase, there was a robust informality. During the Royal hunts, which frequently lasted several weeks, Zizka could study his feudal superiors and make valuable contacts. In 1395, the sport came to an end. Relations between Wenceslas and his leading lords deteriorated. Henry of Rosenberg detained the King for several months at his castle in the south. Rosenberg would not tolerate the centralization of power introduced by the King's father. Eventually, Wenceslas was released but two parties now formed. Rosenberg and his associates were joined by the King's younger brother, Sigismund, King of Hungary, and his cousin, Jost, Margrave of Moravia; Wenceslas could count on the support of his youngest brother, Duke of Gorlitz, and other minor magnates who feared the dominance of Rosenberg.

C.1360—1424

Jan Zizka, blind in one eye from his youth. Stone portrait made by Wendel Roskopf shortly after 1500, now in the National Museum, Prague.

The two factions recruited armed bands and the next few years saw relentless feuding throughout the country. The once stable and prosperous Czech kingdom was torn by mercenary companies causing the kind of havoc experienced by the French during the Hundred Years War.

Zizka demonstrated his loyalty to his King by joining a military company and ravaging the lands of his former overlord, Rosenberg, in southern Bohemia. By 1405, the conflict had cooled and practical survival overcome aristocratic differences. But still the mercenary gangs scoured the land for plunder. Once created, the monster could not easily be dismantled. In 1409, Zizka himself seems to have gone off the rails, Wenceslas signed a letter of amnesty to the townsmen of Budweis, forgiving Zizka all crimes against the Bohemian kingdom. The same year, Wenceslas and his leading warlord, John Sokol of Lamberg, seized upon a means to rid their land of the marauding warrior bands. As in France, the device was to be a foreign campaign. But this time, it was not a crusade, but a war against crusaders – the Teutonic Knights.

Ever since they had left the Holy Land and transferred their base of operations to the Baltic coast, the martial monastic Teutonic Order had advanced east from the Vistula, conquered Prussia and extended its control over Livonia and Estonia. In alliance with the Hanseatic League, the Teutonic Knights dominated Baltic trade and proved militarily awesome. Each year, nobles and mercenary knights from all over Western Europe joined the Teutonic Order on raids against the pagan inhabitants of the eastern Baltic lands. This systematic extermination of these people, dignified and justified by the title of crusade, was almost regarded as a sport; certainly it was a finishing school for young warriors keen on battle experience. The regular influx of western knighthood kept the Teutonic Order aware of the latest military developments and filled its ranks with highly effective young men. Their annual raids continued to devastate Lithuania even after the country had converted to Christianity in 1387. The true brutality of the Teutonic Order could not be made any plainer.

Poland had originally invited the Teutonic knights to the Baltic coast to rid them of troublesome neighbours. But by the beginning of the 15th century, the Order dominated Polish estates and blocked Poland's access to the Baltic sea. In 1385, Jagello, Grand Duke of Lithuania, had been adopted by the Queen of Poland and married her daughter. He became Wladislaw, King of Poland, and the union of Lithuania and Poland proved a powerful counterbalance to the Teutonic Order. It was not long before the two states clashed. In 1409, the still pagan region of Samogitia rose in revolt against the Teutonic Order. Poland and Lithuania supported the revolt, leaving the Teutonic Grand Master no choice but to declare war on Poland. Both sides prepared for a major conflict in 1410.

Naturally, western knighthood rallied to the 'righteous' cause of the northern crusaders. It still considered the Slavs, Christian or not, as 'Saracens'. Poland could only call upon other Slav nations, principally Bohemia. Relations between the two Kings were not good, but Wenceslas could see no political reason not to send his troops, particularly in the light of Sigismund's declaration against Poland. Amnesties were issued to the leading warrior bands of Bohemia and a good many enrolled in Sokol's mercenary army. In Bohemia, there was a deep hatred between the Slavic Czech natives and German immigrants who usually formed the richer, merchant classes. A war in alliance with Polish Slavs against Teutonic Germans encouraged good morale in the warrior bands riding to the standard of the King of Poland. Among these adventurers, Zizka led his own gang of veteran guerrilla fighters.

Wladislaw's army of 1410 consisted of Polish and Lithuanian knights and their retainers, Sokol's Bohemian mercenaries, and the Tatar followers of Witold, governor of Lithuania. The Tatar numbers were not great, but the Germans overemphasised their contribution to the Polish army in order to

Knights of the Teutonic Order battling with Poles and Lithuanians. From Ward Lock's *Illustrated History of the World*, 1885.

create the impression of a pagan enemy. The Polish forces gathered at Czerwinsk on the Vistula, not far from Warsaw. To divert the Teutonic knights from their true path of attack, Wladislaw ordered raids into western Prussia and along the north-east frontier of the Teutonic realm. In July 1410, the Polish army crossed the Vistula by means of a pontoon bridge and advanced northwards into central Prussia. In the meantime, Ulrich von Jungingen, Teutonic Grand Master, awaited the arrival of mercenary troops, among them English bowmen and Genoese crossbowmen. Although commanding a smaller force, von Jungingen was well aware of the superior professionalism of his warriors opposed to the massed, but amateur feudal peasant levies that swelled the Polish ranks. 'Witold's men are more at home with a spoon than a sword,' he sneered.

Marienburg was the castle headquarters of the Teutonic Order and the Poles headed straight for it. Von Jungingen blocked their advance at a site near Kurzetnik. He heavily fortified the nearby riverbanks with palisades and awaited Wladislaw. The Polish King knew better than to attack and sought to outflank the Teutonic army. The Grand Master was determined to bring the Poles to battle and crossed the river Drweca. The armies converged on the open ground between the villages of Tannenberg and Grunwald. The site suited both commanders very well as they both placed great faith in their horsemen. The Poles and Lithuanians numbered some 29,000 horse and 10,000 footsoldiers; the Teutonic army included 21,000 horsemen and about 6,000 footsoldiers.

Handgunners from the *Rudimentum Noviciorum*, Lubeck, 1475. By the early 15th century, firearms were a vital aspect of battle and Zizka soon mastered their employment.

The Teutonic Order was early to rise and their ready formations surprised Wladislaw. As the Polish King attended Mass, Witold and the Polish commanders assembled warriors around 50 Polish banners and 40 Lithuanian banners. Within the Polish contingent, two of these banners consisted entirely of Bohemian soldiers, while a further three contained a good many. Their presence, however, was more important than their numbers. Wladislaw was so impressed by the reputation of Sokol that he offered him overall command of the Slavic army. The Bohemian warlord courteously refused. But throughout the battle, Sokol remained at the King's side. Von Jungingen did not want to initiate the battle: he had dug ditches, erected obstacles, and entrenched his cannon. This gave the Poles time. After three hours of skirmishing, the impatient Grand Master sent forward a party of knights. Refusing to address the Polish King by his title, they offered him their swords: 'We give you these weapons so that you may begin the battle and cease to hide in the woods.' The King and his followers were outraged. A general advance was ordered.

The Lithuanians on the right wing of the Polish army could not restrain themselves. They dashed forward on their small ponies, outstripping the more orderly Polish centre. They overran the Teutonic footsoldiers and cannon, but were soundly stopped by the Germanic men-at-arms. In the centre of the battle, the Teutonic cannon boomed, followed by the thunderous trotting of the Knights of the Order. Whooping, yelping Polish and Tatar horsemen raced to meet them. As collision seemed imminent, the horses of both sides began to shy away from impact. Some slowed down, others tried to pull back, but the blind horses behind urged them on. The formations of the initial charge broke up. By the time both sides made contact, the warriors clashed in little groups scattered across the battlefield. Apparently the more lightly armoured Lithuanians and Tatars were unable to use their steppe tactics to their advantage and suffered in hand-to-hand conflict with knights in plate armour. The Polish right wing wavered and broke. Witold begged Wladislaw to show himself to the remaining warriors to arouse their morale. The King rode among his army. But the Grand

Master piled on the pressure on the Polish centre and sent in his reserves.

The presence of both Wladislaw and Witold on the battlefield reached many of the routed Lithuanians. They reorganised and returned to the battle, hitting the Teutonic army in the rear. Suddenly, the greater numbers of the Slavs began to tell and the Germans were surrounded. In the final struggle, the Bohemians are said to have distinguished themselves. There is no record of Zizka at this battle, but a major combat such as this was a rare occurrence a professional soldier could not afford to miss. Zizka was not getting any younger and he may have considered this battle his last chance to win prisoners, booty, and perhaps some professional acclaim. By early evening, however, there was little opportunity for sparing high-ranking prisoners for ransom. The bitterness between Slav and German ensured that few beaten warriors survived. In the chaos of defeat, the Teutonic Grand Master was slain along with other principal Knights of the Order. The fortified Teutonic camp was quickly overcome. Among the booty were wagons loaded with barrels of wine. To prevent the mass intoxication of his army, Wladislaw ordered the barrels broken and amazingly he was obeyed. Also uncovered in the enemy camp were piles of grease-covered torches with which the Germans had hoped to pursue the defeated Poles into the night. They were now snatched up by the Tatars and Lithuanians hunting the fleeing Germans.

The victorious Poles named the battle after the village of Grunwald, whereas the Germans remembered it as Tannenberg. Five hundred years later, the Germans defeated the Russians on the Eastern Front in 1914. That battle took place nowhere near the medieval site, but the Germans seized upon the name of Tannenberg and proclaimed the victory as a national act of revenge against the Slavs. Certainly, the battle of 1410 was a major defeat for the Teutonic Order and heralded their subsequent decline. In the campaigning following the battle, there is a specific reference to Zizka. Wladislaw went on to capture several castles. Zizka is mentioned as one of Sokol's subordinate commanders in charge of defending the newly captured castle of Radzin. A group of Teutonic knights attempted to storm the fortress but Zizka held on to it, winning the notice he seems not to have gained at Grunwald.

Zizka emerged from the Grunwald campaign a wiser and highly experienced soldier. Polish warfare was determined largely by its geography and Zizka learned much about cavalry warfare. But the Poles also adopted western technology. Against European enemies, they placed their crossbows, handguns, and cannon behind fieldworks. In the more mobile warfare of the eastern plains, however, earthworks were useless. Traditionally, transport wagons had been drawn up into a circle – a laager – to protect camps against Tatar horsemen. Inevitably, these wagons were reinforced and used as frontline defences for footsoldiers bearing firearms and bows. The impetus for this development derived from the increased presence of cannon and handguns on the battlefield at the beginning of the

15th century. Giles Fletcher described a Russian version of these mobile fieldworks used against Tatars in his 16th century account *Of the Rus Commonwealth*.

'If there is to be a set battle, or any great invasion by the Tatars, then footsoldiers are set within the running or moving castle, called *vezha* or *guliai-gorod*. This moving castle is so constructed that it may be set up at whatever length is required. It is nothing else but a double wall of wood to defend them on both sides, behind and before, with a space of 3 yards or thereabouts betwixt the two sides, so that they may stand within it and have room enough to charge and discharge their pieces and other weapons. It is closed at both ends and made with loopholes on either side to lay out the nose of their piece or to push forth any other weapon. It is carried with the army wheresoever it goes, being taken into pieces and laid on carts. It is erected without the help of any carpenter or instrument, because the timber is so framed to clasp together one piece within another.'

Hearing of the destructive impact of such devices on large groups of horsemen, Zizka probably considered it interesting but of little use. So long as he was employed by his King, he and his men-at-arms would continue to

Zizka leading his troops. From the beginning of the Hussite movement, Zizka was a popular leader and favourite of the common people. He carries his famous dagger-in-fist mace. Woodcut from an early 15th century edition of Aeneas Sylvius' *Historia Bohemica*.

396

fight as horse-warriors. Only large armies of footsoldiers, such as rebellious peasants, would require such defences in central Europe. Zizka returned to Bohemia not only rich in experience, but laden with booty. In 1414, he bought a house in the New Town, the Gothic quarter of Prague, not far from the Royal court. He appears to have been employed by the King as an officer of the palace guard, a suitable job for a semi-retired soldier. Frequently, Zizka was responsible for the personal safety of the Royal Family. He regularly accompanied the Queen on her visits to the Chapel of Bethlehem. There they heard the preaching of John Hus.

In a crowded church, Hus spoke out against the corruption of Papal Catholicism. He derided the comfortable life of establishment clergy and demanded a moral decency based simply on the teachings of Christ. It was a common criticism in the 14th and 15th centuries, and a ready congregation pleaser. With three Popes simultaneously occupying the divine throne, how could anyone respect the Catholic hierarchy? But this was not all Hus evoked. Throughout his service hymns were sung. Previously, hymns had been reserved for processions and at the end of sermons. Now, Hus brought singing into the very heart of his service and, above all, the hymns were sung in Czech. This embraced the ordinary, illiterate townsmen as well as the sophisticated courtiers of King Wenceslas. Everyone was raised in a surge of religious reformation combined with Czech national pride. The Czech resentment of German influence in Bohemia has already been stated. Many Bohemians of German background filled positions of power, while the majority of the lower classes were Slavic. In 1409, King Wenceslas ruled that the German element at the University of Prague – the intellectual and religious decision maker – should not be allowed to constantly outvote the Czech faction.

Within Prague, Archbishop Zbynek was chief supporter of Papal authority. Public rows between Zbynek and Hus grew in intensity until the Archbishop excommunicated Hus. The King wished for a quiet life, but public opinion remained excited by his presence. In 1412, he was advised to leave Prague. For the next two years, Hus preached throughout the south of Bohemia, often in the open air. Thus, he widened support for his beliefs among the provincial nobility and rural lower classes. During this activity, Zizka, a Czech of humble background, must have found the teachings of Hus a welcome and overdue expression of all the resentment he had felt towards Germanic overlords. In 1414, an international Catholic conference at Constance in Switzerland demanded that Hus justify his critical beliefs in their presence. King Sigismund of Hungary guaranteed him safe conduct. The meeting became a trial and in 1415 the troublesome Hus was burnt at the stake as a heretic.

Ever after, Sigismund tried to excuse his role in this deception and entrapment. But in the minds of most Bohemians, his broken vow of safe conduct only added to the national outrage of all Czechs. It was probably this aspect, rather than Hus' religious beliefs, that encouraged 452 lords and knights, the majority of Bohemian nobility, to sign an agreement protesting the decision of the Council of Constance and guaranteeing freedom of Hussite preaching on their estates. Defiance of the Council continued when the University of Prague encouraged the giving of both wine and bread in the Eucharist to laymen of both sexes – previously wine had only been allowed to the clergy. A Church of Bohemia had arisen. In the rural communities of the south, followers of Hus took more radical views and founded a group known as the Taborites. Inspired by open air congregations, they took their name from the biblical Mount Tabor. They believed only in what the Bible specifically stated and dispensed with all other religious ritual.

Wenceslas feared for his royal authority and tried to back-track. Hussite churches were closed, but this only encouraged the more committed Hussites to leave Prague for the Taborite communities. Wenceslas was losing control of the situation. As the peasants massed in southern Bohemia, the underprivileged townsmen of Prague were excited by illegal sermons promising them a better life. John Zelivsky, a former monk and acclaimed leader of the street people, realised the inevitability of an armed clash. He needed professional advice and asked a dedicated court follower of the Hussite movement – Jan Zizka. Still chief of security within the royal household, Zizka joined a crowd of Hussite protestors in July 1419. After a powerful sermon by Zelivsky, the angry crowd marched through Prague and broke into the Church of St Stephen where they celebrated Mass in the Hussite manner. They then crowded into the Cattle Market in front of the New Town Hall. The town councillors were asked to release citizens imprisoned in the Hussite crack-down. The councillors refused. A stone was thrown from a window of the Town Hall. The mob exploded. Doors were broken down and councillors thrown out of the building onto the market square where they were slain. The Town Hall was occupied by armed men. Zizka probably commanded the operation.

Throughout this action, Zizka did not believe he was betraying the King. He knew the court favoured Hussite tenets but were compelled by external politics to call a halt to the more radical elements. Zizka had no political commitments. He followed only the truth of God and believed the King would eventually succumb to this righteousness. To the King, however, this was insurrection that threatened his crown. While the Hussites consolidated their position in the New Town, Wenceslas sought help. His court was impatient with the King's mishandling of the crisis and broadly sympathetic to the Hussites. In desperation, Wenceslas called upon his brother, Sigismund of Hungary. The Hussites offered their renewed loyalty to the King in return for recognition of their status. But the shock of the events had been too much for Wenceslas. He suffered a stroke and died. His people were left now to make their own decisions. The lack of royal authority encouraged revolutionary thoughts.

As the only remaining member of the Luxemburg dynasty, Sigismund

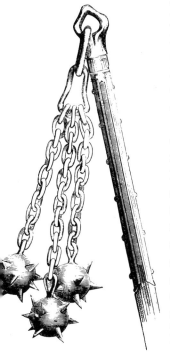

At Tabor, Zizka oversaw the conversion of peasant tools into deadly weapons. The most characteristic polearm of the Hussites was the fearsome flail.

was natural heir to the throne of Bohemia. As King of Hungary and Holy Roman Emperor, his energies were concentrated on other problems, especially Turkish incursions into the Balkans. Nevertheless, Sigismund was attracted to the country to which he had so long been an enemy. For the Hussites, and Czechs generally, there could be no worse candidate for the Bohemian throne. Only a few years previously, Sigismund had founded the Order of the Dragon, a crusading elite dedicated to the destruction of heretics and infidels. Zelivsky seized upon the devilish imagery of the Order in his sermons. Sigismund was the Great Red Dragon of the Apocalypse cast down from Heaven by holy brothers who do 'not hold their lives too dear to lay them down'. Here was a pledge in the Bible to do away with the Dragon of Sigismund even at the cost of one's own life. In an atmosphere of radical change, such fantastic imagery seemed the literal truth.

As the majority of Bohemian nobility supported the Hussite cause, a list of demands was presented to Sigismund: freedom of religious practice; freedom from foreign control; Czech should be the official language of Bohemia. Sigismund was preoccupied with campaigns against the Turks and avoided any definite response to the Czechs. Wenceslas' Queen ruled as regent. Sympathetic to the Hussites, she was also concerned with maintaining royal law and order. Garrisons in Prague were filled with German mercenaries and Taborites forbidden entry into the city. News of an ambush on Taborite pilgrims by a Catholic nobleman outside Prague angered the citizens. In a few days of street fighting, Zizka-led Hussites stormed all the royal garrisons and secured the freedom of Prague for their more radical comrades. Zizka now rode west at the invitation of the city of Plzen. Western Bohemia was fervently Hussite and Zizka felt confident of building an army there to oppose the feared arrival of Sigismund. Several nobles joined Zizka and accepted his command despite his lowly status. Kutna Hora, a largely German mining community in eastern Bohemia, became the centre of Catholic opposition. All Hussite inhabitants of the city were massacred. There would be no quarter on either side.

The Catholics put pressure on the Hussites straight away. Skirmishing around Plzen developed into a constricting siege. Within the city, factions among the community suggested to Zizka they could not withstand the conflict. Reluctantly, he signed an armistice with the Catholics and left the city. He now made for Tabor, the newly established town of the Hussite extremists. With these fanatics, Zizka felt more certain he could create an army. As the small force made its way southwards, the Catholics broke their truce and tried to ambush Zizka before he reached Tabor. Fortunately, his scouts gave Zizka good warning. With only 400 men, he sought a strong defensive position. Using the banks of drained fish ponds as earthworks and then drawing his ordinary supply wagons up on the flank and rear, Zizka compelled the 2,000 Catholic men-at-arms to attack his well-prepared frontal position. The horsemen dismounted, but by evening the hand-to-hand fighting had got the Catholics nowhere and they withdrew. The skirmish at Sudomer raised the morale of Zizka's troops and began his reputation as a giant-killer.

At Tabor, Zizka organized the community along military lines. Four captains, *hejtman*, were elected: Zizka, Nicholas of Hus, a senior leader of the Hussite movement, Zybnek of Buchov and Chval Repicky of Machovice, both competent commanders and faithful Taborites. The four men discussed military decisions but Zizka was the senior commander. In the few months Zizka was at Tabor in 1420, he established the new army he wanted. Raids were carried out on nearby Catholic castles that not only gained military experience for the Taborites but also much-needed stocks of equipment, weapons, and horses. The most ingenious developments, however, took place within Tabor. Peasant tools were converted into weapons. Scythes, forks, and hammers became deadly polearms. Of all the agricultural weapons, it was the flail, used to thresh grain, that became the most characteristic of Hussite arms and the most feared by their enemies. Reinforced with iron bands, chains, nails, and studs, flails were carried by special contingents of warriors practised in the sweeping, swiping strokes of the terrible weapon.

In addition to individual arms, Zizka oversaw the conversion of peasant carts into his famous war wagons. Until his followers had more horses, he knew his army would consist largely of foot soldiers and they had to be protected from the eastern European horsemen of Sigismund. The outsides of ordinary wagons were strengthened with wooden boards. Sometimes the boards were in turn reinforced with iron strips and given loopholes through which bowmen and handgunners could shoot. Within the wagons, tools and equipment were carried to clear roads and dig earthworks. One contemporary account mentions each wagon containing 'two axes, two spades, two pickaxes, two hoes, and two shovels.' In battle, chains linked the wagons together with pavises or stakes placed in the gaps. As the Hussite war progressed, the war wagon became the basic organisational unit around which the foot soldiers concentrated. Each wagon was expected to hold two handgunners, six crossbowmen, two flail-carriers, four halberdiers, two shield-carriers, and two well-armed drivers. But such set tactics had still to be formalised and the offensive use of these wagons lay in the future. In 1420, Zizka simply considered them a necessary defence. The presence of handguns in large numbers, which also became characteristic of Hussite warfare, cannot have been expected at this early stage. Bowmen were still the principal source of fire-power.

At the beginning of 1420, King Sigismund had entered Moravia, the south-east region of the Bohemian kingdom. He tried to win over the Bohemian nobility, but they would not forget his insult to their country, his broken vow, and his accusation of heresy. On 1 March, Sigismund did away with negotiation. A Papal bull proclaimed a crusade against the Hussites. Sigismund mobilised a substantial army. German noblemen and mercenaries flocked to his standard. The bull urged all heretics to be killed and their

Hussite wagon fortress. The chalice and goose emblems of the Taborites are illustrated, as are their firearms, crossbows and flails. The wheels of the wagons are chained together to make a stable base. Pen and wash drawing from a Viennese manuscript of the mid 15th century.

possessions confiscated. This was an open licence to murder and pillage at will. What soldier could resist it? A combined knight and peasant army motivated by a religious and nationalist passion might seem a powerful antidote to this pack of German mercenaries. But the Bohemian nobility were nervous of the trained and efficient army of Taborites. Their successful raids on castles and monasteries were unsettling. Cenek of

Wartenberg, a devoted Hussite and leading aristocrat, was the first to crack.

In return for minor religious concessions, Wartenberg offered Sigismund Hradcany castle, the defending bastion of Prague. The townsmen of Prague were outraged. They tried to storm the fortress but failed. Sigismund made a triumphant entry into Kutna Hora. Fearing his approach, an armistice was signed between Prague and the Hungarian King. But Sigismund demanded unconditional surrender. Prague was desperate and called upon Zizka. The Taborites responded keenly and advanced swiftly on the capital. Warriors from Hradcany and Sigismund's army tried to intercept Zizka but failed to break his wagon fortress. The reception for Zizka's troops in Prague was ecstatic. The Taborites were less enthusiastic about the townsmen: their puritanism shocked by mercantile wealth. Immediately, Zizka reinforced his tight discipline and compelled warriors to attend daily sermons in which the righteousness of their Holy War was preached.

The most immediate threat to Prague was the garrison in Hradcany, on the western side of the city. Zizka ambushed a supply train sent by Sigismund to the castle. The Hungarian King could not afford to lose the valuable foothold. His army approached Hradcany in battle order. Zizka left his general defence of the city and prepared to confront the King. As the two armies faced each other, Sigismund sent food wagons to the Hradcany garrison and thus forced Zizka to abandon his planned assault. Sigismund tightened his hold around the city and cut the roads into Prague one by one. This, Zizka could not allow. He took his stand on Vitkov hill, a narrow ridge just outside the city commanding two routes eastwards. Vineyards covered the southern slope and an old watchtower stood on the summit. Zizka added earthworks and wooden fortifications. Trees and buildings were knocked down to deprive the enemy of cover.

On 14 July, Sigismund's army was ready. Adventurers from all over Europe swelled the force to 80,000. Bohemians, Germans, Hungarians, and eastern Europeans all assembled under the red crusader cross. Principal among Sigismund's military commanders was the condottiere Philippo Scolari. A Florentine by birth, Scolari, better known as Pippo Spano, had taken keenly to the cavalry warfare of the Hungarians and learned the brutality and craft of frontier fighting against the Turks. When he returned to Italy, contemporaries were shocked by his rigorous, ruthless methods. All his prisoners had their right hands chopped off before being released. It was probably Spano who derived the ingenious relief of Hradcany. Now he brought his murderous skills to bear on Prague. Swiftly, while Zizka and the majority of his men rested in the city, a few thousand Hungarian and Geman horsemen rode up the north-east slope of Vitkov hill. They captured the watchtower and then assaulted the recently built barricades. A small Hussite garrison of 26 men and 3 women bravely defended the wood fort. With no bows or guns, they threw stones and spears at the attackers.

Hearing the alarm, Zizka quickly roused himself and made for the danger with his veteran bodyguard. The rest of the Taborite army followed up the southern slope. Climbing over the tangled remains of vineyards, the Taborite army struck the Germans in the flank. Hussite priests strode forward with religious banners bearing the Chalice of the Host. Behind them were archers, and behind them, warriors wielding flails, pikes, and other polearms. Just as singing had been a vital element in Hussite services, so singing raised the fighting spirit of the Taborites.

'You warriors of God and His Law, pray for God's help and believe in him, so that with him you will ever be victorious. You archers and lancers of knightly rank, pikemen and flailsmen of the common people, keep you all in mind the generous Lord. You baggage boys and advance guards, keep in mind that you do not forfeit your lives through greed and robbery, and never let yourselves be tempted by booty. You all will shout "At them, at them!" and feel the pride of a weapon in your hands, crying "God is our Lord!"'

Before the fanatical Taborites, the Germans and Hungarians broke. Many tumbled down the steep north side. Sigismund's losses were only a few hundred, but were severe enough to deter him from any further assaults.

Zizka's warriors fell to their knees on Vitkov, giving hymns of thanks. The day after the battle, the hill's fortifications were strengthened and ever after it bore the name Zizkov. A long siege of Prague now seemed out of the question. It was either an immediate all-out attack or nothing. Catholic Bohemian nobles did not favour a devastating blow against their capital. In negotiations with Sigismund, they persuaded the King it was not worth the cost. As a sign of their support of the Catholic cause, Sigismund was crowned King of Bohemia on 28 July in the Cathedral of Hradcany. By the end of the month, disease and frustration broke up Sigismund's army. With a final payment of booty ripped out of Hradcany, the mercenary forces were ordered home. The first crusade against the Hussites was over.

With the removal of an outside threat, the split between radical and moderate Hussites led to conflict within Prague. By August, Zizka and his Taborite army left the capital and returned southwards. They carried out a guerrilla war against the castles of Ulrich of Rosenberg. Once created, Zizka's fighting machine could not easily be stopped. Having forced Rosenberg into a truce, Zizka began a campaign against the Plzen region in early 1421. Action took place close to the borders of Bavaria and the Upper Palatinate. The Germans feared uprisings in their own countries. As Holy Roman Emperor, Sigismund had to see to the protection of his Imperial vassals. He ordered a counterattack, but the Taborites allied with the Praguers and the King declined the conflict, withdrawing to Hungary. Zizka renewed his attack on Plzen and established control over western and north-west Bohemia. Atrocities on both sides led to the massacring of thousands of innocent Bohemians.

After a pause in Prague, Zizka turned his attention to eastern Bohemia. Terror encouraged many towns to submit before the Taborites reached them. Even Kutna Hora, the base for Sigismund's operations, surrendered. Finally, Hradcany was besieged and the thorn removed from the side of Prague. As Zizka's success grew, so he changed his name to acknowledge the faith that fired him and his men. He dispensed with Trocnov and called himself Jan Zizka of the Chalice. His former family arms of a crab were replaced by the Chalice of the Taborites.

Battles against recalcitrant townsmen and invading German neighbours kept the Taborites busy throughout the summer of 1421. During one siege, Zizka received a serious wound. Directing operations against the castle of Bor, an arrow through remarkable accident struck Zizka in his right eye, the one not already blind. Surgeons tried to save the eye but infection left Zizka blind and seriously ill. For a man in his 60s, this was a terrible blow to his health. Yet the mere presence of Zizka in his Taborite army discouraged enemy forces and kept his own men confident.

At Kutna Hora in September 1421, a Hussite council of regency offered the crown of Bohemia to Witold of Lithuania. King Wladislaw of Poland had already been offered kingship but declined. Witold remained open to the offer and these negotiations must have profoundly irritated Sigismund.

Throughout the autumn of 1421, he gathered a mainly Hungarian army, under the command of Pippo Spano. In October, Pippo crossed the border into Moravia. Sigismund followed and met with German troops from Silesia, Lusatia, the archbishop of Olomouc and Duke Albert of Austria. Several Czech lords, including Ulrich of Rosenberg, rode to Sigismund's banner. Kutna Hora was the inevitable target for the Hungarians. Zizka hurried to its defence. By December, the Taborites were camped outside the city and preparing to confront Sigismund in the open. Zizka commanded the arrangement of his war wagons and 10,000 men took their positions among them. By this stage, the Taborites had acquired many cannon and handguns and were skilled in their use.

Pippo Spano favoured a cavalry assault against the Taborites. His 30,000 soldiers included a majority of Hungarian and Romanian horsemen. He tried to outflank Zizka's right side. Again and again, the Hungarian horsemen rode around the Taborite laager, trying to penetrate any gap or weakness. On each occasion, the Czechs let fly with a blast of handguns and cannon. By nightfall, it seemed as though Zizka could claim another victory. But

405

VS PHI IPPVS HISPANVS DESCOLARIS RELATOR VICTORIE THEVCRO

Pippo had not been so silly as to rely on a cavalry attack against a fortified position. In truth, Pippo had only ordered these assaults to keep the Czechs locked within their wagons. His spies revealed to him that the strong German population within Kutna Hora was guarded only by a small Taborite garrison. Under cover of dark, Pippo sent horsemen past Zizka's right flank to the western city gate. Citizens let them in and began a slaughter of the Taborites.

Zizka had not placed his entire army within Kutna Hora as he did not want to chance a long siege. He had hoped to break the Hungarians in one decisive conflict. But now the loss of the city meant that Zizka was isolated and effectively besieged anyway. His fortified camp held few provisions. Zizka had to counter surprise with surprise and go on the offensive. Horses were harnessed to wagons, and before daybreak the Taborite wagon fort broke ground, rumbling towards Sigismund's lines. When the wagons came within range of the Hungarians, the horses halted and the Czechs fired their guns and shot their bows. A breach was smashed through Sigismund's ring. A mile on, the wagons reformed a square and awaited the pursuing Hungarian cavalry. They never came. Sigismund was happy with his possession of Kutna Hora and would not risk any further engagement with Zizka. The Czech warlord had demonstrated the offensive capabilities of the war wagon, tactics that would be developed further throughout the Hussite wars.

As far as Sigismund was concerned, his campaign was over. His men were sent out to winter billets in surrounding villages. For Zizka, winter meant nothing. He simply awaited reinforcements and in early January struck back. The Taborites defeated a group of enemy soldiers in the nearby town of Nebovidy and marched on Kutna Hora. Pippo Spano realised there was little time to concentrate his troops. He advised Sigismund to evacuate the city. Before he went, the King ordered its complete destruction. Fortunately, Zizka's advanced cavalry forces reached Kutna Hora in good time to extinguish the flames. At first, Sigismund's retreat resembled a rout, but after two days he decided on a stand near the village of Habry. Pippo did not think it wise, morale was low among his soldiers. Sigismund remained obstinate and formed battle lines. Again, unusually, the Taborites took the offensive. Their onrush broke the Hungarians. Now the retreat was a rout. Many warriors died crossing frozen rivers that gave way under their weight. Sigismund was thrown out of Bohemia. The failure sickened him and discouraged crusading plans for several years. As for Zizka, the victory meant official recognition as commander-in-chief of all Hussite forces in Bohemia.

With the expulsion of Sigismund, politics again drove a wedge between radical and moderate Hussites. In the spring of 1423, Zizka could no longer tolerate the more extreme views of his Taborite comrades. He rode with his closest followers to eastern Bohemia and assumed command over the Orebite community, establishing a second Tabor. He invited local nobles and knights to join what amounted to a military brotherhood. He composed a military code for his followers in which order and discipline were stressed: soldiers must remain in the battle groups to which they were assigned; van, rear and flanks must be guarded while marching; fires must not be lit without permission; before every undertaking, the army must kneel down and pray to God. Everyone, from lord to peasant, was equal according to God's law and anyone committing a crime on campaign received equal punishment. Booty was to be pooled and divided justly. Anyone keeping booty to himself would be executed. Under this code, Zizka created an army as effective as the original Taborites.

The independence of the Taborites had long irritated Prague. The emergence of Zizka's Orebite community in a similar style compounded the break between the capital and its chief warlord. Hradec Kralove became the centre of the Orebite region and Prague tried to establish some hold over it by placing their own representative as ruler of the town. In the summer of 1423, Zizka expelled the puppet governor. An army of Praguers left their campaigning in Moravia and rushed to confront Zizka. 'Ark against Ark' was how a chronicler described the conflict. In a battle outside Hradec, Zizka broke the Praguers and personally killed their leading priest. Shocked chroniclers recall that the holy man was brought before Zizka and in a fit of rage the warlord smashed his fist-shaped mace on the priest's head. Civil war broke out. The alliance of some Catholic noblemen with Prague intensified the bitterness.

At the beginning of 1424 occurred the sad sight of Zizka's angry army before Prague. He had spent that spring marching through northern and western Bohemia gathering supporters from all major cities. He intended to return to his base at Hradec, but Prague and her allies decided to intercept him while they possessed superior forces. About 15 miles north-east of Prague, Zizka arranged his war wagons on a low hill. He was hemmed in within the bend of a river and the Praguers felt confident. That night, boats and rafts ferried Zizka across the river to freedom. The exasperated Praguers pursued him eastwards. At Malesov, familiar territory near Kutna Hora, Zizka turned to face his hunters. Again he chose a hill for his wagon fort. But this time he ordered his supply wagons to be filled with stones. When only half the Praguers rode into view, they rashly assumed battle formations and advanced up the slope. Zizka commanded his footsoldiers to roll the rock-filled wagons forward, down the hill. The wagons trundled down the slope, gathering speed, finally tipping over and smashing into the Praguers. Their formations broken, Zizka ordered his guns to fire. As the smoke cleared, Orebite horsemen burst out from among the wagons and completed the chaos. The rout destroyed the rest of the Praguers before they even reached the battlefield: 14,000 enemy were slain and all their arms and booty captured. Eastern Bohemia remained under Zizka's control.

In September, Zizka threatened Prague. An armistice prevented conflict. Political agreements followed and Zizka and Prague sealed a fresh alliance

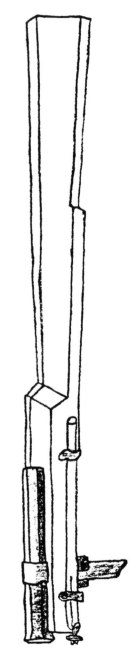

Drawing of a 15th century handgun now in the National Museum, Prague. Length of barrel 30 cm, overall length 113 cm.

Drawing of a 15th century handgun from Plzen in western Czechoslovakia. Length of barrel 30 cm, overall length 105 cm.

Fantastic 16th century version of Zizka's war wagons. His way of war influenced many eastern European and German warlords.

with a new campaign. Moravia remained outside Hussite control even though it formed part of the Bohemian kingdom. A Hussite army of Orebites, Praguers, and Taborites began the march to Moravia in October. On the way, they paused to besiege the castle of a Catholic lord. As preparations were made to assault Pribyslav, Jan Zizka fell ill. He was 64 and had never recovered full fitness since he had lost his sight. He was believed to have contracted plague. Within days, he was dead. Among his last words, he is said to have instructed his lieutenants to 'continue fighting for the love of God and steadfastly and faithfully defend the Truth of God for eternal reward'. Grief racked the entire Hussite army. Zizka's followers proclaimed themselves Orphans, and under this name fought on.

Zizka's body was buried at Hradec Kralove. The subsequent disappearance of his tomb inspired several legends. One story maintains that Zizka asked for his dead body to be flayed and the skin made into a drum that would forever lead his warriors. In reality, Zizka's greatest legacy was his method of war. Until the final defeat of the radical Hussites in 1434, the Taborites and Orphans continued the success of his tactics in battle after battle. On their banners, the warriors painted an image of Zizka in armour on a white horse, holding his famous fist-shaped mace. Wherever the Hussites carried this standard, they were said to be invincible. Even in death, Zizka led his army to victory.

VLAD DRACULA

Within the kingdom of Hungary and the neighbouring realm of Wallachia, Janos Hunyadi was the strong man between 1446 and 1456. Vlad Dracula, in his late teens and early 20s, could only try to survive in the shadow of this mighty warlord. Janos Hunyadi was the most effective military commander against the Turks in the 15th century. He won several major victories that significantly slowed the Ottoman advance in the Balkans. The legend of Hunyadi's success overwhelmed and influenced all ambitious warlords in the region, including Vlad Dracula. Hunyadi had risen from the son of a lowly Wallachian knight to governor of the kingdom of Hungary in ten years. Like his father, he achieved this recognition through martial prowess.

Hunyadi won his most important military experience against the Hussites. He absorbed their tactics and later made effective use of war wagons and firearms, even recruiting Bohemian veterans. Returning to Hungary, he was placed in command of 100 men-at-arms. Through raid and counter-raid he repelled the Turks not only from the Hungarian border but also from his homeland of Wallachia. In the winter of 1443–4, it was thought right to conduct a major offensive against the Turks. Hunyadi led an army of Hungarians, Romanians, Poles, Serbs, Bulgarians, and Bohemians. They crossed the Danube and occupied Nis and Sofia. Through speed and his skill of organisation, Hunyadi prevented the Ottoman forces from uniting and defeated them in a series of battles. By the end of the campaign, he had shattered Ottoman power in the Balkans north of Greece

410

and won himself great fame. Sultan Murad II was forced to accept peace.

Vlad Dracul, Vlad Dracula's father, played an ambiguous role in this campaign. Vlad Dracul was a loyal and successful knight. In 1431, he was made a member of the Order of the Dragon by King Sigismund of Hungary, hence his name. Dracula simply means son of Dracul. The Order of the Dragon was dedicated to the destruction of heretics and infidels. But at the time of Hunyadi's campaign, Dracul was prince of Wallachia, enthroned by Sigismund. He had no wish to ride on a crusade against the Turks. He knew well the power of the Ottomans. Living directly on the Danube frontier of their conquests in the Balkans, he would be the first to suffer from any conflict. Since 1437, Dracul had signed an alliance with Murad II and even accompanied the Sultan on raids into Transylvania, a province of Hungary. In 1441, Hunyadi demanded that Dracul renew his pledge to the Order of the Dragon and resist the Turks. But the next year, Dracul allowed the Turks to pass through Wallachia and ravage Transylvania. Hunyadi defeated the Ottomans near Sibiu, pursued them into Wallachia and at the same time removed Dracul from his throne. Dracul sought sanctuary with the Turks and was forced into even closer agreement with the Sultan. In 1443 he was replaced on the Wallachian throne. To secure his alliance with the Turks, they demanded two of his sons as hostages: Radu and Dracula. They were held in a castle in western Anatolia in Turkey.

In the autumn of 1444, the victorious Hungarians hoped to push the remaining Turkish presence out of Europe altogether. They broke their peace treaty. An international crusader army advanced on the town of Varna on the Black Sea coast to break the Turkish ring around Constantinople. A Venetian-Burgundian fleet endeavoured to occupy the Dardanelles to stop Ottoman reinforcements from Asia. The fleet failed, probably because of Genoese treachery, and the Sultan crossed with a mighty army to confront the Hungarians at Varna. The battle began well for Hunyadi. Bohemians, Italians, and Hungarians armed with handguns blasted the Turkish advance guard. Lightly armoured Hungarian horsemen dashed in among the Turkish warriors, shooting composite bows, throwing javelins, and slashing with their sabres. The Turks panicked. They scrambled out of the havoc. It seemed as though the Ottoman army would break. The Hungarian King and his noblemen were impatient to join the battle. They believed one final charge from their gleaming knights would have the infidels screaming back to Asia. Hunyadi urged caution. The battle was not yet won. The King ignored him. He wished to capture the Sultan, surrounded on a nearby hill by Christian janissary archers. Lances were lowered and horses spurred onwards. Several hundred knights and men-at-arms thundered towards the hill. They had miscalculated. The Turks rallied and shattered the Hungarian onslaught. The King's head was cut off by a janissary. Hunyadi narrowly escaped the slaughter.

Vlad Dracul avoided the catastrophe of Varna by sending a token force of 4,000 Wallachians under the command of his eldest son Mircea. Dracul's

Janos Hunyadi, Hungarian warlord and victorious crusader against the Turks. Woodcut published in Brno in 1488.

part involvement, however, threatened the safety of his two hostage sons. Usually, the life of a noble hostage was a comfortable one. It is likely that the boys were treated with respect, using the occasion to learn Turkish and gain an invaluable insight into Ottoman warfare. With the Hungarian declaration of war, this changed. A Turkish document records that Radu had to defend himself against the perverted sexual advances of the Sultan. He eventually succumbed, becoming a harem favourite of the Ottoman court. In this cruel, anxious atmosphere, the adolescent Dracula learned truths about fear and violence that remained with him for the rest of his life.

Following the disaster of Varna, the failed Burgundian-Venetian fleet sailed into the Black Sea and along the Danube in search of Hunyadi. According to the chronicler Jehan de Wavrin, Dracul aided the fleet with supplies and information. The eight galleys were mounted with cannon and under the command of Walerand de Wavrin, the chronicler's nephew, they assaulted several Turkish garrisons. Noting the amount of booty, Dracul appears to have had few doubts about joining the raiding campaign. On one occasion, he took personal charge of a giant bombard. Inexperienced in its use, he fired it repeatedly without allowing the barrel to cool between shots. Eventually, it burst. The bombard was repaired, but exploded again, killing a gunner. Later, Dracul proposed an ambush on the Turks under the pretence of a safe conduct. Wavrin was shocked at this deception and refused to put his seal to it. Dracul carried on regardless and the Turks were massacred.

With these minor successes behind him, Dracul was scornful of Hunyadi's defeat at Varna. When the Hungarian warlord passed through Wallachia, Dracul had him imprisoned. He laughed at Hunyadi: 'The Sultan goes hunting with more followers than were in your army.' He demanded his execution. Hunyadi's reputation saved him, but the warlord swore vengeance for this humiliation. In 1447, Hunyadi led an expedition against the prince of Wallachia. Dracul and his son Mircea were killed. Hunyadi proclaimed himself ruler of Wallachia. Later he passed the crown to Vladislav II, a loyal retainer. The Turks were angry. Dracul had been a good friend, despite occasional lapses. The next year they released Dracula. They told him to claim the throne of his dead father. Dracula emerged from captivity a bitter, determined man.

At Kosovo, Hunyadi sought revenge for Varna. He placed his German and Bohemian handgunners behind war wagons and fieldworks. He would not be dragged into rash offensives. On his flanks gathered Albanian and Wallachian horsemen, adventuring knights, and Magyar horse-archers. Vladislav II had brought 8,000 warriors and rode alongside Hunyadi. Turkish footsoldiers, still relying on crossbows and composite bows rather than firearms, dug in opposite the Christian centre. Their mail-clad horsemen waited on the wings. Neither side wished to attack first. Eventually, skirmishing broke out between the crowds of cavalry. The battle began. Gangs of horsemen charged forwards, delivered their

Armoured river-boat with cannon. Such craft were employed by the Christians against the Turks along the Danube. From the mid 15th century *Diebold Schilling Amtliche Chronik*, now in the Burgerbibliothek, Bern.

weaponry, and dashed away. Christian gunners sparked their barrels. Iron shot sunk into earth and wood. Through the smoke, crossbow bolts and arrows embedded themselves silently. Again and again the horsemen on both sides challenged each other. Wallachian nerves were strained. They snapped; the Christian centre slowly drew back. The battle lasted two days. It was hard fought. The Turks claimed a victory but gained little advantage. The true winner of Kosovo was riding hundreds of miles to the

Eques Walachus

Wallachian horseman carrying characteristic Balkan shield. A 16th century print, but such shields were common in the 15th century.

north of the retreating Christians. With a small force of borrowed Turkish horsemen, Dracula snatched the opportunity of Vladislav's absence. He rode into Wallachia and assumed the prince's crown. As far as he was concerned, both Vladislav and Hunyadi lay dead at Kosovo.

In the dismal retreat following Kosovo, Hunyadi was imprisoned by a Serbian lord angered at the looting of his territory by the crusader army. Instead of trying to free his patron, Vladislav commandeered the remnants of the Christian army and made for Wallachia. He tracked down Dracula and defeated him. Dracula fled to the court of Moldavia, to the east of

414

Wallachian warrior with composite bow. Wallachians·fought in both Christian and Turkish armies.

Wallachia. In 1455, Constantinople, the bastion of Orthodox Christianity, fell to the Turks. It was a great blow to Hungary and sent a shudder through central Europe. Hunyadi feared a Turkish invasion. Dracula thought it politic to throw himself on the mercy of Hunyadi. Moldavia was too much like exile for Dracula. The court of Hunyadi was the only place for an ambitious young man. Fortunately, Hunyadi had never forgiven Vladislav for leaving him in a Serbian prison while securing his own throne. On top of this, Vladislav had succumbed to Turkish influence. The Wallachians paid a regular tribute and the new Sultan Mehmed II considered the country open land across which he could attack Transylvania. Hunyadi accepted Dracula's pledges of loyalty and employed him to defend the border of Transylvania against Wallachia. It was a golden opportunity. Dracula gathered an army and awaited the time to claim back his princedom.

With typical strategic skill, Hunyadi pre-empted Turkish invasion. He rode to the relief of Belgrade, a powerful fortress controlling the southern Danube border of Hungary. Combining professional warriors with armed peasants, he battered the Turks. It was a remarkable triumph. A few days later, disease broke out among the victorious troops. Hunyadi was one of its victims. His premature death severely weakened Christian resistance in eastern Europe. But at the time, Dracula could only consider it a tremendous relief to be rid of the overwhelming presence of Hunyadi. He saw no obstacle to his ambition. He crossed the Transylvanian mountains into Wallachia. Vladislav was defeated and killed. In September 1456, Dracula became prince of Wallachia. He paid homage to both the Hungarian King and the Turkish Sultan. He already knew the reality of the situation.

Dracula made Tirgoviste in central Wallachia his capital. Within his modest palace, he plotted his initial revenge. When his father and elder brother had fled after their defeat by Hunyadi, they had received no help from the Wallachian nobility: the boyars. In Tirgoviste, Mircea had been captured by hostile boyars, tortured and then buried alive. To verify this tale, Dracula had his brother exhumed. When the earth was removed, he found Mircea face down, his body contorted. In deep silence, Dracula returned to his palace. All the principal boyars were invited to a feast. As the several hundred noblemen assembled, Dracula sent his bodyguard into the palatial hall. One by one, the boyars were dragged out and impaled on stakes outside the palace. In a dreadful night of death, the prince of Wallachia broke the power of the old nobility. The political reasoning was revealed in a question he asked the noblemen before execution. 'How many princes have ruled Wallachia in your lifetime?' None were so young that they had not known at least seven. At this Dracula grew angry. 'It is because of your intrigues and feuds that the principality is weak.' Dracula replaced the massacred boyars with a new nobility. Many warriors were elevated from their free peasant families: the *viteji*. Loyalty mattered above background. The prince surrounded himself with men committed to defending his regime. He raised a personal bodyguard from friendly boyars and mercenaries: the *sluji*.

Despite his control over the nobility, Dracula never felt completely secure. Wallachian subjects were impaled for the most trivial reasons. This method of execution, so characteristic of Dracula, earned him the Romanian nickname Tepes: 'the impaler'. He inflicted on others the misery and pain he had suffered in Turkish captivity. A German print of 1499 records Dracula dining among the dead and dying bodies of Saxon merchants captured in a raid. No execution or torture was too revolting for Dracula to witness with pleasure. The German settlers of Transylvania and especially

Dracula, prince of Wallachia, 15th century woodcut based upon a near contemporary oil painting.

the Saxon merchants of Brasov wielded great economic power. Whenever they refused Dracula's one-sided treaties, the Wallachian brutally destroyed their communities. They never forgave Dracula and relentlessly conspired against him, spreading their accounts of his atrocities to western Europe. At a time of many bloodthirsty warlords, even his contemporaries considered him excessively violent.

The close relationship between Wallachia and the Turks continued into the first years of Dracula's reign. The treaty he signed with the Turks demanded an annual tribute of 10,000 gold ducats. It also expected a constant stream of Wallachian boys for training as Ottoman janissaries. Turkish pressgangs frequently raided the country to ensure the human tribute. Dracula refused to accept this. The raiders were becoming bold and captured several castles along the Wallachian Danube border. Dracula retaliated. To bring an end to the deteriorating relationship, Mehmed II invited the prince to meet one of his representatives on the border. The governor of Nicopolis, Hamza Pasha, prepared an ambush. News of the deception reached Dracula as he approached a frontier fortress called Giurgiu. His horsemen surprised Hamza Pasha. Then, pretending to be Turks, they ordered the garrison at Giurgiu to open its gates. The Wallachians entered with the Turks and slaughtered the defenders. The

Dracula dining among the impaled bodies of his enemies. German propaganda woodcut of 1499 published in reaction to Dracula's atrocities against German settlers in Transylvania.

417

town was set ablaze and the Turks impaled. In respect of his rank, the tallest stake was reserved for Hamza Pasha.

Dracula continued along the Danube to the Black Sea, raiding and destroying. 'We have killed 23,884 Turks and Bulgars,' he wrote to Matthias Corvinus, new King of Hungary and son of Hunyadi. 'That's not counting all those burned in their houses and whose heads were not collected by our officials. Your majesty must be aware that I have broken the peace with the Turk not for my own sake, but for the sake of the honour of your Highness, for the defence of Christianity, and the strengthening of Catholic Law.' None of these considerations had ever been high among Dracula's priorities before, but he was desperate for military aid and hoped the magic of crusade would work. To enforce his request for help, Dracula had two bags of Turkish heads, ears, and noses sent to Buda. The King was not impressed. Dracula's other neighbours also offered only sympathy. Nevertheless, the success of Dracula's Danube campaign did cause excitement in courts further west. Could this be the rise of another Hunyadi? In 1459, Pope Pius II invited Christendom to organise a crusade against the Ottomans. Mehmed II had occupied Bosnia, Serbia, and Peloponnesian Greece. Only Albania continued to resist under the valiant guerrilla leader George Skanderberg. But every major state had its excuses. The French King could do nothing until relations with England had improved. The German Emperor could not depend on his princes. The Polish King was fighting the Teutonic Order. The Venetians asked for too much money. Dracula stood alone.

By the spring of 1462, Mehmed II raised an army some 60,000 strong to strike back at the insolent Wallachian prince. It included Balkan janissaries and Turkish soldiers from Asia Minor; 4,000 auxiliary Wallachian horsemen, among them boyar exiles, were led by Radu. The Sultan considered Dracula's submissive brother an excellent candidate for the Wallachian throne. The realisation of what faced him spurred Dracula to gather an army 30,000 in number. His boyars and their retainers were augmented by Wallachian and Bulgarian peasants. Men who distinguished themselves in battle were instantly promoted to officer rank. These *viteji* shaped the unprofessional mass into an army. The Turks advanced in two parts. The main force, led by the Sultan Mehmed, sailed along the Danube. A supporting land force marched from Philipopolis in Bulgaria. They met at the port of Vidin, one of the few Danube towns not destroyed by Dracula. As the Turks moved along the river, Dracula's horsemen kept them shadowed. When the Ottomans prepared to disembark on the northern bank, the Wallachians burst from the forest and let fly with their bows, forcing the Turks back into their boats. A few miles further on, the Turkish army finally crossed the Danube under cover of night and numerous cannons.

'A few of us first crossed the river and dug ourselves in trenches,' remembered a Serbian janissary, Constantin of Ostrovitza. 'We then set up

418

Mehmed II, conqueror of Constantinople and the Balkans, chief Turkish adversary of Dracula. Portrait attributed to Sinan Bey, around 1475, now in the Topkapi Palace Museum,, Istanbul.

the cannon around us. The trenches were to protect us from their horsemen. After that, we returned to the other side to transport the rest of the janissaries across. When all the footsoldiers were over, we prepared to move against the army of Dracula together with all our artillery and equipment. But as we set up the cannon, 300 janissaries were killed by the Wallachians. The Sultan could see a battle developing across the river and was saddened that he could not join us. He feared we might all be killed. However, we defended ourselves with 120 cannon and eventually repelled the Wallachian army. Then the Sultan sent over more men called *azapi* and

419

Dracula gave up trying to prevent the crossing and withdrew. After crossing the Danube himself, the Sultan gave us 30,000 ducats to divide among us.'

Cannon and handguns were by now a common power in eastern European armies. The development of wet-mixed gunpowder in the 15th century was a key factor in the increased efficiency of these weapons. Saltpetre was allowed to dissolve in water and percolate into charcoal. On drying, the active ingredients resided within the charcoal, rather than separately as they had before, and so produced a finer mixture which ignited immediately. When dried and squeezed through sieves to produce a powder of uniform grain size, it ensured a more consistent reaction. Recent firing tests with simulated medieval handguns revealed that a gun using 14th century dry-mixed powder misfired once in every four shots, whereas a gun using 15th century wet-mixed powder misfired one time in ten. Firing a steel bullet at steel armour, one tenth of an inch thick, a wet-mix gun penetrated five times out of eight, whereas a dry mix gun did not penetrate at all. By the middle of the 15th century, firearms were a vital element in Turkish armies in the Balkans. They gained much from the expertise of captured and bribed Christian gun-makers. The city of Dubrovnik and Venetian gun-runners were frequent suppliers of artillery to the Turks despite Christian bans on supplying arms to them.

Dracula realised the impossibility of confronting the Turks in open combat. He decided upon a guerrilla war with a scorched earth withdrawal. Crops were burned, wells poisoned, livestock and peasants absorbed within the army. The Turks were slowed down by the lack of food and the intense summer heat. It was so hot, the Turks were said to cook shish kebab on their sun-heated rings of mail. At night, the Sultan insisted on surrounding his army with earthworks. The janissary Constantin recalled the frequent raids made by Dracula's warriors. 'With a few horsemen, often at night, using hidden paths, Dracula would come out of the forest and destroy Turks too far from their camp.' The psychological strain of the guerrilla warfare began to tell. 'A terrible fear crept into our souls,' continued the janissary. 'Even though Dracula's army was small, we were constantly on guard. Every night we used to bury ourselves in our trenches. And yet we still never felt safe.' In the Carpathian mountains overlooking Tirgoviste, Dracula planned his most famous night raid. He gathered several thousand of his finest horsemen. Captured Turkish warriors were subjected to hideous torture and precise information extracted from them. Dracula wanted to capture the Sultan.

At nightfall, Dracula's forces assembled in the dim forest. Through ferns and brushwood, they trod silently. Turkish guards were stifled. Suddenly, all hell broke loose. Swinging sabres, yelping like wolves, shooting bows, the Wallachian horsemen descended on the Turkish camp. Slashing through tents and warriors slumped by fires, Dracula's warriors were everywhere. They searched for the Sultan's tent. A particularly grand structure caught their attention. They tore down the rich material, cut down its defenders, two viziers were slaughtered. But they were not the Sultan. While the majority of Turks panicked, Mehmed's janissaries picked up their arms and assembled around their master's tent. If only Dracula's other commander joined the attack, then the loyal but small force could be overcome. But the boyar had lost his nerve. The janissaries raised their bows and handguns. The majority of the Wallachians were content to massacre the more vulnerable Turks and load themselves with loot, before disappearing back into the forest. Dracula was furious. The Sultan had been within his grasp. Mehmed survived the night of slaughter, but he had lost several thousand of his men in a traumatic combat. It was the nearest the two forces would come to a major battle throughout the campaign.

Shaken but undeterred, the Turks advanced on Tirgoviste. Just outside the city, Mehmed came across a mile-long gorge. It was filled with the most terrible of sights. Over 20,000 contorted, rotting bodies, many of them Turkish, were perched on a forest of stakes: impaled on the orders of Dracula. The Sultan was revolted by the scale of the horror. Dracula had finally pierced the Sultan's brutal mind with his terror. 'Overcome by disgust,' wrote the Byzantine chronicler Chalcondylas, 'the Sultan admitted he could not win this land from a man who does such things. A man who knows how to exploit the fear of his people.' The main Turkish army was ordered to withdraw eastwards. The night attacks and the spread of disease among his soldiers were probably the main reasons for Mehmed's reluctance to assault Tirgoviste, but Dracula's terrorism should not be underestimated. Throughout Christendom, the Turkish withdrawal was received as Dracula's victory.

Before leaving Wallachia, Mehmed gave Radu permission to seize Dracula's crown. He left a small force of Turkish warriors under Radu's command. By this stage, Dracula was exhausted. His guerrilla warfare had damaged his own people as much as the Turks. Many of his loyal boyars were disappointed that Dracula had not achieved an outright victory and finished the Turkish menace completely. Radu realised that most Wallachians were desperate for a return to peace. He talked with the leading nobles. They were happy to become a tribute-paying ally of the Turks again in return for an end to hostilities. Radu built on Dracula's resistance of Mehmed to gain greater independence for his country, but chose reconciliation to secure a rapid peace. The boyars proclaimed 'a victory can sometimes be more harmful to the victorious than the defeated.'

German sallet, between 1450 and 1460. Dracula and most eastern European knights wore arms and armour derived from German models. Now in the Wallace Collection, London.

Turkish iron cannons of the 15th century. The Turks were slow to adopt firearms but gained much from their contact with Christian gun-makers in the Balkans and learned to use them to great effect. Outside the Military Museum, Istanbul.

By the end of the year, Radu had been recognised as prince of Wallachia by most boyars and the King of Hungary. The Turks were happy.

Rejected by his people and with few resources, Dracula escaped to the mountains of Transylvania. There, he licked his wounds in the fortress of Arges. Perched among the craggy Carpathian range, this was Dracula's Castle. According to local folklore, Radu pursued his brother along the valley of the Arges river. He set Turkish cannons on a hill opposite Dracula's castle and began to pound it. A final assault was prepared for the next day. During the night, a slave, a distant relative of Dracula, crept out of the Turkish camp to warn the former prince. He attached a message to an arrow and shot it through a window of the castle. Informed of their fate, Dracula's wife declared she would rather have her 'body eaten by the fish than become a Turkish slave'. She threw herself from the battlements, plummeting into the river below. Dracula decided on a less fatal escape. He slipped out of the castle, climbed the rocky slopes, and rode for Brasov, where the King of Hungary had made his headquarters during this crisis. The arrival of the ragged, exhausted, desperate Wallachian was nothing but an embarrassment to the King. Having already recognised Radu as the new prince, the King had Dracula escorted to a prison in Buda.

Dracula remained in prison for 12 years. One chronicler relates that even in his cell he inflicted pain on others. He caught mice and impaled them. But

423

this is propaganda. In reality, Dracula resided at the Hungarian court under house arrest. King Matthias considered it useful to have a claimant to the Wallachian crown among his court. Besides, Dracula's brutal talents might be needed in another crusade against the Turks. Dracula married into the Hungarian royal family. He renounced Greek Orthodoxy to become a Roman Catholic. In Wallachia, this conversion was considered a heresy and all such heretics were said to become vampires after death. Catholicism eased Dracula's path to freedom. He was given the rank of captain in the Hungarian army. Often, King Matthias would have Dracula presented to visiting Turkish envoys to assure them he could be unleashed at any time. The Turks still feared him.

By 1475, Stephen, prince of Moldavia, was keen for an alliance with Hungary. He saw little difference between the Turks and the Wallachians and wished to secure his western and southern borders against them. He proclaimed a crusade and invited the King of Hungary to join him. King Matthias was happy to receive funds for this campaign from the Pope, but created more noise than action. By himself, Stephen moved against Radu and deposed him. Radu received Turkish help and fought back. To protect the Transylvanian border against Wallachian raids, Dracula was placed in command of frontier forces. Once in the saddle, he resumed his war of terror. A papal envoy reported that Dracula cut the Turks to pieces and impaled the bits on separate stakes. At the battle of Vashi, Stephen, with possibly Dracula in his ranks, won a great victory against the Wallachians and the Turks. The triumph was followed by a formal alliance between Stephen and Matthias. The next year, the Hungarian King declared Dracula his candidate for the throne of Wallachia.

In the autumn of 1476, an army of 25,000 Hungarians, Transylvanians, Wallachians, and Serbs assembled in southern Transylvania. Ultimate command lay with Stephen Bathory, a loyal retainer to King Matthias, but the object was to replace Dracula on the throne of Wallachia. At the same time, a force of 15,000 Moldavians prepared to invade eastern Wallachia under Stephen. In November, Dracula descended from the snow covered Carpathians and besieged Tirgoviste. Before the massive army, the Wallachian citizens could do little. It fell without much struggle. The army moved southwards. With the capture of Bucharest, Dracula became prince of Wallachia again. The boyars were seemingly behind him. But the apparent submission of Wallachia to the old tyrant was just that. Within a couple of months, a mutilated, headless body was discovered in marshes near the monastery of Snagrov. The corpse was Dracula. The boyars could not forget the horror of his reign. With a small bodyguard of Moldavians, Dracula was surprised in a skirmish outside Bucharest. Whether it was Wallachians or Turks who delivered the final blows is unknown. Indeed, the exact circumstances of the assassination remain a mystery. What is certain is that Dracula's head was cut off and sent to the Sultan at Constantinople. The Turks rejoiced.

Turkish horse warrior. From Jost Amman's 16th century *Kunstbuchlin*.

The death of Vlad Dracula did little to improve the state of Wallachia. It most certainly weakened its anti-Ottoman stance. Princes came and went and Wallachia depended increasingly on the energetic Stephen of Moldavia to preserve the Danube frontier against the Turks. In the next century, the battle was lost and the Turks surged across the river to Hungary. To the Romanians, Vlad Dracula has remained a national hero, a staunch defender of Christianity against the Turks. In western Europe, his image has undergone a devilish transformation, from triumphant crusader to bloodthirsty vampire. The latter is a creation of the 19th century imagination, consolidated in books and films. But by the late 15th century, western writers had already forgotten Dracula's crusading triumphs and repeated only horrific accounts of his cruelty. German woodcut pamphlets were the principal agents of this image, showing Dracula dining among impaled victims. The Saxon merchants of Transylvania and their German neighbours never forgave Dracula for his raids and crimes against their people. Through their history they forever damned Dracula as the cruellest of medieval warlords.

425

BIBLIOGRAPHY

This is, of necessity, a select bibliography of both primary and secondary sources.

AETIUS:

Flavius Merobaudes, *Panegyrics I & II*. Courtly praise by a contemporary. Translation and commentary by F. M. Clover, Transactions of the American Philosophical Society, vol. 61 pt. 1, pp. 3–78, Philadelphia, 1971.

Renatus Frigeridus, brief biography of Aetius preserved in Gregory of Tour's *History of the Franks*. Translated by L. Thorpe, London, 1974.

Sidonius Apollinaris, *Panegyrics*. References to Aetius and his followers written later in the 5th century. Translated by W. B. Anderson, London, 1936.

Jordanes, *Gothic History*. The most detailed account of the war between Aetius and Attila, 6th century. Translated by C. C. Mierow, Princeton, 1915.

John of Antioch and Priscus. Fragments collected and translated by C. D. Gordon, *The Age of Attila*, Michigan, 1960.

Freeman, E. A., 'Aetius and Boniface', *The English Historical Review*, vol. 2, no. 7, pp. 417–465, London, 1887.

Maenchen-Helfen, J. O., *The World of the Huns*, Los Angeles, 1973.

Thompson, E. A., *Romans and Barbarians*, Wisconsin, 1982.

GAISERIC:

Saint Augustine, letters to Boniface. Translated by M. Dods, Edinburgh, 1875.

Possidius, *Life of St Augustine*. By a contemporary who experienced the seige of Hippo. Translated by F. R. Hoare, London, 1954.

Procopius, *History of the Vandal Wars*. By a 6th century Byzantine. Translated by H. B. Dewing, London, 1916.

Hydatius, *Chronicles*. A 5th century account of Spanish history. French translation by A. Tranoy, Paris, 1974.

Curtois, C., *Les Vandales et l'Afrique*, Paris, 1955.

Casson, L., *Ships and Seamanship in the Ancient World*, Princeton, 1971.

AN LU-SHAN:

Levy, H. S., *Biography of An Lu-shan*. Extracts from the Chiu T'ang-shu. Translated and annotated, Berkeley, 1960.

Pulleyblank, E. G., *The Background of the Rebellion of An Lu-shan*, Oxford, 1955.

Pulleyblank, E. G., 'The An Lu-shan rebellion and the origins of chronic militarism in late T'ang China', *Essays on T'ang Society*, edited by J. C. Perry & B. L. Smith, Leiden, 1976.

des Rotours, R., *Histoire de Ngan Lou-chan*, Paris, 1962.

Twitchett, D. (editor), *The Cambridge History of China*, vol. 3 pt. 1, Cambridge, 1979.

Kwanten, L., *Imperial Nomads*, Leicester, 1979.

OWEN OF WALES:

Jean Froissart, *Chronicles*. Written towards the end of the 14th century and gathered from first-hand witnesses. Several translations.

Davies, J. H., 'Owen Lawgoch-Yevain de Galles', *Montgomeryshire Collections*, vol. 37, pp. 233–256, Oswestry, 1915.

Owen, E., 'Yevain de Galles: some facts and suggestions', *Montgomeryshire Collections*, vol. 36, pp. 144–216, Oswestry, 1912.

Rhys, Professor, 'Welsh Cave Legends and the story of Owen Lawgoch', *Montgomeryshire Collections*, vol. 36, pp. 141–144, Oswestry, 1912.

Anderson, R. C., *Oared Fighting Ships*, London, 1962.

Anderson, R. C., *The Sailing Ship*, London, 1926.

GUESCLIN:

Jean Cuvelier, *Chronique de Bertrand du Guesclin*. Epic poem written about 1380. Edited by E. Charriere, Paris, 1839.

Jean Froissart, *Chronicles*. As above.

Dupuy, M., *Bertrand du Guesclin, Capitaine d'Aventure, Connétable de France*, Paris, 1978.

Thompson, H. Y., *Illustrations from the Life of Guesclin by Cuvelier*, from a manuscript of about 1400, London, 1909.

Vercel, R., *Bertrand of Brittany*, translated by M. Saunders, London, 1934.

ZIZKA:

Aeneas Sylvius, *Historia Bohemica*. Fullest 15th century account of Zizka's life. Several editions, no translation.

Heymann, F. G., *John Zizka and the Hussite Revolution*, Princeton, 1955.

Kaminsky, H., *A History of the Hussite Revolution*, Berkeley, 1967.

Macek, J., *The Hussite Movement in Bohemia*, Prague, 1958.

Wagner, E., *Medieval Costume, Armour and Weapons 1350–1450*, London, 1958.

Joannes Dlugosz, *Historia Polonica*. Fullest 15th century account of the battle of Tannenberg. Several editions, no translation.

Evans, G., *Tannenberg 1410:1914*, London, 1970.

DRACULA:

Florescu, R., & McNally, R. T., *Dracula*, London, 1973.

Stoicescu, N., *Vlad Tepes*, Bucharest, 1978.

Lajos, E., *Hunyadi*, Budapest, 1952.

Petrovic, D., 'Firearms in the Balkans on the eve of and after the Ottoman Conquests of the 14th and 15th centuries', *War, Technology and Society in the Middle East*, London, 1975.

Williams, A. R., 'Some Firing Tests with Simulated 15th century Handguns', *Journal of the Arms and Armour Society*, vol. 8, pp. 114–120, London, 1974.

Index